ADOLESCENT PSYCHIATRY

DEVELOPMENTAL AND CLINICAL STUDIES

VOLUME 24

Annals of the American Society for Adolescent Psychiatry

ADOLESCENT PSYCHIATRY

DEVELOPMENTAL AND CLINICAL STUDIES

VOLUME 24

AARON H. ESMAN

Editor in Chief

LOIS T. FLAHERTY
HARVEY A. HOROWITZ

Associate Editors

THE ANALYTIC PRESS

1999   Hillsdale, NJ   London

Published by The Anayltic Press, Inc.
Editorial Offices: 101 West Street, Hillsdale, NJ 07642

ISBN 0-88163-198-1
ISSN 0226-24064-9

Printed in the United States of America
10 9 8 7 6 5 4 3 2 1

CONTENTS

Editor's Introduction

PART I. DEVELOPMENTAL CONSIDERATIONS: ADOLESCENT DEVELOPMENT RECONSIDERED

Introduction: Shelley Doctors and Harvey Horowitz   1

1   I Am, You Are, and So Are We: A Current Perspective   3
on Adolescent Separation-Individuation Theory
MARCIA H. LEVY-WARREN

2   The Interpersonal Matrix of Adolescent Development   25
and Treatment
ROBERT GAINES

3   The Psychology of Belonging: Reformulating Adolescent   49
Development
GIL G. NOAM

PART II. SCHOOL-BASED MENTAL HEALTH SERVICES: THE FUTURE OF CHILD AND ADOLESCENT PSYCHIATRY

Introduction to Special Section: Irving Berkovitz   69

4   Psychiatric Public Health Opportunities in School-Based   75
Health Centers
STEWART L. ADELSON

5   On-Site School-Based Mental Health Clinics: 15 Years   91
of Experience in Orange County, California
BERNARD A. RAPPAPORT

6   School Mental Health in New Mexico   101
STEVEN ADELSHEIM

7   An Advising Program in a Large Urban High School: 109
The Magic Match
NANCY RAPPAPORT

8   Changing Paradigms in Child and Adolescent Psychiatry: 119
    Toward Expanded School Mental Health
    MARK D. WEIST, OLGA M. ACOSTA, NANCY A. TASHMAN, LAURA
    A. NABORS AND KATHLEEN ALBUS

PART III. FORENSIC ISSUES IN ADOLESCENT PSYCHIATRY

9   Forensic Psychiatry for Adolescent Psychiatrists: 135
    An Introduction
    RICHARD ROSNER
10 Juvenile Justice: An Update   143
    RICHARD A. RATNER
11 Competence in Adolescents   159
    ROBERT WEINSTOCK

PART IV. PSYCHOPHARMACOLOGY IN ADOLESCENCE:
          CURRENT PERSPECTIVES

Introduction to Special Section: Robert L. Hendren

12 Pharmacologic Treatment of Behavior Disorders   179
    in Adolescents
    SRIRANGAM S. SHREERAM AND MARKUS J. P. KRUESI
13 Pharmacologic Treatment of Affective Disorders in   213
    Adolescents
    DWIGHT V. WOLF AND KAREN DINEEN WAGNER
14 Pharmacologic Treatment of Anxiety Disorders   243
    in Adolescents
    ROBINDER K. BHANGOO AND MARK A. RIDDLE
15 Pharmacologic Treatment of Psychosis and Pervasive   271
    Developmental Disorders in Adolescents
    ILEANA BERNAL-SCHNATTER AND ROBERT L. HENDREN

PART V. ISSUES IN ADOLESCENT CONSULTATION-LIAISON

16 Psychiatric Consultation on an Adolescent Medical   297
    Service
    EVERETT DULIT

EDITOR'S INTRODUCTION

AARON H. ESMAN

As *The Annals* approaches both the millennium and its own 25th anniversary, it demonstrates in this volume the broad scope of the field for which it speaks. Rooted as they are in clinical practice and in developmental theory, adolescent psychiatry and its practitioners are engaged in the full gamut of investigative and remedial measures that characterize the mental health professions in today's ever-changing medical universe.

With the invaluable help and cooperation of members of our Editorial Board, we have organized a group of Special Sections to show the ways in which our colleagues are extending the range of concerns and applications of our particular expertise.

The first Special Section, edited by Harvey A. Horowitz and Shelley R. Doctors, consists of three contributions to the continuing effort to reformulate the process of adolescent development in the light of some of the newer conceptual approaches to psychoanalytic developmental theory—an effort that was initiated in Volume 23 with Richard C. Marohn's paper and that will be pursued in Volume 25.

Next are Special Sections on school-based programs, organized by Irving Berkovitz; forensic psychiatry, edited by Richard Rosner; and psychopharmacology in adolescence, developed by Robert L. Hendren. Each describes current, state-of-the-art thinking and practice in these vital areas of concern to the field. Indeed, the section on psychopharmacology constitutes a veritable mini-textbook in this increasingly important area of study and practice.

Finally, Everett Dulit offers a comprehensive statement of the issues involved in consultation/liaison work with adolescents, based on his extensive experience working in a pediatric setting. As psychiatrists are more and more diverted into consultative roles in managed care situations, his chapter takes on greater contemporary relevance.

Editor's Introduction

We believe that the wide range of concerns reflected in this volume testifies to the vitality of adolescent psychiatry today, its continued adaptation to developments both in contemporary culture and scientific advances, and its potential for even greater contributions to the health and welfare of young people in the future.

PART I

DEVELOPMENTAL CONSIDERATIONS: ADOLESCENT DEVELOPMENT RECONSIDERED

SHELLEY DOCTORS AND HARVEY HOROWITZ

At the annual meeting of the American Society for Adolescent Psychiatry (ASAP) in May 1987, Richard C. Marohn presented "A Reexamination of Peter Blos's Concept of Prolonged Adolescence." After his untimely death, his groundbreaking paper was revised and edited by colleagues Shelley R. Doctors and Robert J. Leider and published in Volume 23 of *The Annals*.

Dick Marohn, a self psychologist and former president of ASAP, was the first adolescent psychiatrist of stature to question the basic premises of the prevailing theory of adolescent development. He wrote (1998): "If one sees adolescence as ushered in by an increase in libidinal drive (S. Freud, 1905), and the concomitant developmental task as that of the loosening of infantile incestuous object ties (A. Freud, 1958), then the separation-individuation paradigm follows. That view of adolescence (as a recapitulation of separation-individuation) states that continued psychological contact with the 'infantile objects' is evidence of immaturity. The self–selfobject paradigm offers an alternative—that, throughout adolescence and adulthood, one retains ties to selfobjects. One never separates, individuates, or becomes psychologically independent. One remains psychologically connected. The contrast between these models is dramatic!" (pp. 14–15).

With this contribution, Marohn joined the intellectual ferment emerging in psychoanalysis, as the relational perspective evolved and differentiated itself from the classical tradition. This process and its tensions continue within the vital and illuminating psychoanalytic dialogue of the past decade. This Special Section, inspired by Dick Marohn and dedicated to his memory, proposes to further his work. The following three invited chapters address the question of a revised, updated psychoanalytic theory of adolescent development. Next year's *Annals* will present another such section.

REFERENCE

Marohn, R. (1998), A reexamination of Peter Blos's concept of prolonged adolescence. In: *Adolescent Psychiatry, Vol. 23*, ed. A. Esman. Hillsdale, NJ: The Analytic Press, pp. 3–19.

1   I AM, YOU ARE, AND SO ARE WE: A CURRENT PERSPECTIVE ON ADOLESCENT SEPARATION-INDIVIDUATION THEORY

MARSHA H. LEVY-WARREN

The topic: what we know from mother–infant research that informs our understanding of the development of a sense of intimacy. The place: a college seminar room filled with bright, articulate upper class students. The discussion goes something like this:

"I think that the attunement between caregivers and infants is a key part of the development of a sense of intimacy."

"But do you think that each one has to have a sense of self before real attunement is possible? And, if so, when does that kind of sense of self develop?"

"Hold it, though. Is there really *a* sense of self? Isn't it a dynamic concept? It seems to me that we never really have one sense of self, you know?"

"I think what we all call self changes over time."

"It seems to me that intimacy requires reciprocity between two people, each of whom has a distinct sense of self—people who really know themselves—so that each can be attuned to the other without mistaking his or her own feelings for the partner's."

"Is it mistaking feelings or being overly influenced by the other person's point of view that's the problem?"

"That kind of influence seems related to dependency. To be intimate, does each person have to be able to totally rely on the other?"

"Do you think that being close involves being able to lose yourself in someone else?"

3

Adolescent Separation-Individuation Theory

Late adolescents, perhaps all adolescents—though their concerns change as they move through the adolescent years—are consumed with how to come to terms with who they are and what they want in life, how to be involved intimately with another person, and how they can come to know their deepest thoughts and feelings about these matters. The psychological theories that describe these processes are varied and often at odds with one another (e.g., S. Freud, 1905; A. Freud, 1958; Blos, 1962; Erikson, 1968; Offer, 1969; Wolf, 1982; Kaplan, 1984; Levy-Warren, 1996; Marohn, 1998). The point of view that I put forth in this paper is that achieving genitality is the primary focus of adolescence, that it embraces all of the outlined concerns, and that it develops by means of the separation and individuation processes of this time.

In 1905, Freud introduced the concept of genitality as the last of the psychosexual stages. In the present paper and elsewhere (Levy-Warren, 1996), I attempt to bring this concept into the framework of modern developmental psychoanalytic theory. As I conceive and describe it, genitality encompasses both the integration of adolescents' mature genitalia and the meaning of the functioning of the genitalia. In the evolution of genitality, adolescents come to accept their changed physiology, and they develop the capacity to derive pleasure from their bodies in having an intimate, satisfying relationship. In order to have such a relationship, people need to be able to see themselves and others accurately; they have to evolve from their childhood understandings of themselves to adolescent conceptions of themselves through the progression of their separation-individuation processes. Blos (1962, 1967) denotes this as a second individuation process.

According to Blos, this individuation is modeled on the separation-individuation process of infancy and early childhood first described by Mahler, Pine, and Bergman (1975). Mahler et al. observed that there is a slowly unfolding intrapsychic process that results in (a) a sense of separateness from, and relation to, a world of reality, particularly with regard to children's own bodies and their primary love objects (i.e., separation), and (b) an awareness of achievements that mark children's assumption of their own individual characteristics (i.e., individuation).

The second individuation theory (Blos, 1962, 1967) has come under attack in recent years (e.g., Schafer, 1973; Galatzer-Levy, 1984; Escoll, 1987; Marohn, 1998). Some argue that the separation-individuation processes of early life do not have applicability to adolescence, that the two phases are too different from each other to be compared (e.g., Furman, 1973; Schafer, 1973). Others believe that the "separation" part of this theory de-emphasizes or even ignores the ongoingness of relations with significant others and the necessity for these relationships to be transformed according to the changing needs of adolescents. They argue that there is no disengagement from significant objects, as they read Blos to be suggesting (e.g., Schafer, 1973; Galatzer-Levy, 1984; Escoll, 1987; Marohn, 1998). It often seems that these critics look at separation as if it means a literal detachment from significant others rather than as the intrapsychic separation that both Mahler et al. (1975) and Blos (1962, 1967) so clearly describe.

I imagine a coloring book with a picture of a group of people. The black outlines of their figures are the lines of separation. They bind the figures and show their physical form (i.e., they show where each figure stops and the next one begins). If we color in the figures, we are demonstrating the individuation process. What is inside our physical boundaries—including everything from how strong we are, to how emotional we are, to what we are interested in, to what we believe in—is all aspects of self that provide us with a sense that we have a vivid understanding of who we are. It is this vivid understanding that we bring to our intimate relationships. Without this understanding, it would be difficult to feel truly close to someone else.

What provides us with a sense of knowing and being known is both a sense of who we are as distinct from others and a sense of who we are as we look deeply into ourselves. Feeling known is a critical component of intimacy. To be known by another, we must know ourselves. It is only then that we can trust that what others claim to know of us feels real.

Adolescents are deeply concerned with their outlines (separation), what colors belong within those outlines (individuation), and how their colored-in figures interrelate (relationships). As they move from early to middle to late adolescence, these concerns unfold. They unfold in order, although one concern does not supplant another. There is a cumulative effect, and one set of concerns interacts with the next. Early adolescents are most deeply concerned with the issues of separation, middle adolescents with individuation, and late adolescents with their relationships to each other. In each subphase, however, there is attention paid to the issues that preoccupy adolescents at other times.

Those who take issue with separation theory point to infancy research as offering evidence that even babies act on their environments in ways that imply that they have their own subjectivity right from the time of their birth—that they, therefore, have no need to differentiate themselves from their caregivers. Critics of separation theory see this as proving that there is no need to formulate a separation process (e.g., Galatzer-Levy, 1984; Stern, 1985; Escoll, 1987; Marohn, 1998). This subjectivity, however, does not obviate the need for individuals to come to terms with their separateness. The alone state that becomes particularly and painfully salient during adolescence is a later elaboration of the early version of separateness that Mahler and her colleagues (1975) described. What this research tells us is that our prior idea about babies being unformed is inaccurate; it does not tell us that we have no need to come to terms with the existential state of aloneness, or separateness, that those of us who work with adolescents see on a daily basis. It also does not remove the need to formulate a way of understanding how that alone state works in tandem with the state of being-in-relation-to-others that is a building block of mature genitality.

In this paper, I take the position that the separation and individuation processes of early childhood must continue in order for the maturation of genitality to take place and that we must understand these processes in the context of adolescent development. What I see is that these processes take place in concert with one another during adolescence, but the valence of the importance of each shifts during the three subphases: early, middle, and late adolescence. To restate, then . . . early adolescence is dominated by separation issues, middle adolescence by individuation issues, and late adolescence by the integration of mature genitality. This paper will define these concepts in the ways that I find most useful for adolescence, discuss and illustrate through clinical examples their changing relevance in the three subphases of this developmental period, and conclude by talking about the necessity for us to be aware of these shifts in our work with adolescent patients.

Early Adolescence

When they become pubertal, children must come to terms with the obvious passage of time and the consequent transformations in relationships inside and outside their homes. Their bodies are no longer childlike, and they both see themselves and are seen as in a different place in life. Some are more ready than others for this different place.

Girls enter puberty at the age of 12.5 years (give or take two years), generally two years earlier than boys (Brooks-Gunn and Warren, 1985). Boys, therefore, must contend with female peers who are physically mature before they themselves have begun to develop the relevant changes. As a result, male adolescence often begins (psychologically) before actual physical development takes place. It is not until they are in their midteens that females and males are more on a par in terms of physical, social, and psychological development.

What is singularly important to adolescents in this beginning subphase is the shift from seeing themselves as children to seeing themselves as no longer children. Sometimes, this means that they see themselves as adolescents; sometimes, they just see themselves as beyond childhood. Their reactions are mixed. On the one hand, they welcome this shift. They are proud, excited, and filled with the energy of discovery. On the other hand, they feel sad, frightened, and unsure about how they are supposed to be and what it means that their bodies are changing.

In this context, early adolescents have to redefine not only their sense of self (as a nonchild) but also their relationships with their caregivers. Whereas once caregivers seemed larger than life, capable of all things, now they must be brought into sharper focus for adolescents as the normal (or not so normal) people they are. This deidealization process is one component of what is at the core of the tensions that often arise in families at this time. It is not easy for children to see their parents as less than all-powerful. It is not easy for caregivers to sense that the glow of childhood—in which they had the power to comfort by a touch, the power to relieve their children's distress by a smile—is nearly gone from their relationships with their adolescents.

As children move into adolescence, they must alter aspects of their most basic self-awareness—that of their physical self (e.g., Freud, 1923; Greenacre, 1958; Jacobson, 1964; Stern, 1985). The original feelings of cohesiveness, of boundedness, of security, which derive from feeling that they can predictably know and trust the ways that their bodies work—must shift as they see and feel their bodies change. The physical changes initiated by puberty are far more noticeable to the adolescents themselves and result in adolescents' feeling out of touch with this most fundamental sense of self. They seem all of a sudden to have body parts they previously did not have, mood changes and bodily urges that they cannot explain, new spontaneous bodily emissions, and enlargements in parts of their bodies that they never knew would grow. They sweat, they have hair in new places, and they have pimples.

Sometimes adolescents are pleased about these changes; sometimes these are changes that adolescents would gladly reject. But the changes leave adolescents feeling that they have moved, inexorably, out of childhood. They must, therefore, change their most basic mental representations of self, those that derive from images of their physical being. This is a profound transformation, replete with meaning—a transformation that ultimately incorporates changes in how they are being perceived in their social worlds.

When children have the growth spurts that precede and accompany adolescence, they begin to be perceived differently. Often, those around them react as though the children (now young adolescents) should be acting more maturely. Young but tall kids are not allowed into movies for the under-thirteen rates; developed eleven-year-old girls are ushered into the junior's department in clothing stores, where they are surrounded by much older young women; parents often think their physically mature adolescents are more socially experienced than their kids really are. In turn, these changes in how adolescents are perceived in the social world, particularly by those whom the young adolescents care most about (e.g., their parents, siblings, friends), result in modifications in their self and object representations.

Once the changes of puberty have arrived, those who were once regarded as children are now thought of in different terms. The once-children are often not ready for this shift, and sometimes the significant people in their lives are not quite ready for them, either. The self and object representations of young adolescents have to change in order to accommodate the transformations of this time—both those that the adolescents see and experience and those that are introduced by the surrounding social world. They are responded to in different ways, and they feel different to themselves.

Young adolescents are keenly aware that they have changed—both in the ways that they react to their parents and in the ways that they think of and experience their bodies. They know that their bodies are no longer what they once were and not yet what they will be. It is a clearly a time of transformation about which they are often self-conscious. It is also often a trying time in families, for parents do not know how to react to their ever-changing children, and their children do not quite know how to be. The resultant tension is well-known in families with children at this time of life.

MARSHA H. LEVY-WARREN

Renée is a well-developed thirteen-year-old girl who is "fed up" with a home life in which she is "treated like a baby," "hates" her body, is in the midst of a fight with her best friend, and is, generally speaking, unhappy with her lot in life. She began once-weekly psychotherapy after slashing at her upper arm with a razor while in a fit of anger at her mother. This vignette follows an explosive scene at home, five months into treatment, in which she and her mother ended up in a screaming match. Up until the end of last year, when she began menstruating, she and her mother were very close. At that time, this closeness dissipated, and Renée and her mother became more and more distant and were more and more at odds with each other. The scene at home that preceded this session was a typical one.

R: I hate her. I just hate her. She can't leave me alone. Any time I want to do something, she wants to know where I'm going, who I'm going with, when I'll be back. She doesn't give me any room to breathe. I feel like I'm suffocating.

ML-W: Sounds like she's worried.

R: I don't care whether she's worried or not. She's in my face too much of the time. I can't believe that she won't let me go to the movies later with Tommy. I asked her really nicely, told her it was no big deal—he and I were not going out any more—and she wanted to know what prompted the date, if anyone else was going, why we couldn't go to an earlier show, and on and on and on. Ugh. I just hate her. I feel like she doesn't trust me at all. I mean, what does she think I'm going to do, anyway?

ML-W: Good question. What do you think she thinks you're going to do?

R: [laughing] Probably less than I already have done?!

ML-W: Do you think that she might be concerned that you don't look out for yourself—and she feels that she has to, because you don't?

R: I don't know what she knows, what she thinks. And I don't care. She's just too involved with me. She should be more involved in her own life.

ML-W: Sounds like you have something in particular in mind when you say that. Is there something that she's ignoring in her

R: own life?

R: She's getting fat. She has a belly, she has a double chin, and she has that gross thing that old women get, you know, when their upper arms are all saggy. I can't believe it doesn't bother her. If I looked like that, I'd want to kill myself.

ML-W: Sure sounds like it bothers you . . . almost seems like it gets under your skin.

R: It's embarrassing.

Renée demonstrates the ways in which early adolescents struggle with the process of separation and the sense of separateness that this entails. Right from the moment she slashed at her upper arms—a location that ultimately proved to be related to her disgust with her mother's upper arms and her inability to put that disgust into words—she was showing that she had trouble seeing her mother as distinct from herself. This is not to be understood in the most literal sense, because she certainly knew that her mother was her mother and not her (Renée), but in a more figurative sense—that her attachment to her mother was such that she had trouble dealing with her mother as a distinct person whose existence did not directly affect or reflect on Renée. The disgust she describes is not simple to grasp.

Although it was ostensibly about her mother's "fat," when further explored, it seemed to be about Renée's coming to terms with her mother's aging as well as her own experience of getting older. She was not prepared for puberty when it arrived, as is often the case these days for those girls at the early end of the normal spectrum (the age of onset for puberty has dropped about four months every ten years for the last several decades; Tanner, 1962, 1978).

The separation process as I understand it is not about detachment from significant others, such as mothers; it is not about remoteness; and it is not about disconnection, even though any of these may be outward manifestations of the inner process of separation. It is an awareness of where I stop and you begin, whose feelings are whose, whose thoughts are whose, and whose physical actions are whose. When puberty begins, there is also a shift away from seeing oneself as a child. This means that there is a shift away from, perhaps even a loss of, the self-representations and object representations that stem from being a child (including images of oneself as small—with a body that is hairless and undeveloped, images of being comforted by a parent, etc.).

When children become pubertal, childhood becomes a thing of the past; the former children must now come to terms with their changed outer bodies and inner sensations. Where they stop and the next person begins must be reassessed. Whereas once children were smaller than all those adults who surrounded them, now they meet or even tower over some of them. They become keenly aware that they know things that their parents do not know. They are separate from their parents in ways that they were not aware of in the past. None of these discoveries has to lead kids to disconnect from their parents (although there are often such moments in the lives of families).

Renée is struggling with the adolescent tasks of assuming ownership of her body and her well-being. Her attachment to her mother is such that she feels embarrassed by her mother's appearance and frightened by her mother's aging. Just before she began treatment, she expressed her anger at her mother by cutting herself. This was the act of a daughter who was insufficiently differentiated from her mother—that is, not yet sufficiently intrapsychically separate. Renée's need for her mother interfered with her being able to put her anger and frustration into words. One of the reasons for the overdetermined act of cutting herself was because she could not express her anger directly at her mother. Her claim that her mother is too involved with her reflects her need for her mother to help to regulate her, her own preoccupation with her mother, and an accurate perception of her mother's deep concern.

Renée's sense of "I" is underdeveloped—a common state among adolescents her age. Although there is some continuity of self—predominantly that characterized by Emde (1983) when he spoke of our "affective core"—early adolescents in general lose a distinct sense of who they are in the context of their bodies changing relatively quickly, their social worlds reacting to the changes before they themselves have come to terms with the changes, and their level of self-consciousness being great. They feel out of sorts, unknowing of who they are, and they can be both withdrawn from others and overly influenced by them. This creates the need for a surge of self-focus in which old and new conceptions of themselves are contrasted and compared, and there is ultimately a reintegration of the new conceptions into a current sense of self.

This is the separation process of this time. It involves a move away from the internally represented self and parents of childhood and a move toward representations of self and parents that are more in keeping with the current situations of the now-adolescents. Whereas parents of children may take their children onto their laps, parents of adolescents are more likely to toss them the keys to the car; whereas parents of children may have chosen what their children wore to school each day, parents of adolescents give them allowances and tell them to go buy clothes for school; and whereas children's self-representations may be of pug-nosed children with curly blond hair, adolescents' self-representations may have to change those images into images of larger, Roman-nosed kids with wavy brown hair. Although there is continuity from one set of self-representations or parent representations to the other, there is also a need for a demarcation between the prior set of representations and the current ones—that is, a separation process.

There is a state of aloneness in which adolescents find themselves and with which adults are familiar—a state of being alone with one's thoughts, hearing one's own voice. Development of the capacity for introspection (Piaget, 1947, 1972; Inhelder and Piaget, 1958), in combination with the necessity for adolescents to change their self-representations, is at the foundation for this state of aloneness. This is also an aspect of the adolescent separation process: Adolescents must master this alone state, be able to feel themselves to have integrity of self in the present.

This integrity of self is an important aspect of what permits one person to be intimately involved with another and is, thus, fundamental to the maturation of genitality. If we look back at some of the questions and concerns that were raised in the college seminar described at the beginning of this paper, we can see how quickly late adolescents move to this issue. When one student spoke of attunement as part of intimacy, the next spoke about the necessity of having a sense of self to be attuned. This was followed by a question about whether there is really *one* sense of self or whether it's ever-changing. Then, the importance of knowing yourself, having a distinct sense of self, so you can hold onto it in relationships, was raised. It is clear that the nature of self is of keen interest to these students.

Intrapsychic separateness of the type that deeply concerns all adolescents—but that most deeply concerns those in the earliest subphase, as they move out of childhood—is a critical building block in the development of the capacity to be intimate. Middle adolescence brings with it a continuing focus on separateness but one that elaborates each adolescent's particularity. At this time, adolescents' primary concern is with individuation.

Middle Adolescence

Whereas early adolescents concentrate on moving out of childhood and coming to terms with their changed bodies, middle adolescents are squarely situated in their present lives and want nothing more than to come to know themselves as they now perceive themselves to be. This is no mean task, and they seek out the support of their compatriots in this process of self-discovery.

So, middle adolescents travel in packs. They are consumed with themselves and consumed with one another. Their group activity is a way to consolidate aspects of themselves that they are beginning to focus on as salient to them, aspects of themselves that feel basic to the sense of self that is developing at this time. They join teams, play in bands, wear clothes that resemble those of their friends, listen to the same kinds of music as their friends do, or start writing for literary magazines and newspapers, all in the service of beginning to define a sense of who they are, what is important to them, what they can do, and what moves them. This is the adolescent individuation process in action. It is the predominant force at work in middle adolescent development.

Females and males begin to develop more in tandem in middle adolescence. The earlier discrepancies between them, initiated by the generally earlier onset of puberty for girls, diminish during this middle subphase. These discrepancies tend to draw together young adolescent girls with girls, and boys with boys, in much the same way that thematic support groups are appealing to those who join them. Young adolescents seek out those who are struggling with the same kinds of issues, so they are most drawn to peers who are developing at a pace similar to theirs.

Whereas early adolescents are primarily involved with these same-sex relationships, middle adolescents focus more on getting to know those of the opposite sex. They look for ways in which their opposite-sex peers contrast with them as much as they look for ways they are similar. Developing stronger ties with the opposite sex aids middle adolescents in exploring what it means to be female or male, feminine or masculine, and what it means to have a sexuality.

In this context, I conceive of sexuality in broad terms—to be aware of oneself as a sexual person, of being attracted to someone else, and of being able to enjoy a physical and emotional relationship with that person. Both gender development and sexual development at this middle subphase are important aspects of the adolescent individuation process and, as such, are critical in the maturation of genitality.

Eugene is a tall, athletic, good-looking sixteen-year-old. He came into psychotherapeutic treatment at his own request. He felt he was "obsessing" too much about his long-term girlfriend, Jenny. He was so preoccupied with whether to stay in a relationship with her that he could not concentrate on his schoolwork, was having trouble sleeping, and was constantly at odds with his friends and his parents. All who knew him well were tired of hearing him talk about this conflict. This session took place six weeks after he began treatment.

E: I bet you're getting sick of this, too. But I don't know what to do. My friends think I'm crazy. They say, how can you break up with Jen? She's pretty, she's got a good head on her shoulders, she's athletic, she thinks you're cool. But isn't there more to it than that? Just because she's all these things doesn't mean it's right, does it?

ML-W: Well, maybe we can start by taking a look at what you mean by "right."

E: You know. She's *the one,* the perfect fit, and all that.

ML-W: Hard to know what a perfect fit is. Can you say more about it?

E: Liking the same things, I guess.

ML-W: That didn't sound so wholehearted.

E: Yeah, you're right. I guess it's not really that. The truth is, I feel like she doesn't really know me . . . and I'm not sure I know her, either. There's something off. Hard to believe that after going out for over a year I feel like she doesn't even know what I'm about. But I do feel like that. I know she likes my looks, I know she thinks I'm a good guy . . . but I just don't feel like she knows what matters to me. And I know I don't know what matters to her. The whole thing seems so superficial or something. It just isn't enough that I think she's cute.

ML-W: Sounds like you are looking for some greater depth than you feel you have with Jen.

E: Yeah, definitely. It may be weird to say this, but I actually feel really alone when I'm with her. Like I'm with someone, but I'm not really with someone. It's only my outside that's with her. Inside, I feel like we don't touch each other.

ML-W: What are some of the things that matter to you that you wish she knew?

E: I'm just starting to figure this stuff out for myself . . . but, like, it matters to me to be aware of what's going on in politics . . . and it matters to me that I stay in contact with my friends from out of school . . . and it matters to me to keep in shape . . . and, well, I guess it matters to me to figure out whether I really believe in God or not.

ML-W: Now I'm beginning to wonder whether you and Jen have gotten out of sync . . . you have begun to think of yourself in these more refined terms, and she doesn't see it. I don't know whether that's because she can't or because you haven't told her . . . or what.

E: I think both of those are true. But, also, she just isn't into looking at herself this way. Maybe the fact that she's a sophomore and I'm a junior is part of it. Maybe she's just not into this yet . . . like, she's too young. Seems really strange to say this . . . because when we started going out, even though she was younger, she felt older to me. She just knew more about how to relate. But now, I feel like we're in really different places. I'm thinking about things like college, who I am, who I want to be . . . and she's into how she looks, trying not to fight with her parents, and working out things with Susan, her best friend. It's just different.

ML-W: I can certainly see why you feel like you just don't reach each other. The more you talk about this, the more it seems that you simply are growing in different areas and, therefore, focused on different aspects of life.

Eugene is in the throes of the most significant aspects of middle adolescent development. He is thinking deeply about who he is, who he wants to be, what matters to him, and who matters to him. This is the adolescent individuation process in full gear. He feels lonely in his relationship with Jen because she is struggling more with resolving the issues of early adolescence, issues that he has fundamentally left behind. He does not talk or even think about his parents as much as she does; he is not as concerned with getting along with his same-sex friends; and he feels relatively clear about his physical self.

Individuation is about knowing yourself with specificity; knowing the ins and outs of how your body, mind, and heart work; and knowing the interrelationships among them. Eugene is in the midst of sorting out these issues, and he is troubled about being in a relationship with someone who does not seem to be struggling in the same way.

Sameness–difference is an important theme in middle adolescent relationships. Part of the draw of opposite-sex relationships, whether they are friendships or more romantic/sexual involvements, is that they afford those in them the opportunity to compare and contrast traits and experiences in relationships of obvious difference.

Middle adolescents tend to seek out those who seem to them to share important characteristics, even when they may appear on the outside to be different. It is typical for middle adolescent romantic/sexual relationships, for example, to be with partners who are from markedly different backgrounds. When middle adolescents form such bonds, they come to be able to see themselves in a more individuated manner. What becomes salient is who they are in more fundamental ways than what is represented by the social status of their families, their ethnicities, or their religions. They go beneath the surface to what feels basic and meet their partners in that place. These are often transitory relationships that provide both persons with a more refined sense of themselves. Such relationships contribute to the adolescent individuation process.

When the college seminar students raised questions about how they could be in relationships with others without having a distinct sense of self, without really knowing themselves, it was not only in terms of where they stopped and the other person began. They were also aware of the need to know themselves in some detail, to have a complex picture of themselves, and to be known by others with that degree of specificity. As they brought out, this complex picture keeps each person from being overly influenced by the next. This is where the maturation of genitality dovetails with the individuation process of middle adolescence. The capacity to be intimately involved with someone in a way that incorporates the physical developments of puberty, their meaning, and emotional authenticity—what I regard as the cornerstones of mature genitality—cannot take place without the further development of individuation that occurs at this time. Late adolescence brings with it a renewed focus on family relationships, a concern with establishing personal moral/ethical beliefs, a consolidation of the separation and individuation processes of early and middle adolescence, and a deep concern with forming committed, intimate relationships. When the separation and individuation processes of the earlier subphases have been negotiated with some success, the transition into late adolescence is filled with excitement and promise.

Late Adolescence

Late adolescents stand alone, especially when you compare them with middle and early adolescents. They are far clearer about who they are, what they want, and with whom they want to spend time. They are involved in groups but to a much lesser degree than their younger counterparts. The need for group affiliation as a way of solidifying aspects of their identity is greatly diminished. The experimentation with group connection that is typical of middle adolescence has usually provided late adolescents with sufficient clarity about themselves that these group involvements are less necessary.

What does concern this age group is what they believe in, what they feel is right or wrong, and how they can come to terms with these issues. They look to their friends and they look to mentors—both in the form of people and in the form of the written word—often including their parents in this category of relationship. The relative distance between middle adolescents and their parents, as compared to their relationship of earlier years, is now supplanted by a renewed interest in seeing who their parents are, what they think, and how they relate to each other and the world.

Late adolescents are in the throes of synthesizing their adult identifications. In so doing, they look to their parents in a new way, seeing them as adults out in the world, in intimate relationships, and with defined belief systems. Late adolescents renew efforts at getting to know their parents as people: whereas, in early adolescence, this getting-to-know process was motivated by the need to move away from childhood dependencies, in late adolescence it is motivated by their renewed appreciation for their parents' roles in their lives and a need to identify with them as adults.

In the context of leaving childhood behind, early adolescents struggle to look at themselves for the first time as having a past. Middle adolescents, living very much in the present, try to take a good, hard look at who they are and who their friends are. Late adolescents, looking ahead, wonder about how they will fit in society, what they will do, and with whom they will move into adult life.

Marie is an attractive, bright eighteen-year-old who is highly anxious about finding a boyfriend, doing well in school, and maintaining her weight. She is thin but feels she must be constantly vigilant to stay that way. She exercises every day, usually to an excessive degree (e.g., two hours). Both of her parents are overweight, her younger sister is slightly pudgy, and Marie "doesn't want to go there." She is in her last year of high school and is worried about whether she will get into the college of her choice. Indeed, she is so worried about most things that she is having trouble eating, sleeping, and concentrating on her schoolwork. Her mother suggested that she consult with a psychotherapist, and she readily agreed. This session took place three months into treatment.

M: I'm freaking out. Absolutely freaking out. I just can't stop thinking that I am going to blow up into a balloon, get rejected at Yale, and end up being alone all year. I think about these things all the time. Day and night. I still can't sleep. And my mother is concerned about my not eating.

ML-W: Are you actually not eating?

M: Well. You know me. I'm not big on eating in the first place, but being stressed all the time doesn't help.

ML-W: You know, you say that your mother is concerned about your not eating, but what about you?

M: Let's put it this way. I'd rather not eat than eat, so it suits my larger purpose to be so nervous that I can't eat.

ML-W: Well, that's honest . . . even if it's not the most self-protective of attitudes. It also puts you in the position of having your mother worried about you.

M: Frankly, I wish she'd worry more about herself. And my father. And my sister. They are all so fat, it totally disgusts me.

ML-W: Pretty strong feeling, that disgust. I wonder if that's all you feel.

M: Well, you should see them . . . but, you know, you're right. It isn't just disgust. It's also that they worry me. I feel like I'm the only one in the house that has any control over eating. She's constantly telling me to eat more, and I'm constantly trying to hint to everyone that they should eat less and exercise more.

ML-W: So, maybe the control you try to maintain over your eating and exercising are partly aimed at sending a message to the rest of your family.

M: Well, you know, I worry about what's going to happen when I go away next year. They're so out of control. I look at my parents, then I look at my sister, and I can't imagine how they can help her to get her act together about this stuff, and I can't imagine how they're going to keep from getting heart attacks just from being too fat.

ML-W: Sounds pretty frightening. Wonder if your concern about leaving them to their own devices contributes to your general level of anxiety.

M: Totally. No question. I suppose if I didn't care so much, it would help.

ML-W: Hard to imagine that caring about your family is the problem. Maybe the degree to which you keep all this to yourself increases your stress, though. Do you feel that there is a way to talk about some of these things more directly at home?

M: You know me. I hate confrontation.

ML-W: This would have to be a confrontation?

M: I don't know. I always think of it that way. But maybe I'm exaggerating, I don't know. My parents are actually pretty reasonable about talking about hard things, even when it has to do with them. I just wish they could help each other more about this eating thing, no less my sister. I sometimes wonder how they got to be so oblivious about how they look. Don't they care about being attractive to each other, for example? Or, have they just made some kind of compromise . . . you know, like I won't care if you won't? Seems weird to me.

Marie is looking at herself and her parents with a high degree of insight and objectivity. She is quite concerned about her future, including what it will be like at home when she goes away to college. Her issues are clearly those of someone her age, although the degree of anxiety she is experiencing is higher than would be present for most of her contemporaries. She is suffering with worries about how to leave home, how to see her parents as individuals and as a couple, how much to let them see who she really is (including how she looks at them), and how she thinks about the world.

Marie's adolescent separation process has taken place, as she seems squarely located in this time in her life and experiences her family members as distinct from her. Although she shows us that she is concerned about telling her parents something that might hurt or anger them ("confronting" them), she is willing to think about trying to do so; this tells us more about where she is in her adolescent separation process. She is worried about causing her parents displeasure or pain but not enough to completely stop her from trying to tell them something that might be of help to them.

Her individuation process is also reflected in this brief anecdote. She is knowledgeable about herself, as evidenced by her insight about her eating, her love of her parents, and her difficulties with confrontation. This makes clear that she is developing a picture of how she operates in the world—an important aspect of individuation at this age. She is looking at her appearance—another aspect of individuation—but she has a distorted view of it. These are individuation problems that we have to look at in her treatment, but they are problems with which most late adolescents contend.

Adolescents in this last subphase need to enter adulthood with as clear as possible a view of who they are when they look at themselves alone, who they are in relation to those around them who most matter, and how they view the most significant people in their lives. It is only when they have squarely confronted these issues that they can be viewed as having a mature genitality. Marie shows us that she is concerned about these issues, but she is having difficulty coming to some peaceful resolution of them. The college seminar students—in the fluidity of their movement from discussing issues of the self with boundaries to issues of the complex picture of self to issues of relationship—show us what the maturation of genitality looks like.

In order to move into adulthood, late adolescents need to feel relatively clear about who they are, who the important people in their lives are, and how the significant relationships of their lives work. This is mature genitality; it incorporates the separation and individuation processes of adolescence. In order for a late adolescent to have an intimate, committed relationship with another person, as the students in the college seminar suggested, each person must be self-aware, aware of the other, and aware of the boundary between them. Separation and individuation processes must, therefore, have moved beyond those of childhood. Without the further developments in these areas that adolescence brings, the changes that are intrinsic to this time would not be incorporated into self-representations and object representations—that is, the sense of self.

Conclusion

If we compare Renée, Eugene, and Marie, we can see how developmental issues change over the course of adolescence. All three adolescents are concerned with who they are, how they are seen, what their relations with their parents and friends are like, and what it means to be close to people. There are shifting emphases, however, as we look at these adolescents as they are engaged in the different subphases of adolescent development.

Early adolescent Renée is preoccupied with her relationship with her mother and struggling in her capacity to see herself as distinct from her mother. She hurts herself as a way of expressing her discontent with her mother; she is furious about her mother's concerns about her but is unable to establish clearly that she is able to care adequately for herself; and she cannot express any of the preadolescent closeness that she felt toward her mother. All of these are problems of separation.

Eugene is upset that his girlfriend is unaware, except in the most superficial sense, of who he is. He wants to know himself in a complex way and wants to be seen by those with whom he is intimate in this complex way. This exemplifies the unfolding of the individuation process that is characteristic of middle adolescence.

The integrative processes of late adolescence as they contribute to the maturation of genitality are demonstrated by Marie's focus on her parents, their relationship with each other, and how she is the same and different from them. She is looking at who she is and how she compares to the rest of her family—evidence of adolescent versions of separation and individuation processes. Her focus on the nature of her parents' relationship with each other is an important component of the maturation of her genitality, as it gives her an opportunity for thinking through what it means for two people to be intimate.

These case anecdotes are examples of how the concerns of adolescents change as they move through this developmental phase. All are involved with the issues of their maturing genitality, but how they are involved shifts as they move through the subphases. As adolescents move through their subphases, they struggle to define who they are in relation to others, who they are in their particularity, and how they wish to be in relationships. Their capacity to do so exponentially increases during this phase of life.

To be attuned to the needs of patients, clinicians must know what their patients are trying to accomplish at each stage. We need to meet them where they are and respond to them as they show us what they are trying to understand about themselves and the world. Knowing what the predominant developmental needs are for each of the adolescent subphases helps immeasurably in these efforts.

The clinical relationship is itself a laboratory for the development of the capacity for intimacy. In the psychotherapeutic process, we draw the outlines of our patients—who we are in relation to them, who they are in their specificity, and how we interrelate. We outline, we color in, and we talk about the picture we have drawn together. This affords us the opportunity to bolster the processes of development that may not have taken place as fully as they needed to for these adolescents to progress without our intervention. I hope that this paper has provided us with a more vivid picture of what it is we are trying to accomplish in our therapeutic labs.

REFERENCES

Blos, P. (1962), *On Adolescence: A Psychoanalytic Interpretation.* New York: Free Press.
———— (1967), The second individuation process of adolescence. *The Psychoanalytic Study of the Child,* 22:162–186. New York: International Universities Press.

Brooks-Gunn, J. & Warren, M. P. (1985), Measuring physical status and timing in early adolescence: A developmental perspective. *J. Youth Adolesc.*, 14:163–189.

Emde, R. (1983), The prerepresentational self and its affective core. *The Psychoanalytic Study of the Child*, 38:165–192. New York: International Universities Press.

Erikson, E. H. (1968), *Identity, Youth and Crisis*. New York: Norton.

Escoll, P. (1987), The psychoanalysis of young adults. *Psychoanal. Inq.*, 7:5–30.

Freud, A. (1958), Adolescence. *The Psychoanalytic Study of the Child*, 13:255–278. New York: International Universities Press.

Freud, S. (1905), The transformations of puberty. *Standard Edition*, 7:207–243. London: Hogarth Press, 1953.

——— (1923), The ego and the id. *Standard Edition*, 19:30–66. London: Hogarth Press, 1953.

Furman, E. (1973), A contribution to assessing the role of infantile separation-individuation in adolescent development. *The Psychoanalytic Study of the Child*, 28:193–207. New York: International Universities Press.

Galatzer-Levy, R. (1984), Adolescent breakdown and middle-age crises. In: *Late Adolescence: Psychoanalytic Studies*, ed. D. D. Brockman. New York: International Universities Press, pp. 29–51.

Greenacre, P. (1958), Early physical determinants in the development of the sense of identity. *J. Amer. Psychoanal. Assn.*, 6:612–627.

Inhelder, B., & Piaget, J. (1958), *The Growth of Logical Thinking from Childhood to Adolescence*. New York: Basic Books.

Jacobson, E. (1964), *The Self and Object World*. New York: International Universities Press.

Kaplan, L. J. (1984), *Adolescence: The Farewell to Childhood*. New York: Simon & Schuster.

Levy-Warren, M. H. (1996), *The Adolescent Journey: Development, Identity Formation, and Psychotherapy*. Northvale, NJ: Aronson.

Mahler, M. S., Pine, F. & Bergman, A. (1975), *The Psychological Birth of the Human Infant*. New York: Basic Books.

Marohn, R. C. (1998), A reexamination of Peter Blos's concept of prolonged adolescence. *Adolescent Psychiatry*, 23:3–19. Hillsdale, NJ: The Analytic Press.

Offer, D. (1969), *The Psychological World of the Teenager*. New York: Basic Books.

Piaget J. (1947), *The Psychology of Intelligence.* New York: Harcourt Press.

———— (1972), Intellectual evaluation from adolescence to adulthood. *Human Development,* 15:1–12.

Schafer, R. (1973), Concepts of self and identity and the experience of separation-individuation in adolescence. *Psychoanal. Quart.,* 42:42–59.

Stern, D. N. (1985), *The Interpersonal World of the Infant.* New York: Basic Books.

Tanner, J. M. (1962), *Growth at Adolescence.* Springfield, IL: Thomas.

———— (1978), *Fetus to Man: Physical Growth from Conception to Maturity.* Cambridge, MA: Harvard University Press.

Wolf, E. (1982), Adolescence: Psychology of the self and selfobjects. *Adolescent Psychiatry,* 10:171–181. Chicago: University of Chicago Press.

2   THE INTERPERSONAL MATRIX OF ADOLESCENT DEVELOPMENT AND TREATMENT

ROBERT GAINES

The development of principles of technique for working psychoanalytically with adolescents has been hemmed in on many sides. Adolescents frequently do not want our help. Approaches designed for a willing and cooperative patient have to be modified. They do not play like children, and they do not talk like adults. Finally, the very developmental theory that might inform clinical innovation has remained largely dominated by rather orthodox Freudian thinking.

Richard Marohn's (1998) paper shows how thoroughly we have mistaken theoretical assumptions for facts and how the emerging relational point of view opens up new vistas. I welcome the opportunity to continue his line of thought.

Operating from a self-psychological orientation, Marohn (1998) points out that adolescence is not just a recapitulation or reworking of the oedipal complex or of the phases of separation/individuation but a time of new experiences. Interpersonal theory concurs and attempts to demonstrate how all the biological, cognitive, family, and social system changes of adolescence have their impact through the new interpersonal possibilities they create. Marohn argues further that adolescence is not a process of detachment from the parents but a transformation of the adolescent–parent relationship that continues on. Interpersonal theory again concurs and adds some observations and conceptualizations that specify how the relationship transforms and what kind of new experiences adolescent and parent need to have with each other. Marohn suggests that we consider possible new selfobject experiences that become needed in adolescence, and interpersonal the-

25

ory replies that important new modes of relating emerge in relationships to peers. Finally, Marohn tentatively proposes that the therapist fulfills selfobject functions for the adolescent patient. Interpersonalists firmly state that the multiple ways the real relationship with the therapist meets the adolescent's developmental needs are central to therapeutic action.

I also welcome this opportunity to discuss the relationship of interpersonal developmental theory to other points of view and to update and extend interpersonal developmental thinking, particularly as it pertains to adolescence. Sullivan (1940, 1953) clearly felt that developmental theory was quite important to clinical work, but succeeding generations of interpersonalists focused more on the implications of Sullivan's foundational concept, the interpersonal field, and its application to treatment, participant observation, without reference to developmental considerations. I will try to show how these developmental considerations help adapt the contemporary interpersonal stance—the mutual analysis of the mutually created relationship—to work with adolescents.

Interpersonal and Relational Theories

Interpersonal theory, as developed by Sullivan in the 1930s and early 1940s, was one of the first attempts to reformulate psychoanalytic theory to eliminate the centrality of the drives and, instead, to emphasize the role of interpersonal experience (Sullivan, 1940, 1953). It was a brilliant innovation, absolutely novel and penetrating in its broad strokes, although not a comprehensive theory of human development by today's standards. Interpersonal developmental theory is simultaneously a bold and creative synthesis of ideas from psychoanalysis, sociology, anthropology, linguistics, physics, and philosophy of science and a somewhat sketchy theory built largely on Sullivan's own life experience. Its enduring legacy is a fresh way of looking at people and a conceptual structure that can accommodate and integrate many contemporary developments.

As originally demarcated by Greenberg and Mitchell (1983), the relational group of theories included interpersonal theory, self psychology, attachment theory, and various object relations approaches. As Mitchell (1988), in particular, has gone on to discuss, each relational approach has distinctive emphases, or, we might say, relative to each other, they each have strengths and weaknesses. A synthesis of the

26

various contemporary relational approaches may yield a more useful and comprehensive theory than any single version. The creation of such a synthesis is underway. At this stage in the process of integration, it is still useful to talk about the individual contributions of each theory to highlight those distinctive aspects that deserve a place in the broader synthesis.

INTERPERSONAL THEORY OF DEVELOPMENT: BASIC CONSIDERATIONS

Like all relational theories, interpersonal theory assumes that the human organism is related from birth onward and that maintaining satisfactory connectedness is the prime motivation. Also, like other relational theories though perhaps with stronger emphasis, interpersonal theory sees the individual's actual experience with significant relationships as the crucible of development. Realities, not instinct or fantasies, are decisive in development. Interpersonal theory does take account of individual differences in temperament and endowment as well as other biological, cognitive, and broad cultural factors in development, but these are integrated by the interpersonal contexts in which they occur and have their impact in terms of the interpersonal possibilities they open up or foreclose (Gaines, 1995).

Interpersonal theory in general, and of adolescence in particular, is distinctive in several respects—a strong emphasis on active growth and the emergence of new relational needs at each developmental stage; a rich appreciation of the role of peer relationships, individual and group; a sharp focus on the critical role of parents in fostering or impeding adolescent development; and a sophisticated understanding of the intertwining of individuality and connectedness in relationships. Before discussing adolescent development in detail, I briefly review some of its conceptual underpinning.

Developmental Progression

The foundation in actual experience commits interpersonal theory to emphasizing that each individual's developmental trajectory must be formulated in terms of the specific particulars of his life (Zucker, 1989). Common fantasies or configurations, such as the classic oedipal complex, are not assumed to be universal. Development occurs through participation in an expanding series of interpersonal fields. As a result of cognitive growth, biological maturation, the progression of cultural and familial expectations, and the results of experience in previous periods of development (including emerging relational needs), the individual is presented with a succession of new possibilities for relating at each step along the way to maturity. These possibilities offer the opportunity for growth but also pose tasks that must be mastered. The nature of the resulting developmental change can be conceptualized as a continual process of differentiation, both within the ongoing child–parent relationship and within the child's represented interpersonal world.

To help organize observations of developmental progression, Sullivan (1953) proposed the following epigenetic sequence of stages: infancy, childhood, juvenile, preadolescence, early adolescence, and late adolescence. However, contemporary interpersonalists recognize that not all aspects of development fit neatly into stage theory. Some aspects of development are more continuous, others more event-specific, still others more idiosyncratic.

The interpersonal way of thinking about development is both highly inclusive, taking seriously the concept of multiple interacting forces, and quite open ended, allowing for many different patterns (Shapiro, 1995–1996). One individual's movement into adolescence may be strongly colored by a clash between a dramatic, early appearance of secondary sexual characteristics and a sexually repressive family culture, whereas another's may be more influenced by a pseudosophisticated, "fast" peer group coupled with a parent's overly narcissistic investment in the child's popularity.

Development Leading up to Adolescence:
Infancy, Childhood, Juvenile Stages

Infancy is about the establishment of mutual regulation in the mother–child dyad in the service of meeting the infant's needs and establishing the relationship bond (Schecter, 1973). From virtually the moment the relationship bond is established, it begins to evolve. Both baby and mother, in the process of enriching the dialogue, promote differentiation and autonomy. Movement from closer, more responsive, and established modes of relating to more loosely regulated, less responsive, newly emerging modes always entails some period of disequilibrium and anxiety. The familiar must be left before the novel can become reliable, and so there is always some tug of war between wanting to move forward and wanting to stay the same. This powerful separation/individuation dynamic echoes through life and is highly relevant during adolescence, when child–parent relationships are radically restructured.

As differentiation in the parent–child relationship proceeds, the focus shifts from securing the relationship bond to using it to shape the child. With and without awareness, parents now systematically use the power of affirmation, attunement, and anxiety to mold the child's personality. The parents become authority figures in the child's life. As the child becomes more differentiated within himself, with a subjective sense of his own inner world of thoughts and feelings, a new relational need for recognition of and participation in imaginative play emerges. During this time, the child experiences the loss of the exclusive tie to each parent, and oedipal dynamics enter the picture (Schecter, 1968). Using his increasing cognitive equipment, the child becomes aware that mother and father have other significant relationships—to other children perhaps, to their jobs, to each other. In his wish to hold onto exclusivity, the child may focus particularly on the parent bond as his obstacle, with attendant feelings of jealousy, wishes to remove one parent, and consequent fears of retaliation. The conceptualization of the parents' closeness, as well as the wish to be especially close to each parent, may be sexualized to varying degrees depending on the dynamics of the family group. The multiple frustrations the child faces in dealing with this more complex relational network make him wish to be like his parents or other adults—fostering identifications and opening up future plans and dreams as a psychologically alive space.

As differentiation proceeds, the juvenile begins his emergence from embeddedness in the family. He develops an understanding that there is a special cohort of children out there—his age/life space mates—who, individually and collectively, can include or exclude him, and new relational needs for peer relationship and group affiliation evolve. This kind of group is different from the family; it is self-selected for membership, and in it all are equal and conflict resolution is on a reciprocal basis. In his desire to affiliate, the child must master new relational skills of cooperation, tolerance of differences, and competition.

The juvenile also begins differentiating authority figures and authority situations. Juveniles are learning both to subordinate their personal needs to new authorities and to free themselves from the absolute rule of authority, especially parental authority. The school society offers opportunities for observing child–authority relationships (what works and does not work in their own and in other children's relationships to teachers) and opportunities for comparing authorities to one another, teachers to other teachers, their parents to their teachers, and their parents to other children's parents. This is the beginning of a process, which accelerates in adolescence, of developing a more realistic image of one's parents (Gaines, 1996–1997). This process of renegotiating the relationship to parents and modifying their internal representation has nothing to do with a need to defend against a supposed regressive revival of an incestuous tie to the parents initiated by the upsurge of drives in early adolescence. It is part of the general process of self–other differentiation that began in infancy and continues throughout life.

Adolescence

Development in adolescence is multifaceted and can be described from a variety of conceptual angles. No single exposition can address all the relevant issues. For example, Sullivan and many theorists following him approached adolescence as a progression of subphases, with early adolescence being the most concerned with leaving childhood behind, sexuality arriving powerfully in midadolescence, and late adolescence the time when identity and a future adult role loom large. However, interpersonal theory also emphasizes that these developments are not linked in any simple, direct way to underlying biological maturational process, and therefore there can be considerable overlap and individual variation. Instead of following phase by phase, I will focus on four developmental themes and task areas identified as particularly salient by interpersonal theory: cognitive maturation, peer relationships, the interpersonal context of puberty, and renegotiation of the adolescent–parent relationship.

COGNITIVE MATURATION

Cognitive maturation, which has been part of earlier development, becomes particularly important in adolescence. Interpersonal theory conceives of the individual growing through his experience of relationships. Experience is not a photocopy of events but a cognitive construct, so growth of cognitive capacities opens up new relational possibilities. Adolescents' ability to think about thinking and the products of thought, rules, values, self-concepts, relationship patterns, political and family organizations, and so on throws many things into question and gives perception and experience a striking sense of being fresh and new. The ability to reflect on one's identity can be troubling, but it also creates surges of feelings of self-discovery. The adolescent's new capacity to observe and question his own and others' personalities can be used to direct himself toward change and constructive experience in a way that was not possible before.

PEER RELATIONSHIPS

Throughout adolescence, experiences with friends, individually and in groups, are extremely important. Except for the relatively few isolated adolescents, most spend a lot of time with their peers, and sometimes this is taken for granted. Interpersonal theory reminds us that constructive friendships are not automatic. There is a lot of learning about relationships—learning that is necessary for progressive development—that may or may not be taking place.

At the very beginning of adolescence, before the peak of pubertal changes, a new relational need for intimacy emerges. By intimacy, Sullivan was referring to a close relationship to one person, at this age usually of the same sex, that is characterized by a collaborative mode of relating and sharing many thoughts and feelings, including one's perception of oneself and the other. By collaborative, Sullivan meant a relationship in which the security and satisfaction of the other are as important as one's own. Sullivan (1953) felt that this relationship, which he called "chumship," was extremely important in development. It is a wonderful opportunity to find validation of many aspects of one's personality that have not been affirmed at home or in the juvenile peer group. It is a chance to discover how powerful a personal relationship can be in alleviating anxiety. Moving forward, it will provide a way to "normalize" the experience of the unfamiliar and rapidly changing inner states associated with puberty by discovering that one's peers are having the same experiences (Shapiro and Esman, 1992). It is a chance to learn about intimate sharing and caring before the complications of sexuality set in. On the other hand, difficulties in moving toward collaborative relationships can have serious consequences. Some individuals remain arrested in the juvenile stage and are only dimly aware of what they are missing. Others may attempt to integrate intimate relationships with inappropriate partners, which may lead to rejection or exploitation, sexual and otherwise.

Lack of fulfillment of the need for intimacy creates loneliness, which Sullivan felt was one of the most painful states. The need not to feel lonely can drive the adolescent past anxiety into relationships, which can work out well and lead to enhanced self-esteem but which are inherently risky and can sometimes lead to disaster. The need to attenuate feelings of loneliness, often compounded by persisting feelings of deprivation by parents and rejection by the juvenile peer group, can lead to detachment, drug use, or frantic activity.

The progression to an intimate/collaborative mode of relating is not a defense against or a reaction to threatening pregenital dependency or oedipal fantasies. It grows out of the progressive momentum of self-differentiation and evolution of relational needs. If earlier development, and parents' reaction to current behavior, has left the adolescent with great restrictions in his ability to grow, he may feel imprisoned by a dependent or sexualized tie to a parent and may reactively try to overthrow this bondage. This activity may move in the direction of peer relationships but will not have the characteristics of collaboration and intimacy.

Another aspect of adolescent peer relationships is the forming of social gangs. The two-person chumships tend to link together into larger groups. These groups bear many similarities to the kinds of social and work groups individuals will participate in throughout adult life. The adolescent gangs differentiate roles—leaders, followers, diplomats, independents, entertainers. Experimentation with different roles and role relationships provides opportunities to explore new aspects of oneself—to find validation for previously undervalued traits—or may reinforce negative aspects of one's self-image. The specific friends one finds and chooses, and the group dynamics that develop, can make a considerable difference as to whether this experience is growth-promoting or destructive. Very important in these groups is the issue of conformity to the group culture. The issues of affiliation and acceptance that emerged in the juvenile era are still potent, perhaps intensified, yet adolescents must at the same time begin to learn how to stand apart—to use their own judgment and listen to their own inner voice of conscience. Often, each gang has a group identity (e.g., nerds, jocks, socialites, druggies) and a consistent pattern of activity that supports that identity. The gang's identity has meaning within the larger preadolescent society and the wider community. This social recognition and this endorsement of gang identity can have beneficial or negative effects on the individual child.

THE INTERPERSONAL CONTEXT OF PUBERTY

As adolescence progresses, the pubertal changes in body size, shape, coordination, and capacity for genital arousal and discharge arrive. Actually, the latency myth has tended to blind us to the fact that both conscious experience of sexual attraction and genital arousal have existed for years. The experience of peremptory desire for actual genital contact is the strikingly new element.

Interpersonal theory recognizes puberty as a momentous occasion but emphasizes that its meaning will derive from the interpersonal context in which it occurs. Past relationship history and current interpersonal context give shape and meaning to physical changes that have a great deal of psychological plasticity. For instance, a glance at a group of seventh- and eighth-grade boys and girls will reveal that degree of interest in the opposite sex is not perfectly correlated to pubertal physical development. Psychological dynamics can significantly amplify or attenuate the influence of hormonal shifts and probably even the course of the biological events. Another example: research has shown that the pubertal changes in body size and shape are welcomed by boys but experienced negatively by girls (Peterson, 1988). As there is nothing intrinsically negative about the girls' changes, this finding (along with the larger phenomenon of the drop in self-esteem among adolescent girls; Gilligan, 1982) points up the overriding importance of the interpersonal context in defining the subjective experience of the puberty changes.

For interpersonalists, sexuality has its developmental impact through the new relationships it makes possible and necessary. The advent of sexuality in the individual and in the peer group brings about many relationship transitions. Chumships may dissolve painfully as one member moves into heterosexual relating before the other does. There may be peer group pressure to pursue sexual relating before an individual is ready. Because sexuality requires not only inner integration but successful social performance, the individual who is slow to mature or who has difficulty attracting a partner may suffer a serious setback to his self-esteem. Sexuality also demands a change in the parent–adolescent relationship. Many relationships that have been adequate up to this point begin to unravel, and some that have been struggling fall apart entirely. Successful integration of sexuality requires creating a relationship with a suitable, willing partner and doing so on more or less the timetable expected by one's peer group and surrounding culture. Delays in this movement, as well as difficulties attracting and keeping a partner, can have lasting effects.

RENEGOTIATION OF THE ADOLESCENT–PARENT RELATIONSHIP

Renegotiation of the adolescent–parent relationship is central to all other developments at this time. The relationship must expand to allow the adolescent room to grow, and the parents need to take an active part in guiding and supporting that growth. Even with all of the other involvements the adolescent has, the ongoing, evolving relationship to the parents remains the foundation of development.

Freudian theory has conceptualized this as a process of emancipation from the contemporary parents and a detachment from inner infantile object ties. The goal is autonomy and independence. As Schafer (1973) points out, this is a rather concrete, all-or-none way of thinking. The so-called infantile objects are not like old dolls—to be played with one last time and then brought to the curb to be thrown out. The internal representations of the child–parent relationship, and the relationship itself, have been continuously revised and reorganized throughout childhood. Adolescence will merely continue this process at an increased pace. This is not just a mix-up of reified metaphors. It is a fundamental difference in the view of human life. Classical psychoanalytic theory has bought into, if not helped create, a vision of maturity as complete self-reliance. Interpersonal theory, on the other hand, views individuals as interdependent at every stage of life, with only the dimensions of connectedness evolving. The individual who has successfully traversed adolescence still needs and makes use of a continuing relationship to his parents but needs less frequent direct contact and help and is more capable of using the parental relationship as an inner resource. What we see, during adolescence, is not detachment but a process in which the dimensions of individuality and connection are modified, with the end result being both greater individuality and more mutual interconnectedness for all parties. Traditional theory has set up a false dichotomy between autonomy and dependence. Increased capacity for individuality (self-direction, self-regulation, self-assertion, self-expression) makes possible a more fluid and mutual connectedness, a connectedness with more permeable boundaries, a connectedness that can take place on the representational level. Interpersonal theory emphasizes that this process of renegotiation of the dimensions of connectedness is a two-way process, with significant contributions or impediments from the adolescent and the parents.

The adolescent's contribution to forward movement in the parent–adolescent relationship is quite apparent in the assertive desire to make decisions, explore new roles, assume new responsibilities, and establish greater privacy and freedom from supervision. This is usually described as striving for autonomy and independence, although, from an interpersonal point of view, such a formulation of the adolescent's aims is inaccurate and misleading. These concepts imply a freedom from relationship, whereas interpersonal theory sees a striving for a new kind of relating. The aim of the adolescent is to be accepted by adults as an almost equal, as an adult-in-training. Oddly enough, in our language there is no term that describes this relationship precisely. Something in between apprenticeship and partnership would be just right. The essence of the adolescent's new relational need is recognition by adults of his capacity to function cognitively, emotionally, and physically at a fully adult level. Obviously, the adolescent does not function steadily at this level or relate consistently on the collaborative/intimate level. These are relational modes that are emerging in adolescence and that will continue to develop over many years. In the meantime, they alternate with relational modes characteristic of earlier developmental levels.

In the context of this discussion of the adolescent's push to redefine his relationship to adults, it is important to state that interpersonal theory does not see regression or marked ambivalence as part of the normal adolescent process. The emergence of new relational needs arises out of the progressive momentum of self and self–other differentiation. It is not a compensatory thrust against a regressive undertow. At every period of developmental transition, there is always trepidation about leaving established ways of maintaining connectedness and avoiding anxiety for a beckoning but unfamiliar new level of relatedness. In adolescence, the rapidity of change, and the feeling of being at one of life's turning points, guarantees that there will be some vacillation between wanting to be treated like the grown-up one is becoming and the child one does not want to leave behind, but forward movement will never stop for long. One does not need to posit a reluctance to give up infantile dependency to account for this. Going from twelve to nineteen is hard enough. If anxiety severely constricts an adolescent in accessing his inner resources, and he feels small and weak, or if there is a persisting sense of unmet needs from earlier stages, forward movement may be blocked. Then we may see stubborn clinging to, or angry demands for, earlier modes of relating. This is a deviation from a healthy developmental path.

Whereas the adolescent's contribution to the transforming parental relationship has been somewhat taken for granted, the parents' vital role has been mostly overlooked. Interpersonal theory places great stress on the parent's role. The parent's contribution can be described in terms of two crucial processes—*permission* and *promotion*. Permission refers to the parents' allowing the adolescent room to grow. One aspect of this involves permitting the parent–adolescent relationship itself to grow. The parent needs to accept the adolescent's new strengths and competencies, to acknowledge when he is right or has won, to accept his help, to be stimulated by his intellect. Another aspect is permission to become involved in relationships outside the family. Interpersonal theory places great emphasis on the importance of relationships to peers and new adults, and this leads naturally to the realization that parents sometimes try to block these relationships. Sullivan (1953) rather caustically described how parents' own anxiety about change can lead them to disparage any friend or sexual partner their adolescent may find or to ridicule the adolescent for trying to reach out to others.

Promotion refers to all the extra help beyond mere permission that adolescents need in finding and tackling new experiences. Although vastly more competent than they were only a few years ago, adolescents still need information, guidance, modeling, and limit setting. Promotion refers to all of the ways parents help adolescents function on their highest possible level. Promotion can take the form of locating opportunities for participation outside the family world, providing information about how the adult world works, or challenging a youngster to greater effort in pursuit of his goals. Trad (1991, 1992) illustrates this with his concept of *previewing*—parents' presenting to a child, in an age-appropriate way, a model of an imminent developmental step while indicating how this step will change the parent–child relationship in a positive way. For example, a mother might talk to her fourteen-year-old daughter about some of the experiences that she will have when she begins dating and how much fun it will be to talk about it together when it happens. Through this conversation, the mother helps the daughter to see herself in that future role and provides a wealth of information about how to go about it and what feelings to expect—at the same time indicating that she welcomes the change it will bring about in their relationship.

Also relevant to the promotion of adolescents' involvement in the outside world are formal aspects of the family dialogue that move the relationship to a higher level of differentiation. For example, research with a family decision-making task found that the adolescents whose parents actively solicited and responded affirmatively to their suggestions showed more active and productive exploration of identity issues in their life (Grotevant and Cooper, 1998).

Permission and promotion have their concrete, day-today aspects, and a less tangible aspect. This less tangible aspect has to do with how the parent creates, holds in mind, and presents to the adolescent a vision of his future, an image of his fully realized adult state. This affirmation and respect for the person the parent knows the adolescent can be is perhaps the most important ingredient of all.

The adolescent's normative ambivalence about change is matched by parents' similar feelings. Parents may have separation issues of their own, aging and death concerns activated by their children's growth, or issues with competition or envy. In their forward and backward movements, parents and adolescents react to each other in a complex interplay that I have barely explored here. And that is precisely the point I wish to emphasize—that every day there are myriad adolescent–parent transactions that can promote or hinder development.

Another important part of the renegotiation of the adolescent–parent relationship concerns the role of the parents' authority in the adolescent's life. Challenge to authority is not unique to adolescence. As soon as parents begin asserting their authority, their children start challenging it. What is new in adolescence is the force and penetration of the challenge: The child may question specific decisions, but the adolescent questions the parents' right to make rules at all. Adolescents also question and criticize the parents' way of making decisions as well as the clearness and consistency of the rules applied. They are much more acute observers, and they jump on inconsistencies in the application of rules and discrepancies between what parents say should be done and what they actually do. These challenges are aimed at gaining more freedom and responsibility, but they are also part of the way adolescents go about learning how to conduct themselves. Lack of response leaves them feeling abandoned to flounder in their own limited experience. The struggle with parents' rules is the active process of understanding and assimilating these rules. Occasionally, breaking rules is the adolescents' way of trying to learn from their own experience At the same time, parents' maintaining standards and expectations that adolescents must meet to keep their approval is necessary to continue the process of identification with the parents. A balance must be achieved between allowing for experimentation (and learning from mistakes) and leaving the adolescent alone in a vacuum. Although it is vital for parents to continue to assert authority and present direction, these must be done in new ways that are congruent with the adolescent's growth. Parents must still, at times, enforce rules and expectations with negative consequences. But they must also respect the adolescent's greater capacity to understand the reasoning and purpose of various regulations and be willing to endlessly discuss and debate them. Because of the adolescent's new ability and interest in scrutinizing their parents' behavior, more than ever it is not sufficient to take a "do as I say, not as I do" approach. Adolescents need leadership along with dialogue.

New relationships with peers and adults are triangulated into the ongoing renegotiation with the parents. The peer group and peer culture become a way station on the path to self-definition. The shared standards, protocols of dress and behavior, and group narcissism (each adolescent group feels it is the latest and greatest) provide a replacement for parental connectedness while the adolescent learns to do more for himself and to establish connectedness to the parents on a new level. However, if parental connectedness becomes too attenuated, the adolescent is at risk for submerging himself and his good judgment in the peer group. Relationships to elders can play a similar role, but they have the additional function of providing relationship experiences that are temporarily or permanently unavailable with parents. Temporary unavailability results when the parents are slow to adapt to developmental changes in the adolescent or when the adolescent needs to push the parent away to define dimensions of individuality. Permanent unavailability stems from parental limitations. The heroes and heroines of early adolescence offer a vicarious participation in invincible self-esteem, which the parents, not being superstars and already somewhat cut down to size in the juvenile era, cannot provide. The later role models and mentors of middle and late adolescence usually combine qualities very similar to the parents' with qualities that balance or modulate the parents' more troublesome aspects. The adolescent usually is aware only of the differences between him and his parents, but, from a more distant vantage point, we can see how these relationships serve to maintain a continuity with the past while opening up new dimensions of relating.

Distinctive Features of the Interpersonal View of Adolescence

Emphasis on the powerful progressive momentum of development and on the appearance of new developments throughout the growth cycle is one of the distinctive features that the interpersonal view can bring to a synthesis of relational theories. For the adolescent, there is an enormous sense of newness, of discovery, of expanding horizons and self-creation. A developmental theory that orients us to growth and new experience helps us attune to this dimension of adolescent life, to affirm it when we see it, and to detect it when the adolescent himself is defensively trying to remain unaware of it. The generation gap arises, in part, because the adolescent, in the midst of self-discovery but still rather egocentric, cannot conceive that the adult generation can understand what he is going through. His experience is so new that it cannot have anything to do with what his parents or therapist went through. The interpersonal point of view can help us bridge this gap and avoid invalidating the adolescent's experience.

This orientation to new experience and growth in interpersonal theory also stands in sharp contrast to the "recapitulation theory" that had been at the core of the heretofore dominant Freudian theory (Jones, 1922; Blos, 1967, 1979). In this point of view, the essence of the adolescent process is the regressive revival of incestuous infantile object ties and the struggle to detach from these ties and invest in new objects. In this theory, the emphasis on regressive, infantile wishes and on the tendency to see the significance of the adolescent's forward movements mainly as defensive maneuvers against these infantile wishes amounts to a devaluation of the adolescent's capacities and growth process. It mirrors the process, almost universal in human history, of the older generation's feeling threatened by adolescents and needing to keep them down (Bryt, 1979; Kaplan, 1984). In treatment, this is a serious countertransference impediment. A more positive stance was described by Sullivan (1972) way back in the 1920s:

The epoch of adolescence seems to me the locus of hope. Preadolescents and adolescents seek assistance and welcome knowledge
of people. . . . That which we can accomplish with adolescents is
a preface to the future, to parenthood and the second generation.

Clinical Applications

The derivation of clinical principles from thinking about any one
stage of development is in some ways artificial, because we always
deal with the sum total of development, past and current. Further,
adolescents who most need treatment have problems most heavily
influenced by unfavorable early experience. Those who had "good
enough" earlier development and who are struggling with an adolescent
issue are much more likely to be able to solve it with help from friends,
family, or indigenous community helpers such as teachers, coaches, or
clergy. Nevertheless, some generalizations from interpersonal theory
can be made. I will take up three issues—the kind of help adolescents
seek, the nature of the therapeutic relationship, and work with parents.
Interpersonal theory emphasizes the emergent aspects of adolescent
development—in particular, the process of finding and mastering a
variety of new relationship experiences. This emphasis on new experience alerts us to expect that adolescents will seek or, as is more usually
the case, will accept help only when it seems relevant to their current
relationship problems. Adolescents may be brought for treatment for
underperforming in school, not getting along with siblings, abusing
drugs or alcohol, or being involved in delinquent behavior, but these
are not likely to be what concerns them most. What adolescents want
help with is their feelings of loneliness, their inability to fit into the
desired social group, their desperation to succeed with the opposite
sex, or their feelings of rejection by their parents. Connecting with
these current concerns is the surest way to engage the often reluctant
adolescent; characterological issues, behavior problems, and other
symptomatic activities must come later. Of course, this is easier said
than done, because the treatment relationship is situated primarily in
the context of the parent–adolescent relationship. The same degree of
tension and mistrust that are operating there, which is usually considerable, will pervade the treatment relationship and make the adolescent

reluctant to discuss these concerns. This brings us to consider the nature of the therapeutic relationship.

Adolescents bring their new relational needs and the difficult experiences they are having with them into the therapy relationship. They seek intimacy and collaboration, acceptance of their sexuality, and promotion of their emerging capacities but are wary that they will find the opposite. Although this dilemma can eventually be discussed directly, the more powerful generator of therapeutic action is the real relationship with the therapist, which differs in significant respects from the current relationships of difficulty. In trying to be a "better parent" or a "good chum," we must keep in mind that we are not saviors, we do not make up for all lost experience, and we cannot replace the significant others with whom the adolescent lives his life. What we can do is try to provide new relationship experience that can generalize and that can open up new possibilities with the people available in the adolescent's world. Particularly with regard to the parents, we must remember that, although we are trying to differentiate ourselves from the negative parental representation and the actual parents of today, with whom the adolescent is locked in conflict or by whom he feels rejected or deprived, we also need to align ourselves with the good parental representation and help the adolescent revive that representation for himself.

Beginning with Aichhorn (1925), the icon of adolescent treatment, therapists have been concerned with differentiating themselves from the parents and creating a new kind of relationships. Often they have relied on dramatic maneuvers such as ostentatiously throwing the adolescent's medical record in the garbage, quietly informing the sullen, suicidal teenager that he is free to leave if he pleases, or spending the first session discussing the merits of communism versus capitalism. All adolescent therapists have their ways of sending the message, "Look, I'm different from the other adults you know." Accounts of the seriously disturbed adolescent who is told that therapy must be his own choice and who gets up and leaves only to return the next day asking for help (Anthony, 1976) are seductive. In my experience, it rarely happens that way. Nor should it. Too much of an effort to disavow any alliance with parental figures and adult standards of behavior is, and will be perceived as, disingenuous, and it can promote splitting and acting out. The adolescent's initial wariness is slow to melt and frequently reappears. Exploring it is not to be bypassed, for that exploration will promote a genuine therapeutic dialogue and will reveal his

41

significant difficulties in making relationships. The relationship must be addressed openly, gently, consistently.

Rather than using dramatic maneuvers, the interpersonal therapist relies on trying to establish a really new kind of relatedness and is guided by his conceptualization of the emerging relational modes of intimacy, collaboration, and apprenticeship. He endeavors to demonstrate how to put the other person's security and self-esteem before his own. He actively tries to validate aspects of the adolescent's personality that prior experience neglected or judged unacceptable. The interpersonal therapist strives to interact with the adolescent in ways that recognize and promote his highest level of functioning. This translates into an active engagement, an open sharing of thoughts and feelings within the session, and efforts to evoke the patient's curiosity about himself. The therapist actively solicits the teenager's observations and formulations about whatever is being discussed and gives them equal value with his own. In exploring enactments or relationship snarls, he acknowledges equal participation and responsibility for making changes to work them out. He is willing to share and expose for scrutiny his own values, life experiences, and approaches to difficult interpersonal situations, so that the adolescent can learn from them, be free to choose to be different or to identify. The therapist's goal is not to explain the adolescent to himself but to expand his field of observation about his relationships. He realizes that the adolescent, the drag racer of developmental progression, is not that interested in the past and cannot find meaning or safety in a context that fosters regression. The adolescent requires a real, knowable person who actively demonstrates his concern, interest, and respect (Kantor, 1995).

The final area I will take up is direct work with the adolescent's parents. Many therapists, including some interpersonalists (Schimel, 1979), advocate a tight boundary around the relationship with the adolescent, with only the minimum of contact with the parents necessary to retain their support of the treatment. I believe that an interpersonal perspective suggests otherwise. First, the amount of contact necessary to create and sustain genuine support for treatment is usually considerable, not minimal. To truly trust the therapist and "get behind" the therapy, parents must have sufficient opportunity to get to know the therapist really well, including his values and feelings about their child. Also, given the pivotal role in the adolescent's development that interpersonal theory assigns to the parents, it is imperative to try to make some constructive changes with them. Whether it is in trying to ameliorate hostile, destructive interactions or, in more benign situations, sharpening parents' awareness of the need to actively promote their adolescent's development, a little change in the parents goes a long way. In this era when parents feel that adolescents are supposed to be "independent," there is much confusion about how actively to get involved. Whether it is a question of what role parents should play in supervising a seventh grader's homework or what they should know about a seventeen-year-old's friends and activities, parents need a lot of direct coaching on how to promote development.

Some clinical material from the first interview and early phases of work with a tenth-grade boy can illustrate these features of the interpersonal approach. Fred reluctantly came (was brought) to therapy after many years of being angry and oppositional at home, passive–aggressively undermining himself at school, and suffering with being socially isolated and needy. Fred is the oldest sibling; next in age is a brother, then a sister. The key dynamic in Fred's family has been the inordinate amount of time, effort, and emotional energy the parenting of his severely learning disabled, emotionally vulnerable brother requires.

At our first meeting, Fred immediately declared that therapy was for people who are weak, which he was not. He could take care of his problems, which he planned to do by forgoing college, moving out of home, and getting a job as soon as he graduated high school. I said it sounded to me that he was making some very big commitments rather prematurely. I also wondered how he would feel talking to me if he didn't want to be there. He said that wasn't a problem—he was comfortable talking to all kinds of people, and, besides, he planned to come only a few times to satisfy his parents. He acknowledged being very angry, which he attributed to his mother's continual appeasement of his volatile, learning-disabled younger brother. I said that his parents had mentioned that as a source of his unhappiness, which I could see as well, and perhaps he too wanted some help with that? He suggested I could help by talking to his mother, not him. He did mention a fear of death, but mainly he spoke nonstop about not wanting treatment. He felt no one really wanted therapy unless they were desperate, and he challengingly stated that he was sure I had never been in therapy. I matter-of-factly corrected his assumption. His fear of death related to a fear of abandonment, and, in discussing this, he spoke of his reluctance to become attached to anyone and his belief that it did not matter anyway, because he could not spend more than two days with anyone, including friends, without fighting. When I suggested I might be able to help him with that, he seemed genuinely surprised but said nothing. In subsequent sessions, without ever directly acknowledging my comment, he began to discuss aspects of his hair-trigger temper and his idea that only weaklings come for therapy. Early in our meetings, Fred asked that I talk to his parents about his desire to have more self-direction of his academic commitments. They were reluctant because of his poor track record, but I suggested that an attempt to meet his initiative with a positive compromise would be better than a flat turndown.

This session illustrates several features of the interpersonal approach just outlined. I try to make explicit the interpersonal field in which we are operating and my contribution in creating it. I acknowledge my partial sympathy with the patient's parents' point of view and quickly try to make this aspect of our relationship something we can discuss. The patient declines this invitation but may return to it in the future. While respecting his ideas about solving his problems, I offer my opinion about a possible better alternative. I disclose some personal information, which he seems to need to know. In all these ways, I am trying to be a real and knowable person so that he can use me to explore himself. My responses indicate that I am a nonauthoritarian authority but that I am willing to hold a position and disagree. At every turn, I approach the patient with respect, encourage him to express his thoughts, and demonstrate that I can see things from his point of view. I am trying to promote his highest level of functioning. Later in the interview, my genuine curiosity about the patient's fear of death activates his own curiosity, and he reveals more of his inner concerns. When I hear, as I have been waiting hopefully for, a statement of a problem with which he wants help, I leap to offer that help, and a moment of unguarded meeting takes place. Similarly, I seize the first opportunity to talk to the patient's parents about something they can do to promote his developmental need for recognition of his higher level functioning.

I do not expect that this one session will melt the patient's unwillingness, but I feel that I engaged him in a pattern of relating that will move in that direction. In fact, many subsequent sessions returned to themes relating to his unwillingness to be there—including his concerns about weakness, his fear of being diminished or submissive by being compliant, and his taking pride in being oppositional and different. Many times he announced he was through, and yet he came back for more.

Summary

Interpersonal theory can be summarized as emphasizing the role of actual experience in development and treatment. This simple formula has extensive ramifications. In regard to adolescent development, interpersonal theory underscores the importance of adolescence as a developmental stage and highlights the role of peer relationships and renegotiation of the adolescent–parent relationship in that development. Applied to treatment, interpersonal theory leads us to emphasize that therapy needs to be a real relationship that creates a new relationship experience. At the same time, active efforts to modify parental behavior are critical.

REFERENCES

Aichhorn, A. (1935), *Wayward Youth*. New York: Viking Press.

Anthony, E. J. (1976), Between yes and no. In: *Adolescent Psychiatry*. Chicago: University of Chicago Press, 4:321–344.

Blos, P. (1967), The second individuation process of adolescence. In: *The Psychoanalytic Study of the Child*. New York: International Universities Press, 22:162–186.

——— (1979), Modifications in the classical psychoanalytical model of adolescence. In: *Adolescent Psychiatry*. Chicago: University of Chicago Press, 7:6–25.

Bryt, A. (1979), Developmental tasks in adolescence. In: *Adolescent Psychiatry*. Chicago: University of Chicago Press, 7:136–146.

Gaines, R. (1995), The treatment of children. In: *The Handbook of Interpersonal Psychoanalysis*, ed. M. Lionells, J. Fiscalini, C. Mann & D. B. Stern. Hillsdale, NJ: The Analytic Press, pp. 761–769.

——— (1996–1997), Psychotherapy with children and juvenile era tasks. *Rev. Interper. Psychoanal.*, 2:21–25.

Gilligan, C. (1982), *In a Different Voice: Psychological Theory and Women's Development*. Cambridge, MA: Harvard University Press.

Greenberg, J. & Mitchell, S. (1983), *Object Relations in Psychoanalytic Theory*. Cambridge, MA: Harvard University Press.

Grotevant, H. D. & Cooper, C. R. (1998), Individuality and connectedness in adolescent development: Review and prospects for research on identity, relationships, and context. In: *Personality Development in Adolescence*, ed. E. Skoe & A. von der Lippe. New York: Routledge, pp. 3–37.

Jones, E. (1922), Some problems of adolescence. In: *Papers on Psychoanalysis*. Boston: Beacon Press, 1961.

Kantor, S. (1995), Interpersonal treatment of adolescents. In: *The Handbook of Interpersonal Psychoanalysis*, ed. M. Lionells, J. Fiscalini, C. Mann & D. B. Stern. Hillsdale, NJ: The Analytic Press, pp. 771–792.

Kaplan, L. (1984), *Adolescence, the Farewell to Childhood*. New York: Simon & Schuster.

Marohn, R. C. (1998), A reexamination of Peter Blos's concept of prolonged adolescence. *Adolesc. Psychiat*, 23:3–19. Hillsdale, NJ: The Analytic Press.

Mitchell, S. (1988), *Relational Concepts in Psychoanalysis*. Cambridge, MA: Harvard University Press.

Peterson, A. C. (1988), Adolescent development. *Annual Review of Psychology*, 39:583–607.

Schafer, R. (1973), The concepts of self and identity and the experience of separation-individuation in adolescence. *Psychoanal. Quart.*, 42:42–59.

Schecter, D. (1968), The Oedipus complex: Considerations of ego development and parental interaction. *Contemp. Psychoanal.*, 4:111–137.

——— (1973), The emergence of human relatedness. In: *Interpersonal Explorations in Psychoanalysis*, ed. E. Witenberg. New York: Basic Books, pp. 17–39.

Schimel, J. (1979), Adolescents and families. In: *Adolescent Psychiatry*, Chicago: Chicago University Press, 7:362–377.

Shapiro, R. (1995–1996), Infant, mother, and bathwater: An interpersonal perspective. *Rev. Interper. Psychoanal.*, 1:12–13.

Shapiro, T. & Esman, A. (1992), Psychoanalysis and child and adolescent psychiatry. *J. Amer. Acad. Child Adolesc. Psychiat.*, 31:6–13.

Sullivan, H. S. (1940), *Conceptions of Modern Psychiatry*. New York: Norton.

——— (1953), *The Interpersonal Theory of Psychiatry*. New York: Norton.

——— (1972), *Personal Psychopathology*. New York: Norton.

Trad, P. (1991), Previewing: A developmental phenomenon and a therapeutic strategy. *Psychoanal. Psychol.*, 8:283–304.

——— (1992), Previewing and its relation to self formation in the systems of Kohut, Sullivan, and Stern. *Contemp. Psychoanal.*, 28:199–227.

Zucker, H. (1989), Premises of interpersonal theory. *Psychoanal. Psychol.*, 6:401–419.

THE PSYCHOLOGY OF BELONGING:

REFORMULATING ADOLESCENT

DEVELOPMENT

GIL G. NOAM

Adolescent Identity Development: A Historic Sketch

Erik Erikson, Peter Blos, and many other psychoanalytic contributors have provided us with enormously creative and influential insights into the adolescent years. So important was the evolving understanding of adolescent identity formation that it became the nexus of Erikson's theory of the entire life cycle. And, so successful have been the contributions of Erikson and the entire generation of psychoanalytic thinkers that, in the past 50 years, adolescent development has become synonymous with the task of forming a unique, self-chosen identity (e.g., Erikson 1950, 1968). It has also become established wisdom that adolescents need to transform childhood identifications with significant others (e.g., parents, grandparents, teachers) into a new and more elaborate unity we have come to call identity. That this process entails a painful set of crises and losses and represents a "second separation-individuation phase" (e.g., Blos, 1962; see also Mahler, Pine, and Bergman, 1975) has also become part of the accepted canon of psychoanalysis and an accepted wisdom of popular psychology.

But are adolescents still dealing with the same issues faced by their counterparts 30, 40, or even 50 years ago, when these theories were first introduced? Are youth still preoccupied with defining who they are and what they want to stand for? If so, have the significant political and cultural shifts of the past decades made any impact on how we understand or should understand adolescents today? To attempt to answer these questions, we can benefit from the historical context in which these ideas about adolescent identity development first germinated.

Identity theory was a curious product of a number of worlds. One world was shaped by prescribed norms of life in the 1950s; there still was a clear sequence when one studied, got married, had children, retired, and so forth. Another world was shaped by the rebellion and social upheaval of the 1960s. In a way, identity theory of the 1950s was culturally ahead of its time. Erikson introduced his grand synthesis, *Childhood and Society*, in the middle of this century (1950), before these ideas were refined through observation of and dialogue with many young people during the decade of flower power, black power, and anti-Vietnam protests.

Psychoanalytic identity theory had its roots in an even earlier world. It derived many elements from the European (especially German) experience of the youth movement between the two World Wars and the even earlier Romantic tradition of the adolescent "wanderlust." Both of these traditions profoundly shaped Erik Homburger's life (before he gave himself his new name in his new country—the quintessential identity statement). They also deeply influenced his friend, Peter Blos, who had introduced him to the world of psychoanalysis in Vienna.

Erikson and Blos brought from Europe to the United States a tremendous cultural and experiential wealth but also the social turmoil that had entered every family between the two wars. This social crisis added responsibility to the young to define their future. The Jewish youngsters, many of whom later became the psychologists, psychiatrists, and psychoanalysts who define our present-day understanding of adolescence, had to make monumental decisions: When should they emigrate? How should they define themselves in the face of being officially viewed in the most negative terms possible? Should they be Zionists, communists, or liberals? Should they prepare for departure to Palestine, move to the United States, or flee to another country or continent? Or should they wait it out in Germany or Austria? These decisions were often fateful. They were, of course not only about identity; often they were also quite situational (Whom did one know in what country? What visa could one still get?). Nevertheless, there was that important identity component (Who was one? What was one's relationship to religion and to the great ideologies of the century?). The shape of one's identity, in other words, was not only an adolescent issue of experimentation but a fateful process that enhanced or decreased the chances for survival.

This European turmoil, which included a far greater time span than the Nazi years, was the most important experiential backdrop against which the psychoanalysts developed their theories of adolescence. It is worth exploring separately how the immigration experience of Anna Freud and others in England shaped a path of understanding adolescent development different from the American path of the psychoanalytic "family" (e.g., A. Freud, 1936). In the United States, the synthetic and adaptive nature of the ego shaped a long phase of psychoanalytic thinking and provided the theoretical foundation on which identity formation was built.

One can only guess how much the Euro-American analysts had to work against the very nature of their own experience to posit such a unified and synthetic ego and identity. Most immigrants live in two experiential worlds and see the world through a multitude of lenses (see Suarez-Orozco and Suarez-Orozco, 1995). They know most intimately how impossible it is to develop a truly integrated identity. Of course, even under these conditions, important work to bridge these worlds is performed and makes a concept of an ego or self quite important. But equally important (and far less developed in the theoretical literature) are the fluctuations of experience—the lack of integration that comes from living in multiple worlds.

Erikson knew much of this, but he was always the revolutionary (with a new way of "looking at things") who wanted to remain in the fold. He attempted to overcome many of Sigmund Freud's notions (e.g., S. Freud, 1915) while trying to remain a loyal Freudian (e.g., he overcame the preoccupation with early childhood and instead focused on the entire life cycle). Identity formation represented a bold theoretical declaration of independence: The central point in the life span had shifted from the preoedipal and oedipal time to a youth era in which choice, morality, ideology, and future orientation were central. It also represented a shift away from the psychoanalytic psychology of the family and the parents to a psychology of the generation and the peer group. It further represented a shift away from the "timeless" unconscious time to historic time, what Erikson called the historic moment. And, it represented a shift away from destiny and reflection to choice and action. In the process of making these essential shifts, Erikson and some of his psychoanalytic ego psychology colleagues transformed Freud's theory of nonresolution of human drives and conflicts into an adaptive theory of social and ethical solutions, exemplified by religious men like Luther and Gandhi.

Erikson's contribution was so sweeping and his integration abilities (shaped by his and Joan Erikson's artistic predilections) so great that all the distinctions I just introduced apply only partially. He knew and wrote about the power of early childhood, he saw conflict reemerge at every level of development (the "versus" in his stages), and he certainly saw the limitations history and biology imposed on individual choice. Still, we find in his work a great transformation—one that has yet to be fully incorporated into the field of psychoanalysis.

THE IDENTITY CONCEPT CHALLENGED

Especially because his transformation of psychodynamic principles included a new understanding of the role of culture and history in human development, we need to ask ourselves whether Erikson's and his generation's ideas of adolescent development are still valid. Influenced by these theories, the general public, or at least the media, still seems to accept the notions of adolescence as a time for young people to find themselves, to chose among different possible selves, and to seek a space in which to experiment and take risks. Autonomy is still the great buzzword for parents, teachers, and adolescents discussing homework, dating, or work. But the reality of youth today, I believe, is represented less and less by these constructs, and so it is time to realign our theoretical focus.

In fact, even in the past, the adolescent moratorium often required some money in the bank as well as some educational capital in the home. Youngsters who joined the work force right out of school, who were not given a college education, or who were drafted into the army had very different experiences. For them, the time of questioning, experimenting, and finding themselves seemed socially removed. Building a life and a family came much earlier, and the process of identity formation most likely followed a very different rhythm. This was found to be true as well when researchers began to focus on race and ethnicity and noticed many different paths of identity development during the adolescent years (e.g., Cohler, Stott, and Musick, 1995; Ogbu, 1985; Appiah, 1996).

Similarly, many feminist theorists (e.g., Gilligan, 1982, 1996; Jordan, in press) have resisted the notion that identity formation is needed for the creation of true intimacy in adulthood. For them, the search for intimacy is simultaneously the road toward a jointly established identity.

If that is so, then forming an identity is less an adolescent task than an adult one and less a task focused on individual choice than on interpersonal and communal connections.[1]

Another critique, empirically supported by a survey, comes from Offer, the Chicago-based developmental psychiatrist, and his colleagues (Offer and Schonert-Reichl, 1992). Offer rejects the notion of the adolescent identity crisis as normative and tries to shift it into the realm of serious adolescent psychopathology. His work indicates that the great majority of adolescents continue to be identified with their parents and follow their parents' political and life-style preferences and goals. Crisis and identity formation in antagonism to one's earlier identifications are the exception, he claims, not the rule.

There is always the danger of different methods producing different outcomes. Erikson treated and observed young patients and would have been appropriately hesitant to accept survey data as the fountain of wisdom regarding the adolescent identity experience. Identity formation is a deep process that can occur even if acceptance of the parents' values is reported on the surface. And what are the long-term consequences of an unquestioned childhood in adulthood?

Even if we agree with Offer's conclusions that today's adolescents define themselves less against their parents and their pasts, we lose a great deal by pathologizing the large minority of young people who are struggling to find themselves. How can Offer be so sure that they are in the throes of serious psychopathology? Indeed, he still owes us the longitudinal research necessary to distinguish between crises that are resolved in the process of transitioning into adulthood and crises that represent a beginning of a chronic state of depression, delinquency, and so forth. What distinguishes these paths? In the midst of adolescent turmoil, it still remains difficult, if not impossible, to make these distinctions in a meaningful way.

These challenges to identity theory and research—the social class argument, the gender differences perspective, and the medical model point of view—are contributing to a search for a new perspective. Such a search is well under way and has become part of a larger shift to the relational perspective now widely accepted in psychoanalysis (see Noam, Higgins, and Goethals, 1982), infancy and attachment research

---

[1]Some Erikson scholars have responded to this critique by suggesting that this concept of identity development includes a strong relational component (Horst, 1995).

(e.g., Ainsworth, 1982), and feminist psychology. It is also part of a new "historic moment" when cultural identity politics plays an increased role in defining identity (e.g., Appiah, 1997) and when psychologists are placing greater emphasis on social and cultural context in identity development (e.g., Penuel and Wertsch, 1995; Vigil, 1988).

Furthermore, a general consensus about the phases of the life cycle has broken down because there are today so many acceptable life cycles, so many pathways of development (e.g., Noam and Fischer, 1996). Choice is not anymore adolescent choice alone but continued life-style choice throughout development: childbearing, with marriage and without, at fifteen, 25, 35, or even 45 years of age; gay or heterosexual coupling; remaining in one career or making frequent changes and geographic reallocations; and so forth. And yet, most of our teaching about adolescent development and most of our clinical tools are still strongly influenced by the theories of identity formation that began to evolve about 50 years ago, when the life cycle that defined all was mostly white, American, middle-class, and suburban.

FROM TODAY'S PERSPECTIVE: A MISSING DEVELOPMENTAL EPOCH IN THE LIFE CYCLE

The adolescents Erikson studied were moving into a world in which commitment and ideological stance were at the fore, as were the questions "Who am I?" and "What do I stand for?" We stand today on the shoulders of Erikson and many others of his generation. In the most general of terms, today's adolescents are still identity-seeking, but new themes have evolved that motivate and define them maybe even more profoundly than the issues of choice and stance. One central new theme of the adolescent experience I want to label a sense of belonging—identity less self-chosen and individualistic and more a form of group identification. So powerful is this desire/motivation that it needs to be not only described as a modern (many would call it postmodern) phenomenon but introduced as a developmental epoch that has been missing in Erikson's brilliant description of the life cycle. In this section, I will discuss this developmental process.

The Mutual-Inclusive Self: Belonging Versus Rejection

Although I believe that we have benefited greatly from the perspective that all clinical and developmental matters—and all learning, for that matter—are fundamentally relational (see also Noam and Fischer, 1996), we need to focus on a life-cycle era in which the experiential and existential theme of "belonging" becomes so powerful that it over-shadows most other concerns. This is a period that we need to locate between the latency age and Erikson's adolescent/early-adult period.

Erikson's epigenetic model of the life cycle went directly from the latency tasks of acquiring concrete knowledge and skills to the adoles-cent tasks of questioning identifications, taking a perspective on the past, and developing a new sense of self. Most textbooks have accepted this sequence, and so have most clinicians using developmental theory. But this is not really how we progress from the early school years to the college years—the time frame that is covered by these two developmental stages. We do not move from latency-age industry to identity formation with a sequence of steps that include some mixtures of negative identity, moratorium, and identity crisis.

Let us remind ourselves of Erikson's (1968) definition of the latency period: "Competence, then, is the free exercise of dexterity and intelli-gence in the completion of tasks, unimpaired by infantile inferiority. It is the basis for co-operative participation in technologies and relies, in turn, on the logic of tools and skills" (p. 124). Here we see a strong cognitive and skill orientation that shapes this developmental era.

Erikson's description of the next stage, adolescence, includes not only finding oneself, but "in puberty and adolescence all sameness and continuities relied on earlier are more or less questioned again" (1950, p. 261). This period is also defined by a new set of motivations, abilities, and virtues:

> a high sense of duty, accuracy, and veracity in the rendering of reality; the sentiment of truthfulness, as in sincerity and convic-tion; the quality of genuineness, as in authenticity; the trait of loyalty of "being true"; fairness to the rules of the game; and finally all that is implied in devotion—a freely given but binding vow, with the fateful implication of a curse befalling traitors [1968, p. 125].

But most of these virtues are actually only found in late adolescents and adults. Authenticity requires a knowledge of the self; truthfulness requires something one stands for. Similarly, a "binding of the vow" has a strong component of choice and commitment. We know that these are the hallmarks of Erikson's ideas of adolescent fidelity and identity.

But for many adolescents I have treated or taught, interviewed or researched, the question is less "Who am I?" or "What am I committed to?" and more "Where do I belong?" "What am I part of?" "Who accepts me?" "Who likes me?" "Who provides me with self-esteem?" These adolescents want to know that they are popular, wear the right clothes, and listen to "cool" music.

To recapitulate, Erikson painted a picture of the life cycle that went from latency industry stage to a late adolescent identity development stage. In between these two developmental worlds are not only different phases (i.e., early, middle, and late adolescence researched in great detail by developmental psychologists) but a fundamental set of adolescent experiences that deserves the status of a developmental level. I have termed this developmental level, which emerges in early adolescence, as mutual-inclusive and have researched it as it relates to normal development and psychopathology (e.g., Noam, 1988a; Noam et al., 1990; Noam and Borst, 1994). If we want to stay with Erikson's terminology, we could call this the belonging-versus-rejection stage—a label that will become clearer when I list some of the ingredients that typically mark this developmental world:

- Self strongly defined by group.
- Self defined through others' eyes.
- Sense of belonging essential to well-being.
- Hypervigilance about being liked and accepted.
- Great conflicts over divergent opinions of significant people; avoidance of anger, confrontation, and differentiation.
- Identity, collective and interpersonal, humorously referred to as "wego" instead of "ego."
- Conflicts arising out of being a different person with different friends or trying to be close to parents and close to friends when they do not accept each other.
- Prone to feeling anxiety, guilt, depression; increased risk for suicidality.

Again, being the keen observers of adolescence that Erikson, Blos, and others really were, they knew about these dimensions. For example, in his description of identity development in the life cycle, Erikson did

56

not completely ignore the importance of relationships (Horst, 1995; Seligman and Shanok, 1998). But they emphasized a different set of psychological processes, a "second separation and individuation process," when we emphasize here a new level of inclusion and connection, an identification of self with the needs and wishes of others. This new level of identification is often misunderstood as part of a primitive, even borderline self—a block in the way of establishing autonomy, inner security of self, and productive boundaries. But this level of identification is not primitive at all (although it usually has echoes from the past and regressive potentials). It relies heavily on the new psychological abilities to understand the world from the perspective of others and to view the self from that point of view.

These cognitive capacities, which usually set in around ages eleven to thirteen (often referred to as "early formal operations"), have been observed and researched in a variety of developmental theory traditions that build on Piaget, Kohlberg, Loevinger, and others (for a review, see Noam, Kohlberg, and Snarey, 1983). Despite their great significance for an in-depth understanding of development, they have not received sufficient attention in psychoanalytic circles. But I am not suggesting a simple import of Piagetian principles. Instead, the work I am introducing here has also reshaped Piagetian developmental principles by integrating analytic ones:

• Developmental forward movement is usually accompanied by regressions and developmental repetitions.
• Each developmental accomplishment can create a new set of developmental vulnerabilities.
• Developmental risks and psychopathology are not necessarily signs of delay or arrest but can be signs of developmental complexity.
• Development is not a linear or stepwise progression but a transforming developmental movement forward and a simultaneous (and often related) return to earlier productive periods as well as unresolved conflicts.

It is important to note that this period of the mutual-inclusive self, when the yearnings for belonging and acceptance are at the apex of importance, is not bound to only one age in a person's life. Many people never move to a developmental world that matches Erikson's identity development. When age and stage are inseparable, as they are in Erikson's model—each stage is an age, a set of psychological tasks, and a psychological organization—remaining in this developmental mode of identification rather than "self-choice" becomes a negative attribute. As everyone seen through the lens of his theory has to develop identity in youth, we are left to call the person who resists this movement someone who "forecloses" identity (Erikson, 1968). But why limit ourselves to a negative formulation when in fact so many positive attributes define this era of mutual-inclusive psychological self-definition, which can last a lifetime? (This is not just as a Blosian "prolonged adolescence" but an adult version of mutual inclusiveness.)

If it is true that this developmental focus or level can last a lifetime, then we need to do more than insert a new stage into Erikson's model (although doing so represents an important first step). Joan and Erik Erikson, with whom I had the great privilege to discuss many of these issues over the years, began to use Joan's weavings to exemplify the theory of the life cycle. What became very clear from this visual representation of their model was that all developmental issues of the life cycle always preexist and exist long after the specific stage disappears. In the weaving, the stages are represented by key colors, and these colors are made up of a specific combination of horizontal (psycho) and vertical (biological-makeup and life-history) threads. (For a visualization and description, see Hulsizer et al., 1981.)

Thus, we focus here on identification and belonging as key adolescent issues, not just childhood leftovers that become issues for the entire life cycle (the threads continue to live on beyond that phase). To understand these yearnings of belonging in adolescence is to understand throughout different phases of life. Without a clear understanding, we have tended either to devalue these complex psychological processes as remnants of the past or subsumed them as part and parcel of adolescent identity development. Before addressing these issues further, I will briefly introduce Rosa and an early part of her twice-a-week psychotherapy.

Clinical Example: Rosa.   I began to see Rosa, a Hispanic sophomore at a college in the northeast United States, after she had been hospitalized in the student infirmary for serious suicidal ideation, a suicide attempt, and increasingly intrusive thoughts (her father's voice: "You should kill yourself! You are worthless like I am!").

Rosa had grown up in a large immigrant family with three brothers and three sisters in an urban center under poverty conditions. Her father was an alcoholic, in and out of jobs; her mother took good care of the children but was constantly overwhelmed and at times depressed.

An avid reader and a good writer, Rosa had excelled throughout her twelve years of school. In fact, she was the only family member who had done well academically. Although she was proud of her admittance to a good college, leaving home left her feeling displaced, and she experienced the separation from her family as a tremendous loss. She was an adolescent without a home, but she felt college to be a cool place. Soon after her arrival, she ended up on academic probation. Although she was clearly able to perform well, her conflicts interfered with her ability to finish papers and pass exams.

Rosa's recovery took many years, punctuated by long periods of separation, when she needed to be away. Treatment provided a window into the relationship among trauma, culture, and identity development, as it became apparent that Rosa had been sexually abused during her childhood. What I focus on in this short vignette, though, is her tremendous longing to belong. Although Rosa's family wanted her to succeed academically, they were also threatened by her new world. They never came to visit and gave Rosa the impression that she had lost the powerful, though highly dysfunctional, foundation of her life.

Meanwhile, at college, she felt that she did not fit in. She tried to develop intimacy through short-lived sexual relationships, which left her feeling extremely vulnerable, even self-loathing. Additionally, she felt more identified with the janitors and other workers than with the students and professors. The conflict of living between two worlds and belonging to neither—a topic of much discussion during our sessions—became so pronounced that she decided to take a leave of absence.

Rosa had actually decided on a very creative strategy for the next six months. She was going to cross the United States setting up events for the college's alumni association—that is, she was going to be a worker! This represented an important compromise of dealing with her various sets of identification. Rosa could simultaneously belong to the college and conform with her family by becoming a worker rather than a student while being away from her family. This plan had important implications for her treatment, too.

Rosa needed to break off therapy. I remember the dramatic moment when she came to my office with flowers to announce that she was leaving for an indefinite amount of time, maybe even forever. She did not want me to consider her "terminated," though. "Keep the file open," she said teasingly, "I will stay in touch." It was essential for the future success of the treatment that I allowed this to happen (against the urging of the clinic staff, worried about liability). Part of the need to belong is to continue to belong during separations. Rosa needed the affirmation that she had a home base while exploring the world. It was also a blessing that the college had a very liberal policy for leave-taking.

One could say that Rosa was in the middle of developing a new identity. But she really was most concerned about finding a way to remain connected to the different relationships that defined her. She sought contexts of affirmation that would not make her lose other contexts of belonging. In the process, she suffered from not belonging anywhere. She could understand this conflict, but her solutions were less insight oriented and more focused on rearranging the context in which she lived. She was also working hard not to lose any part of herself, but she was not particularly interested in transforming her identifications into a new unity that could hold all of these different relationships in a new way. Most important to her was the capacity to belong to multiple worlds, to live with them, and to be able to travel between them. In the course of her treatment, after she returned from her sabbatical, she became increasingly able to experience these multiple worlds and to belong to them in new ways. We will now return to some theoretical reflections.

Identification and Identity

This positive focus on identifications and on the essential nature of relationships has been with us for a long time, even though it had not been attended to much theoretically. For Harry Stack Sullivan, the transition to adolescence is a time of a powerful new experience, the "chumship" through which children experience friendship by being like one another. Most of development, for Sullivan, is a struggle to overcome loneliness while avoiding interpersonal engulfment. Erikson (1959) was far more suspicious of "identifications," even when they created interpersonal closeness, and saw them as less productive than self-chosen identities:

> The limited usefulness of the *mechanism of identification* becomes at once obvious if we consider the fact that none of the identifica-

tions of childhood (which in our patients stand out in such morbid elaboration and mutual contradiction) could, if merely added up, result in a functioning personality. . . . As every cure attests, "more desirable" identifications tend to be quietly subordinated to a new, a unique Gestalt which is more than the sum of its parts. The fact is that identification as a mechanism is of limited usefulness [p. 112].

But the themes that seem to represent our times—the search for belonging and community as well as the politics of identity and multiculturalism—have become increasingly important for our vision of the life span (found, as mentioned earlier, in different variations in the attachment literature, object relations psychoanalysis, self psychology, and feminist theory). Cognitive, autonomous, self-selected identity is increasingly under attack; contextual, fluctuating, relational identifications are increasingly "in" (e.g., Lifton, 1993; McAdams, 1997). Once our focus becomes the interpersonal field, the relational matrix, or a coconstructed reality, what exactly is this "crown jewel of internalization"—the unit we have learned to call identity?

For present-day identity and relational theorists, we are all destined to live out a multitude of group identifications that can never really be synthesized. Cultural psychologists and modern research into the immigrant experience have also shaped this kind of view. Thus, I posit that the developmental telos is not necessarily to integrate and synthesize various experiences and self states but to let different parts of the self live in different, often contradictory and "unintegrateable" relationship contexts. As we have seen in the case of Rosa, the task is not necessarily integration, because the worlds are often not integrateable, but toleration of contradiction and inherent disorganization and support of a new sense of belonging.

From this vantage point, a psychology of identifications can in fact be developmentally equally complex as one focuses on identity formation. Identifications with persons and groups allow a certain fluidity, an emotional openness—letting the world of the "other" impress itself on the self. To yearn for belonging is to be able to risk relationship and loss. The gross exaggeration of this yearning is masochism, loss of self and perspective, and a level of social conformity that can easily be exploited.

But identity development can lead to a brutal act of integration—a way to demand from the self and others to cohere and to shape noncongruent experiences so they fit. This would not be called a flexible form of identity, but who ever said that identity is necessarily open and evolving instead of rigid and totalitarian? The benefit is a higher order sorting capacity—a way to stand back and make all personal and group identifications adjust to a chosen blueprint of what is considered most and least important. The self is strengthened by this formed identity and can often better deal with inevitable rejections and losses; one can view them as a necessary aspect of "being oneself." But how often is one blindsided? How difficult it is to draw the line between identity and the false self?

Interestingly, this focus on multiple experiences, multiple worlds, and multiple realities brings us back to traditional psychoanalysis when adaptation and integration took a back seat. The unconscious is always creating a different reality and can never be truly integrated with the waking self. It can be partially understood, but it can never be controlled (the weak ego-rider on the powerful id-horse).

We go in and out of our childhood, adolescent, and adult worlds. The goal is not to integrate but to ensure that childhood conflicts don't dominate adult functioning. But within such a formula, there is a great deal of room for continuous fluctuations and regressions—movements in and out of different experiential and relational worlds, real and imagined.

Maybe we should not only elevate identifications to a new level of developmental acceptance, but we should also redefine identity as a far more relational and contextual construct (see also Penuel and Wertsch, 1995). We should meld the principles of group identification and relational contextualism with identity as choice, commitment, and autonomy. They belong together, complement one another, and are different aspects of our everyday lives.

Understanding Adolescent Development as a Way to Evolve
New Clinical Tools

More than ever—with managed care here to stay—we need the strongest possible developmental theories. Why? As we see our young patients for increasingly short times, we have to rely more heavily on the inherent restorative capacities that they bring to their psychological distress. One important support can be provided through a greater understanding of how to encourage developmental abilities that are often dormant under the weight of psychological distress, an insecure future, and an unworked-out relationship to the past.

Adolescent mental health is fundamentally a clinical developmental activity (e.g., Bowlby, 1982; Winnicott, 1965; Wolf, 1988). Anna Freud had taught the clinical principle that the psychoanalytic approach to children is fundamentally developmental. Understanding the developmental motion, movement, and rhythm is essential to help youth find their way. Adult psychotherapy is only beginning to fully grasp that treating adult disorders not only involves reconstructing and revisiting past trauma but also follows the specific rhythms of adult development (e.g., Vaillant, 1997; Noam, Chandler, and LaLonde, 1995). What are the clinical implications of focusing on this mutual-inclusive adolescent world? I will briefly address this issue in this last section of this paper.

At this developmental level, the therapist is prone to overestimate the capacities for insight because all of the developmental capacities for such an approach appear to be in place (see also Noam, 1998). But when we listen carefully to what these adolescents have to tell us, we do not, as in the case of Rosa, encounter identity development in the making. The adolescent can certainly experience a great deal of crisis but does not take a perspective on his identifications to transform them into a new identity. Instead, identifications are sought and lived—the self is mutual, at home with idealized friends and adults. Group conformity is at its height, and so is the constant fear of losing the "relationship base," of being abandoned by parents, teachers, and friends. It is this fear of losing those who define the self—and of not fitting in and of being rejected—that is a core feature of this adolescent.

The ability of these youngsters to frame experiences in psychological terms—to describe feeling states and detailed interactions with important others—encourages most therapists to explore patterns and motivations, autonomous self-observation, and critical judgment about self and relationships. These explorations usually lead to surprisingly superficial descriptions that frustrate both therapist and client. Surprised by this "lack of self," the therapist may interpret this state as an early and primitive manifestation of a separation-individuation problem. The patient consequently feels incompetent and senses that he is not living up to expectations. Feeling inadequate leads to feeling hopeless, and the patient is thereby silenced. The silence, in turn, often makes the therapist and client feel quite uncomfortable, which increases the potential for low self-esteem and depression.

63

There is no therapeutic model that clearly fits this adolescent, which is surprising in light of the fact that so many adolescents who enter therapy function at this level. One reason might be that we did not know about this developmental gestalt (see also Noam, 1985, 1988b).

Existing therapy methods that use supportive strategies run the risk of underchallenging the patient. The relationship can easily become stale as the adolescent waits for some challenge or some guidance in framing the problems in new ways.

Insight-oriented therapy, on the other hand, requires an observation of systematic patterns of the self that is not available to adolescents in this developmental world. Following a set of goals that is experienced as self-chosen—and questioning existing conventions and creating new ones—requires a differentiation between the part of the self steeped in prescribed pathways and conventions and the part that is reflecting, doubting, and questioning. The therapist can be sure that she has an ally in the patient who can cognitively contain, at least under supportive conditions, both sides of the self. For that reason, more traditional psychodynamic therapy can be applied with people who have these capacities—but not so at the mutual-inclusive level.

Between these two therapy forms—supportive and insight oriented—we need to establish new, developmentally guided methods. The adolescent at the mutual-inclusive level is apt to observe one set of processes with great care—the fluctuations in the relationship, the feelings of inclusion and protection, the sense of abandonment and despair. These adolescents respond vigilantly to the wishes and desires of others and lack anger and self-assertion. Help is needed to deal with these strengths and vulnerabilities. As was the case with Rosa, therapy is not and will not be viewed as a manifestation of inner conflicts and life themes. But therapist and client can focus on the pattern of their relationship and of others. They can wonder together about the lack of anger when the self has been violated and share, almost as friends, the adolescent's victories and disappointments. Table 1 describes dimensions of clinical work relevant to this developmental world.

I remember one adolescent patient who always asked me about my opinions, what I considered normal and pathological, and what I would do in a given situation. At the time, I pursued a position of not answering these questions and noticed the girl becoming more and more disappointed and removed. I explained the reasons but to no avail. She wanted to end therapy. Out of desperation, I began to answer more and more questions, and our relationship became unstuck. I felt powerful

TABLE 1

CLINICAL-DEVELOPMENTAL INTERVENTIONS WITH ADOLESCENTS:
IDENTITY-SEEKING SELF-COMPLEXITY LEVEL

Treatment Focus

- Insight-oriented therapy supporting the emerging capacities to "choose" a self from among many different possibilities.

Setting

- Individual treatment often effective as the therapist can become an ally in reviewing the past relationships and be a sounding board in creating life goals and plans.
- Including the context (friends, family, etc.) can be useful, but focus has to be not only on being part of relationships but also on the need for differentiation.

Support

- Person needs to be supported through the inevitable confusions of wanting to be close to others and be like them while trying to come to terms with being different and standing up for a life project that might not be in line with others' expectations.

Insight

- Taking a perspective on the dilemma of needing approval from significant others while listening to an inner direction.
- Coming to terms with the fact that pursuing one's identity can mean making unpopular decisions and being excluded.
- Focus on potential for being overly differentiated and becoming "ideologically pure" but isolated.

Typical Therapeutic Binds

- Difficulty in handling conflicts that arise from experimenting with identity (e.g., risk-taking to prove that one is different from family, searching out experiences of self through drugs, ideological struggles with authorities, etc.).
- Leaving important relationships for the sake of "finding oneself," including the therapeutic relationship, without adequately thinking through the consequences of isolation and lack of support.

---

and effective, and she felt pleased and acknowledged. Only I noticed that we did not move forward and that many of my answers cemented her insecurities. As a supervisor, I see many young clinicians fall into this same trap.

Since then, I have learned to find a different path. I turn the questions into a joint exploration. I try not to overchallenge or underchallenge the patient. The adolescent's insecurities are often related to a long history of insecure attachments and should not be repeated in the therapy. A strategy must be found that locates the power of finding solutions neither in the patient nor in the therapist but in their relationship. It is not that the therapist has to find his answers, which pulls for the identity-seeking position not yet reached, and it is not that the therapist will answer for the patient, which supports the nonassertive and dependent attitude that the therapy tries to address. Instead, therapist and patient together will find solutions that are, at least in part, located in their relationship.

In conclusion, expanding our focus on adolescent identifications and changing our notions of identity will help provide better treatments. We are at an exciting point: A new era in our understanding of adolescents is combining with a new theoretical view focused increasingly on context, relationships, and multiple worlds. It is also a critical time for creating new psychoanalytic tools for adolescent psychotherapy.

REFERENCES

Ainsworth, M. (1982), Attachment: Retrospect and prospect. In: *The Place of Attachment in Human Behavior*, ed. C. Parkes & J. Stevenson-Hinde. London: Tavistock, pp. 3–30.

Appiah, A. (1996), Multiplying identities. *Crit. Inq.* 18(4).

———— (1997, October 9), The multicultural misunderstanding. *New York Rev. Books*, 44:30–36.

Blos, P. (1962), *On Adolescence: A Psychoanalytic Interpretation*. New York: Free Press.

Bowlby, J. (1982), *Attachment and Loss Vol. I. Attachment*. New York: Basic Books.

Cohler, B. J., Stott, F. M. & Musick, J. S. (1995), Adversity, vulnerability, and resilience: Cultural and developmental perspectives. In: *Developmental Psychopathology Vol. 2: Risk, Vulnerability, and Resilience*, ed. D. Cicchetti & D. J. Cohen. New York: Wiley, pp. 753–800.

Erikson, E. (1950), Growth and crises of the health personality. *Psychological Issues*, 1:50–100.

———— (1968), *Identity, Youth, and Crisis*. New York: Norton.

Freud, A. (1936), *The Ego and Mechanisms of Defense*. New York: International Universities Press, 1950.

Freud, S. (1915), Introductory Lectures on Psycho-Analysis. *Standard Edition*, 15. London: Hogarth Press, 1963.

Gilligan, C. (1982), *In a Different Voice: Psychological Theory and Women's Development.* Cambridge, MA: Harvard University Press.
———— (1996), The centrality of relationship in human development: A puzzle, some evidence, and a theory. In: *Development and Vulnerability in Close Relationships: The Jean Piaget Symposium Series,* ed. G. G. Noam & K. W. Fischer. Mahwah, NJ: Lawrence Erlbaum Associates, pp. 237–261.

Horst, E. (1995), Reexamining gender issues in Erikson's stages of identity and intimacy. *J. Counsel. Development,* 73:271–278.

Hulsizer, D., Murphy, M., Noam, G. & Taylor, C. (1981), On gererativity and identity: From a conversation with Joan and Erik Erikson. *Harvard Educ. Rev.,* 51:249–269.

Jordan, J. (in press), *Clarity in Connection: Empathic Knowing, Desire, and Sexuality.* Wellesley, MA: Stone Center.

Lifton, R. J. (1993), *The Protean Self.* New York: Basic Books.

Mahler, M. S., Pine, F. & Bergman, A. (1975), *Psychological Birth of the Human Infant.* New York: Basic Books.

McAdams, D. P. (1997), The case for unity in the (post)modern self: A modest proposal. In: *Self and Identity: Fundamental Issues, Vol. 1,* ed. R. D. Ashmoe & L. J. Jussim. New York: Oxford University Press, pp. 46–78.

Noam, G. G. (1985), Stage, phase, and style: The developmental dynamics of the self. In: *Moral Education: Theory and Application,* ed. M. Berkowitz & F. Oser. Hillsdale, NJ: Lawrence Erlbaum Associates, pp. 321–346.
———— (1988a), A constructivist approach to developmental psychology, In: *Developmental Psychopathology and Its Treatment,* ed. E. Nannis & P. Cowan. San Francisco: Jossey-Bass, pp. 91–122.
———— (1988b), The theory of biography and transformation: Foundation for clinical-developmental therapy. In: *Cognitive Development and Child Psychotherapy,* ed. S. R. Shirk. New York: Plenum, pp. 273–317.
———— (1988c), Clinical-developmental psychology: Towards developmentally differentiated interventions. In: *Handbook of Clinical Psychology, Vol. 4,* ed. I. Sigel & K. Renninger. New York: Wiley, pp. 585–634.
———— & Borst, S. ed. (1994), *Children, Youth, and Suicide: Developmental Perspectives.* San Francisco: Jossey-Bass.
———— Chandler, M. & LaLonde, C. (1995), Clinical-developmental psychology: Constructivism and social cognition in the study of

psychological dysfunctions. In: *Developmental Psychopathology: Vol. 1. Theory and Methods*, ed. D. Cicchetti & D. J. Cohen. New York: Wiley, pp. 424–464.

———— & Fischer, K. W., ed. (1996), *Development and Vulnerability in Close Relationships: The Jean Piaget Symposium Series*. Mahwah, NJ: Lawerence Erlbaum Associates.

———— Higgins, R. & Goethals, G. (1982), Psychoanalytic approaches to developmental psychology. In: *Handbook of Developmental Psychology*, ed. B. B. Wolman & G. Stricker. Englewood Cliffs, NJ: Prentice-Hall, pp. 23–43.

———— Kohlberg, L. & Snarey, J. (1983), Steps towards a model of the self. In: *Developmental Approaches to the Self*, ed. B. Lee & G. G. Noam. New York: Plenum, pp. 59–142.

———— Powers, S., Kilkenny, R. & Beedy, J. (1990), The interpersonal self in life-span developmental perspective. In: *Life-Span Development and Behavior, Vol. 10*, ed. P. B. Balts, D. L. Featherman & R. M. Lerner. Hillsdale, NJ: Lawrence Erlbaum Associates, pp. 59–104.

Offer, D. & Schonert-Reichl, K. (1992), Debunking the myths of adolescence: Findings from recent reviews. *J. Amer. Acad. Child Adolesc. Psychiat.* pp. 1003–1014.

Ogbu, J. U. (1985), A cultural ecology of competence among inner-city blacks. In: *Beginnings: The Social and Affective Development of Black Children*, ed. M. B. Spencer, G. K. Brookins & W. R. Allen. Hillsdale, NJ: Lawrence Erlbaum Associates, pp. 45–66.

Penuel, W. R. & Wertsch, J. V. (1995), Vygotsky and identity formation: A sociocultural approach. *Educational Psychologist*, 30(2):83–92.

Seligman, S. & Shanok, R. (1998), Erikson, our contemporary: His anticipation of an intersubjective perspective. In: *Ideas and Indentities: The Life and Work of Erik Erikson*, ed. R. S. Wallerstein & L. Goldberger. Madison, CT: International Universities Press.

Suarez-Orozco, C. & Suarez-Orozco, M. (1995), *Trans-formations: Immigration, Family, Life, and Achievement Motivation Among Latino Adolescents*. Stanford, CA: Stanford University Press.

Vaillant, G. E. (1977), *Adaptation to Life*. Boston: Little Brown.

Vigil, J. D. (1988), Group processes and street identity: Adolescent Chicano gang members. *Ethos*, 16:421–445.

Winnicott, D. W. (1965), *The Maturational Processes and the Facilitating Environment*. New York: International Universities Press.

Wolf, E. S. (1988), *Treating the Self: Elements of Clinical Self Psychology*. New York: Guilford Press.

PART II

SCHOOL-BASED MENTAL HEALTH SERVICES: THE FUTURE OF CHILD AND ADOLESCENT PSYCHIATRY

IRVING H. BERKOVITZ

That the school-based health center (SBHC) is the wave of the future in delivery of mental services to children and adolescents reflects the opinions of many professionals in the mental health field. As of 1998, there were more than 1,100 SBHCs functioning in 49 U.S. states and more being added each month (Lear and Schlitt, 1998). Most SBHCs have about 1,500 to 2,000 students each—or a total of about 1.5 million children and adolescents whose medical and psychiatric needs are being cared for thus far. Managed-care firms are also currently developing ways to work with SBHCs (Koppleman and Lear, in press). The wave is spreading. It behooves psychiatrists, especially those treating children and adolescents, to become more involved. The following examples show how some psychiatrists are achieving a high degree of involvement.

Commonly, staff in SBHCs include a medical assistant, a nurse practitioner or physician assistant, and a mental health professional (usually a master's-level social worker) who addresses the psychosocial needs of the students. SBHCs are almost always run by outside community agencies such as local health departments. The model SBHC offers age-appropriate and comprehensive physical and mental health services through a multidisciplinary team of health professionals. Mental health services provided in schools are often dramatically different from services provided in community mental health centers. Among other differences, the school therapist has contact with students not only in the therapy office but in the hallway, at schoolwide events (e.g., assemblies), at athletic games, in the cafeteria, and so forth. Given these environmental factors, it is not uncommon for school-based therapists to see ten to twelve children in a seven-hour day.

This section presents a variety of mental health approaches to improving the mental health of adolescents in secondary schools, including the SBHCs. Many other equally excellent programs could have been described. Space did not permit presenting more. The approaches described in the five chapters of this section will be seen to have many similarities but also significant differences. The order in which the chapters are presented has no qualitative relevance. The programs are all excellent. It has been exciting to organize this section and to be able to present these advances in provision of services to children, adolescents, and their families, many of whom might otherwise have fallen through the cracks and never have received necessary interventions.

The section begins with a chapter by Stewart Adelson, who presents an excellent overview of the opportunities in SBHCs. The next two chapters describe programs that are different from the SBHC. They are not part of a medical facility, as with most SBHCs, but do have more exclusively a mental health focus. Although unlike the usual SBHC, they are of interest as examples of the provision of mental health services when a SBHC is not available or when a special focus is desired. Nancy Rappaport describes the program in Cambridge, Massachusetts—a unique intensive nonclinical program. Two adolescent psychiatrists were asked by the personnel of Cambridge Rindge and Latin High School to design an advising program for the 2,000 students of this large urban school. The primary role of the psychiatrists was to supervise teachers to develop effective mentoring relationships in advisory groups attended by all the students. As part of this curriculum, students were asked to keep a weekly journal as well as an ongoing Personal Development Plan to encourage them to begin making future goals and planning steps to achieve them. The impact of these groups is being evaluated by different measures of success.

As described in Bernard Rappaport's chapter, in Orange County, California, the emphasis was directed primarily to mental health services. The school district and the mental health department have undertaken efforts to reduce the use of high-end services. The county mental health department established clinics for children at school sites in some areas of the county. The buildings for these sites generally were supplied by the schools; the county relied on volunteer efforts for renovations. In some cases, gang members were involved. The clinics housed county and contract staff, including psychiatric staff, and operated year-round. The staff served children attending school at the clinic site and visited other sites to see children attending different schools. A large majority of the children receiving treatment at the clinics were eligible also under federal special education funding. In addition to providing services needed by individual children, each therapist spent 5% or 10% of his or her time consulting with the school district housing the clinic, with the particular activities determined by the district. Consultation activities could include, for example, short-term therapy to individual students identified by the schools, teaching social skills to groups of students, responding to crises in the schools, and assisting with behavior management. Outcome is still being evaluated, but effects seen thus far are the greater involvement of Hispanic students, reduction of hospitalization needs, and no suicides.

The chapter by Mark Weist and colleagues, as well as describing the program in Baltimore, Maryland, presents provoking and cogent questions about some assumptions in child and adolescent mental health—derived in large part from experiences in the SBHCs. Currently, Baltimore has programs in place in 60 schools. It is notable that these SBHCs were the first sites for expanded school mental health services. Since then, mental health services have been added to schools without health centers, based in large part on lessons learned from the SBHCs. In the Baltimore programs, mental health services in

71

SBHCs are offered in the context of a range of other primary-care health services including on-site medical screening and physical examinations, treatment for accidents and minor illnesses, family planning services, immunizations, and a range of health education programs.

Yet another type of program occurs in New Mexico. New Mexico is one of five states with a federal Maternal and Child Health grant to develop school mental health infrastructure. New Mexico also has one of the highest rates of poverty and uninsured children in the country. This state is using school mental health models to integrate school health services and education reform to relieve students' barriers to learning and to improve educational outcomes. Through the expansion of school mental health services, legislation, and statewide coordination of funding, communities throughout the state are expanding school–community collaborations in behavioral mental health. Steve Adelsheim's chapter presents the exciting experience of integration of state departments of health, education, and children's services around school mental health and the school–community mental health pilot programs. School-based mental health expansions resulting from this collaboration are described.

Details of an exemplary SBHC program in Dallas, Texas, were described by Glen Pearson and colleagues in volume 23 of *Adolescent Psychiatry*. To show similarities to and differences from the programs described in the current volume, I shall describe the main features of the Dallas program here. Youth and Family Centers are a network of sixteen high-school-cluster-based centers providing health and mental health services to children and families in 200 schools. Targeting early intervention for students with discipline problems, failing grades, and poor attendance, school-based mental health care provides psychiatric evaluation for students and their families. Parenting programs engage the families in activities that strengthen and empower them. In coordination with the psychiatrist and the family, the treatment team develops an individualized service plan for each student. The service plan includes actions for the school (classroom management, schedule changes, academic support, teacher consultation, and student support groups), the family (individual therapy, family therapy, couples therapy, medication, and parent training and education), and the community (after-school programs, social service agencies, etc.) that ensure maximum school success. The Youth and Family Centers are open one or two days/nights a week for psychiatric evaluation. All services are provided at the school-based center by professionals and school staff. Child and Adolescent Services, part of Dallas Mental Health/Mental Retardation Center, provides the psychiatrist and additional therapists for each center.

As time goes on, changes will undoubtedly occur in these models. Other models may be developed as well. Additional SBHCs are being opened every year. At the moment, the services being rendered are exciting, health-promoting, and essential for many children and adolescents and their families. The satisfaction and pride of the personnel involved are additional elements that can be sensed between the lines of each chapter.[1]

REFERENCES

Koppelman, J. & Lear, J. G. (in press), The new child health insurance expansions: How will school-based health centers fit in? *J. School Health.*

Lear, J. G. & Schlitt, J. (1998), Late breaking findings on school-based health centers in the United States. Presented at meeting of the Center for School Mental Health Assistance, Virginia Beach, VA.

[1]Several of these chapters were presented at the annual meeting of The American Academy of Child and Adolescent Psychiatry in Anaheim, California, October 1998.

4 PSYCHIATRIC PUBLIC HEALTH OPPORTUNITIES IN SCHOOL-BASED HEALTH CENTERS

STEWART L. ADELSON

The majority of children and adolescents suffering from mental illness receive no specialized care for their emotional and behavioral problems (Offord et al., 1987; Leaf et al., 1996). These youth are not reached by traditional models of psychiatric care such as outpatient clinics and hospital-based programs. As emotional and behavioral problems and their sequelae are the major causes of morbidity and mortality among adolescents (Bass, Gallagher, and Mehta, 1985), the failure to reach large segments of psychiatrically ill youth is a major limitation of American health care (Ellickson et al., 1993). As the result of concern about this fact, there is currently great interest in developing new models for the delivery of mental health services that can reach underserved groups efficiently. Child and adolescent mental health programs provided through school-based health centers (SBHCs) may be one promising new model for delivering such services (American Medical Association Council on Scientific Affairs, 1989; Lear et al., 1991; Dryfoos, 1994; Weist, 1998). One hundred years ago, school-based public health programs dealt with such causes of morbidity and mortality among youth as infectious and nutritional diseases. Current programs contend with new causes of morbidity and mortality among youth—violence, suicide, depression, substance abuse, teen pregnancy, sexually transmitted diseases including HIV, and delinquency and school failure—the "new morbidities." As many as one fourth of youth engage in multiple high-risk behaviors such as drug and alcohol use, teenage sexual activity, and truancy; another fourth engage in one of these activities (Dryfoos, 1990).

Improved access to needed mental health services for children and adolescents is a particularly important public health issue for several reasons. First, several epidemiologic studies in child and adolescent psychiatry over the past ten years have found that 18% to 22% of youth under eighteen years of age suffer from a diagnosable psychiatric disorder (Offord et al., 1987; Bird et al., 1989; Velez, Johnson, and Cohen, 1989). Among causes of mortality in adolescence, accidents, homicide, and suicide account for approximately 80% of deaths among thirteen to eighteen-year-olds in the United States (Bass, Gallagher, and Mehta, 1985). These causes of adolescent mortality are often associated with mental disorders including depression, conduct disorder, and alcohol and substance abuse (Douglass, 1983; Halperin, Bass, Gallagher, et al., 1983; Friedman, 1985; Goldstein et al., 1990; Shaffer et al., 1996). Mental disorders cause severe handicap in about half of afflicted youth and are the leading cause of disability among ten- to eighteen-year-olds (National Center for Education in Maternal and Child Health, 1990; National Institute of Mental Health, 1990). In addition, the natural histories of many common, often treatable child and adolescent psychiatric disorders—such as hyperactivity, depression, substance abuse, and conduct disorder—include chronic or relapsing courses, high degrees of comorbidity, and poor long-term outcomes (Kovacs, 1985; Cantwell, 1985; Kovacs et al., 1988; Burke et al., 1990; Rohde et al., 1991; Kovacs, 1996). Given the high prevalence of youth with psychiatric illness, the chronicity of these illnesses, and the high morbidity and mortality associated with them, the public health burden of psychiatric illness among children and adolescents is quite high. Access to care and successful treatment or prevention of psychiatric disorder among youth is an important public health goal in its own right, and so the very large proportion of youth not receiving treatment for psychiatric illnesses is a matter of great public health concern.

In addition to the importance of access to mental health services for youth in order to lower the rates of adverse psychiatric outcomes in adolescents—such as suicide, depression, and substance abuse—mental health is also central to the control of a number of related adverse outcomes affecting youth. Many nonpsychiatric public health and social problems affecting U.S. adolescents—including violence, child abuse and neglect, high-risk behavior for HIV, other sexually transmitted diseases and teen pregnancy, and school failure and dropout—have in common psychiatric disturbance associated with or a factor in the transmission of illness (Lewis, Shanock, Pincus, et al., 1980; Robbins et al., 1983; Tallmadge and Barkley, 1983; Dryfoos, 1990; Moffitt, 1993). Addressing psychopathology associated with these problems is an important strategy to consider in efforts to ameliorate these nonpsychiatric problems as well. Thus, psychiatric illness among adolescents is an important public health issue due both to epidemics of psychiatric disorders per se and to nonpsychiatric problems associated with emotional and behavioral disturbance.

Overcoming Barriers to Mental Health Care

Despite these compelling reasons for ensuring that youth have adequate access to psychiatric services when needed, in some areas fewer than one in four youth with disability due to diagnosable psychiatric illness receives specialized mental health services (Leaf et al., 1996). One barrier to care is the lack of adequate health insurance among a significant proportion of youth (Newacheck, McManus, and Gephart, 1992). However, even in areas where there is universal coverage of services by government plans, such as Ontario, a large proportion of youth with psychiatric illness is still not in care (Offord et al., 1987), which suggests that there are barriers to appropriate use of child and adolescent mental health care other than financial ones. These barriers may include difficulty gaining access to care, failure to accept available services, inappropriate allocation of services, inadequate number of treatment sources, language barriers, cultural factors including stigma associated with psychiatric illness and care, poor case-finding practices, and individual resistance and family dysfunction interfering with appropriate help-seeking for children in need, among others.

Providing mental health services in schools is thought to lower several of the barriers to mental health care. For example, by placing mental health services in schools, one may gain access to underserved youth with or at risk for emotional and behavioral problems. School-based services do this within a socially accepted institution in the community where many of those in need are already to be found. Many of these health centers are supported through novel funding streams, such as by state health department grants that allow care to be provided to uninsured youth (Dryfoos, 1994, pp. 171–204). Therefore, SBHCs may be a promising model for improving access to mental health care for underserved youth.

In addition to the public health concerns, an independent set of educational imperatives has brought mental health into schools. As a result of growing awareness that social, medical, and emotional problems create barriers to effective learning for many youth, society is increasingly calling upon schools to teach not only by imparting information but also by promoting the conditions necessary for effective learning. The past several decades have seen a broadening of the goals by which schools are expected to achieve their fundamental mission of education. In recent years, many influential nonprofit organizations as well as governmental agencies at various levels have encouraged the involvement of schools in novel models to deliver health and social programs that reduce health-related barriers to learning for underserved groups (Dryfoos, 1994, pp. 1–18). Thus, society increasingly invests in schools the responsibility for the medical, emotional, and social well-being of youth. One model devised in response to this broadened mandate has been the concept of *full-service schools*. These schools provide on-site medical and social programs to promote health, emotional well-being, and prosocial values among students in need who might not otherwise receive these services.

History

The idea of delivering health and medical programs through schools has historical precedents dating to 1892 with the inception of a public health program delivered through schools to children in need in New York City. Over the past 100 years, various public health programs delivered through schools have been devised in response to different epidemics and community needs. Early programs focused on the exclusion from school of children with communicable diseases and were seen as a way of combating infectious epidemics. Gradually, models of school-based health care evolved that incorporated linkage with treatment, follow-up, or limited services for sick children; the emphasis of most school-based health programs continued to be health screening. School-based public health programs have flourished during times of immigration and high density of poor urban populations with endemic illness; the programs have tended to lose the support of the organized medical community during periods of relative social affluence (Lear et al., 1991; Dryfoos, 1994).

The past two decades have seen a rapid resurgence in medical care provided to underserved youth through full-service schools. As part of this resurgent interest, there has been an extremely rapid growth in primary health care for children and adolescents delivered in SBHCs, which have proliferated rapidly since the inception of two experimental programs in the late 1960s and early 1970s (Lear et al., 1991; Weist, 1998). SBHCs are health centers located in schools that provide comprehensive adolescent medical services, such as pediatrics, health promotion, family planning, and mental health care. By virtue of their location in schools—which allows high community acceptability, ready access, and unique funding streams for underinsured youth—they are intended to improve access to care. By virtue of their comprehensiveness, relevance to adolescents of the services offered, and integration with school functions and school-based community and social services, such health centers are intended to improve problem finding, treatment, interinstitutional collaboration, and health and social outcomes among underserved youth (Earls et al., 1989).

Combining Public Health Approaches with Child and Adolescent Psychiatry

There is a natural affiliation between the fields of public health and child and adolescent psychiatry by virtue of the emphasis that each places on a long-term perspective—in the case of child and adolescent psychiatry, the perspective of individual development, and in the case of public health, the perspective of the longitudinal analysis of factors associated with the development of or protection from disease in populations over time. From a public health standpoint, delivering mental health care through schools makes sense because of the ability to reach and follow over time a large population at risk for the development of mental illness. This population at risk includes both youths who are psychiatrically symptomatic but not in treatment and youths who are not currently psychiatrically ill but at risk for becoming so due to their exposure to risk factors associated with the development of psychiatric illness.

By providing mental health practitioners with the opportunity to intervene early in the developmental course of psychopathology and to follow individuals over long periods of time as they progress through school, SBHCs provide an opportunity to design, test, and implement programs for the primary and secondary prevention of illness—the traditional goals of the public health approach. The conceptual framework for such interventions is embodied in *causal chains* (Robins, 1970), the idea that a psychiatric illness occurring at one point in the developmental course may lead to a second psychiatric illness by influencing the course of development, which may in turn lead to another, and so on over time. This concept may account for the high comorbidity of psychiatric conditions in children and adolescents.

Child and adolescent psychiatrists have a unique set of skills to bring to school-based mental health programs because of their knowledge about individual development, psychopathology, etiologic factors in mental illness, and diagnosis and treatment of various mental illnesses. They are also able by virtue of their clinical training and knowledge to devise techniques for the screening of populations at risk, to target services and programs appropriately, and to engage and treat those in need.

By giving access to large populations of children and adolescents at risk for mental illness, school-based programs provide a unique opportunity not only to treat underserved groups but to implement programs for the prevention of child and adolescent mental disorders (Shaffer, Philips, and Enzer, 1989; Ellickson and Bell, 1990). Further, such programs can provide a unique opportunity to learn which interventions are most effective at ameliorating or protecting against psychiatric disorders—knowledge that is required for development of prevention programs (Offord, 1987). SBHCs thus provide unique treatment, prevention, and research opportunities in public health initiatives to combat burdensome epidemics both of psychiatric illness and of other conditions associated with behavioral and emotional disturbance.

Need for Models of School-Based Mental Health Care

The model by which child and adolescent psychiatric services should be integrated into school-based clinic programs is an important consideration. Apart from mental health services provided to youth through SBHCs, there are many other ways of providing mental health services in schools. In the field of child and adolescent psychiatry, several traditional models of psychiatric intervention in communities have been used in schools and other settings. Some of these may be successfully adapted in whole or in part to activities of SBHCs. In the mental health consultation model (Caplan, 1970), a psychiatrist helps a school or teacher to educate by providing consultation about a student or school system without assuming any medicolegal rights or responsibilities for the student. In the community consultation model (Comer, 1980), the psychiatrist facilitates a process of social change and community involvement in schools to ameliorate ecological factors impinging on the mental health of students. In the behavioral consultation model, a mental health practitioner uses concepts of behavioral psychology to assist educators with the management of pupils in classrooms (Alpert, 1976). In the special education model of specialized settings for psychiatrically disturbed youth, a staff psychiatrist may assume a role similar to that in traditional clinic settings, including the diagnosis and treatment of youth identified as having a psychiatric illness.

Beyond these traditional models of psychiatric intervention in schools, there are many other types of programs and interventions in schools that fall under the rubric of mental health. Examples include structured programs to prevent substance abuse, to promote the nonviolent resolution of conflict, to improve study and work habits, to support the development of prosocial values, and to cope with stress adaptively (Bond and Compas, 1989). Some aim to diminish or prevent dysfunction, others to support positive psychological functioning and wellbeing. Some are targeted to special groups at risk for adverse outcomes; others are designed to be administered to a general population. Broadly construed, the term mental health may be understood to subsume such school-based activities as guidance and peer-counseling programs.

Recent epidemiologic investigation of the pattern of service use in diverse communities for mental health problems has found that schools are now one of the most common places where mental health services are provided to children and adolescents (Leaf et al., 1996). However, these studies find little agreement between children or adolescents and their parents about whether they have received mental health services— indicating widely divergent perceptions of what constitutes such services. In addition, a large proportion of mental health services are provided to children and adolescents without *DSM* diagnoses.

There is thus a wide variety of activities—provided by several different professions and staff of differing training—that may be broadly construed as "mental health programs" and that are already implemented in schools, most outside the framework of school-based clinic programs.

Some of these have been rigorously studied to determine their effectiveness before their implementation, whereas many others have not. For example, at a time when about 170,000 students were exposed to suicide prevention programs designed for school-based implementation (Garland, Shaffer, and Whittle, 1989), there was little objective, scientific evidence for the effectiveness of such programs (Vieland et al., 1991). Therefore, research on effective and safe ways to use school-based opportunities for mental health care is crucial.

With as many as 21% of SBHC visits being for problems related to mental health (Lear et al., 1991), the rational structuring of mental health services in SBHCs is crucial to ensure appropriate prioritization and efficient allocation of resources to youth in need of them. Ideally, mental health services in schools would be delivered with maximal cost effectiveness to those with greatest need and with the greatest chance of benefiting from them. The best model for the provision of school-based mental health services is thus still to be determined. Prototype school-based mental health programs may incorporate conceptual elements from diverse disciplines, including not only clinical psychiatry but also developmental and educational psychology, teaching, social work, and others. These programs may have prevention or treatment orientations and may be narrowly targeted or broadly focused (Bond and Compas, 1989; Taylor and Adelman, 1996).

As a result of there being many disciplines involved in the design of school-based mental health programs and there being concerns about overdiagnosis of psychopathology, one question will inevitably be asked: What role should a medical model, including psychiatric concepts such as diagnosis of illness, play? However, given the large proportion of psychiatrically ill youth not receiving mental health care found in epidemiologic studies, it is likely that a large number of psychiatrically ill and disabled youth who are not receiving any current treatment will present to SBHCs. Although concerns about overdiagnosis may indeed be appropriate in regard to the 80% to 90% of youth in the general population without psychiatric disorder, for the 10% to 20% of youth with psychiatric conditions, underdiagnosis of disorder is of equal concern. In light of the evidence for the effectiveness of specific treatments for many psychiatric disorders, it is useful and important to provide early and accurate diagnosis of conditions such as attention deficit hyperactivity disorder, depression, learning disability, substance abuse, eating disorders, and others. Thus, child and adolescent diagnostic and treatment services will inevitably be one important component of the mental health services provided in SBHCs.

Recommended Components of New Models

Traditional models of psychiatric intervention in schools (cited earlier) may have many aspects well suited to adaptation in SBHCs. For example, child and adolescent psychiatrists working in these settings may incorporate some aspects of mental health consultation, community consultation, and behavioral consultation to teachers and school administrators. In addition to these traditional activities, however, school-based clinic programs will bring mental health practitioners into direct clinical contact with large segments of youth in need of mental health services but not cared for by any other model of mental health care delivery. These youths may need to be engaged in new ways. Models of child and adolescent psychiatric services provided in SBHCs may need to contain the following elements:

1. *Case finding.* In order to allocate psychiatric services appropriately to those in need of them, it is necessary to have systems to identify those in need. Screening programs administered to students in classrooms have been developed by which students in need of more intensive diagnostic or other services can be identified (Vaughan et al., 1996). Such techniques allow for the efficient allocation of intensive services to those in need of them.

2. *Linkage to services.* If methods are devised for the identification of students in need of psychiatric services, it is crucial that case finding be linked to clinical treatment. After being identified, students in need of care may not be willing to accept treatment in traditional psychiatric settings due to stigma and other concerns. Research is needed on the types of mental health service that school-based populations are willing and able to use. It may be necessary to make available on-site treatment in schools and special services such as case management for complex cases. It would be crucial to have such services in place and available before the implementation of any screening program.

3. *Strategies to overcome barriers to care (e.g., language, cultural bias and stigma, financial barriers).* Given the large proportion of students in need of care but not receiving psychiatric treatment, it is

apparent that many barriers exist to the use of care. Programs may be necessary for youth in need of financial assistance with treatment, of culturally sensitive and bilingual services, and of psychoeducation. Mental health services research may help to define the precise nature of the barriers to care and the best way to overcome them.

4. *Mechanisms for engaging students in mental health treatment.* When working in schools, where mental health problems may be identified in youths who have not come voluntarily requesting psychiatric services, health centers will encounter patients and families posing a significant risk to self or others but not willing to immediately accept help. A variety of mechanisms, ranging from intensive case management to mobile crisis services, may be necessary. Mechanisms must be put into place in order to coordinate these special outreach services with school and other agencies.

Parsons (1951) described the sociological phenomenon of the *sick role*, a special, socially recognized status of ill persons comprised of three phases: recognition that one is sick, acceptance of appropriate dependency on others for care, and eventual resumption of normal social responsibilities. One of the greatest differences between individuals who come to a clinic voluntarily for help and those with illness identified in schools is that those in health centers have gone through a process whereby they recognize that they are ill and accept some degree of appropriate dependency, albeit sometimes ambivalently. By contrast, students and families identified through screening programs in schools may be quite ill but lacking in insight or the inclination to accept help. For this special situation, which can be expected frequently in school settings, special policies and programs may be necessary to encourage acceptance of treatment by those identified as being in need of it or to deal with those who need treatment but refuse it.

5. *Medicolegal policies to address special issues.* Many special medicolegal situations pertain to school-based mental health (English and Tereszkiewicz, 1989). For example, in school-based settings, mental health practitioners often encounter youth in mental health crisis in the context of a reproductive health issue such as pregnancy or a sexually transmitted disease. Health law may require involvement of parents in the mental health crisis but prohibit their involvement in the reproductive health issue, and disentangling these from each other may be clinically difficult. Standards of practice must be clarified or established as they relate to difficult situations involving confidentiality

among student, family, and school; medicolegal responsibility of practitioners; and other special issues that arise in school settings.

6. *Research.* Research is needed to define the types of case-finding, prevention, and treatment strategies to be used in schools. Research questions to be considered include those about the nature, timing, and effectiveness of different interventions applied over the course of development while youth are in school.

7. *Training.* Clinical training programs for medical students, residents, and fellows in pediatrics, psychiatry, and affiliated fields will need to incorporate curricula pertaining to the public health opportunities and unique clinical and administrative roles of child and adolescent psychiatrists working in schools.

One final important aspect of school-based child and adolescent psychiatry programs is the uniquely extensive collaboration required with a broad array of other disciplines, agencies, and organizations. For example, specialists in pediatrics, family planning, obstetrics and gynecology, public health, and other disciplines may be involved in the development and implementation of school-based programs for drug prevention, pregnancy and sexually transmitted disease prevention, and other public health problems. Although the outcomes targeted by these programs, such as lowered pregnancy rates or delayed pregnancy, may be quite different from traditionally measured psychiatric outcomes, child and adolescent psychiatrists may have a crucial role to play in the design and implementation of these programs, as psychopathology may be a significant mediating variable in the targeted outcome. Other disciplines may be involved in support, coping, and health promotion programs aimed at those students not psychiatrically ill but under stress and at risk for adverse mental health or other outcomes. Finally, close collaboration will of course be necessary with educators and the education system, whose work is the *raison d'être* of schools and at whose invitation and under whose responsibility any SBHC or mental health program exists.

Summary

In summary, SBHCs present a unique opportunity to reach the very large proportion of youth in need of psychiatric services but not receiving care. This opportunity may make it possible to achieve important public health goals in diminishing the morbidity and mortality due to untreated psychiatric illness and associated with important epidemics of other conditions affecting youth. Child and adolescent psychiatrists, by virtue of their unique knowledge of development, psychopathology, and etiologic factors in mental illness, have a crucial role to play in the organization and practice of school-based mental health care. As a result of the unique opportunity presented by SBHCs and the access they provide to large populations of healthy but at-risk children, these practices go well beyond the traditional activities of psychiatrists in schools—such as school consulting or acting as staff psychiatrist in a special education program. New models are needed for the provision of mental health care in schools in order to take full advantage of the public health opportunities they provide.

REFERENCES

Alpert, J. L. (1976), Conceptual bases of mental health consultation in the schools. *Prof. Psychol.*, 7:619–626.

American Medical Association (AMA), Council on Scientific Affairs (1989), Providing medical services through school-based health programs. *J. Amer. Med. Assn.*, 261:1939–1942.

Bass, J. L., Gallagher, S. S. & Mehta, K. A. (1985), Injuries to adolescents and young adults. *Pediatr. Clin. North Amer.*, 23:31–39.

Bird, H. R., Gould, M. S., Yager, T., Staghezza, B. & Canino, G. (1989), Risk factors for maladjustment in Puerto-Rican children. *J. Amer. Acad. Child Adolesc. Psychiat.*, 28:847–850.

Bond, L. A. & Compas, B. E., ed. (1989), *Primary Prevention and Promotion in the Schools.* Newbury Park, CA: Sage.

Burke, K., Burke, J., Regier, D. & Rae, D. (1990), Age at onset of selected mental disorders in five community populations. *Arch. Gen. Psychiat.*, 47:511–518.

Cantwell, D. P. (1985), Hyperactive children have grown up: What have we learned about what happens to them? *Arch. Gen. Psychiat.*, 42:1026–1028.

Caplan, G. (1970), *The Theory and Practice of Mental Health Consultation.* New York: Basic Books.

Comer, J. P. (1980), *School Power: Implications of an Intervention Project.* New York: Free Press.

Douglass, R. (1983), Youth, alcohol and traffic accidents: Current status. *Recent Dev. Alcohol.*, 1:347–366.

Dryfoos, J. (1990), *Adolescents at Risk: Prevalence and Prevention.* New York: Oxford University Press.

———— (1994), *Full Service Schools: A Revolution in Health and Social Services for Children, Youth and Families.* San Francisco: Jossey-Bass.

Earls, F., Robins, L. N., Stiffman, A. R. & Powell, J. (1989), Comprehensive health care for high-risk adolescents: An evaluation study. *Amer. J. Public Health*, 79:999–1005.

Ellickson, P. L. & Bell, R. M. (1990), Drug prevention in junior high: A multi-site longitudinal test. *Science*, 247(4948):1299–1305.

———— Lara, M. E., Sherbourne, C. D. & Zima, B. (1993), *Forgotten Ages, Forgotten Problems: Adolescents' Health.* Santa Monica, CA: RAND.

English, A. & Tereszkiewicz, L. (1989), *School-Based Health Clinics: Legal Issues.* Washington, DC: Center for Population Options; San Francisco: National Center for Youth Law.

Friedman, I. M. (1985), Alcohol and unnatural deaths in San Francisco youths. *Pediatrics*, 76:191–193.

Garland, A., Shaffer, D. & Whittle, B. (1989), A national survey of school-based, adolescent suicide prevention programs. *J. Amer. Acad. Child Adolesc. Psychiat.*, 28:931–934.

Goldstein, P. J., Brownstein, H. H., Ryan, P. J. & Belluci, P. A. (1990), Crack and homicide in New York City: A case study in the epidemiology of violence. In: *Crack in America: Demon Drugs and Social Justice,* ed. C. Reinarman & H. G. Levine. Berkeley, CA: University of California Press, pp. 113–130.

Halperin, S. F., Bass, J., Gallagher, S. & Mehta, K. (1983), Unintentional injuries among adolescents and young adults: A review and analysis. *J. Adolesc. Health Care*, 4:275–281.

Kovacs, M. (1996), Presentation and course of major depressive disorder during childhood and later years of the life span. *J. Amer. Acad. Child Adolesc. Psychiat.*, 35:705–715.

———— (1985), The natural history and course of depressive disorders in childhood. *Psychiatric Annals,* 15:387–389.

———— Paulauskas, S., Gatsonis, C. & Richards, C. (1988), Depressive disorders in childhood: III. A longitudinal study of co-morbidity with and risk for conduct disorders. *J. Affective Disord.*, 15:205–217.

Leaf, P. J., Alegria, M., Cohen, P., Goodman, S. H., Horwitz, S. M., Hoven, C. W., Narrow, W. E., Vaden-Kiernan, M. & Regier, D. A. (1996), Mental health service use in the community and schools: Results from the four-community MECA study. *J. Amer. Acad. Child Adolesc. Psychiat.*, 35, 889–897.

Lear, J. G., Gleicher, H. B., St. Germaine, A. & Porter, P. J. (1991), Reorganizing health care for adolescents: The experience of the school-based adolescent health care program. *J. Adolesc. Health*, 12:450–458.

Lewis, D., Shanock, S., Pincus, J. & Glaser, G. (1980), Violent juvenile delinquents: Psychiatric, neurological, psychological, and abuse factors. *Annual Prog. in Child Psychiat. and Child Devel.*, 1980:591–603.

Moffitt, T. E. (1993), Adolescence-limited and life-course-persistent antisocial behavior: A developmental taxonomy. *Psychol. Rev.*, 100:674–701.

National Center for Education in Maternal and Child Health. (1990), *The Health of America's Youth.* Washington, DC: National Center for Education in Maternal and Child Health.

National Institute of Mental Health (NIMH), (1990), *National Plan for Research on Child and Adolescent Mental Disorders: A report requested by the U.S. Congress*, Submitted by the National Advisory Mental Health Council. Rockville, MD: U.S. Department of Health and Human Services.

Newacheck, P. W., McManus, M. A. & Gephart, J. (1992), Health insurance coverage of adolescents: A current profile and assessment of trends. *Pediatrics,* 90:589–596.

Offord, D. R. (1987), Prevention of emotional and behavioral disorders in children. *J. Child Psychol. and Psychiat. and Allied Disciplines,* 28:9–19.

———— Boyle, M. H., Szatmari, P., Rae-Grant, N. I., Links, P. S., Cadman, D. T., Byles, J. A., Crawford, J. W., Blum, H. M., Byrne, C., Thomas, H. & Woodward, C. A. (1987), Ontario Child Health Study: II. Six-month prevalence of disorder and rates of service utilization. *Arch. Gen. Psychiat.*, 44:832–838.

Parsons, T. (1951), *The Social System.* Glencoe, IL: Free Press.

Robbins, D. M., Beck, J. C., Pries, R., Jacobs, D. & Smith, C. (1983), Learning disability and neuropsychological impairment in adjudicated, unincarcerated male delinquents. *J. Amer. Acad. Child Adolesc. Psychiat.,* 22:40–46.

Robins, L. N. (1970), Follow-up studies investigating childhood disorders. In: *Psychiatric Epidemiology*, ed. E. H. Hare & J. K. Wing. London: Oxford University Press, pp. 29–68.

Rohde, P., Lewinsohn, P. M. & Seeley, J. R. (1991), Comorbidity of unipolar depression: II. Comorbidity with other mental disorders in adolescents and adults. *J. Abnorm. Psychol.*, 100:214–222.

Shaffer, D., Gould, M. S., Fisher, P., Trautman, P., Moreau, D., Kleinman, M. & Flory, M. (1996), Psychiatric diagnosis in child and adolescent suicide. *Arch. Gen. Psychiat.*, 53:339–348.

———— Philips, I. & Enzer, N. (1989), *Prevention of Mental Disorders, Alcohol and Other Drug Use in Children and Adolescents*. OSAP Prevention Monograph 2. Rockville, MD: National Clearinghouse for Alcohol and Drug Information.

Tallmadge, J. & Barkley, R. A. (1983), The interaction of hyperactive and normal boys with their fathers and mothers. *J. Abnorm. Child Psychol.*, 11:565–579.

Taylor, L. & Adelman, H. S. (1996), Mental health in the schools: Promising directions for practice. In: *Adolescent Medicine: State of the Art Reviews*, 7(2). Philadelphia: Hanley & Belfus, pp. 1–15.

Vaughan, R. D., McCarthy, J. F., Walter, H. J., Resnicow, K., Waterman, P., & Armstrong, D. (1996), The development, reliability, and validity of a risk factor screening survey for urban minority junior high school students. *J. Adolesc. Health*, 19:171–178.

Velez, C. N., Johnson, J. & Cohen, P. (1989), A longitudinal analysis of selected risk factors for childhood psychopathology: The New York Study. *J. Amer. Acad. Child Adolesc. Psychiat.*, 28:861–864.

Vieland, V., Whittle, B., Garland, A., Hicks, R. & Shaffer, D. (1991), The impact of curriculum-based suicide prevention programs for teenagers: An 18-month follow-up. *J. Amer. Acad. Child Adolesc. Psychiat.*, 30:811–815.

Weist, M. (1998), Mental health services in schools: Expanding opportunities. In: *Handbook of Child and Adolescent Outpatient, Day Treatment and Community Psychiatry*, ed. H. S. Ghuman & R. M. Sarles. Philadelphia: Brunner/Mazel, pp. 347–357.

5 ON-SITE SCHOOL-BASED MENTAL HEALTH CLINICS: FIFTEEN YEARS OF EXPERIENCE IN ORANGE COUNTY, CALIFORNIA

BERNARD A. RAPPAPORT

During 1997, there were more than 25 children and youth mental health outpatient clinics located throughout the four service-delivery regions of the Orange County, California community mental health system. Sixty percent of these clinics were on-site, within the county's public school districts. The county is the fifth largest county in the United States. It has a culturally and politically diverse population of about 2.7 million residents. Therefore, it took many years of program planning (and much prior evidence of successful program operation) before the development of such a widely dispersed regional school-based outpatient clinic system could be established throughout all of the different areas of this densely populated urban county.

The first regional school-based program started in 1983 with the building of an on-site school-based clinic in the southern portion of the county. This program received extensive support and acceptance from the community and the schools. Its success stimulated program development in the other regions of the county. This paper describes the county's experience with the original program. The success of that program helped establish the countywide continuum of school-based regional mental health outpatient/hospital/residential treatment services.

This first program began with only one half-time staff person in a single school. Fifteen years later, the program was serving eleven cities and communities. By 1997, six outpatient clinics had been established. One clinic was located in a United Methodist Church; five were located in one of the 46 schools of two unified school districts (Capistrano, Laguna Beach).

These two school districts are a study in contrast. Their student enrollment is about 43,000. Seventy-five percent of the students are Caucasian, 17% Hispanic, 5% Asian, and 2% African American. Capistrano Unified is a large, rapidly growing urban school district with innumerable space problems. It is situated in one of the more socially and politically conservative areas of the county. The contiguous district, Laguna Beach Unified, is the smallest unified district in the county. It has a stable student enrollment and serves the residents of an affluent, socially and politically liberal coastal resort village.

Staff were initially stationed in the offices of an Indian Education Resource Center school building. This caused school and mental health personnel to begin interacting in new and different ways. Subsequently, the community became comfortable with the concept of a mental health clinic on school grounds. Community leaders wanted to preserve family values and to prevent their emotionally disturbed children from having to undergo unnecessary or prolonged institutional care. They wanted their children to be treated in the community and to continue to live in their own homes.

School districts donated space, volunteers funded and built clinics, and treatment teams developed techniques for providing services to children in nonclinic settings. They learned how to reach out to children, even when parental or social supports were minimal or unavailable.

The mental health staff and the schools devoted much time determining where additional services were most needed and which communities most strongly supported establishing new clinics. Working relationships were developed with parent–teacher associations, religious organizations, and service clubs. The community's culture and family values were incorporated into the planning process.

Youth groups held car washes and bake sales. Some parents held fundraisers to pay for supplies; others volunteered to help with construction, furnishings, and décor. Each clinic opened with a gala event that recognized the community's hard work, diversity, talent, and dedication to mentally and emotionally ill children.

Because the clinics were outgrowths of community commitment, they became integrated into the community's service system. Once started, they continued to receive ongoing support from the community. During the county's recent bankruptcy, when supplies were hard to obtain, volunteers donated needed items. Some citizens even left supplies, anonymously, in gift baskets at clinic doors.

The clinics are used exclusively for mental health services. Volunteers constructed the offices with privacy in mind (e.g., they added soundproofing). The décor is noninstitutional. Patients usually believe that the clinics are part of the school guidance program. A casual observer might not recognize these as mental health clinics. A young patient once stated of the first clinic that the waiting room looks like "grandma's house." This helps patients who require mental health services to receive services with little or no stigmatization.

Staffing

All of the clinics house county and contract agency staff as well as local private mental health practitioners (the latter being employed on a part-time/as-needed basis in order to eliminate waiting lists while maintaining high standards of care).

During 1997, there were more than 30 full-time-equivalent professional staff. Staff ethnicity was reflective of the local community. However, there is a relatively large number of bilingual staff, particularly Spanish-speaking therapists. About half of the staff are clinical psychologists; more than one third are clinical social workers. There is a volunteer services coordinator. The program director is a licensed clinical social worker.

Fifteen percent of staff are psychiatrists, including child and adolescent psychiatrists. Psychiatrists provide consultation services to the schools. They also provide much training, consultation, and support service to clinic staff and are always available to provide second opinions upon parent or school request. Their expertise and special medical training are also used to treat parents of child patients in individual sessions when appropriate. Psychiatrists are encouraged to maintain a small psychotherapy caseload of young patients.

Description of Patients and Families; Age and Number of Patients

A wide range of patients is served year-round—from children who walk in or are brought by parents to children in severe crisis brought by the police. Patients who need county outpatient services have obtained all of these services from this school-based clinic system. This is because, in 1997 and during the previous years of program operation, there were no other county-funded resources serving children in the catchment area.

Staff see children at the local school's clinic site and then visit other sites to provide services to children who attend other schools. They also visit area nonschool sites (e.g., hospitals, police stations), are available at night or on weekends to see patients who may be brought to these facilities, and act as the gatekeepers for patients who are referred to the program's contract or extra-help private practitioner staff. Each year, more than 1,000 children and adolescents are served.

Referrals of patients younger than thirteen are more numerous than referrals of older patients. However, the majority of patients in the program are adolescents. This is because chronically ill patients and/or those with inadequate support systems are placed in continuous case management with the patient's therapist. This special case-management program has been very effective and contributes to the low number of recidivistic patients.

Many of the program's children are aggressive and/or behaviorally disturbed. Significant minorities have suicidal ideation and/or before admission to treatment have made suicide attempts. A few are psychotic and/or suffer from pervasive developmental disorders. Many of the program's children have educational disabilities and attention and learning problems and are eligible for services under the Individuals with Disabilities Education Act (IDEA).

Many parents, when first seen by the program, are not motivated to have their children treated. Other parents appear motivated but, because of work schedules and/or other time constraints, indicate difficulty in participating in treatment sessions or arranging for treatment for their children. In such cases, the flexible and/or extended hours of operation and the geographical accessibility of the clinics allow for schedules to be arranged or rearranged so that treatment impediments can be eliminated.

Children who are from families with such difficulties and/or dynamics can be difficult to assess and/or treat in traditional mental health outpatient clinics. However, in this on-site school-based program, such parents/caretakers are usually most amenable to having their children treated; after a while, they may even become enthusiastic about participating in the treatment.

Services

TREATMENT

There is a large variety of multimodality treatments including consultation, outreach, and volunteer mentor services. Volunteers work with families as special friends and role models and take a lead role in children's entry or reentry into the community social system. Treatment-service intensity is based on clinical need. It is not uncommon for severely ill children and their families to receive five or more outpatient and collateral or family therapy sessions a week. On occasion, some patients and their families may receive nine or more hours of service a week.

All of the services have a family focus. However, the clinical approach is individualized and child centered. High priority is placed on diagnosis and assessment. Initial evaluations are designed to be as complete and comprehensive as possible. Clinical care and treatment are designed to establish a bond of emotional closeness among the program staff, parents, and patients and to emphasize continuity of care. If during the course of treatment there are changes in children's living situations, therapists are expected to follow their patients into the new setting(s) and continue to provide care as is appropriate.

Initially, it was believed that suicidal children or those from violent or rejecting homes could not be diverted from hospitalization. As the program matured, however, it became possible to develop a system that provided such diversion in a therapeutic manner. This came about when all of the program participants—school staff, parents, and volunteers—formed working alliances to maximize everyone's strengths and abilities first to stabilize and then to help children benefit from mental health care in the schools. This system was administratively supported by a flexible on-call/overtime system and a caseload structure that gave clinicians sufficient time to provide as much intensive care, emergency case management, and coordination as were necessary.

The role of the psychiatrist in supporting this new type of care situation was of crucial importance. However, every team member's role was also important. Everyone, including contract agency staff, worked as a team, sharing resources and cases to best help the patients. It was found that, when this happened—for example, when there could be immediate supportive response from school staff, with classroom changes—not only was intensive outpatient therapy possible, but an overall therapeutic milieu could be created that was equal to or better than that in a hospital. In such a supportive environment, it becomes possible to create a uniformly consistent, therapeutic milieu not just at school but at home and in the after-school setting.

CONSULTATION

Much time is spent consulting with the school district. Consultations have contributed to school and mental health staffs' understanding and respect for each other's very different realms and to a greater appreciation for how the balance of strengths and differences can forge a strong, effective team.

A special interagency mentorship program was developed when the consultation program first began. School staff were assigned as mentors to mental health staff. Education staff then helped the clinicians learn school district policies, procedures, and systems. Consequently, when working on school campuses, mental health staff know how to obtain assistance and guidance from principals and school administrators. As a result of this process, education staff also become increasingly knowledgeable of mental health staff's treatment capabilities and of the value of referring disturbed students earlier, when mental health staff's treatment techniques are usually more efficacious.

Consultations have included a continuum of activities, with the school districts determining the specific types of activities. At one end of the continuum may be short-term therapy for individual students identified by the schools; at the other end may be the teaching of social or goal-setting skills to groups of students or the helping of students to avoid gang life. Mental health staff also assist school staff with behavior management. In addition, they are available to provide group support services for children coping with loss and grief.

A major value of this arrangement is that mental health staff become available on a continuous basis to respond to crises occurring in the schools. They are available for comprehensive, on-site response to disasters and, during such events, are able to provide assistance to teachers and children during the school day or, if necessary, in the evenings or at night.

An extreme example of such a capability occurred when a firestorm threatened Laguna Beach in 1993. Because of the close working rela-

WE ARE PLEASED TO SEND YOU THE
ENCLOSED VOLUME FOR REVIEW:

title: Adolescent Psychiatry
Volume 24

editor: Aaron H. Esman
associate editors: Lois T. Flaherty & Harvey A. Horowitz

pages: 396pp.

price: $55.00

publication date: 1999

ISBN: 0-88163-198-1

tionship with the Laguna Beach school district, mental health staff were able to quickly develop a coordinated response to this disaster, even as flames approached the city. As the firestorm subsided, mental health staff teamed with the schools and implemented a comprehensive follow-up program, which has since received national acclaim. If at the time of the firestorm this working relationship had not existed, such a response would not have been possible.

Service Delivery: Process, Coordination, Monitoring, and Results

Extensive ongoing coordination in regard to service delivery occurs on a daily basis between the program's staff and the school personnel. There are procedures for unanticipated crises or emergencies. The mental health service chief and key school officials exchange home telephone numbers and/or pager numbers; when the need arises, they do not hesitate to call one another at any hour of day or night, weekdays or weekends.

To ensure that patients receive appropriate care, an extensive follow-up and monitoring system was instituted through a system of multidisciplinary case reviews and a specially developed integrated case-management system. Each patient has a mental health case manager, usually the patient's therapist. These managers oversee services and make sure there is coordination without duplication of services.

Treatment plans and coordination plans specify what services are in place at the school-based clinics and elsewhere. Impairment and Support Scale rating forms are also attached to the treatment plans. These forms describe a child's degree of psychosocial impairment and the status of the child's psychosocial support system. The forms rate progress and assist in ensuring that care is effective and time-efficient. "Problem-case reviews" are conducted any time patients are not progressing at the expected rate, as determined by clinical judgment and/or by information obtained from the forms.

The result has been excellent clinical response, improved long-term patient outcome, and minimal use of high-end services such as psychiatric hospitalization or inappropriate or unnecessary segregation of emotionally disturbed children in nonpublic (or private) schools because of emotional problems and instability. During these fifteen years of operation, the annual psychiatric bed utilization of the program has averaged significantly less than one bed/100,000 children. During these years, no patient has been admitted to the state hospital, and no patient has committed suicide.

Privacy and Confidentiality

Parents are always asked to sign releases of information so that mental health staff may speak to school staff on an ongoing basis. The defined goal for these releases is to authorize mental health staff's provision of information to school staff to help them assist patients in their school functioning. Content or process information may be involved—data that mental health staff believe may be appropriately shared with school staff without jeopardizing a family's privacy. School staff recognize that some of mental health staff's work involves issues that do not directly relate to school functioning—issues that are personal and private for patients and their families and that should not be shared with the school.

Identifying Students in Need

A major strength of the program has been its ability to facilitate the identification and referral for treatment of a wide variety of emotionally disturbed students in all types of need at an earlier stage of impairment, when treatment can be more efficacious and more cost-effective. Specifically:

1. Children with major mental illness are usually identified early and referred for services. When this happens, such children usually respond to treatment, as they are especially able to benefit from the program's ability to mainstream patients.
2. The program also identifies children who are not aggressive but who may benefit from specialized services earlier. During school consultations and school visits, there are many opportunities for mental health staff to observe students in need. Mental health staff can then advise their school liaisons of these observations. Consequently, school staff are helped to recognize students who,

although not disruptive, appear to have problems that may indicate the presence of serious mental health conditions.

3. There is much focus on young, aggressive children and those with anger-management problems. With these children, it has been found that early intervention can help preserve self-esteem, enable educational and social success, and teach verbal ways of expression. Quick screening is given to any child who threatens others, is easily angered, is more aggressive than peers, or is too interested in or "plays" at mass destruction. Such patients usually respond to treatment and improve when they can be seen in the normative environment of the school setting.

4. There has been considerable success in serving Hispanic children with disabilities who are eligible for mental health services under IDEA. The percentage of special education Hispanic children receiving related mental health services in these school districts is statistically much greater than the statewide average. Staff have been pleased that the "penetration rate" of the two school districts for obtaining related mental health services for their Hispanic special education children may be the best in the state. They are proud of the program's ability to consistently foster successful response to treatment in this patient population. This response, in turn, has facilitated appropriate mainstreaming. The program's special education Hispanic patients seldom require treatment in psychiatric hospitals, placement in residential treatment institutions, or incarceration in juvenile justice system institutions. They are not inappropriately segregated in nonpublic schools.

Summary

Developing on-site school-based clinics is a complicated, time-consuming, and labor-intensive task. However, fifteen years of experience gained from operating these programs indicate that developing such programs can be of much value, especially if members of the community are involved in the process of establishing the clinics. Experience has demonstrated that such involvement leads to the community's developing feelings of pride of ownership, which in turn leads to its developing an interest in being educated further about mental health issues. This in turn leads to the community's becoming advocates for serving larger numbers of children.

Consequently, the school-based clinics described in this paper have been able to serve a wide variety of children. Their location on school sites has the effect of reducing the stigma of treatment, improving service accessibility, increasing patient referrals, correcting ethnic imbalances in the referral rate, helping to develop culturally competent continuums of care, identifying children needing mental heath services at earlier stages of impairment, increasing parental involvement in the treatment of their children, and increasing the numbers of children who are treated in mainstreamed settings.

Our experience has been that, when we compare school-based clinics with traditional clinics in the same system of care, treatment outcomes are much improved in the school-based clinics. Comparisons of the use of high-end inpatient services with managed-care systems would, we believe, be similarly favorable. Members of the community who have expressed concerns about recent trends in managed-care treatment state that they would not have the same concerns if children could receive treatment in the types of school-based clinics described in this paper. In such school-based clinics, in which all community members can feel the pride of ownership and become involved in intervening in the emotional illnesses of their children, the finest principles of managed care can be seen in action.

6   SCHOOL MENTAL HEALTH IN NEW MEXICO

STEVEN ADELSHEIM

New Mexico's children currently face some of the highest rates of poverty, substance abuse, suicide, and school dropout of any children in the United States. Daily, children come to school with multiple problems that make it hard for them to focus on their education, to learn, and to become the productive members of society we all would like them to be. Many teenagers face problems such as homelessness, drug abuse, pregnancy, mental health issues, and domestic violence. These problems make it difficult for them to stay in school, and often these teens end up dropping out of school and later finding themselves in the juvenile justice system. The work of Abraham Maslow reminds us that, in order for children to be able to reach the levels of motivation to be educationally successful, their physiological, safety, nurturing and self-esteem needs must first be met. Without meeting these needs, we cannot expect children to succeed.

The recent document by the New Mexico Department of Health, *The Status of Children's Mental Health in New Mexico*, shows that we have many children whose mental health problems are not being identified and treated successfully. When we look at the prevalence of expected mental health diagnoses for 12- to 21-year-olds, we find a minority of children whose mental health problems are being adequately identified and addressed. Community-based services have not yet been expanded to a great degree under Medicaid managed care, and we still see our public systems having difficulty identifying and bringing children into treatment services.

Fortunately, New Mexico has been taking active steps to alleviate many of these difficulties. School health has become a high priority within our state. New Mexico has an active Office of School Health with twenty staff members in the Public Health Division of the Department of Health. New Mexico has been the recipient of two federal grants—one from the Centers for Disease Control (CDC) to expand school health statewide and one from the federal Maternal and Child Health Bureau to develop school mental health infrastructure within the state.

The Office of School Health has many collaborative partners in these efforts. Within the Department of Health, we work closely with the Behavioral Health Division and with the Division of Health Improvement, which monitors the effectiveness of interventions. The New Mexico Department of Children, Youth, and Families is responsible for many children's mental health services and for juvenile justice and child protective services. Our partnership with children's mental health programs in this department has increased over the years and has brought many collaborations in school mental health. The Department of Human Services has been actively involved in school health issues because of its administration of both Medicaid-managed care and the Medicaid in the Schools Program. Furthermore, under welfare reform in New Mexico, children are required to stay in school in order for their family to continue to receive financial benefits, so school health has become a critical issue in this area as well. The New Mexico Department of Education is not under the governor but is under the state Board of Education and works as a separate department. We have active collaborations with the School Health Unit in the state Department of Education, funded largely through our CDC grant and through the Special Education Division, which is actively working with us to expand awareness and training for teachers on how to identify children's mental health issues and intervene successfully in the classroom.

School-based health centers (SBHCs) are important components of our school health interventions in New Mexico. Although most states with SBHCs have a large majority of mental health providers in them, our state has mental health providers in only one third of our facilities. One of our goals in the year 2000 is to expand the capability of these sites to provide mental health support by linking them more effectively with community children's mental health providers. Our SBHC data collection system has been improved over the course of the 1998–1999 school year. We hope to receive more accurate data on the number of children being served and on their diagnoses. Nationally and in New Mexico, about one third of children who come to SBHCs have a primary mental health condition that becomes clear after several visits. Thirty-seven percent of the students who visit the six University of New Mexico SBHCs have a mental health diagnosis or problem. The numbers are particularly large at middle schools, where more than 50% of students have primary mental health or substance abuse issues. The most frequent diagnoses are depression and dysthymic disorders, general counseling needs, family disruptions, and academic problems leading to potential adjustment disorders. Many of our children face high rates of poverty, lack of support at home, and multiple stresses that make it hard for them to be successful in a school environment. Consequently, many children also exhibit underlying symptoms of posttraumatic stress disorder (PTSD) and anxiety.

Studies done over the last several years have shown that many of the children not successful in our schools go on to have difficulty within our legal system. A snapshot of children incarcerated in New Mexico—taken by our Department of Children, Youth, and Families in 1995—showed that a vast majority (67%) of children in our youth detention facilities have a history of school failure, 63% have a history of substance abuse, 52% have a mental health history, 36% have a history of special education, and 34% have a history of abuse and neglect. These data fit closely with other, national data regarding youth with conduct disorders and substance abuse problems, as seen in the work of Paula Riggs (at the University of Colorado) and in the work of Steiner et al. (at Stanford University), who looked at PTSD in juvenile offenders in the California Youth Authority.

In 1997, the New Mexico Office of Epidemiology in the Department of Health surveyed 28,000 public school students (grades seven to twelve) about issues relating to substance use, self-esteem, depressive symptoms, and school behaviors. The numbers of children abusing substances other than alcohol increased from those of the previous, 1993 study. Of particular note were that both boys and girls were equal in their cigarette use, marijuana use increased to about 25% of boys and 22% of girls, and the abuse of other drugs (particularly inhalants and crack cocaine) continued to increase. Many of our youths have had difficult experiences in school, including having their belongings damaged or stolen, being harassed or picked on, ditching school, shoplifting, and putting others down.

In a further review of these results, there appears to be a relationship between the problem behaviors and mental health and substance abuse issues of these youth. Many of the children with more severe problems are students who more frequently complain of feeling depressed, hopeless, and sad and are also more frequently students who report higher rates of substance use, particularly marijuana or other drugs of abuse.

When we look at prevalence of past-year experiences and at mental health indicators, it is clear that the children who reported feeling more discouraged or hopeless all or most of the time were much more likely to have stolen something, ditched school, put someone down, or hit someone on purpose than were children who did not have a positive response to that question. Furthermore, students who frequently used drugs were even more likely to have engaged in similar behavior than were students with no history of drug use. In addition, students who more frequently used drugs had higher mean depression scores, and these scores increased in severity based on higher frequency of drug use.

Clearly, we are seeing children facing multiple barriers to their successful learning and achieving in our schools and in our communities. It has become critical within our state to focus on these barriers to learning if our students are to achieve successfully in school and become productive members of our communities later. Our state has taken an approach of working to expand school–community collaboration in multiple areas in order to bring together parents, schools, community providers, and other community members to increase the support for children to have their social and emotional needs addressed so they can have more productive futures.

The New Mexico School Mental Health Initiative (SMHI) is working actively on ways to expand the focus and collaboration on these school mental health issues throughout the state. Three workgroups have focused on these issues. The Advocacy Workgroup has been promoting school mental health legislation to look at expanding support in many ways for these issues. The Training Workgroup has focused on developing school mental health assessments for at-risk children so they can be properly screened and directed to interventions through our schools; in addition, this workgroup has focused on expanding university linkages for preservice and in-service training for our school and community providers. The Families, Schools, and Communities Linkages Workgroup has been actively involved in trainings on Section 504, a component of the 1973 Rehabilitation Act providing general education classroom intervention for children with behavioral and physical disabilities.

Through collaborative efforts with the Behavioral Health Division of the New Mexico Department of Health and with the New Mexico Department of Children, Youth, and Families, we have four state pilot sites working on children's mental health school–community collaboration. Furthermore, additional sites are receiving regular technical assistance in order to expand their services and programs in these areas. Finally, a primary-care pilot site was developed in one community; local primary-care providers were given additional training in how to identify and treat children's mental health issues in an isolated, rural area of the state.

The SMHI has also conducted multiple statewide training sessions; these are in addition to the more than 40 local-community sessions conducted in 1998. The Office of School Health coordinates a yearly school health conference now attended by 400 people from around the state. We have provided grant-writing workshops for school–community collaborative partners to learn how to find additional funds to provide for the community interventions that they want to develop. Through our Section 504 training in collaboration with the state Department of Education, Special Education Division, more than 375 teachers and administrators from throughout the state were trained in implementation of Section 504. We have also provided additional statewide training in adolescent substance abuse and, in the fall of 1998, with the governor's Mental Health Planning Council, cosponsored the first state Summit on Children's Mental Health.

We are working to develop additional state infrastructure for school mental health. Our SMHI staff, who works statewide, includes a child psychiatrist director, a master's-level social worker program director, and a special education teacher. Within the Public Health Division, we have developed regional School Mental Health Advocate positions. As our state is divided into four public health districts, each district now has one advocate who works on a regional basis providing technical assistance and support to schools and communities to expand their ability to provide school mental health prevention and early intervention support for children throughout each of those districts. These advocates work in collaboration with other district health professionals, educational specialists, and mental health providers in their communities.

In addition, the SMHI has multiple state collaborative partners. We work closely with New Mexico's universities to expand preservice and in-service training for school personnel and mental health providers who will later go to work in the schools. We work closely with parent organizations to advocate on their behalf for increased support for children's mental health and substance abuse intervention. We work with the state Pupil's Services Alliance to link with school nurses, school social workers, school psychologists, school counselors, and child psychiatrists to bring a collaborative effort to expand support for

105

school health professionals. Finally, we work with youth organizations to give youth a more active voice in policy and legislation in the state.

As New Mexico has moved to Medicaid-managed care, the SMHI has developed relationships with our Medicaid-managed care providers. We are working closely with them to expand community providers into schools through the behavioral health systems of Medicaid-managed care. We are in the process of developing pilot projects in both Albuquerque and Santa Fe to expand the community mental health component of the Medicaid behavioral health services. We are working on the complex tasks of negotiating the reimbursement mechanisms for the SBHC providers as well as distinguishing which special education services schools need to provide for children separate from Medicaid treatment services. We are working on these issues with our schools and our local Medicaid partners.

Finally, New Mexico is working to make a commitment to expand both behavioral health assessments in schools and school health, mental health, and substance abuse services through our State Children's Health Insurance Plan (SCHIP). New Mexico has the highest percent of children in poverty of all states; however, New Mexico Medicaid eligibility is already at 185% of the poverty level. Many of our uninsured children are eligible for Medicaid but are not currently enrolled. Our plan involves two phases—increasing Medicaid eligibility to 235% of poverty and expanding wraparound services for all children under 235% of poverty.

These wraparound services include home-visiting services for first-time mothers; behavioral health early identification, assessment, and intervention services; school-based health services; increased support for children with developmental disabilities; behavioral health respite care; medical day-care services; and dental services. The SCHIP assessment component would focus on identifying risk factors in children and would serve as a gateway to other SCHIP wraparound services and to Medicaid-managed care services, school interventions, and/or community resources and services. This assessment would take place in child-care, day-care, or school settings whenever possible. A mental health professional or a paraprofessional with supervision and training would complete the assessment. SCHIP school health services would focus on identifying individual risk factors for children that might lead them to need more intensive treatment through Medicaid-managed care. SCHIP interventions would be individual and group risk-reduction interventions with funding tied to the existence of school health advisory committees that would identify each community's school health services needs. Children not in school—whether home-schooled, suspended, or expelled—would also be eligible for these services. The various school health intervention categories include risk reduction for depression and suicide risk; abuse and neglect services; substance abuse risk reduction; tobacco use risk reduction; nutrition, obesity, and malnutrition prevention; and pregnancy, HIV, and STD risk reduction.

Although New Mexico's children face multiple issues, we are actively working to address their many needs. Our state is taking an active approach using school health, mental health, and substance abuse intervention to provide accessible care for our children and their families. We are making school- and community-level collaboration a priority throughout the state and are working to develop the needed infrastructures to make these interventions feasible. Although we have a lot of work to do, we are optimistic that these interventions will increase the prevention and early intervention services for all our children and will help those children who need more intensive support to gain access to that treatment.

7   AN ADVISING PROGRAM IN A LARGE URBAN HIGH SCHOOL: THE MAGIC MATCH

NANCY RAPPAPORT

I am going to describe a four-year effort to introduce an advising program into an urban public high school in Cambridge, Massachusetts. It is, alas, not a success story with numbers that dazzle. If one works in schools, one develops a certain amount of humility from the struggle and effort that go into implementing a program. Rather, I have slowly built a program that I hope will affect students. Why am I doing this? In asking myself this question, I look for inspiration from some of the more visionary doctors in our field. Dr. Elvin Semrad (1948) was instrumental in improving the lives of many patients in state hospitals when he encouraged staff to create caring environments in which patients could be more self-reflective. I believe that therapists can help many disengaged adolescents in this country in a similar way. Advising programs that help teachers create a "holding environment" for adolescents will allow these teens to become more self-reflective and to take a more active role in their own education.

Fortunately, most of us can point either to our parents or to a caring adult who helped us navigate our teen years. If teenagers have family support or are lucky enough to go to an alternative or private high school, they will probably benefit from this type of relationship, which research shows is key to mental health. I want to find a way of adapting advising to large public high schools. The average public high school contains 2,000 to 4,000 students—a troubling arrangement by any standard.

In spite of adults' recognition that a good high school education is a key to a productive future, many urban adolescents continue to do poorly—skipping classes, failing courses, and showing many other signs of apathy toward academics. Teachers and administrators are searching for new, effective ways of motivating students to care about their education and to take steps to plan constructively for their future. Lawrence Steinberg (1996), a prominent education researcher on motivation, has written that as many as 40% of American students of all social classes are disengaged from school. This apathy translates to poor performance on international tests and other well-known signs that indicate that our high schoolers are ill-prepared to meet the challenges of adulthood. Poor motivation is a formidable barrier to learning. There is an urgent need to develop effective interventions that prompt students to invest effort in their education. Academic engagement has also been identified as a critical protective factor against adolescent violence. Therefore, this is a promising prevention strategy.

Eccles et al. (1993) have critically analyzed the precipitous decline in performance as students move from elementary to high school. Two factors are known to limit student motivation: low confidence and the belief that one's ability to learn is predetermined. Students who believe that they are incompetent may decide that academic success is irrelevant rather than accept the belief that they are inadequate. The cycle begins when these same students fail to invest effort in their class work, avoid difficult classes, and redirect their energies to nonacademic activities. This guarantees failure and only confirms their lack of confidence and helplessness. Researchers and writers, including Lisa Delpit (1994), Louise and George Spindler (1988), Feldman and Elliott (1993), and Taylor, Gilligan, and Sullivan (1995), have documented extensive evidence that adolescent minorities and girls are especially at risk for failing or showing mediocre performances in high school.

Research by Meier (1995) and McDonald (1997) has demonstrated that, in general, learning is enhanced when constructive relationships are built between students and adults in a school. In small, alternative high schools, well-planned advisory programs have made a difference in outcomes for these at-risk populations. However, larger advising programs in public high schools have not been consistently executed or sufficiently evaluated to ensure similar success, or, in most cases, programs have not even been tried at all. This leaves a serious gap in our knowledge and understanding of how teacher–student connections in an advising program can effectively translate into increased motivation to learn. In Sarah Lawrence Lightfoot's (1983) eloquent examination of good high schools, she repeatedly comes back to what she calls the "magic match"—the crucial connection between a great teacher and a struggling student. If we know that this kind of contact is critical, what can be done to make sure that as many students as possible in public high schools have the chance to make connections with caring adults?

Starting an Advising Program in Cambridge

Let me give some background to explain how I got involved in advising. Since 1995, I have worked as a mental health director at the Teen Health Center, a school-based clinic at Cambridge Rindge and Latin High School (CRLS) in Cambridge, Massachusetts. Of its 2,000 students, about 60% are from racial or ethnic minorities. More than half are eligible to receive free lunch, and one third speak a first language other than English. Often, poor academic performance is only one of many problems confronting these teenagers. Teen pregnancy, substance abuse, broken homes, and numerous detentions and suspensions are all part of their troubled lives. The number of CRLS students who are failing is alarming: 30% of all students fail at least one class every semester. Even more disturbing is that the percentages for minorities are even higher: 47% of African American students and 38% of Latino students are experiencing such failures. It is not uncommon for failing students to be ignored and to be moved to the next grade (unless they provoke some disciplinary action, for which they are suspended or expelled).

Advising is an effort to address this cycle. Phase 1 took place over a five-month period in 1996 that teamed all 2,000 students with 200 adult volunteers from the school. The program evolved into phase 2 during 1997–1999—in which only ninth graders are targeted, and groups are led only by teachers who, in exchange for a lighter course load, meet weekly with students. There are currently 26 advisors teamed with 490 ninth graders. There is an effort to have each advisor also have the students in daily homeroom and an academic class. We anticipate expanding in the next two years to include tenth grade. All through the school year, groups of about fifteen students meet weekly with a caring teacher. The meetings are held during the regular school day and last for a typical class period. There is a specific curriculum, but there is also plenty of room for advisors to adapt to the needs of the students. I meet regularly with advisors to talk about how groups are going and about how they might successfully intervene with troubled kids. We have done five surveys to learn more about students' experience of advising and to help determine how to improve advising. Although we do not have dramatic results to show changes in student achievement, I would offer that advising is necessary but not sufficient to support changes such as these. What I anticipate is that we may see changes over time after three to four years, when the program could affect how students use resources in high school and their improved attitudes toward learning. This may indirectly translate to students' higher grades and increased motivation.

We may find that 26 advisor meetings per year may not be intensive enough. However, we draw our satisfaction from the small steps we see happening in terms of students' knowing themselves better. When the program works, we see small, subtle shifts in student perceptions. We have learned from surveys that students value information that they receive in advising, especially about graduation requirements, how they manage their time, identifying learning styles, reviewing report cards, and learning how to work out problems in class. Although advisors provide concrete information, it is also an opportunity in a safe place for students to talk about school—from the prosaic, everyday hurdles to the more significant obstacles. Students may talk about a conflict that they may be having with a teacher and try to come up with strategies for dealing constructively with the conflict versus blowing up or going on strike. Or, they may discuss mundane things such as trying to figure out how to fit their books into a locker or how to understand credits. A full range of topics gets covered. The program is designed to help all students—those labeled nonlearners and learners alike. By providing students with more consistent discussion with an advisor to help them get the most from school, we hope to improve students' performance.

I have also learned why it is so hard to work in schools. Absolutely everything is open to debate. Some areas are easy to resolve; some are not.

To give an example of the process of debate, even naming the program was difficult. During our site visit to another advising program in Philadelphia, we learned that they called their program Family Group. Some staff at our high school referred to our initiative as Family Group too. Among some vocal Cambridge parents, this quickly was interpreted as a subversive effort by teachers to uncover family secrets and to supplant the role of parents. So, we thought that we would be accommodating and changed the name to Small-Group Discussion Program, but this was criticized as being too "shrinky." So, next came Academic

Advising Program, which sounds about as innocuous as you can get. This was attacked by school guidance counselors, who complained that academic advising was their territory. In the end, we decided to go with the most generic name—the Advising Program. This example gives a flavor of what it is like to work in the schools.

Without going into great detail, my advice to anyone interested in starting a similar program is to make sure the power brokers are identified and acknowledged when planning begins. This can save an enormous amount of time. Also, get the guidance counselors into the process so they won't see it as a threat to their job security. Define early on how the role of the advisor who is a teacher is different from that of a guidance counselor. The latter is seen as complementary to the efforts of the teacher. The guidance counselor comes into each advising group three times a year and provides concrete information about graduation requirements, transcripts, and how to decide course selection. The difference in responsibility is that guidance counselors usually have a load of 150 to 250 students, and the teacher is making a commitment to fifteen students.

The hardest decisions have been in determining (a) which students should participate in advising and devising the curriculum as a vehicle for establishing meaningful relationships between students and advisors and (b) how to train high school teachers (who specialize in delivering content) to become effective advisors.

It is critical to accept that there are a lot of trade-offs and no easy answers. For example, we faced the decision whether to involve all students or to select those students at risk. This is something that any of us working in schools wonders about: Do you run a preventive program or target those students at risk? Those who argued that advising should be reserved for high-risk students saw it as overkill to provide advising for stable, directed students who would be better served by focusing on academics. The additional concern was that students could be forced to work with an advisor they didn't like.

The proponents of including all students in the advising program gave several arguments. They saw advising as a preventive intervention. To preselect students would defeat this purpose. Also, many students who needed to examine their attitudes toward learning and their investment in school might not choose to participate, but they would be the very students we needed to engage. Also, by selecting only nonachieving students for the advising program, we would also be running the risk of stigmatizing them. They might feel more inadequate as a result.

If the goal is to build on students' strengths, then, ideally, all students will have something to offer. Also, the benefit of self-reflection is not reserved for failing students. An example of the strength of having an inclusive model in which all students participate follows. In one of the groups, students discussed homework and how sometimes they "totally blew it off," which can ensure failing a class. Having a mixed group of achieving and nonachieving students resulted in a profound conversation about the fact that some students didn't hand in homework and that it reflected the fact that they didn't have any adult in their life to monitor them. Those kids who routinely handed in homework had a parent or someone who was invested in making sure that they performed.

CRLS resolved this conflict by making a reasonable compromise. All students were expected to participate, but there was a mechanism for students to opt out after meeting with an administrator. The fantasy was that we would have a mass exodus of students opting out. What we found was that, of 2,000 students in phase 1, only two went through the formal route of opting out. This is consistent with a survey result that 85% of students said that they wanted to figure out how to do better in school. Advising was seen as a vehicle for helping students to achieve this result.

Our decision to write a formal curriculum came out of concerns that surfaced in phase 1 of the program. In phase 1, we found that, although students enjoyed meeting with advisors, they saw little connection between advising and academics. Our goal in the curriculum is to help ninth graders make a smooth transition to CRLS in two basic areas—orientation and academic support. In orientation, they learn, for example, to locate key areas in the high school, to understand the roles of adults in the building, to understand the rules and policies (especially the policies about attendance, school tardiness, and graduation requirements), to begin charting self-progress, and to ask for support from teachers. In academic support are opportunities to learn effective organizational strategies for keeping up with the classes, to get an introduction to time management, to develop a four-year plan, to generate quick writing samples, and to identify their learning styles and potential career interests. The curriculum is ideally used as the scaffolding to build a caring relationship by conveying certain information and showing interest in students' decisions.

In working with teachers, I have been impressed by their resourcefulness. A lot of the curriculum comes from suggestions that teachers and

I worked on together. For example, in terms of orientation, a group of teachers figured out a clever way of doing orientation. While advising, they asked, "Are you oriented?" The students replied that they knew where things were located. This meant that they could chart themselves from one class to the next, but they did not have a clue about the various resources that were available in the school (e.g., Teen Health Center, tutoring service). So, the teachers set up a game. Advising groups interviewed school personnel to find out about different resources. If the school personnel thought that the students had performed well, then they would give them advising money. The students who earned the most "advising money" were then allowed to go out to lunch with their advisors. This is a very clever way of forging a positive relationship with shy ninth graders.

I would suggest that, of the teachers who are advisors, probably 30% can do advising in their sleep. However, 30% to 40% of teachers are awkward with moving from their role of being a teacher and delivering content to being an advisor. One thing is clear after four years: Staff development needs to be more intensive and individualized for teachers who lack classroom management skills that are helpful in engaging teenagers.

After experimenting with several formats that included afternoon workshops featuring inspirational speakers from outside the high school, we shifted our focus to give advisors time each week to meet and simply talk about how they ran their groups. Concurrently, I am spending more time observing the groups. The goal is to observe each of the 25 groups twice a year to identify concrete strategies that work with this student population.

We were surprised that we did not always find the problems that teachers anticipated. Before starting the program, many advisors worried that students would reveal overwhelming intimate details about their lives (e.g., abuse, abortions). What really happened was that teenagers were cautious and did not share readily. So, the most common problem for advisors wasn't an outpouring of deep, dark, secrets but rather dealing with the silence they encountered in 80% of the groups.

For students, the biggest problem we identified was how to relate the conversations in advising groups to everyday classroom experience. For example, one survey identified that, although most students expect to go to college, they do not always make the connection between hard work and attaining this goal. Eighty-one percent of students with D averages and 79% of students with F averages reported that they intended to go to college. We are working to emphasize the necessity of hard work to reach goals.

The most troubling finding to emerge from student surveys related to the comfort level students had when dealing with adults in the high school. Black students were far less likely to rely on an adult in the high school than white students were, according to our survey responses. Two thirds of white students versus less than a third of black students relied on adults. This will be an important variable to track over time; it will also be important to see if black students begin to see an advisor as a potential resource. We anticipate that addressing the alienation of these black students may take more than making adult relationships available. Mark Freedman, in *The Kindness of Strangers* (1993), recognizes the limitations of mentoring with some alienated black teenagers. He points to difficulties including the "generation gap," lifestyle differences, and class differences. He warns that mentors must bridge this gap before they can make a connection. If not, mentors run the risk of having goals that are irrelevant to the youngsters and of misunderstanding the indifferent pose that ultimately isolates these kids from the kind of support critical for their development.

Another finding was, predictably, that the students who indicated that they had never seen their advisors one-on-one or that they had seen them less than two times a year one-on-one were less likely to state that their advisor got to know them.

There are some days that I feel that our program still has a long way to go. So far, it has failed to translate into better student–teacher relations among minority populations and even to convince some teachers of the need to interact with their students beyond subject matter. For example, 46 students out of 240 surveyed stated that they never spoke with the advisor one-on-one. The one-on-one interactions were often as simple as stopping in the hall for a quick check-in. The students' answers on the survey were consistent with advisors' observations that, if they had students for core subjects and/or homeroom, they felt much more effective in their efforts to understand and support students. Therefore, we made every effort this year to pair the advisors with their homeroom students. In staff development this year, I am working with teachers to structure one-on-one discussions with students.

In closing, I want to share a favorite quotation. Maybe part of my interest in working with adolescents is that I am still one at heart and I am still searching for the perfect yearbook quotation. William Sloane Coffin (1993), in *A Passion for the Possible*, writes, "Hope makes us persistent when we can't be optimistic, faithful when results elude us. For like nothing else in the world, hope arouses a passion for the possible, a determination that our children not be asked to shoulder burdens we let fall." I am sure that each one of us has a commitment to providing opportunities for children, and in my own small way I am trying to extend that guarantee in the schools. It is not easy, but schools are the right place for applying our type of professional skills because where the kids are is the best place to do preventive care.

REFERENCES

Coffin, W. S. (1993), *A Passion for the Possible.* Louisville, KY: Westminster/John Knox Press.

Delpit, L. (1994), *Other People's Children: Cultural Conflict in the Classroom.* New York: New Press.

Eccles, J. S., Midgley, C., Wigfield, A., Buchanan, C. M. & Reuman, D. (1993), Development during adolescence. *Amer. Psychol.,* 48:90–101.

Feldman, S. & Elliott, G. R., ed. (1993), *At the Threshold: The Developing Adolescent.* Cambridge, MA: Harvard University Press.

Freedman, M. (1993), *The Kindness of Strangers.* San Francisco: Jossey-Bass.

Lightfoot, S. L. (1983), *The Good High School.* New York: Basic Books.

McDonald, J. (1997), *Redesigning Schools.* San Francisco: Jossey-Bass.

Meier, D. (1995), *The Power of Their Ideas.* Boston: Beacon Press.

Semrad, E. (1948), Psychotherapy of the psychoses in a state hospital. *Dis. Nerv. Syst.,* 10:105–111.

Spindler, G. & Spindler, L., ed. (1988), *Doing the Ethnography of Schooling: Educational Anthropology in Action.* Prospect Heights, IL: Waveland Press.

Steinberg, L. (1996), *Beyond the Classroom: Why School Reform Has Failed and What Parents Need to Do.* New York: Simon & Schuster.

Taylor, J., Gilligan, C. & Sullivan, A. (1995), *Between Voices and Silence, Women and Girls, Race and Relationship.* Cambridge, MA: Harvard University Press.

8 CHANGING PARADIGMS IN CHILD AND ADOLESCENT PSYCHIATRY: TOWARD EXPANDED SCHOOL MENTAL HEALTH*

MARK D. WEIST, OLGA M. ACOSTA, NANCY A. TASHMAN,
LAURA A. NABORS, AND KATHLEEN ALBUS

Questionable Assumptions in Child and Adolescent Mental Health

On a recent flight, one of us (Mark Weist) came across a *Forbes* article, "Management's New Paradigm," by Peter S. Drucker (October 5, 1998). In discussing business management's reliance on old ideas, Drucker stated, "We are preaching, teaching and practicing policies that are increasingly at odds with reality and therefore counterproductive. . . . Basic assumptions about reality are the paradigms of a social science. These assumptions about reality determine what a discipline focuses on. The assumptions also largely determine what is pushed aside as an annoying exception. Get the assumptions wrong and everything that follows from them is wrong." Drucker went on to point out that many standard practices in business are based on problematic assumptions (e.g., multiple layers of management with those on lower layers treated as "subordinates") that serve to constrain the growth of the business.

What is striking about Drucker's comments is how applicable they are for the child mental health field. Much of what we do in child mental health is based on fundamental assumptions that may in fact be faulty and outdated. Here are examples of some of these assumptions:

*Supported by project MCJ24SH02-01-0 from the Office of Adolescent Health, Maternal and Child Health Bureau (Title V, Social Security Act), Health Resources and Services Administration, U.S. Department of Health and Human Services.

1. *Families will seek services in community mental health centers (CMHCs).* We know that this statement is generally not true. Although some families will seek services in these centers, many will not. Pervasive barriers to using CMHCs include stigma, transportation problems (cost, inconvenience), limited knowledge about available services, and long waiting lists. As a result, only a small proportion of the many youth who have mental health needs will receive services in these centers. Although it is reported that up to 20% of youth under age 20 exhibit psychosocial problems severe enough to warrant intervention, it is estimated that less than one third actually receive mental health services (Office of Technology Assessment, 1991). Even when the need for mental health services is identified and referrals to CMHCs are made, families frequently fail to seek these services. Of those families who actually complete the intake process, many will drop out of treatment before it is completed (Weist et al., 1999). Yet, in spite of these limitations, providing services through CMHCs remains perhaps the dominant model of service delivery in child mental health.

2. *Professionals are always experts and unbiased.* Mental health professionals, whether they come from psychiatry, social work, nursing, or psychology, often interact with their "patients" with an attitude of professional superiority (see Flaherty et al., 1998). These professionals do not treat children and their parents as partners or knowledgeable consumers of care. They may blame the children's problems on the parents or on the children themselves. Such a focus alienates families and discourages change. Clinicians often work in isolation from their colleagues and rely on their own skills and experiences to formulate treatment plans. These mental health providers may neglect to recognize the expertise that nonprofessionals and families may be able to offer.

Further, some clinicians place inappropriate confidence in their case formulations and do not realize the range of biases that threaten the validity of their assessments. Human information processing is characterized by significant biases, and these same biases (e.g., asking questions that lead to responses that confirm hypotheses) operate on mental health professionals (see Weist, Finney, and Ollendick, 1992). It goes without saying that, if the assessment is biased, the treatment will likely be ineffective. Clinicians need to be aware that they, as everyone else, are subject to biases in their information processing, particularly when they are forming clinical interpretations or predicting future behavior (Meehl, 1954; Faust, 1986).

3. *Services should be provided by professionals.* In spite of findings that comparable outcomes from mental health intervention can be obtained by paraprofessionals and even nonprofessionals (Strupp and Hadley, 1979; Burlingame and Barlow, 1996; Cowen et al., 1996), we continue to throw a mental health professional at every problem. As a result, costly professionals often engage in activities that could be done by other staff (e.g., case management), and the amount of services to children and adolescents is unnecessarily delimited. In fact, Emory Cowen's Primary Mental Health Project (PMHP), a school-based program for early detection and intervention of young children's school adjustment problems, uses nonprofessional *child associates* as their primary mental health providers. The PMHP is hailed as one of the most carefully researched and pioneering prevention programs for children. Cowen and his colleagues (1996) view the use of nonprofessionals as one of the most important distinguishing features of their program.

It is very clear that children's mental health needs far surpass the current system's ability to meet them. Dryfoos (1994) estimated that ten million children ages ten to seventeen can benefit from mental health services. This is an astronomical figure. Meeting such a need will require significant collaborative efforts among all those interested in children's mental health. The concept of collaboration can be traced back to Lightner Witmer, who is the first recognized clinical psychologist. In his work, Witmer used a team approach in which individuals from various professions worked together to formulate comprehensive treatment plans for individuals in need (Nietzel, Bernstein, and Milich, 1994). There is a need for analysis of when and in what situations paraprofessionals or nonprofessionals should be used instead of professionals.

4. *The 50-minute session.* Providing mental health services to youth and families for 50-minute sessions predominates in spite of the fact that it has never been proved that youth should be treated for this amount of time. It has been argued that the 50-minute session is an arbitrary standard imposed on the therapeutic relationship. In fact, some recommend that the 20- or 120-minute session is a more appropriate use of time, depending on the therapist's orientation and the client's needs. As Lazarus and Fay (1990) point out, "Many other therapists are still disinclined to adjust treatment time to suit the individual needs of their clients. Unfortunately, this factor is probably governed by economic considerations" (p. 43). Maintaining the 50-minute session may also trace to differential rates of reimbursement through managed-

care companies. Within managed care, longer sessions are often reimbursed at higher rates than shorter sessions. Such a reimbursement system fails to recognize the reality that quantity of session time does not ensure quality of services.

5. *Diagnosis is essential and unharmful.*   As already mentioned, biases operating on information processing affect mental health diagnosis. The reliability of diagnosis is generally poor even when done by trained professionals using structured diagnostic interviews (Hickey, 1998). In addition, we have all noticed how some centers are known for high frequencies of certain diagnoses, whereas others are noted for other diagnoses. Further, as contrasted with medical diagnoses, which have a clear physiological anchor, most mental health diagnoses are based on circular reasoning. For example, how do you know a child has attention deficit hyperactivity disorder (ADHD)? Because he's impulsive and out of his seat. Why is he impulsive and out of his seat? Because he has ADHD (see Goodman and Poillion, 1992).

Moreover, we know that mental health diagnoses may not be confidential. For example, insurance companies share some databases that include youth diagnoses. Diagnoses are stigmatizing and self-fulfilling. For instance, a teacher may put more effort into helping a child when the child's problem is framed as an adjustment disorder rather than a chronic condition—inadvertently creating more alienation and stress for the child labeled with the chronic condition. Of further concern is that diagnoses can have lifelong negative effects on youth (e.g., future denial of insurance coverage or military service). As Thomas Szasz (1974) has argued, "The rules of the medical game define health—which includes such things as a well-functioning body and happiness—as a positive value; and they define illness—which includes such things as a badly functioning body and unhappiness—as a negative value. It follows, then, that insofar as people play the medical game, they will, at least to some extent, dislike and demean sick persons" (p. 197). Yet, in spite of these problems, diagnosis remains the ticket into mental health care for youth in most communities and is often a requirement for reimbursement.

6. *Episodes of mental health care should be provided.*   Nicholas Cummings (1990), an acknowledged genius in health and mental health systems and predictor of managed care some 20 years ago, recommended that we provide brief, intermittent therapy to individuals throughout their life spans. That is, people should establish long-term relationships with mental health care providers. As problems arise, the

provider helps the child and family address them. When problems have improved, the provider does not "terminate" the family (only in mental health do we use this very negative word) but rather remains in the background, available to the family should a need arise. Cummings (1995) refers to this lapse in treatment as a therapy interruption, not a termination, and asserts that the mental health professional "should function as a primary care physician not subject to a gatekeeper" (p. 10). This model of care makes sense to many providers, to youth, and to families, and yet we continue to provide mental health services to youth episodically.

7. *Teachers are not mental health staff.* In our work in the schools, the difference between the amount of contact that we have and that teachers have with youth is often striking. For example, over the course of a school year, clinicians may see an individual child for a total of six or seven hours; a teacher will see the same child for six or seven hours a day for 180 days. Further, teachers encounter a larger number of students than clinicians encounter. Although a large therapy group may have ten children, a typical classroom may have 30 children. Also, whereas clinicians can identify youth with common issues, teachers are often faced with the challenge of dealing with a room full of children with varying abilities and skills. Teachers can represent the front line in school mental health. They may be the first school staff to recognize serious emotional and behavioral problems in students. Their ability to recognize problems, make appropriate referrals, help implement treatment, and keep the clinician informed of progress is a critical aspect of effective treatment. Given the diversity of students and complexity of issues that teachers encounter, they need to be knowledgeable about mental health issues.

Given our relatively limited time with children, mental health professionals must be viewed as specialists—which contrasts with the more general role teachers usually have in the lives of youth. If teachers had knowledge of mental health issues in children and adolescents and skills in managing behavior and enhancing protective factors in them, interventions could be powerful (Weist et al., 1998). A classroom setting offers a natural opportunity to develop and reinforce skills learned in therapy. But, the reality is that most teachers know very little about mental health, and most mental health professionals, even those who work in schools, spend very little time interacting with and consulting with teachers. To better serve children and adolescents, teachers and mental health providers need to view themselves as part of the same team (Waxman, Weist, and Benson, 1999).

This is only a sampling of child and adolescent mental health assumptions that may be at least partly erroneous. It is unclear why these assumptions continue to exert such a strong influence on the field. Fortunately, we are in a period of intensive analysis and redesign of mental health programs for youth, with a number of prospects pointing to significantly enhanced funding of these programs (e.g., State Children's Health Insurance Program; see Koppelman and Lear, 1998). Expanded school mental health (ESMH) programs, which provide comprehensive mental health services to youth in schools, hold the potential to be centerpieces in children's mental health reform. Although not a panacea, ESMH programs move beyond many of the faulty assumptions just reviewed. In this chapter, we draw on experiences from a national technical assistance center and a program in Baltimore that are focused on ESMH.

CENTER FOR SCHOOL MENTAL HEALTH ASSISTANCE

The Center for School Mental Health Assistance (CSMHA) is one of two national technical assistance centers (the other is at the University of California, Los Angeles) funded by the Maternal and Child Health Bureau of the U.S. Department of Health and Human Services to provide support to the growing ESMH movement. The five objectives of the CSMHA are to provide technical assistance, offer national training and education, identify and analyze critical issues, develop relevant resources, and promote networking between people and programs interested in improving children's mental health services.

SCHOOL MENTAL HEALTH PROGRAM

The University of Maryland's School Mental Health Program (SMHP) was established in 1989 due to concerns by Baltimore leaders in education and health that youth in need of mental health services generally could not access these services. That year, services were provided at two middle and two high schools, and the program essentially represented a CMHC in the school. Since then, the program has broadened services to include prevention, case management, and consultation and has added schools every year (the current total is 20—eight elementary, two elementary/middle, six middle, and four high schools).

In the next section, we describe ESMH programs and discuss how questionable assumptions in child mental health are addressed in these programs. Two themes guide our discussion: (a) issues related to stakeholder involvement and collaboration and (b) providing a full range of services that mesh with the needs of youth. The chapter concludes with ideas for increasing the involvement of child and adolescent psychiatrists in this emerging field.

Expanded School Mental Health

ESMH programs involve the provision of a full range of services, including evaluation, prevention, therapy, case management, and consultation to youth in special and regular education in schools. These programs often involve close collaboration between school-hired mental health professionals (e.g., school psychologists, social workers, guidance counselors) and mental health professionals from community settings (e.g., clinical psychologists, child and adolescent psychiatrists). Ideally, these programs are also closely connected to programs that address physical health needs of youth in schools such as school-based health centers (SBHCs; Flaherty, Weist, and Warner, 1996; Weist, 1997). Related to growing disenchantment with providing mental health services at inaccessible sites and to growing awareness of the advantages of comprehensive mental health care for youth in schools (CSMHA, 1996), ESMH programs are growing progressively in the United States.

Of the 20 schools in the SMHP, four are connected to SBHCs, and in other schools clinicians from our program maintain a close working relationship with Baltimore City Health Department nurses, nurse practitioners, and health aides who work in these centers. As the number of SBHCs has grown to more than 1,100 nationally (Lear and Schlitt, 1998), they have called attention to the need for mental health services. Once these services are added to an SBHC, they quickly become one of the most used (if not the most used) groups of services. This is related to simple epidemiology—significant emotional and behavioral problems in youth far outnumber significant physical health problems.

Thus, health staff are a significant source of referrals to our mental health program. The relationship between physical and mental health providers is collaborative, mutually supportive, and mutually enhancing of services delivered to students (see Waxman et al., 1999).

Our Department of Psychiatry has benefited from the opportunity to deliver state-of-the-art services as part of a broader movement that has the potential to reform service delivery in children's mental health care. Most important, through working in the school system, we have gained unparalleled access to children and adolescents in need. This is underscored by the fact that, in the schools, clinicians often see ten or more children a day—in contrast to the three to five that clinicians see in the CMHCs. In school settings, clinicians are able to observe and interact with youth in a variety of settings (e.g., hallway, cafeteria, gym, special event) and as a result can gain a greater understanding of important factors in the lives of children and adolescents with whom they are working.

ISSUES RELATED TO STAKEHOLDER INVOLVEMENT AND COLLABORATION

In our program, family involvement in treatment is considered an integral aspect of care. We must emphasize that, in many schools, involving parents or guardians in care is a real challenge. To illustrate, some parents may be resistant to their child's receiving services that they did not themselves initiate. Others may have the same difficulty accessing school services that they have accessing community-based services. For these reasons, children may be more likely to be seen in schools with minimal parental involvement (beyond consenting for services) than in other settings such as CMHCs. Nonetheless, meaningful family involvement is an important goal for all ESMH programs, and a range of efforts needs to be made to engage families as partners and collaborators in the treatment process (CSMHA, 1997).

Inherent in working within a complex system is school mental health clinicians' recognition of the expertise that other professionals and families offer. In developing the range of services provided through the SMHP, we have turned to primary stakeholders (e.g., parents, teachers, students, principals, health staff) to help us identify the most pressing needs of the community. In addition, we continue to rely on feedback from our stakeholders to ensure that children are receiving quality services and that services remain accessible to the entire school population. Many of our clinicians have benefited from observing and having the opportunity to collaborate with experienced school staff (e.g., teachers, guidance counselors, social workers), who are viewed as peers with important skills, experiences, and knowledge to share.

The school is also an optimal arena for clinical training. The use of individuals in training and paraprofessionals allows for an increase in the provision of services by extending the person hours and outreach of the program. According to recent satisfaction surveys conducted in our program, students were highly satisfied with treatment from both professionals and trainees. Our Department of Psychiatry has established affiliations with local graduate programs and the medical school as a training site for residents, interns, and "externs" in medicine, social work, and psychology. We try to have our interactions epitomize the collaborative model of working together—experienced staff, trainees, students, and families, shoulder to shoulder, in a mutual problem-solving and supportive effort (Weist, 1997; Waxman et al., 1999).

Clinicians also work collaboratively with school administrators and other school mental health providers (e.g., school social workers, psychologists, guidance counselors) in schoolwide efforts to address pressing problems. For instance, our efforts include the development of crisis intervention plans for use after tragedies such as the violent death of a student, which unfortunately occurs in many of our schools one or more times a year. In addition, we act as a bridge for the school—helping to connect the school, its students, and its staff to a full range of community resources.

PROVIDING A FULL RANGE OF SERVICES THAT MESH WITH THE NEEDS OF YOUTH

In developing a structure for seeing children and adolescents for psychotherapy within the schools, we discovered that we needed to adapt traditional therapy models to better meet the needs of school and students. Our experience has been that 50 minutes is a good amount of time for assessment and group therapy sessions but that many individual sessions are more appropriately conducted in 30 minutes or less. Frequency of sessions should also be considered. We have found that some youth seem to benefit more from several shorter sessions within a week than from one longer session. Perhaps this parallels the shorter attention spans of some youth. Similarly, just as some youth may need several shorter sessions a week, some may need less frequent contact, like once a month.

Our program strives to proactively and preventively provide services to the many youth who are at risk for not receiving needed services. Our mission is to provide services to youth and families regardless of ability to pay and diagnostic status. Although many of the children we serve could receive formal diagnoses, this is not an emphasis of our program. We recognize that related to the pervasive stress that most of our students encounter is the fact that most of them would benefit from mental health services, and a diagnosis that will potentially stick with them for life should not be their ticket to receiving services (see CSMHA, 1998a). Our clinicians work to become active members of the school team and work to educate staff and students about mental health services and how they can be best used. Over time, we have found that receiving mental health services is no longer viewed with stigma; in fact, once the program is established in a school, services are often sought by "popular" students.

Within our program, we have been able to provide long-term care as youth progress from one grade to the next. Not only have we been able to help youth within the same school, we have also been able to successfully transition some of these children to the clinician at the next school level and thereby ensure continuity of care. Although we do close cases on some youths, we continue to see other youths intermittently throughout the current and future school years. Some of these intermittent contacts clearly involve therapeutic services, whereas others are more appropriately described as mentoring (e.g., helping a student make decisions about college). As Cummings (1990) suggested, this ongoing relationship, with intermittent therapy over time, may be the most effective method for delivering services and no doubt is a more natural approach than "terminating" cases. Intermittent therapy also appears to be cost-effective, as future episodes of need are less time-consuming and involve less regression than would be required if treatment had been terminated completely.

Schools are the ideal location for developing prevention programs (Durlak, 1997; Weist, 1997). One way in which clinicians have been able to successfully implement prevention programs has been to collaborate with teachers. Clinicians and teachers can work together to conduct prevention activities, including classroom presentations to students on stressors, emotional and behavioral problems, and ways to cope and

succeed. We also provide training to school staff on the early identification of youth who may need assistance. As mentioned, in our program,
teachers are viewed as equal and important collaborators in developing
a range of programs for individual students, classrooms, and the school.

Schoolwide approaches to prevention include key activities, performed by our clinicians, that offer opportunities to teach all students
about factors related to prosocial behavior and positive mental health.
However, it is often difficult for clinicians to carve time out of their
schedules, and, clearly, these activities require a team effort. Conducting
classroom prevention activities, with teachers playing a primary role, is
one way in which prevention activities can be implemented. Moreover,
considerable efforts are needed to integrate proven-to-be-effective prevention research programs and the ESMH field (CSMHA, 1998b).

Toward a More Expansive Role for Child and Adolescent Psychiatrists in Expanded School Mental Health

In this chapter, we have offered our critique of mental health services
for youth and have attempted to capture the pragmatics and the promise
of ESMH programs in advancing services for children and adolescents.
Unfortunately, with some exceptions (e.g., in New Mexico and Texas),
child and adolescent psychiatrists have not been involved in or are
only minimally involved in ESMH. For psychiatrists to assume the
role that they should assume in this national movement, a few challenges
need to be addressed. First, we need to overcome funding challenges,
as child psychiatrists are the most expensive mental health professionals, and, with so many schools in need, the tendency is toward hiring
less costly staff. However, this challenge can be overcome if communities look to reapportion mental health services out of CMHCs (not
completely) and into the schools. Second, child psychiatrists need to
recognize the importance of joining teams involving other mental health
professionals, teachers, and community stakeholders as equal players
in the effort to improve services for youth. As reviewed earlier, attitudes
of professional superiority and aloofness, which can characterize professionals from all disciplines, are lethal in school mental health. Third,
although consultation is important, child psychiatrists need to move
beyond consultation alone to providing primary care and preventive
services in schools. Adding psychiatry to the interdisciplinary work of

129

ESMH, in many communities, may be the needed impetus to move services forward. Further, most child psychiatrists will find the primary-care (e.g., assessment, therapy, psychopharmacology) and preventive (e.g., schoolwide violence prevention) aspects of ESMH to be personally and professionally rewarding. Finally, child psychiatrists are natural leaders and advocates for youth in communities. For those psychiatrists who are unable to work in the schools, an important contribution can be made in helping a community develop ESMH programs as part of a full continuum of mental health care for its children and adolescents.

REFERENCES

Burlingame, G. M. & Barlow, S. H. (1996), Outcome and process differences between professional and nonprofessional therapists in time-limited group psychotherapy. *Internat. J. Group Psychother.*, 46:455–478.

Center for School Mental Health Assistance. (1996), *Documenting the Effectiveness of School-Based Mental Health Programs.* Baltimore, MD: Author.

Center for School Mental Health Assistance. (1997), *Family Involvement and School Mental Health.* Baltimore, MD: Author.

Center for School Mental Health Assistance. (1998a), *Addressing Unique Legal and Ethical Issues of School-Based Practice.* Baltimore, MD: Author.

Center for School Mental Health Assistance. (1998b), *Integrating Prevention Research and Expanded School Mental Health Programs.* Baltimore, MD: Author.

Cowen, E. L., Hightower, A. D., Pedro-Carroll, J. L., Work, W. C., Wyman, P. A. & Haffey, W. G. (1996), *School-Based Prevention for Children at Risk.* Washington, DC: American Psychological Association.

Cummings, N. A. (1990), Brief intermittent psychotherapy throughout the life cycle. In: *Brief Therapy: Myths, Methods, and Metaphors*, ed. J. K. Zeig & S. G. Gilligan. New York: Brunner/Mazel, pp. 169–184.

——— (1995), Impact of managed care on employment and training: A primer for survival. *Prof. Psychol.: Res. Prac.*, 26:10–15.

Dryfoos, J. G. (1994), *Full-Service Schools.* San Francisco: Jossey-Bass.

Durlak, J. A. (1997), Primary prevention programs in schools. *Adv. Clin. Child Psychol.*, 19:283–318.

Faust, D. (1986), Research on human judgement and its application to clinical practice. *Prof. Psychol.: Res. Prac.*, 17:420–430.

Flaherty, L. T., Garrison, E. G., Waxman, R., Uris, P. F., Keys, S. G., Siegel, M. G. & Weist, M. D. (1998), Optimizing the roles of school mental health professionals. *J. School Health*, 68:420–424.

———— Weist, M. D. & Warner, B. S. (1996), School-based mental health services in the United States: History, current models and needs. *Community Ment. Health J.*, 32:341–352.

Goodman, G. & Poillion, M. J. (1992), ADD: Acronym for any dysfunction or difficulty. *J. Spec. Educ.*, 26:37–56.

Hickey, P. (1998, March), DSM and behavior therapy. *Behav. Ther.*, pp. 43–55.

Koppelman, J. & Lear, J. G. (1998), The new child health insurance expansions: How will school-based health centers fit in? *J. School Health*, 68:441–446.

Lazarus, A. A. & Fay, A. (1990), Brief psychotherapy: Tautology or oxymoron? In: *Brief Therapy: Myths, Methods, and Metaphors*, ed. J. K. Zeig & S. G. Gilligan. New York: Brunner/Mazel, pp. 36–51.

Lear, J. G. & Schlitt, J. (1998, September), Late-breaking findings on school-based health centers in the United States. Presented at meeting of the Center for School Mental Health Assistance, Virginia Beach, VA.

Meehl, P. E. (1954), *Clinical Versus Statistical Prediction*. Minneapolis: University of Minnesota Press.

Nietzel, M. T., Bernstein, D. A. & Milich, R. (1994), *Introduction to Clinical Psychology*, 4th ed. Englewood Cliffs, NJ: Prentice-Hall.

Office of Technology Assessment. (1991), *Adolescent Health*. Washington, DC: U.S. Government Printing Office.

Strupp, H. H. & Hadley, S. W. (1979), Specific vs. nonspecific factors in psychotherapy: A controlled study of outcome. *Arch. Gen. Psychiat.*, 36:1125–1136.

Szasz, T. S. (1974), *The Myth of Mental Illness*. New York: Harper & Row.

Waxman, R., Weist, M. D. & Benson, D. (1999), Toward collaboration in the growing education–mental health interface. *Clin. Psychol. Rev.*, 19:239–253.

Weist, M. D. (1997), Expanded school mental health services: A national movement in progress. In: *Advances in Clinical Child Psychology*, ed. T. H. Ollendick & R. J. Prinz. New York: Plenum, pp. 319–352.

———— Finney, J. W. & Ollendick, T. H. (1992), Cognitive biases in child behavior therapy. *Behav. Ther.*, 15:525–538.

———— Myers, C. P., Hastings, E., Ghuman, H. & Han, Y. (1999), Psychosocial functioning of youth receiving mental health services in the schools vs. community mental health centers. *Community Ment. Health J., 35:69–81.*

———— Olsen, L., Shafer, M. E. & Jackson, C. (1998, September), Mental health education: A promising direction for prevention. Presented at meeting of the Center for School Mental Health Assistance, Virginia Beach, VA.

PART III

FORENSIC ISSUES IN ADOLESCENT PSYCHIATRY

9   FORENSIC PSYCHIATRY FOR ADOLESCENT PSYCHIATRISTS: AN INTRODUCTION

RICHARD ROSNER

There is increased public concern about violent youth. There is increased political pressure to have juvenile offenders tried in adult courts. Many of the adolescents in the juvenile justice system and in the adult criminal justice system suffer from mental disorders. The interests of adolescent psychiatrists and forensic psychiatrists converge in the assessment and management of troubled teenagers. In order that adolescent psychiatrists may function more effectively on those occasions when they are asked to work in forensic settings or to collaborate with specialists in forensic psychiatry, this paper will provide adolescent psychiatrists with an introduction to forensic psychiatry—including an explanation of how it differs from therapeutic psychiatry, a four-step conceptual framework for understanding how forensic psychiatrists approach their work (i.e., how to think like a forensic psychiatrist), and an example of how the conceptual framework may be applied to the assessment of whether a teenage defendant is competent to stand trial.

Differences Between Forensic Psychiatry and Therapeutic Psychiatry

"Forensic psychiatry is a subspecialty of psychiatry in which scientific and clinical expertise is applied to legal issues in legal contexts embracing civil, criminal, correctional or legislative matters; forensic psychiatry should be practiced in accordance with guidelines and ethical principles enunciated by the profession of psychiatry" (Amer. Acad.

of Psych. and the Law, 1998, p. X). This is the definition initially adopted by the American Board of Forensic Psychiatry, Inc. and subsequently adopted by the American Academy of Psychiatry and the Law. Whereas clinical psychiatry is directed to therapeutic issues in health care contexts, forensic psychiatry is directed to legal issues in legal contexts. Because the ends of law differ from the ends of health care, forensic psychiatry differs from clinical psychiatry.

In the health care context, a relationship exists between the examining clinical psychiatrist (doctor) and the person (patient) who is the focus of his examination. In the legal context, there is often no doctor–patient relationship between the examining forensic psychiatrist and the person (defendant/appellant/claimant/litigant) who is the focus of his examination. Because there is no doctor–patient relationship, the forensic psychiatrist has an ethical obligation (and often a legal obligation) to clarify for the examinee the nature of the forensic examination (i.e., at minimum, by whom he has been employed, what the legal purpose of his evaluation is, that no confidentiality of communications exists, and that the forensic psychiatrist is not necessarily concerned with doing what will be of assistance to the person being examined). This ethical obligation to clarify the nature of the forensic examination is important because, regardless of who has paid for the physician's time and skills, most people have come to expect that a physician is going to help them, that a physician will keep their communications in confidence, and that a physician has the best interests of the patient as his primary concern.

Forensic psychiatry is not unique in medicine in having obligations in addition to, or other than, the welfare of the individual as a patient. All physicians have a societal obligation to report gunshot wounds and child abuse to the proper legal authorities. To ensure the scientific integrity of their work, research psychiatrists may properly withhold potential treatments from patients in a study's control group and may conceal during the course of the study which patients are receiving a placebo as opposed to the active drug. Administrative psychiatrists may properly place the interests of a health care system as a whole above the interests of an individual health care consumer. Military psychiatrists may have an obligation to maintain the fighting capacity of a soldier rather than the safety of that particular soldier. In all of these fields, the psychiatrist must be aware of the limitations of his commitment to the person he examines and of his ethical obligation to reveal those limitations.

Forensic psychiatrists must be able to present their clinical and scientific knowledge effectively in legal contexts. That may entail testimony and cross-examination. In a court, the issue is not the sincerity of the psychiatrist; it is whether he can support his opinions with relevant facts sufficient to compel the assent of the majority of rational persons. Much of clinical medicine remains an art rather than a science. The court may require that the forensic psychiatrist reveal to what extent his opinions are based on science and to what extent they are not. For many clinicians, it is uncomfortable to be obliged to explain the exact database from which their opinions are derived, the exact scientific literature that supports the inferences they make from their database, and the logical process of reasoning by means of which they reach their opinions. Unlike some overly compliant patients, the court demands that the doctor demonstrate that he actually has knowledge and has correctly applied that knowledge—not merely that the doctor is honest and benevolent. Physicians for whom this type of logical rigor is an attractive challenge, rather than a daunting confrontation, will enjoy forensic work.

The Four-Step Approach to Forensic Psychiatry

In order to organize their consideration of practical problems in their subspecialty, forensic psychiatrists use a four-step conceptual framework: What is the exact legal issue? What are the exact legal criteria for the issue? What data are relevant to the legal criteria? What reasoning process has led to the forensic psychiatric opinion?

Legal Issue. The range of issues that confront forensic psychiatrists is extensive. In civil law cases there are, for example, conservators and guardianships, testimonial capacity, competence to make a will, personal injury litigation, competence to make a contract, and disability determinations (for social security, worker's compensation, and private insurance coverage). In family law and domestic relations law, there are, for example, divorce, child custody, spouse abuse, child abuse, child neglect, elder abuse, termination of parental rights, and delinquency. In criminal law, there are, for example, competence to confess, competence to stand trial, competence to waive representation by counsel, competence to enter a plea, not responsible by reason of insanity, diminished

137

capacity, diminished responsibility, and guilty but mentally ill. In legal regulation of psychiatry, there are, for example, treatment over objection, voluntary hospitalization, involuntary hospitalization, confidentiality, the right to refuse treatment, competence to consent to treatment, competence to authorize do-not-resuscitate orders, malpractice, and ethics.

Legal Criteria. The various forensic psychiatric issues are presented in various legal contexts. To the surprise of many citizens, there really is no such thing as "the Law" in the United States. Rather, there are 51 different legal contexts and 51 different sets of law. Each state, as well as the federal government, has its own constitutional laws, its own legislated laws, its own judge-made case laws, and its own administrative laws. The legal criteria that will determine how any of the various forensic psychiatric issues will be decided differ depending on in which of the 51 legal contexts the specific case at hand will be considered. This matter of different legal criteria for any single forensic psychiatry issue is not initially easy to grasp.

By way of analogy, consider the clinical psychiatry issue of whether a patient meets the diagnostic criteria for schizophrenia. The diagnostic criteria in *DSM–I, DSM–II, DSM–III, DSM–III–R,* and *DSM–IV* may be different. Whether a patient meets the diagnostic criteria for schizophrenia will depend on which diagnostic criteria are used. Analogously, consider the forensic psychiatry issue of whether a patient meets the legal criteria for not guilty by reason of insanity (NGRI). The legal criteria in Washington, DC, Virginia, New York, and Michigan, for example, may be different. Whether a defendant meets the legal criteria for NGRI will depend on which jurisdiction's legal criteria are used.

Relevant Data. No matter how complete a forensic psychiatry report may be in other respects, it will be of no value if it does not contain information relevant to the legal criteria for the specific issue. In the same way that the diagnostic criteria determine what data are relevant to resolve a particular diagnostic issue, the legal criteria determine what data are relevant to resolve a particular legal issue. If the clinical psychiatric report does not contain information relevant to the diagnostic criteria, there will be no data upon which to decide the diagnostic issue; if the forensic psychiatric report does not contain information relevant to the legal criteria, there will be no data upon which to decide the legal issue.

For example, consider the legal issue of competence to make a will. The law usually will include some variation of the criteria that the person making the will (a) should know what a will is, (b) should know the nature and extent of his property, (c) should know who are the "natural heirs of his bounty," and (d) should know that he is making a will. Unless the forensic psychiatrist has asked questions directed to these legal criteria and has included the data in his report, the court will not be able to decide whether the person was competent to make the will.

Reasoning Process. The basic model of reasoning in forensic psychiatric reports is to state (I) the legal criteria for the issue, (II) the data relevant to the legal criteria, and (III) the conclusion. For example:

I. A person is mentally competent to make a will if he knows what a will is, knows the nature and extent of his property, knows the natural heirs of his bounty, and knows that he is making a will.

II. Mr. John Doe knows what a will is (e.g., he said, "A will is a legal instrument to ensure that, after my death, my property is distributed in accordance with my wishes"), knows the nature and extent of his property (e.g., he said, "I own my home and have $257,000 in savings and securities"), knows the natural heirs of his bounty (e.g., he said, "My natural heirs are my wife and my son"), and knows that he is making a will (e.g., he said, "This document I'm signing is my last will and testament").

III. Therefore, Mr. John Doe is mentally competent to make a will.

This four-step conceptual framework for forensic psychiatry is not merely a convenient method of structuring the data in forensic reports and testimony. It helps the forensic psychiatrist to organize and focus his thinking, facilitates communication about cases, and makes sure that the essential forensic psychiatric matters have all been appropriately addressed.

A Practical Example: Assessment of an Adolescent's Competence to Stand Trial

Legal Issue. In applying this four-step conceptual framework, the forensic psychiatrist who receives a request to evaluate an adolescent for competence to stand trial would first clarify if that was the only legal issue or issues that need to be addressed. For example, a single teenager could have several forensic psychiatric legal issues under consideration: At the time of the alleged offense, was the teenager not criminally responsible by reason of mental disease or mental defect? At the time that he was arrested, was the teenager mentally competent to confess to the police? Is he suffering from a mental disease or mental defect that makes him more likely to be a danger to the public if he were to be granted bail? At the present time, is the teenager mentally competent to stand trial? At the present time, is the teenager mentally competent to enter a plea to the charges against him? At the time he will be sentenced, will the teenager be competent to abide by the terms of probation, and/or will he be competent to be incarcerated in prison? If this is a capital case, is he suffering from a mental disease or mental defect that renders him incompetent to be executed? The referring attorney, court, or probation officer should be able to advise the forensic psychiatrist regarding exactly which issue or issues need to be considered.

Legal Criteria. After the legal issue or issues to be considered have been clarified, the forensic psychiatrist must determine what the legal criteria are for each of the issues that must be decided. For example, if the issue is competence to stand trial, the legal criteria will include some variation on these questions: Does the teenage defendant have the capacity to understand the charges against him? Does the teenage defendant have the capacity to assist in his own defense? Does the teenage defendant suffer from a diagnosable mental disease or mental defect? If the teenage defendant lacks the capacity to understand the charges against him or lacks the capacity to assist in his own defense, is that lack of capacity due to his diagnosable mental disease or mental defect? The forensic psychiatrist needs to know both the legislated criteria and how the courts have interpreted the criteria in prior cases. The referring attorney or the court should be able to provide the forensic psychiatrist with (a) the legislated statute establishing the criteria for competence to stand trial in the particular state or the federal jurisdiction and (b) the prior judge-made case-law decisions establishing how the court has interpreted the legislated statute establishing the criteria for competence to stand trial in the particular state or federal jurisdiction.

Relevant Data. After the forensic psychiatrist has determined the legal criteria and how the court has interpreted them, he is in a position to obtain the legally relevant information. For example, in an evaluation

140

of a teenage defendant's competence to stand trial, the forensic psychiatrist would need to ask the adolescent questions such as these: What crime are you accused of having committed? Do you have an attorney? What is your attorney supposed to do for you? What is the district attorney supposed to do in your case? What is the judge's job in a court case? What does a jury do in a court case? What is a plea bargain? What plea have you entered, if any? What are the consequences of being found guilty? What happens if you are found not guilty? In addition, the forensic psychiatrist would have to evaluate the adolescent's capacity to rationally understand such questions and their answers (as contrasted to the teenager providing mere rote responses) and the adolescent's capacity and motivation to assist in his defense. If the teenage defendant demonstrates a lack of capacity to understand the charges against him or to assist in his own defense, the forensic psychiatrist needs to determine if the teenager is suffering from a diagnosable mental disease or mental defect. If the adolescent defendant has a demonstrated lack of capacity to understand the charges or to assist in his defense and also has a diagnosable mental disorder, then the forensic psychiatrist must evaluate whether the lack of capacity is directly caused by the mental disorder or if it has some other cause (e.g., lack of familiarity with the legal system, coming from a foreign nation, willful oppositionalism, socio-political motivation).

Reasoning Process. The forensic psychiatrist must organize his data in a logical manner to support his opinion. For example:

I.   A person is competent to stand trial if he has the capacity to understand the charges against him and the capacity to assist in his own defense.

II.   Mr. John Doe, a sixteen-year-old male defendant, has the capacity to understand the charges against him (he said that he was charged with "rape, forcing a girl to have sex with me against her will") and the capacity to assist in his own defense (he said that he had an attorney and that the job of his attorney was "to help me, to defend me in this case, to protect my rights"; that the job of the district attorney was "to convict me, to get me sent to prison"; that the job of the judge was "to keep things fair in the courtroom, to pass sentence if I'm found guilty"; that the job of the jury was "to decide if I'm guilty or not guilty"; that he would "go to prison for a long time" if he were found guilty and that he would "go free" if found not guilty; that a plea bargain meant "guaranteed less time in prison than if convicted at trial, in exchange for pleading guilty instead of going to trial"; and that he had "not decided yet" whether to enter a plea of guilty). He demonstrated no diagnosable mental disorder.

III. Mr. John Doe is competent to stand trial.

There is no such thing as a single, comprehensive forensic psychiatric evaluation. There is only a series of individually focused specific forensic psychiatric assessments. Each specific forensic psychiatric issue would be addressed in a similar systematic method. For each individual issue, the legal criteria would be set forth, the legally relevant data would be obtained, and a logically structured opinion would be offered.

Conclusion

It is impossible to condense all of forensic psychiatry into a brief discussion. This presentation has been designed to provide adolescent psychiatrists with an introduction to forensic psychiatry—including an explanation of how it differs from therapeutic psychiatry, a four-step conceptual framework for understanding how forensic psychiatrists approach their work (i.e., how to think like a forensic psychiatrist), and an example of how the conceptual framework may be applied to the assessment of whether a teenage defendant is competent to stand trial. To learn more about forensic psychiatry for adolescent psychiatrists, see Rosner (1994, in press) and Rosner and Schwartz (1989).

REFERENCES

American Academy of Psychiatry and the Law. (1998), *Membership Directory*. Bloomfield, CT.

Rosner, R. (1994), *Principles and Practice of Forensic Psychiatry*. New York: Chapman & Hall.

——— (in press), *Textbook of Adolescent Psychiatry*. Washington, DC: American Psychiatric Press.

——— & Schwartz, H. (1989), *Juvenile Psychiatry and the Law*. New York: Plenum.

RICHARD A. RATNER

The Juvenile Court System: Origins and Principles

The societal impulses that led to the creation of the first juvenile court system in the state of Illinois in 1899 can be detected as early as 1825 with the creation of the New York House of Refuge. They reflected a nation in which the elite, or at least the wives of the elite, had begun to have time for charitable enterprises, and the condition of children who offended became a prime focus of concern. These elite were directly responsible for the establishment of institutions that aimed to teach young offenders how to grow up and lead moral lives. However, not only was "treatment" harsh and moralistic, but, as the years went by, those who ran these institutions became corrupt (Levine, Ewing, and Hager, 1987). Toward the end of their existence, many of these institutions had become little more than sources of cheap labor, with payoffs going to those who ran them.

The juvenile court system, an attempt to improve this failed system, united two principles that together formed the basis of the court's philosophy—the so-called *parens patriae* (function of the state) and the notion of rehabilitation rather than punishment. The former is the principle by which the state operates as the wise parent of a minor and as such may do things on his or her behalf. The latter, rehabilitation, was the war cry of the "child savers," a group of women, active in the late nineteenth century, who recognized that the Houses of Refuge had deteriorated beyond help. Soon after the establishment of the first juvenile court, Dr. William Healy, who studied with Freud at one point, was responsible for creating the first Child Guidance Clinic, which was meant to work in conjunction with the court. These clinics, which followed the spread of the juvenile court system throughout the country, are widely understood to have been the crucibles out of which the modern science of child psychiatry has emerged.

In the area of juvenile justice, there has always been a tension between the principles of punishment and rehabilitation. Typically, these principles have sorted out along political lines, with people we think of as more liberal behind the push to rehabilitate and people we think of as more conservative more concerned with punishment. The pendulum of popularity has over the years swung back and forth, in lengthy cycles, between these two approaches. The advent of the juvenile court system with its attendant Child Guidance Clinics signified that, in the early years of the 20th century, rehabilitation had become the dominant approach to youth crime. By 1920, only three states did not have juvenile court systems modeled after the Illinois experience, and, by the 1940s, all states were accounted for. Further, in 1974 the federal government established, through the Juvenile Justice Act, the Office of Juvenile Justice and Delinquency Prevention. As an example of the continued importance of the rehabilitative impulse, one of the prime purposes of this act was to convince states to keep juvenile offenders separate from their adult counterparts.

DIFFERENCES FROM ADULT COURTS

Because the juvenile courts were dedicated to the principle of rehabilitation rather than punishment, significant differences occurred in court procedure relative to adult courts. In fact, an entirely new language was developed in order to distinguish passage through juvenile court from passage through adult courts. For example, rather than "felon," "convict," or "criminal," juveniles who had offended were referred to as "delinquents." Rather than undergoing a "trial," juveniles went through an "adjudication." Rather than a "sentence," they received a "disposition." These differences in language were not merely cosmetic; they pointed to major differences in how the juvenile court was run. One major difference was that the juvenile court, unlike its adult counterpart, was informal. The purpose was both to help guarantee the confidentiality of the proceedings (onlookers were not allowed to sit in, and juvenile court records were sealed) and to allow the judge wide discretion and flexibility in his disposition of the offender. For better or (as we shall see) for worse, there was no obligation on the part of the court to keep transcripts of juvenile court proceedings and no guaranteed right to counsel. Further, the standard of proof used to adjudicate a delinquent was by a preponderance of the evidence rather than beyond a reasonable doubt.

In addition to these innovations in juvenile court processing, the intent and nature of the juvenile court's dispositional phase were also changed. In light of the commitment to rehabilitation rather than punishment, it became the intent of the court to treat and heal juveniles, who were generally seen as troubled youth rather than evil offenders. Thus, mental health workers were integrated into the operations of the court and its dispositions. Not only were pains taken to divert youth from court altogether, but, when serious crimes were adjudicated, adolescents began to be sent to state "schools" rather than adult prisons. This system remained in place essentially unchanged until the late 1960s when, not surprisingly, things changed dramatically.

Juvenile court intake is handled by probation officers or social workers assigned to that task. This phase differs from adult court in that intake workers have considerable authority to dispose of matters before a juvenile ever comes before a judge. Depending on prior record, on the seriousness of the crime, and on whether the juvenile is willing to admit his complicity, his case may be diverted from a formal proceeding. Any number of informal dispositions (including community service, restitution, family therapy, or even a warning and reprimand) may end the involvement of the juvenile with the court. However, if the alleged crime is more serious, if there is a prior record, and if the juvenile denies responsibility for the delinquent act, the case will be scheduled to be heard by a judge. In this adjudicatory phase, which is the juvenile court's version of a trial, witnesses are presented, and if the judge makes a finding of delinquency (i.e., guilt), the juvenile moves on to the dispositional phase. The range of dispositions is wide, extending from incarceration in a juvenile institution to probation, from residential treatment to restitution.

In extremely serious cases, there has always been the possibility that the juvenile could be "waived," or transferred, to adult court. Such a decision would indicate that the court felt that the juvenile had likely committed a truly serious crime such as murder, that he was old enough to bear responsibility for his acts, and that he was beyond its ability to rehabilitate. The 1966 *Kent v. United States* decision, one of several that changed the juvenile courts dramatically (discussed later), mandated that no juvenile could be sent to adult court without a full investigation by the juvenile court. This investigation was meant to include a comprehensive review of the juvenile's record and to focus on the issues of amenability to treatment and rehabilitative potential.

The juvenile's situation is also unique in that there is a whole category of behaviors that would not be considered crimes if committed by adults. These misbehaviors (e.g., being truant from school, being uncontrollable by one's parents, attempting to buy alcohol), based only on the status of the offender as a juvenile, are termed status offenses. Logically, misbehaving teens would be expected to be different from more serious adolescent offenders, and typically they would more likely be treated by the court without a formal adjudication. One mandate of the Juvenile Justice Act (discussed later) was to avoid "institutionalizing" such offenders and to deal with them more mildly.

THE ERA OF GAULT

In an ideal world, the operation of the juvenile court would serve a benign purpose—to keep juveniles out of the public eye and from stigmatization as felons. In the meantime, they would be given other chances or sent for treatment. Either way, they would have real chances to get their lives together and to join society as productive adults. As with many other well-intentioned social changes, however, the system did not fulfill the fondest hopes of its supporters. For one thing, the so-called state schools (i.e., "reformatories"), although initially having a "therapeutic" orientation, tended over time to degenerate into snake pits that were scarcely an improvement over adult settings. By the 1970s, influenced by movements toward deinstitutionalization and community-based services, the Commissioner for Youth in Massachusetts, Jerome Miller, concluded that the "reform schools" in his state were not redeemable. He closed them summarily and replaced them with a network of community-based alternatives.

With respect to the operation of the juvenile court itself, the very absence of many of the trappings of adult court also opened the door to abuse. The very informality and confidentiality meant to protect juveniles made it easier for judges to ignore the due-process protections enshrined in the Sixth Amendment to the Constitution and thus fundamental to adult criminal procedure.

These kinds of abuses typified the case of Gault (*In re Gault*, 1967). Gault was a 15-year-old Arizonan who was arrested because of an accusation that he had made lewd telephone calls. Without even the

146

opportunity to confront his accuser, an elderly lady, and on the flimsiest evidence, a judge sentenced him to confinement in a state school for up to six years. Had Gault been an adult, the same crime, if proved, would have resulted in a fine of $5 to $50 or imprisonment for not more than two months. In essence, after its review of this case and several others at about the same time, the Supreme Court concluded that the juvenile courts as they then functioned routinely and often profoundly violated the constitutional rights of juveniles.

Further, during its investigation of juvenile justice, the Supreme Court could not help but become aware of the decline in quality and safety of those facilities where juveniles were incarcerated. Although these facilities were meant to be primarily for treatment, years of neglect and budgetary tightening on the part of state and local governments had resulted in their steep decline. Contemplating this problem along with that of how justice was administered to juveniles, the court observed, "There must be grounds for concern that the child receives the worst of both worlds: that he gets neither the protection accorded to adults nor the solicitous care and rejuvenative treatment postulated for children" (*Kent v. United States*, 1966).

In a series of landmark decisions, the Supreme Court responded by dramatically overhauling the administration of juvenile justice in this country. In *Gault*, the court granted juveniles many of the rights that are standard in adult court—the rights to counsel, to notice of proceedings, to a written record of the proceedings, to confront and cross-examine one's accuser, to subpoena witnesses, and to protection against self-incrimination. In *Winship* (*In re Winship*, 1970), the court added that the adult standard of proof (i.e., beyond a reasonable doubt) must be used in finding culpability; in *Breed v. Jones* (1975), protection against double jeopardy was extended to juveniles; and in *Kent*, the court required that a transfer hearing be held in juvenile court before a minor could be transferred to adult court for trial. Indeed, one of the few rights not extended to juveniles (*McKeiver v. Pennsylvania*, 1971) is the right to a trial by jury.

Inevitably, in extending these due-process rights to juveniles in juvenile court, the Supreme Court made the juvenile court more adversarial. Lawyers, transcripts, Fifth Amendment protections, and a higher standard of proof combined to make juvenile proceedings much more like adult court. However, adversariality and due-process rights turn out to be two sides of the same coin, at least in our system. Given the depths to which juvenile justice could—and did—fall without those protections, most accept the reality of a more adversarial court as a practical necessity.

RECENT HISTORY

Despite these changes in juvenile court, the rehabilitative impulse was by no means dead. One major manifestation was the 1974 passage of the Juvenile Justice Act, which created the Office of Juvenile Justice and Delinquency Prevention. This act, among other things, funded research into juvenile delinquency and the problems of runaway and homeless youth. Innovative delinquency treatment programs were also funded. In order to receive money from the federal government, however, states had to follow the four "mandates" of the act: deinstitutionalization of status offenders; sight and sound separation of juveniles from adult offenders; removal of juveniles from adult jails and lockups; and reduction of disproportionate minority confinement. The theory was that status offenders ought not to be locked up with juveniles who had committed more serious crimes, and, by the same token, juveniles who had committed crimes ought not to be confined with adult felons who would either provide a bad influence or abuse them physically. Nearly every state has complied with these mandates in order to receive funding for their programs, and, although much progress has been made, it is not unheard of, depending on local conditions, for these principles to be violated, at least for short periods.

In the 1980s, a combination of a political shift in the country and a very visible increase in juvenile crime caused the public to lose faith in the rehabilitative approach and to call for harsher punishments for youthful offenders. Between 1982 and 1991, the number of murder arrests of ten- to seventeen-year-olds increased by 93%; between 1992 and 1993, arrests of male minors on charges of murder and nonnegligent manslaughter jumped by 13.5% (LIS, Inc., 1995). Disturbing cases of young people killing still younger children caused sadness and anger and contributed to the fervor for more retribution and less rehabilitation in the treatment of juveniles.

It is always a matter of speculation as to what the causes for these increases and decreases are. The availability of handguns is certainly one factor. Teens who once settled matters in a less lethal way now resort to shootings. The wider availability of drugs of abuse is another. The very size of the adolescent cohort at a particular point in time is another factor. Economic conditions must also be taken into account: In the past couple of years, we have had nearly full employment and a generally healthy economy; before that, we were in recession. Despite these most recent changes, many states have been rewriting their juvenile justice statutes typically to tighten up sentences and increase the likelihood that certain juvenile offenders would be tried in adult rather than juvenile court settings.

Waiver to Adult Court and the Death Penalty

A major consequence of changes in these statutes has been the much increased likelihood that a serious juvenile offender would be tried in an adult court. Between 1988 and 1992, for example, there was a 68% increase in juveniles waived to adult court (Aron and Hurley, 1998). The reason is that state legislatures simply put new procedures in place to make this happen. In particular, states created or expanded two means of getting to adult court (*statutory waiver* and *prosecutorial waiver*), both of which bypassed the juvenile court transfer hearing, which had been mandated by the *Kent* decision. In statutory waiver, teenagers are automatically sent to adult court based on age and the nature of the charged crime. These criteria are written into the appropriate juvenile justice statutes of each state. Prosecutorial waiver results when the state gives the prosecutor the discretion to bring the case to adult court if he or she deems it proper to do so. Indeed, it has become so common now for juveniles to be transferred to adult court when a serious crime is committed that a recent *San Diego Union Tribune* article was headlined "Teens Won't Stand Trial as Adults in a Skateboarder's Death" (March 7, 1998). Most of the increase in waiver proceedings has been due to this second process, which has been severely criticized for its mainly discretionary quality. A study of the behavior of prosecutors in one jurisdiction substantiates many of these concerns (Bishop and Frazier, 1991).

In light of the fact that capital punishment has been restored in many states, waiver to adult court opens up the possibility that a juvenile could be sentenced to death. A brief history of the death penalty begins in 1972 with the case of *Furman v. Georgia,* which had to do with adults and the death penalty. In this case, the Supreme Court, throwing out all existing death penalty statutes, said that none of them met constitutional muster. However, instead of throwing out the death penalty once and for all as an example of cruel and unusual punishment, as the death penalty antagonists had hoped, the court said in effect that, if a state wished to have a death penalty, it had to observe due process in seeking it. Accordingly, it laid out a blueprint for exactly what had to take place if death sentences were to be constitutional in the future. So, if a state like Texas or Florida, which were among the first to get back into the business, wanted to have a death penalty statute that passed constitutional muster, the way to do it was to follow the blueprint that the court had laid down.

At this point, executions stopped completely in this country, because the process by which all death row inmates had arrived there had been declared unconstitutional. It took four years before the court upheld the constitutionality of a newly written death penalty statute (*Gregg v. Georgia*, 1976). As a result, by the mid to late 1970s, the death penalty was again up and running. Thereafter, it would only be a matter of time before a juvenile committed a capital crime and was waived into adult court.

After capital punishment was reinstated, the first major Supreme Court case to deal with the issue of how old is old enough for the death penalty was the case of *Thompson v. Oklahoma* (1988). Thompson was a fifteen-year-old who, with some older men, committed a murder. He had a waiver hearing, which resulted in his transfer to adult court. He was tried as an adult and was given the death penalty. However, the sentence was appealed on the basis that it was cruel and unusual punishment (and thus unconstitutional under the Eighth Amendment) to give someone so young the death penalty. Among other bases for a finding that a punishment was cruel and unusual were three notions—that a societal consensus exists that the punishment "offends civilized standards of decency," that the punishment is out of proportion to the severity of the crime, and that it makes "no measurable contribution to acceptable goals of punishment" such as retribution or deterrence.

The American Society for Adolescent Psychiatry (ASAP), in one of the high watermarks of its advocacy, sponsored an amicus *curiae* brief to the Supreme Court in which ASAP took the side of Thompson and his lawyers and basically argued on two grounds—developmental and pathological. The pathological argument was based largely on the work of Dorothy Lewis, who had studied 14 juvenile death row inmates and found significant and substantial neurological and psychological deficits (Lewis et al., 1988). The developmental notion was based on the concept that a 15-year-old was not yet a fully responsible adult cognitively, judgmentally, or psychologically, and therefore someone so young should not qualify for the full weight of adult punishment (McLaughlin et al., 1987).

Four members of the court, siding with ASAP, concluded that execution of a fifteen-year-old offender would violate the Eighth Amendment. Their plurality opinion argued that such an execution would constitute cruel and unusual punishment both because it would violate contemporary standards of decency and because it would fail to contribute to acceptable goals of punishment. Although ASAP's arguments were taken into account, the court's decision regarding standards of decency was based largely on a survey of existing state laws on the theory that these laws defined the states' beliefs about those standards. The court found that thirteen states and the District of Columbia did not allow the death penalty for anybody and that, of the 37 states with death penalty laws on their books, eighteen had set the minimum age at sixteen (i.e., if a juvenile committed a capital crime before reaching his sixteenth birthday, he or she could not be executed).

Adding these eighteen states to the fourteen states that prohibited capital punishment altogether, the plurality came up with the number of states, 32, that did not permit those younger than sixteen to be executed. Because this constituted a majority of the states, the plurality concluded that there was a consensus, expressed by these state laws, that evolving standards of decency no longer supported executions of those so young. The plurality prevailed, however, only because of the concurrence of Justice O'Connor, but hers was not full agreement. She concluded that the consensus noted here was probable but not absolute, and she did not feel ready or able to extend a blanket prohibition on such executions. Her view was that such executions were prohibited only in those states that had not set a minimum age for executions in its own laws (Bassham, 1991). In her view, in other words, if a state had established, say, fourteen as the age below which offenders could not be executed, then a fifteen-year-old offender could be executed.

A couple of years later, in the cases of *Stanford v. Kentucky* and *Wilkins v. Missouri* (1989), the perpetrators were not so lucky. They were sixteen and seventeen, respectively, and the same arguments that saved Thompson did not save them. ASAP and many other organizations again submitted *amicus* briefs, and again the four justices forming the plurality in Thompson agreed, stating that to execute someone who committed crimes when under the age of eighteen was invariably disproportionate. However, Justice O'Connor voted this time with the conservatives in the belief that executing these older adolescents did not violate contemporary standards of decency.

It is interesting, however, that the majority opinion made specific mention of the transfer hearing as a safeguard that would protect juveniles. It seems to have assumed that every teenager who reached adult court in the first place would not get there without passing through a transfer hearing. As has been noted here, this is no longer the case.

So, that is where the matter stands. There is little popular interest in doing anything about it at this point. The American Psychiatric Association has been unable to pass position papers rejecting the death penalty in recent years, and, in light of the pendulum's continuing swing toward punishment and away from treatment, that's probably the way it's going to be for the time being. If anything, attempts to create even harsher penalties and further opportunities to place juveniles in adult court continue.

Most Recently

Interestingly, in the most recent period, since 1994, the American Bar Association (ABA, 1998) reports that arrest rates of youth for murder fell 14% annually through 1996. The overall juvenile crime arrest rate fell 9.2% in 1996, the second year in a row that juvenile crime rates fell. Despite this most recent downturn in juvenile crime, conservative elements in the Congress have continued to push for more punitive legislation. At the time of this writing, the Violent and Repeat Juvenile Offender Act of 1997, which had been resuscitated in 1998 as Senate bill S.10, had again failed in the Senate. Among other things, this act, if passed, would mandate that juveniles as young as fourteen could be tried as adults for certain crimes at prosecutorial discretion. It would severely weaken the protections enunciated by the Juvenile Justice Act to isolate juveniles from adult felons and by allowing status offenders to be locked up in any correctional facility for up to two weeks. In essence, the new act would have turned the Juvenile Justice Act on its head by offering block grants to states only if they obeyed these new mandates, which means abandoning the old protective ones. A broad coalition of organizations has been opposing the passage of the so-called S.10, and, as of the end of 1998, this coalition had succeeded in keeping the bill from becoming law.

In light of the current tendency to expand the use of transfer to adult courts, it is interesting that studies are beginning to appear comparing the recidivism rates of juveniles sent to adult courts and the recidivism rates of juveniles retained in juvenile court (Fagan, 1995; Bishop et al., 1996). These studies tend to show that juveniles sent to adult courts are more likely to reoffend after release than are those retained in juvenile courts, which is not surprising to many of us. This is even more apparent given that progress has been made in the management of juvenile criminal behavior on many fronts. Not only has our knowledge of teen criminality increased, but a new approach to community-based treatment—multisystemic family therapy (MST), originated by Scott Henggeler in South Carolina—shows great promise (Henggeler, Melton, and Smith, 1992). MST is cost-effective and has been validated by numerous controlled studies, which have proved it to be a remarkably economical and effective form of treatment for juveniles who get themselves tied up in the system.

The Role of the Psychiatrist

Despite all of the changes in juvenile justice over the years, there has been little change in the kinds of issues that draw psychiatrists into these proceedings since the publication of our *Handbook of Psychiatric Practice in the Juvenile Court* (Kalogerakis, 1992). In that publication, I laid out several issues that come up at different stages of the juvenile court process that can involve a psychiatric evaluation. These include competency for trial, insanity, amenability to treatment, and rehabilitation potential. Such evaluations may be requested at various points along the way, depending on specific juvenile court functioning and the needs of court personnel. Another area beyond the scope of the current chapter includes cases in which the juvenile is a victim (e.g., of abuse or neglect) rather than the perpetrator (sometimes he is both). In this case, an evaluation of how badly the juvenile has been damaged may be requested; in other cases, issues of the fitness of parents to remain parents may come to the fore.

What is competency to stand trial? Competency to stand trial is governed by a Supreme Court case, *Dusky v. United States* (1960). In that case, the court laid out the criteria such that, if one is going to make a determination of competency, one has got to determine whether the person being interviewed satisfies these criteria. Unlike the insanity defense, in which each state has its own standard (to be discussed), *Dusky* serves as a national standard. To satisfy these criteria, one must show that the person has a rational and factual grasp of the charges and the proceedings against him or her and is able to cooperate with his or her attorney in the defense with a reasonable degree of rational understanding. Of course, whether an individual meets these criteria is the issue in such examinations.

Note that these criteria for competency have nothing to do with the person's state of mind at the time of the crime but rather constitute a "present state" evaluation—having to do only with the person's state of mind at the time of evaluation. Is this person able to participate meaningfully and effectively in his or her defense? In contrast, when one is called to discuss the insanity defense—whether an insanity defense is, or is not, appropriate—the evaluation is retrospective. In different jurisdictions, a finding of incompetence due to the presence of a mental disease or defect may lead to dismissal of the case altogether or merely to postponement of the charges until the juvenile returns to competency. Grisso, Miller, and Sales's (1987) article remains the best and most comprehensive discussion of competency as it pertains to the juvenile court.

Although still uncommon in juvenile court, the insanity defense remains possible in certain jurisdictions and certainly may come into play with a juvenile in adult court. Before the changes brought about by Gault and other cases, adjudication in juvenile court was not considered equivalent to an adult conviction. Thus, because the insanity defense represents an acquittal, there seemed no point in acquitting someone who had not been convicted. Some jurisdictions have felt that it is unconstitutional to raise an insanity defense in juvenile court, but, with the general expansion of due-process rights, the insanity defense has made an appearance in some jurisdictions. Interestingly, the insanity defense is based on the concept of being not responsible, so that the "insane" person is considered analogous to a child who is too young to be responsible for his or her acts. For a seven-year-old who discharges a gun and kills a sister, we continue to assume that someone this young simply could not possess criminal intent. But, this nearly automatic assumption certainly does not apply to older children (e.g., those fourteen and older). For them, insanity defenses are likely to appear, if not in juvenile court, then in the adult court to which they have been transferred (Harrington and Keary, 1980).

In contrast to competency, "insanity" refers to a situation in which the perpetrator of a crime is not held criminally responsible by virtue of mental illness. It means that the individual did not possess the ability to form the intent to commit the crime and therefore is not responsible for it. Although different jurisdictions spell this out in different ways, some more restrictively and some more liberally, the state of mind at the time of the crime is the ultimate issue. One widely used standard is based on the American Law Institute Model Penal Code, in which the concept is defined via two different criteria. According to the code, one may be considered not guilty by reason of insanity if, by virtue of mental illness, one is either unable to appreciate the wrongfulness of the (criminal) act or is unable to conform one's behavior to the requirements of the law. The first criterion is the so-called cognitive prong; the second is the volitional prong. The federal government, which once adhered to this standard, has subsequently amended federal insanity statutes to remove the volitional prong on the theory, supported by the American Psychiatric Association, that it is nearly impossible to judge whether a person could control his or her behavior at the time of the event. The implication, of course, is that it is possible to gauge whether a person could appreciate the criminality of his or her acts at the time—which some people feel is equally questionable. It is often very difficult to feel certain about either type of determination, and this explains why most insanity defenses that go forward have one expert on either side of the aisle.

In any case, the evaluation of a person's state of mind at the time of a crime is the centerpiece of the insanity defense evaluation. That someone is competent for trial months after an event in no way means that he or she was mentally intact earlier. Clearly, such an evaluation requires not only a solid psychiatric evaluation such as one would perform for any reason but also special emphasis on the behavior at the time of the crime. For this purpose, police reports, affidavits of involved individuals, witnesses, and so forth—as well as family reports of the individual's mental state around the time of the crime—assume additional importance.

As it turns out, very few insanity defenses succeed. In only one fourth of 1% of cases in which they are tried are they successful, and in many of these cases it is because the prosecutor does not contest the finding. I am unaware of any survey that has been done of insanity defenses in juvenile court, in part because they remain rare.

The third reason a psychiatrist might be called into juvenile court is to assist in deciding on waiver. This is considerably more important for us because it will come up more and more often and will turn out to be crucial for the future of the accused adolescent as a result of the changes in the laws noted here. The evaluation must be aimed at whether any kind of progress can be made with the juvenile—whether he or she can really give up a life of crime and be rehabilitated.

In light of recent changes in the law, it seems likely that on occasion we will be testifying in adult court regarding "reverse waiver" (a juvenile is sent to adult court but is then considered for return to the juvenile setting). One can expect that essentially the same issues will be brought up as in waiver hearings—but this time in an adult setting.

Conclusions

The juvenile court system remains in flux. Not only do forces of the right and left feel that the system is respectively too soft and too harsh on crime, but many respected critics feel that, in its present form, it is a mishmash of conflicting ideologies and ineffective procedures (e.g., Springer, 1991). Further change can be expected as these ideologies battle each other on the national stage.

Nonetheless, the psychiatrist who wants to make a difference in the life of individual adolescent offenders may have little choice but to deal with the juvenile court as it exists in his or her community. To do so effectively, the psychiatrist must understand the basics of juvenile court process and must learn the details of how these courts function in one's own community. If one accepts responsibility for evaluating a teen, one must have a clear sense of the questions that need to be answered and must be prepared to describe the basis for one's opinions in a cogent, jargon-free manner. One must also be prepared for cross-examination (Ratner and Nye, 1992). I hope the information I have provided here will make it easier for psychiatrists to involve themselves in these matters and thereby make a contribution to the futures of those youth whose lives come afoul of the law.

REFERENCES

American Bar Association. (1998), *Questions and Answers About Juvenile Justice Policy & the Violent and Repeat Juvenile Offender Act of 1997 (S.10).* Washington, DC: American Bar Association.

Aron, C. & Hurley, M. (1998, June), Juvenile justice at the crossroads. *The Champion,* 22(5):10–12, 62–65, 73.

Bassham, G. (1991), Rethinking the emerging jurisprudence of juvenile death. *Notre Dame J. Law, Ethics and Public Policy,* 5:467–501.

Bishop, K. & Frazier, C. (1991), Transfer of juveniles to criminal court: a case study and analysis of prosecutorial waiver. *Notre Dame J. Law, Ethics and Public Policy,* 5: 281–302.

——— ——— Lanza-Kaduce, L. & Winner, L. (1996), The transfer of juveniles to criminal court: Does it make a difference? *Crim. & Delinq.,* 42:171–191.

Breed v. Jones 421 U.S. 519 (1975).

Dusky v. United States, 362 U.S. 402 (1960).

Fagan, J. (1995), Separating the men from the boys: the comparative advantage of juvenile versus criminal court sanctions on recidivism among adolescent felony offenders. In: *A Sourcebook on Serious, Violent and Chronic Offenders,* ed. J. C. Howell, B. Krisberg & D. Hawkins. Thousand Oaks, CA: Sage, pp. 238–260.

Furman v. Georgia, 408 U.S. 238 (1972).

Gregg v. Georgia, 428 U.S. 153 (1976).

Grisso, T., Miller, M. O. & Sales, B. (1987), Competency to stand trial in juvenile court. *Internat. J. Law Psychiat.,* 10:1–20.

Harrington, M. & Keary, A. (1980), The insanity defense in juvenile delinquency proceedings. *Bull. Amer. Acad. Psychiat. Law,* 8: 272–279.

Henggeler, S., Melton, G. & Smith, L. (1992), Family preservation using multi-systemic therapy: An effective alternative to incarcerating serious juvenile offenders. *J. Consult. Clin. Psychol.,* 60:953–961.

In re Gault, 387 U.S. 1 (1967).

In re Winship, 397 U.S. 358 (1970).

Kalogerakis, M., ed. (1992), *Handbook of Psychiatric Practice in the Juvenile Court.* Washington, DC: American Psychiatric Association.

Kent v. United States, 383 U.S. 541 (1966).

Levine, M., Ewing, C. & Hager, R. (1987), Juvenile and family mental health law in sociohistorical perspective. *Internat. J. Law Psychiat.,* 10:91–110.

Lewis, D., Pincus, J., Bard, B., Richardson, E., Prichep, L., Feldman, M. & Yeager, C. (1988), Neuropsychiatric, psychoeducational, and family characteristics of 14 juveniles condemned to death in the United States. *Amer. J. Psychiat.*, 145:584–589.

LIS, Inc. (1995), *Offenders Under Age 18 in State Adult Correctional Systems: A National Picture*, Special Issues in Corrections 1. Longmont, CO: National Institute of Corrections Information Center.

McKeiver v. Pennsylvania, 403 U.S. 528 (1971).

McLaughlin, J., Epstein, J., Weisburg, H., Freeling, K., Peabody, R. & Pincus, S. (1987), *Brief of the American Society for Adolescent Psychiatry and the American Orthopsychiatric Association as Amici Curiae in Support of Petitioner William Wayne Thompson*. New York: Counsel Press.

Ratner, R. & Nye, S. (1992), Court testimony: the psychiatrist as witness. In: *Handbook of Psychiatric Practice in the Juvenile Court*. Washington, DC: American Psychiatric Association.

Springer, C. (1991), Rehabilitating the juvenile court. *Notre Dame J. Law, Ethics Public Policy*, 5:397–420.

Stanford v. Kentucky, Wilkins v. Missouri, 109 S. Ct. 2969 (1989).

Thompson v. Oklahoma 487 U.S. 815 (1988).

11   COMPETENCE IN ADOLESCENTS

ROBERT WEINSTOCK

Adolescents are in a stage cognitively and emotionally intermediate between childhood and adulthood. Their moral development generally also is intermediate. Adolescence is the period in which adolescents move cognitively from Piaget's concrete operational thinking stage to what he called the formal stage of operational cognitive thinking. Even though an adolescent may be able to pass many simple cognitive tests, the law in most spheres recognizes that adolescents are immature both cognitively and emotionally.

Such recognition is the likely rationale for denying adolescents many rights and privileges. For example, they are denied the rights to vote, drink alcohol, drive below a specific age, and engage in voluntary sex with an older adult. The law does not allow adolescents to take any cognitive test that would enable them to demonstrate their cognitive ability to engage in specific activities. For example, a bright adolescent may know more about political candidates than most adults but still is not allowed to vote. Additionally, an adolescent may demonstrate an unusual sense of responsibility—and knowledge of the dangers of alcohol, knowledge of the problems with voluntary sex with an adult, and how to drive a motor vehicle—but the law still does not permit these activities. This practice highlights the law's tendency to recognize the emotional and cognitive immaturity of adolescents regardless of simple cognitive abilities.

In contrast, there is growing impetus in the criminal arena to treat adolescents as adults if the crime is serious or the adolescent shows recidivism. Even in the death penalty area, there has been a movement toward executing adolescents deemed competent on the basis of simplistic cognitive tests despite the law's restricting adolescents' privileges in many areas. Some politicians have advocated executing adolescents even as young as fourteen years. In the legal arena, there seems to be a tendency to make the adolescent suffer both ways. The adolescent is denied many adult privileges but is punished as an adult. In a criminal trial, adolescents are given most but not all the rights of an adult defendant (in re Gault, 1967).

Some of these discrepancies may be a reflection of a tendency for adults in general to be hostile to adolescents. Most generations are ready to disapprove of the adolescent life styles of the time—the music, dress, drug or alcohol use, strong commitment to unconventional ideas, and radical policies. Frequently, adults in each generation see the new generation as the worst ever. The current trend is to blame adolescents for most of the crime in our society. There is an increased fear of crime and a desire for ever harsher punishments, even though the general crime rate has been diminishing. In the less highly charged civil venue, there is a greater readiness to recognize adolescents' intermediate functioning capacities and a greater emphasis on the best interests of the adolescent. As part of analyzing adolescent competence, a number of developmental issues are relevant.

Piaget's Stages of Cognitive Development

The preoperational phase in Piaget's scheme occurs from ages two to seven. Remnants of such thinking occur in adolescents—and even in some adults when they regress, especially under stress. Concrete thinking in a schizophrenic adolescent also involves some early-stage cognitive conceptions. Although recent studies have shown Piaget's stages not to be as discrete as he had thought, with development of some capacities occurring earlier than others, his scheme still is very helpful in delineating cognitive development and describing the development of more complex thinking.

This preoperational stage (Flavell, 1963) is egocentric—displaying an inability of the individual to understand the perspective of another person. For example, a child is able to view a physical object from one position but cannot envision what it would look like from another position. The child can perceive a situation only from his or her own viewpoint but is unable to adapt to understand the needs of the other person in a conversation. Another characteristic of the preoperational phase is centration—the tendency to focus attention on one striking feature and thereby neglect all other features. This can lead to illogical thinking. It is a factor found in paranoid patients who focus on one aspect of a situation and thereby lose their perspective of the entire situation. Preoperational thinking considers changes irreversible insofar as the child cannot analyze a change or understand how each change could be annulled by its inverse (what would compensate for it). Preoperational thinking is imagistic and intuitional as opposed to schematic or abstract. The reasoning is called transducive, meaning that the child proceeds from particular to particular, centering on one salient aspect of an event and ignoring all others. Reasoning is neither deductive nor inductive. Associative connections are made by juxtaposition rather than by a true causal relationship—similar to the thinking of many schizophrenic patients.

The next phase is the stage of concrete operations, usually achieved from ages seven to eleven. The child at this stage has developed a coherent integrated cognitive system to organize, manipulate, and understand the world. The present is structured in terms of the past without frequently stumbling into contradiction and perplexity. By learning from frustrating interactions with peers, the child comes cognitively to appreciate differing perspectives and viewpoints. Reciprocal interactions develop among peers.

An example involving physical objects might help illustrate the difference between operational and preoperational children. If a liquid is poured from one vessel into a differently shaped vessel, the preoperational child will focus on one aspect (e.g., height, width) and conclude that one vessel contains more than the other; the operational child can see each transformation that would annul the alteration by pouring the liquid from the second vessel back into the first one and understand that both vessels contain the same amount of liquid.

Structuring and organizing activity in the concrete stage is directed toward concrete things and events in the immediate present. There is little extrapolation as to what is not there. The ability to interpret and organize lacks its full potential. In contrast, in the formal operational stage, the real becomes a special case of the possible. Children in the concrete phase cannot use the "all other things being equal" method. They cannot control and vary factors as needed to test cause and effect or to consider the hypothetical. By imagining all that might be there, the formal-stage adolescent is better equipped to find what is there by imagining all the possibilities. The child in the concrete stage can focus on only one solution to a problem and is unable to conceive of alternative solutions that may be preferable to the one that comes initially to mind. Careful, reasoned thought about a problem is not possible.

Although the formal stage of thinking can be achieved during adolescence, not all adolescents or even adults achieve it. Recent studies do not indicate any sharp demarcation between stages, but the ability to engage in more complex aspects of thinking increases with maturity in a gradual way with remnants of earlier thinking still present during the later stages.

Formal-stage adolescents, in contrast to concrete-stage adolescents, are capable of examining more than one way of achieving their goals. They are able to consider the future and the hypothetical. Clearly, knowledge of these abilities can be important when assessing the true cognitive capabilities of an adolescent and when assessing whether he or she is able to think at the same level as an adult, yet simplistic cognitive tests increasingly are being used to assess juveniles with criminal behaviors. These tests do not assess the complex areas of cognitive immaturity and are likely to give a misleading assessment of the adolescent's true capacities and incapacities. A juvenile's inability to consider alternative options can lead to impulsivity and emotional immaturity.

Conceptions of Moral Development—Kohlberg and Gilligan

Kohlberg expands on Piaget. His scheme focuses on the establishment of cooperative relationships with an emphasis on the concept of justice (Kohlberg, 1981). His earliest stages involve basing morality on obeying external rules, with some rudimentary concept of egalitarianism and reciprocity. His middle stage involves taking actions for the purpose of being thought good by others. Good things also are done to help the current social order survive. The highest stage, according to Kohlberg, employs social contract theory. Principles of forming a better society are used. Universal principles are considered. Highest stage individuals try to determine how impartial people would organize a good society. This framework is based on the assumption that the highest morality is not based on following rules or on trying to impress others. The highest morality is based on considering what would be best in an ideal society or on doing what you would expect others to do in a good society. Such morality appreciates the need to think out each ethical dilemma, as the rules of our current society may not always be "right."

Gilligan's (1982) conception involves a morality of caring. She feels that Kohlberg places too much emphasis on moral principles. She believes that his framework describes the way men think but that women, in contrast, are more concerned about caring and the responsibility to help those they care about. Obviously, men also are concerned about these issues, but they do not give them as great consideration in decisions about what is right than do most women. Gilligan is concerned that Kohlberg's pure abstract morality may be good for society but could lead to cruel, harmful acts toward those we care about.

Civil Competence in Adolescents

In the civil area, many specific rights, privileges, and responsibilities are denied to adolescents until they reach a definitive age. The age cutoffs are rigid and remain in effect regardless of the adolescent's ability to pass any cognitive test, even a complex one. Although such age cutoffs are somewhat arbitrary, they do demonstrate recognition of adolescent immaturity. The only exceptions are made for emancipated minors when there is no one better able to make a decision or in some states for things like contraception, when it is felt that parental involvement would be counterproductive.

Although legal competence is determined by the courts, psychiatrists can express opinions on these issues. If psychiatrists prefer, they can discuss capacities to make certain decisions. By doing so, they can address all of the issues of competence under the rubric of capacity yet clarify that only courts or legal statutes can determine whether an adolescent is competent for a specific civil purpose.

Informed Consent

Informed consent (or informed refusal) requires the ability to weigh the risks and benefits of a treatment and alternatives, including the no-treatment option. Informed consent for an adolescent's treatment usually requires not only getting the informed consent of the parent but, if possible, the adolescent's informed consent or at least assent.

Assent, according to the Committee on Bioethics (1995) of the American Academy of Pediatrics (AAP), should be an interactive process between physician and patient and should not involve routine legalistic procedures or development of assent forms. Assent at minimum requires helping the adolescent to achieve a developmentally appropriate awareness of the condition and explaining what to expect with tests and treatment. A clinical assessment of the adolescent's understanding of the situation should be made. Care should be made to ensure that inappropriate pressure is not influencing how the patient is responding. Efforts should be made to help the adolescent willingly accept the proposed care as well as to obtain parental consent. However, the adolescent should not be deceived. The patient's views should be solicited only if they really will be weighed seriously. If the patient is to receive medical care regardless of his or her wishes, the physician should simply tell the patient what will happen, consistent with the patient's ability to understand.

Age alone, although legally important, may not be the most significant ethical factor in determining to what extent adolescents should be involved in the process. Issues such as cognitive and emotional development are crucial. Economic and psychological dependence on parents also affects legal and ethical determinations of whether informed consent should be obtained from the adolescent in addition to a parent or, in the case of an emancipated adolescent, instead of the parent. For adolescents sufficiently independent and mature, the law may recognize the adolescent's ability to give valid independent consent (i.e., emancipated or mature minor). When parents make decisions clearly harmful to adolescents, the situation should be brought to the attention of an appropriate agency or court. The adolescent psychiatrist ethically should do whatever is possible to obtain clearly needed treatment for an adolescent. Generally, courts have not permitted parents to refuse life-sustaining treatment for adolescents even if they legally are permitted to make such decisions for themselves. Courts usually appoint a surrogate decision-maker.

According to the tradition of English common law, children under the age of majority were deemed to lack the legal capacity to give consent to medical treatment or services, necessitating consent by a parent, guardian, or other legally authorized representative. There was an assumption that a child lacked the capacity to give informed consent and that the parent or guardian would act in the child's interest. However, in recent years it has become increasingly clear that in some cases parents do not act in the child or adolescent patient's interest. Nevertheless, absent an emergency or under legally specified circumstances, providing medical care to an adolescent without the consent of an authorized person can constitute a battery.

Legislation over the past half century has produced general emancipation statutes for lawfully married minors, minors on active military duty, and minors older than 15, living apart from parents or legal guardian, and financially independent from them. There also are limited medical emancipation statutes for specific, designated conditions. The Committee on Bioethics (1995) of the AAP has stated that adolescents, in contrast to children, generally have the capacity to give informed consent, so in most instances informed consent and not merely assent should be obtained. Examples include performing a pelvic examination, honoring a request for oral contraceptives, and prescribing long-term antibiotic treatment for acne. The committee states that adolescent patients have both the decision-making capacity and the legal authority to accept or reject interventions such as these and that no requirement exists to obtain parental permission even though parental involvement in such cases is recommended. Such adolescents, though, may not really have the full cognitive capacity or emotional maturity of an adult to make these decisions. Also, there may be a growing tendency to use the same kinds of simple cognitive tests used for adults in these civil situations. However, some adolescents may be better able to decide what is in their interest than a parent or legally appointed guardian.

The age of majority varies by state, ranging from sixteen to 21 (Macbeth, 1992). Besides this absolute demarcation, in some situations adolescents who have not attained the chronological age of majority and are not legally emancipated may still have certain decision-making rights and privileges. For example, in California, unemancipated adolescents are legally able to consent to oral contraceptives, abortion, and outpatient psychotherapy on their own without parental consent, but they generally need parental consent for psychotropic medication, absent an emergency. They can obtain hospital, medical, and surgical care related to pregnancy; medical care related to the diagnosis and treatment of any infectious, contagious, or communicable disease including a sexually transmitted disease; and medical care related to rape or sexual assault. Medical care and counseling related to the diagnosis and treatment of a drug or alcohol problem can be obtained by individuals twelve or older without parental consent. The likely rationale is that, if parental consent were necessary, many such patients out of embarrassment or fear of parental response might defer needed treatment. States differ in their laws regarding the ability of adolescents to consent to abortions without parental consent or judicial authorization—a highly politicized issue.

The AAP, strongly supportive of respecting an adolescent's ethical right to give consent for medical procedures, entered and recently prevailed in a lawsuit against the state of California. In *American Academy of Pediatrics v. Lungren* (1997), the California Supreme Court ruled that the state could not require that a pregnant minor (under eighteen) secure parental consent or judicial authorization before obtaining an abortion. This decision was based in part on the explicit right to privacy found in the California constitution but not in the federal constitution. However, Judge Mosk, in a dissenting opinion, stated that there is no presumption of competence in adolescents, and the medical emancipation statutes were designed to apply to limited circumstances and conditions. The AAP notes that empirical data suggest that adolescents, especially age fourteen and older, may have attained adult-level decision skills for making informed health care decisions. It is likely, though, that the AAP did not consider the cognitive and emotional maturity issues discussed earlier. Moreover, out of legal and ethical concern for an adolescent's welfare, it may be necessary sometimes to oppose adolescents who wish to make seriously unwise decisions.

Research

Research on adolescents is essential but has many special ethical and legal considerations. The problems with doing research on adolescents have led to a paucity of relevant scientific data. For example, there is very little research on the use of most medications for adolescents, particularly with regard to efficacy or side effects.

The Code of Ethics of the American Academy of Child and Adolescent Psychiatry (1980) distinguishes between research that has potential therapeutic benefit for an adolescent and research that does not. In cases of potential therapeutic benefit, an understanding of the risks and benefits should be communicated to the parents or guardians as well as to the involved adolescent—just as would happen in the usual treatment situation.

In research not related to potential therapeutic benefit for the adolescent or to other direct, positive outcomes, the level of risk becomes critical. When the risk is minimal (e.g., as in standardizing new psychological tests or obtaining urine or blood samples for analysis), only parental consent and adolescent assent are needed. If the risk is more than negligible (e.g., as in taking a biopsy or administering a chemical agent), the adolescent, if developmentally capable of understanding the procedure, the risks, and the larger benefits, should have the right to refuse to participate regardless of parental or guardian consent.

Civil Commitment

Civil commitment of adolescents presents its own issues and challenges. Adolescents have some legal rights but not as many as adults in such situations. In *Parham v. J. R.* (1979), the U.S. Supreme Court held that the risk of error inherent in parental decisions to institutionalize children for mental health care is sufficiently great that some kind of inquiry by a "mental fact finder" is necessary. Although a hearing by a judicial or administrative official is not required, the decision maker must have the authority to refuse admission. Unlike court decisions for adults, the Supreme Court decision regarding minors gave a higher priority to patient well-being than to liberty.

States, though, are not prohibited from requiring hearings and giving greater legal protection to an adolescent's liberty. For example, the California Supreme Court in *In re Roger S* (1977) held that minors old enough independently to exercise their right to due process could not be deprived of their right to a hearing. However, they were not entitled to all of the same procedural protections accorded an adult in the same situation.

Adolescent Sex

The law about sex between adolescents is complex and somewhat arbitrary. For example, the legality of sexual relations between an eighteen-year-old and a sixteen-year-old or between underage adolescents is not always clear, despite the similar conceptual capacity of both parties. The general rule is that voluntary consensual sex with an adolescent becomes abuse only when there is more than a five-year age difference unless such behavior is a result of parental neglect (abuse) or there is exploitation. However, some overzealous prosecutors have pursued such cases. It is necessary to be aware of the case law in a specific jurisdiction, as not all states always follow this unofficial rule. In California, voluntary and consensual sexual behavior between minors under fourteen need not be reported absent other indicia of abuse (Planned Parenthood Affiliates v. Van de Kamp, 1986). However, all sexual contact with persons under fourteen is prohibited regardless of consent if the older adolescent is over fourteen (People v. John L, 1989). In California at least, these court decisions make an arbitrary distinction that could result in a finding that it is reportable child abuse and criminal for a fourteen-year-old to have sex with a thirteen-year-old but not for a thirteen-year-old to have sex with a twelve-year-old.

Ethics in Forensic Psychiatry

It is essential to know the legal criteria before expressing an opinion on a legal issue and applying the clinical data to the legal issue. Many forensic psychiatrists limit themselves to interpreting the many legal criteria in simple ways that are easy for courts to use. Their opinions can be based on simplistic cognitive tests and not on more complex assessments that take the adolescent's cognitive and emotional immaturity into account. The approach of trying to figure out how the courts previously interpreted a legal issue—and not going beyond that—was followed by forensic psychiatrist Seymour Pollack (1974) and is still followed by many forensic psychiatrists (Rosner, 1990; Appelbaum, 1997).

However, many legal issues are vague and the criteria ambiguous. When simplistic interpretations of legal criteria do not address the central issue of an adolescent's immaturity, adolescent psychiatrists should, in my opinion, use broader interpretations that take aspects central to a case into account. The reasoning for the opinion should be presented to the court. A forensic adolescent psychiatrist should not misleadingly imply that a simplistic cognitive test of an adolescent is sufficient. However, if an adult test is not the only one used, the test or interpretation employed should be explained to the trier of fact. A judge or jury may reject this expanded interpretation. However, if the information is clearly identified when given, at least triers of fact have an opportunity to consider the data if they wish to do so in a specific case. They may or may not accept the expanded interpretation, but at least they have an opportunity to consider the issue and are not misled into thinking a simple cognitive test used for adults is sufficient.

Such an approach to participation in court cases was used by the eminent and highly respected forensic psychiatrist, Bernard Diamond (1992). His participation in cases in which definitions were expanded to encompass the facts of a case led to modification of many laws by the California Supreme Court. He was most influential in the development of diminished capacity, in which the inability to have a required criminal intent because of mental illness and intoxication resulted in conviction on a lesser included crime. He tried to participate in the legal system when he could educate the court about mental illness and some good could be done consistent with medical values. Many forensic psychiatrists agree that traditional medical ethics should retain an important role in forensic work (Weinstock, Leong, and Silva, 1990; Weinstock, 1998).

Juvenile Death Penalty

Special legal considerations apply to adolescent death penalty sentences and evaluations. In 1988, the U.S. Supreme Court in *Thompson v. Oklahoma* prohibited a juvenile death penalty for those adolescents under sixteen at the time of the crime. In subsequent cases (*Stanford v. Kentucky, Wilkins v. Missouri*, 1989), the Supreme Court explicitly permitted individuals sixteen or older at the time of a capital crime to be executed if a state should choose to do so. Individual states nevertheless can require a higher minimum age at the time of the crime for a death penalty verdict or can prohibit capital punishment altogether. In those states with a juvenile death penalty, adolescence can be a mitigating factor that the defense can present during the penalty phase of a trial in which the prosecution is seeking a death penalty.

It has been stated that the arguments against a juvenile death penalty may not be valid because most adolescent defendants are able to meet the minimum cognitive standards necessary for an adult defendant to be competent to be executed (Leong and Eth, 1989). Moreover, because of appeals, most adolescents become adults by the time a death penalty sentence would be carried out. Therefore, it has been argued that, at the time of execution, they would be as competent as an adult to be executed, regardless of their immaturity at the time of the crime.

Although most adolescents can meet cognitive tests for competence to be executed and competence to stand trial and can meet the cognitive test precluding a M'Naghten insanity defense (Miller, 1994), these are examples of the problems with tests that do not take emotional and cognitive immaturity into consideration. Achievement of Piaget's formal stage of reasoning, necessary for reflective thought, makes conceptualization of alternative courses of action possible. In contrast, preformal adolescents are unable to conceptualize alternatives and therefore may act impulsively. Formal thought makes regulation of affect and behavior possible (Overton et al., 1992). It is important to keep in mind that such issues can be introduced at least as a mitigating factor in the sentencing phase of a death penalty trial even if they are not deemed relevant earlier in the case for a diminished *mens rea* defenses capacity type or an insanity defense.

The United States is the only western democracy still retaining the death penalty. According to the United Nations, except for China, our country has most expanded the use of the death penalty (Crossette, 1997). Here, capital punishment remains a source of continuing debate that is reflected in an ongoing ethical controversy within American psychiatry (Foot, 1990; Weinstock, Leong, and Silva, 1992; Leong et al., 1993) and medicine (Michalos, 1997). In the absence of a consensus, there are no clear ethical guidelines for most aspects of psychiatric participation in capital cases, except for the prohibition against participation in the execution process itself. Opinions differ regarding the ethical propriety of many death penalty roles for psychiatrists based on personal ethical, moral, or religious considerations or an individual views regarding what should be ethically acceptable or desirable on a professional basis.

Despite the legal permissibility of most professional roles in capital cases, adolescent psychiatrists must become aware of the ethical considerations involved when they participate in such cases. Facilitating death is in conflict with traditional medical roles. Psychiatrists can be asked to present aggravating circumstances to help obtain a death penalty verdict, present victims' impact statements, or treat adolescents to make them competent to be executed. In the absence of a consensus or clear, generally accepted ethical guidelines for most facets of death penalty case involvement, adolescent psychiatrists must make their own determinations of what is professionally and personally ethically acceptable or desirable.

Conclusion

Because mental capacities during adolescence are in flux and do not lend themselves to simple categorization, it is essential to become aware of developmental issues and problems in order to assess properly an adolescent's competence for legal and other purposes. If specified, the relevant legal tests must be used, but additional information about the emotional and cognitive immaturity of an adolescent should be given if a strict, narrow interpretation does not take such factors into account. As adolescent psychiatrists are most familiar with adolescent development both cognitively and emotionally, they have much to contribute to the assessment of the competence of adolescents.

REFERENCES

American Academy of Child and Adolescent Psychiatry Code of Ethics, 1980.

American Academy of Pediatrics v. Lungren. California Supreme Court No. 884574, filed August 5, 1997.

Appelbaum, P. S. (1997), A theory of ethics for forensic psychiatry. *Bull. Amer. Acad. Psychiat. Law*, 25:233–247.

Committee on Bioethics (American Academy of Pediatrics). (1995), Informed consent, parental permission, and assent in pediatric practice. *Pediatrics*, 95:314–317.

Crossette, B. (1997, September 30), UN monitor investigates American use of death penalty. *New York Times*.

Diamond, B. L. (1992), The forensic psychiatrist: Consultant vs. activist in legal doctrine. *Bull. Amer. Acad. Psychiat. Law*, 20:119–132.

Flavell, J. H. (1963), *The Developmental Psychology of Jean Piaget*. Princeton, NJ: Van Nostrand.

Foot, P. (1990), Ethics and the death penalty. In: *Ethical Practice in Psychiatry and the Law*, ed. R. Rosner & R. Weinstock. New York: Plenum, pp. 207–217.

Gilligan, C. (1982), *In a Different Voice: Psychological Theory and Women's Development.* Cambridge, MA: Harvard University Press.

In re Gault, 387 US 1, 87 S.Ct. 1426 (1967).

In re Roger S, 19 Cal. 3d 921 (1977).

Kohlberg, L. (1981), *The Philosophy of Moral Development.* San Francisco: Harper & Row.

Leong, G. B. & Eth, S. (1989), Behavioral science and the juvenile death penalty. *Bull. Amer. Acad. Psychiat. Law*, 17:301–309.

Leong, G. B., Weinstock, R., Silva, J. A. & Eth, S. (1993), Psychiatry and the death penalty: The past decade. *Psychiatric Annals*, 23:41–47.

Macbeth, J. A. (1992), Legal issues in the psychiatric treatment of minors. In: *Clinical Handbook of Child Psychiatry and the Law*, ed. D. H. Schetky & E. P. Benedek. Baltimore, MD: Williams & Wilkins, pp. 53–74.

Michalos, C. (1997), Medical ethics and the executing process in the United States of America. *Med. Law* 16:125–167.

Miller, R. D. (1994), Criminal responsibility. In: *Principles and Practice of Forensic Psychiatry*, ed. R. Rosner. New York: Chapman & Hall, pp. 198–215.

Overton, W. R., Steidel, J. H., Rosenstein, D. & Horowitz, H. (1992), Formal operations as regulatory context in adolescence. In: *Adolescent Psychiatry* 18:502–518. Chicago: University of Chicago Press.

Parham v. J. R., 99 S.Ct. 2493, 442 U.S. 584 (1979).

People v. John L, 209 Cal. App. 3d 1137 (1989).

Planned Parenthood Affiliates v. Van de Kamp, 181 Cal. App. 3d 245 (1986).

Pollack, S. (1974), *Forensic Psychiatry in Criminal Law*. Los Angeles: University of Southern California.

Rosner, R. (1990), Forensic psychiatry: A subspecialty. In: *Ethical Practice in Psychiatry and the Law*, ed. R. Rosner & R. Weinstock. New York: Plenum, pp. 19–29.

Stanford v. Kentucky, Wilkins v. Missouri, 109 S.Ct. 2969 (1989).

Thompson v. Oklahoma, 101 L.Ed. 2d 702 (1988).

Weinstock, R. (1998), Response to Appelbaum PS: A theory of ethics in forensic psychiatry [letter to the editor]. *J. Amer. Acad. Psychiat. Law*, 26:151–155.

Weinstock, R., Leong, G. B. & Silva, J. A. (1990), The role of traditional medical ethics in forensic psychiatry. In: *Ethical Practice in Psychiatry and the Law*, ed. R. Rosner & R. Weinstock. New York: Plenum, pp. 31–51.

———— ———— & ———— (1992), The death penalty and Bernard Diamond's approach to forensic psychiatry. *Bull. Amer. Acad. Psychiat. Law*, 20:197–210.

PART IV

PSYCHOPHARMACOLOGY IN ADOLESCENCE: CURRENT PERSPECTIVES

ROBERT L. HENDREN

This Special Section consists of four excellent chapters reviewing state-of-the-art psychopharmacologic treatment of adolescents with mental disorders. Each chapter describes a cluster of disorders (disruptive behavior disorders, affective disorders, anxiety disorders, pervasive developmental and psychotic disorders) and the pharmacologic agents currently used to treat these disorders and concludes with recommendations for future study and research. The chapters are written by authors who are leading experts in the diagnosis and treatment of these disorders.

The application of pharmacologic treatments to mental disorders in youth has grown rapidly in the past decade. Although certain outcome measurements clearly demonstrate improvement with pharmacologic treatment, heated controversy exists around the application of this treatment to problems as complex as mental disorders in young people. What are the effects of these medications on the developing young person? What is the role of family and individual psychotherapy? What are the influences on treatment from the social environment, including pressures from third-party payers to treat quickly at the lowest cost? Are we aggressively using these powerful medications to the long-term detriment of our young people?

These are interesting and important questions to be considered when we think about prescribing a medication, give informed consent to young people and their families, or get together with colleagues to discuss how we practice. These questions are not addressed directly in the following chapters, but the early and evolving science supporting the use of psychopharmacologic agents in youth is comprehensively reviewed. After reading this review, there can be little doubt that medications improve symptoms or that improved symptoms lead to improved relationships that in turn lead to further improvement in symptoms.

The first chapter in this section, "Pharmacologic Treatment of Behavior Disorders in Adolescents" by Drs. Srirangam S. Shreeram and Markus J. P. Kruesi, is a comprehensive review of the disruptive behavior disorders seen in adolescents—with thoughtful critiques of the recent significant pharmacologic treatment studies. The disorders covered are attention deficit/hyperactivity disorder, conduct disorder, and oppositional defiant disorder. The medications discussed include psychostimulants, tricyclics, and other antidepressants; alpha-adrenergic agonists; neuroleptics; mood stabilizers; and beta-blockers. The authors present a thoughtful approach to pharmacotherapy including combination treatments. Recommendations for further research include pharmacokinetic studies and studies of the complexity of comorbidity and the use of combination treatments.

Major depression, dysthymia, and bipolar disorder are covered in the next chapter, "Pharmacologic Treatment of Affective Disorders in Adolescents," by Drs. Dwight V. Wolf and Karen D. Wagner. Studies using tricyclic antidepressants (TCAs), selective serotonin reuptake inhibitors (SSRIs), monoamine oxidase inhibitors (MAOIs), newer antidepressants, and mood stabilizers in the treatment of affective disorders in adolescents are reviewed. Treatment and augmentation strategies are offered in a concise, useful manner in this straightforward chapter.

In "Pharmacologic Treatment of Anxiety Disorders in Adolescents," Drs. Robinder K. Bhangoo and Mark A. Riddle describe the 10 anxiety disorders encountered in adolescents and their overlap with one another and with other common comorbid conditions. The pervasiveness of anxiety symptoms and the differing expression of anxiety at different levels of development are thoughtfully presented. The four groups of medications commonly used to treat anxiety disorders—benzodiazepines, TCAs, buspirone, and SSRIs—are discussed, and the published studies are reviewed. The authors' recommendations for future research include studies to improve diagnostic clarity, controlled medication trials, and longitudinal studies.

The fourth chapter, "Pharmacologic Treatment of Psychosis and Pervasive Developmental Disorders in Adolescents," by Drs. Ileana Bernal-Schnatter and Robert L. Hendren, provides a review of the diagnosis and treatment of the psychotic disorders and pervasive developmental disorders (PDD) found in adolescents. The category of PDD has been newly defined in the fourth edition of the *Diagnostic and Statistical Manual of Mental Disorders* and will likely see further refinement in the future. In this chapter, difficulties in the differential diagnosis of PDD and psychosis, especially in younger adolescents, are discussed. Treatment studies are reviewed but are limited due to the evolution of the diagnosis and the difficult differential diagnosis. Based on a practical decision tree, the uses of conventional or typical neuroleptics and of the newer and more frequently used atypical neuroleptics are presented.

Together, these chapters provide a thorough and thoughtful review of the psychopharmacologic treatment of mental disorders in adolescents and make recommendations for good diagnosis and treatment practices. Mental health practitioners working with adolescents increasingly need to have current knowledge of this area in order to weave an effective treatment program for young people. Knowing when and how to use these medications in the context of an adolescent's environment continues to be an art that relies on the good training and judgment of the practitioner.

12   PHARMACOLOGIC TREATMENT OF BEHAVIOR DISORDERS IN ADOLESCENTS

SRIRANGAM S. SHREERAM AND MARKUS J. P. KRUESI

Disruptive behavior is among the most frequent causes for adolescents to be referred to mental health professionals. Many of these adolescents referred for psychiatric evaluation are diagnosed with attention deficit/ hyperactivity disorder (ADHD), oppositional defiant disorder (ODD), and conduct disorder (CD). These disorders are classified under the section, "Attention Deficit and Disruptive Behavior Disorders," in the *Diagnostic and Statistical Manual of Mental Disorders, Fourth Edition* (*DSM–IV*; American Psychiatric Association, 1994). Despite the frequency of these disorders, there is a relative paucity of literature on pharmacological treatment specific to adolescents. As of 10 years ago, there were only three controlled studies of pharmacotherapy exclusively for ADHD in adolescents (Wilens and Biederman, 1992). There was growing recognition of the persistence of ADHD, the treatment of which was increasingly being extended into adolescence. In the previous decade, medication treatment of CD was described as speculative, and CD in itself was not considered to be an indication for pharmacotherapy (Rapoport and Kruesi, 1984). Because of the overlap between CD and ADHD populations, questions were raised as to whether one or both disorders were responding to treatment.

The focus of this chapter is on recent developments in the pharmacological treatment of ADHD, ODD, and CD in adolescents. This decade's development in the classification, epidemiology, and clinical presentation of ADHD, ODD, and CD, as they relate to current trends in treatment, is reviewed.

Classification/Nosology

The nosology and conceptualization of disruptive behavior disorders have undergone significant change in the past decade. *DSM–IV*, pub-

179

lished in 1994, resulted in several changes over the revised third edition (*DSM–III R*), published in 1987. ADHD in *DSM–IV* is viewed as a unitary disorder with different predominating symptom patterns— predominantly inattentive type, predominantly hyperactive type, and combined type. Some provisions added in *DSM–IV* minimize the chances of overdiagnosing ADHD. These include the requirement that some impairment from the symptoms be present in two or more settings and before age seven.

Despite controversy over whether CD and ODD constitute a continuum of the same disorder or are in fact distinct entities (Rey 1993), *DSM–IV* maintained ODD and CD as two separate diagnoses. The differentiation of CD and ODD in *DSM–IV* is consistent with the growing consensus that the distinction between predatory versus affective quality of the aggression (rather than the distinction between aggressive and nonaggressive disruptive behavior) is salient to pharmacological treatment. Vitaro et al. (1998) view the *DSM–IV* CD-criteria aggressiveness items as more proactive or predatory and the ODD items as more anger-like and reactive.

Epidemiology

In a recently published community survey of psychiatric disorders in upstate New York, Cohen, Cohen, and Kasen (1993) found the prevalence of ADHD, CD, and ODD among 14- to 16-year-old boys to be 11.4%, 15.8%, and 15.4%, respectively. For 14- to 16-year-old girls, the rates were 6.5%, 9.2%, and 15.6%. Whereas the rate of ODD in both sexes and the rate of CD in girls seemed to peak in this age group, a steady decline with age was noted in the rate of both ADHD and CD in boys. Specifically, the rate of ADHD in boys declined about 20% each year from more than 20% at age 10 to about 2% at age 20. In comparison, the rate of ADHD in girls remained fairly constant through this age range. As pointed out by Boyle et al. (1996), estimates of ADHD and CD prevalence vary widely (from 0.1% to 39.2%), depending on the threshold set for diagnosis.

The apparent steep decline in prevalence of ADHD with increasing age in epidemiological studies may not be applicable for clinically identified samples. Although one analysis of data from previous prospective studies (Hill and Schoener, 1996) suggested that ADHD de-

180

clined exponentially with increasing age—with a 50% drop in prevalence every five years—another prospective study found a much higher stability in the ADHD diagnosis (Barkley et al., 1990).

Epidemiological studies have recently focused on the phenomenon of comorbidities and pharmacoepidemiology. In a community study, Bird et al. (1988) reported that about 45% of youth diagnosed with either ODD or CD have a comorbid diagnosis of ADHD—consistent with the range of 30% to 50% reported by Biederman, Newcorn, and Sprich (1991) in their review of the literature. In a study of community prescribing practices for CD, 78% were comorbid for other disorders including ADHD, mood disorder, and posttraumatic stress disorder (PTSD; Stoewe, Kruesi, and Lelio, 1995). In a school survey, Safer, Zito, and Fine (1996) reported a 2.5-fold increase in number of youth receiving methylphenidate prescriptions between 1990 and 1995. This was attributed partly to treatment's being extended increasingly into high school and beyond.

Clinical Presentation

Over the past decade, recognition of ADHD in adolescents and of its wide-ranging manifestations has increased. Several studies that have followed clinically identified hyperactive children into their teens have dispelled the notion that hyperactivity is outgrown in adolescence (Barkley et al., 1990). Between 30% and 50% of hyperactive children continue to be impaired by ADHD manifestations. In adolescents, inattention and hyperactivity may present in a muted way compared to how they present in younger children (Wender, 1995). ADHD adolescents make careless mistakes and fail to complete their schoolwork. Other associated characteristics described include laughing excessively, "fooling around" without regard for the feelings of others, and overreacting to teasing. On some clinical parameters like age of onset, mean number of symptoms, and comorbidities (except substance use disorders), ADHD adolescents may be similar to ADHD children (Biederman et al., 1998), although family history of ADHD is more common in adolescents. Teachers may complain of social immaturity, unpopularity, fighting with peers, and self-destructive behaviors. Vandalism, assault, possession of a weapon, and suspensions and expulsions from school were all more frequent among the ADHD group (Barkley et al., 1991).

Studies consistently note the high rates of comorbidity within disruptive disorders. Comorbid PTSD (McLeer, Callaghan, and Henry, 1994), Tourette's disorder (Comings and Comings, 1987), specific learning disorders (Semrud-Clikeman and Hynd, 1990), and bipolar disorder (Biederman et al., 1996) have been described.

Male and female adolescents with ADHD and CD are significantly more likely than their peers to commit traffic offenses (Nada-Raja et al., 1997) and to have more crashes (Barkley, Murphy, and Kwasnik, 1996). In both sexes, CD is a major risk for adolescent substance abuse (Weinberg et al., 1998) and for being sexually assaulted (Bagley, Bolitho, and Bertrand, 1995). ADHD probands had a significantly shorter period between the onset of substance abuse and dependence compared with controls (Biederman et al., 1997).

DIAGNOSTIC ASSESSMENT

Practice parameters for ADHD and CD have been published by the American Academy for Child and Adolescent Psychiatry (Dulcan, 1997). The diagnostic assessment of an adolescent with attention deficit and/or disruptive behavior should be aimed at differential diagnosis and documentation of all comorbid conditions. As with children, the interview with adolescents may not in itself yield information sufficient for confirmation of an attention deficit/disruptive disorder diagnosis. However, important information needed for differential diagnosis, assessment of comorbidities, and psychosocial factors contributing to the clinical picture is frequently elicited. Interviews with parents, teachers, and other caregivers including psychotherapists, case workers, and school counselors are appropriate. A higher index of suspicion should be maintained for substance abuse and suicidality in adolescents compared to children.

Failing school performance, rule violations, or aggressive behaviors in a previously well-adjusted adolescent should arouse suspicions of substance abuse. Even in the absence of such signs, a toxicology screen is appropriate in the presence of new-onset or erratic symptoms. However, routine blood tests for thyroid function are not indicated (Weiss et al., 1993; Spencer et al., 1995) because of the low general-population incidence of thyroid abnormalities with associated ADHD. CD adolescents with severe-aggression histories are particularly likely to have histories of head trauma. For example, a study of 25 homicidal youths found that 43% of the subjects had a history of head trauma and 8% had a history of seizures (Myers et al., 1995). Nonetheless, it should be noted that CD/ODD children are less likely to have clear pathology on clinically read MRIs than are youth with schizophrenia spectrum diagnoses (Hendren et al., 1991). Currently, imaging by CT, MRI, or SPECT should not be thought of as routinely indicated for assessment of disruptive behavior (Peterson, 1995).

Pharmacologic Agents

In this section, we review the evidence that supports the use of specific agents in the treatment of adolescents with attention deficit and disruptive disorders. We have focused on controlled studies that have been done exclusively on adolescents in the past decade. Where no such studies are available, we have discussed open studies and those including adolescents. The list of agents discussed here was compiled from those most frequently reported as used for ADHD, ODD, or CD in an ongoing epidemiological study of psychotropic medications currently prescribed for children and adolescents in Illinois (Stoewe and Kruesi, 1997). This list is consistent with the list of frequently prescribed drug classes in hospitalized adolescents (Kaplan and Busner, 1997).

PSYCHOSTIMULANTS

As of 10 years ago, there were only three published double-blind placebo-controlled studies of stimulants for ADHD adolescents (Wilens and Biederman, 1992). Over the past decade, at least five other double-blind studies have been published, all of which used methylphenidate (MPH). Three of these studies (Klorman et al., 1990; Evans and Pelham, 1991; Smith, Pelham, Evans, et al., 1998) used samples comprised entirely of adolescents, whereas one study (Pelham et al., 1991) compared matched groups of adolescents and children; the fifth study (Smith, Pelham, Gnagy, and Yudell, 1998) reported on a group of adolescents who had been previously studied during their childhood. Klorman et al. (1990), studying previously untreated ADHD adolescents, found that the clinical effect of MPH treatment in adolescents was of moderate degree and less than the effect found in children. On the other hand, Smith, Pelham, Evans, et al. (1998), studying unselected adolescents, found an average response rate of 75%, which is roughly equivalent to the 70% response rate typically reported in children. Of the two studies that compared childhood MPH response with adolescent MPH response, Pelham et al. (1991) found an unusually low response rate of 50% in both children and adolescents, whereas Smith, Pelham, Gnagy, and Yudell (1998) concluded that the stimulant effect size does not change significantly from childhood to adolescence.

One recently published double-blind crossover study evaluating the efficacy of Adderall (a racemic mixture of amphetamine salts) in ADHD included adolescents up to age 14 (Swanson et al., 1998). Although significant improvements in attention and objective measures of math performance were observed, it is not clear if adolescents responded to the same degree as children.

Outcome measures like rule violations, oppositionality/defiance (Evans and Pelham, 1991), and behavioral noncompliance (Smith, Pelham, Gnagy, and Yudell, 1998) failed to show significant medication effects in adolescents. This raises the possibility that these characteristics are truly less stimulant-responsive in adolescents as compared to children. These characteristics are more likely to be present in subjects comorbid for CD or ODD. Consistent with this hypothesis, adolescent ADHD studies that have excluded ODD and CD (Varley, 1983) have reported a rate of MPH response higher than that reported in other adolescent ADHD studies that have included these diagnoses (Klorman, Coons, and Borgstedt, 1987). However, in a recent study of 84 children with CD (Klein et al., 1997), MPH was superior to placebo in improving CD ratings even after its anti-ADHD effects were discounted. In a similar fashion, a double-blind placebo-controlled study of nine adolescent males comorbid for ADHD and CD found MPH effective in reducing physical aggression (Kaplan et al., 1990). Riggs et al. (1996) reported on an open trial of pemoline in 13 male adolescents who had substance use disorders, CD, and ADHD and who showed significant improvement in mean Conners Hyperactivity Index scores.

In conclusion, although the adolescent response rate to stimulants and predictors of response are far from being conclusively established, it is reasonable not to discontinue prescribing stimulants for ADHD children automatically with the onset of adolescence. Although it is possible that the rate of response decreases in adolescence and that certain symptoms might become less responsive within individual patients, stimulants appear to have a role in many adolescents and in the amelioration of ADHD symptoms. Even in ADHD adolescents with no prior stimulant treatment, there might be as much as a 50% stimulant response rate and a theoretical possibility that a greater proportion will respond over several weeks. Stimulants may also have a role in treatment of CD, aggression, and ADHD with comorbid substance abuse.

Dosing

Early studies on ADHD adolescents (Varley, 1983; Brown and Sexon, 1988) found a linear relationship between MPH dose and therapeutic response on various measures. There was incremental improvement from 0.15 to 0.3 to 0.5 mg/kg per dose. These results do not rule out the possibility of deterioration in cognitive functioning at doses higher than 0.5 mg/kg. Recent studies are consistent with these findings. Smith, Pelham, Evans, et al. (1998) found that the greatest improvement with minimal side effects was achieved at MPH doses of 0.18 to 0.36 mg/kg/day. Most studies dosed MPH at breakfast and at noon; some added a third, smaller dose in the afternoon. The only study evaluating Adderall (Swanson et al., 1998) found doses of 10, 15, and 20 mg to produce significant improvements in attention.

Side Effects and Adverse Effects; Medical Monitoring

The most common side effects of psychostimulants are loss of appetite, insomnia, nervousness, abdominal pain, tachycardia, and weight loss (during prolonged therapy). Efron, Jarman, and Barker (1997) found many of these symptoms to be preexisting ADHD characteristics that actually improved with stimulant treatment. In a placebo-controlled double-blind design, Brown and Sexon (1989) found significant increase in diastolic blood pressure in the MPH group. Careful monitoring of weight, height, heart rate and blood pressure is therefore needed when prescribing stimulants. Paranoia, nightmares, and even frank psychosis have been reported with the use of stimulants and may necessitate reduction in dosage, if not complete withdrawal.

TRICYCLIC ANTIDEPRESSANTS

As of 10 years ago, there was only one open study of a tricyclic antidepressant or TCA (desipramine) in the treatment of adolescent

ADHD (Gastfriend, Biederman, and Jellinek, 1985). Five other studies that included adolescents reported robust response of ADHD to antidepressants, but none specifically mentioned age effects (Spencer et al., 1996).

There has been one double-blind placebo-controlled study of desipramine (Biederman, Baldessarini, Wright, et al., 1989) and one retrospective chart review of nortriptyline (Wilens, Biederman, Geist, et al., 1993) since then. The rate of treatment response in these studies (70% to 90%) is higher than usually reported in ADHD adolescents. Also, the patient sample in both studies had high rates of previously failed medication trials. The double-blind study noted that baseline depression (as assessed by parent) did not predict treatment response; the retrospective study had high rates of comorbid "mood disorder" (60%) and concurrent treatment with other medications including MPH, lithium, and clonidine. The findings of these studies may at best be generalizable to ADHD adolescents who failed previous medication trials.

Dosing

In the Wilens, Biederman, Geist et al. (1993) study, the dose of nortriptyline ranged from 0.4 to 4.5 mg/kg/day. However, there was a high rate of concomitant treatment with other medications in this study. Earlier literature seemed to suggest that lower doses of TCAs were required to treat ADHD compared to depression and that time to response was relatively short (Green, 1995). Both of these beliefs were contradicted by the findings of the Biederman et al. (1989) study, in which the doses were titrated upward to an average daily dose of 4.6 mg/kg/day of desipramine, a relatively high dose. The subjects seemed to require three to four weeks to show significant clinical improvement. An arbitrary maximum dose limit of 5 mg/kg/day was recommended in the wake of reports of sudden death in subjects taking desipramine.

Side Effects and Adverse Effects; Medical Monitoring

There has been at least one reported sudden death in an adolescent (and five deaths in children) taking TCAs (Green, 1995). Five of these deaths occurred in patients taking desipramine. One child who died was taking imipramine. Although the cause of the deaths has not been

186

established, and restrictions on the use of desipramine have been debated, there is agreement that, at the very least, certain precautions need to be taken while prescribing TCAs for adolescents (and children).

When treating an adolescent with TCAs, besides the routine baseline measures (complete blood count with differential, heart rate, and blood pressure), an electrocardiogram (ECG) should be obtained at baseline and with dose increases to monitor changes. The following parameters for monitoring cardiovascular function while on TCAs were suggested by Elliott and Popper (1990/1991):

1. PR interval: less than or equal to 210 milliseconds.
2. QRS interval: widening no more than 30% over the baseline.
3. QTc interval: less than 450 milliseconds.
4. Heart rate: maximum of 130 beats per minute.
5. Systolic blood pressure: maximum of 130 mm Hg.
6. Diastolic blood pressure: maximum of 85 mm Hg.

Monitoring serum levels of TCA is also being recommended. Wilens, Biederman, Baldessarini, et al. (1993) found that combined serum levels of desipramine and 2-OH-desipramine of over 250 ng/ml increased the risk of cardiovascular toxicity.

Side effects reported by adolescents receiving desipramine were trouble sleeping, higher heart rates, and delayed urination (Boulos et al., 1991; Kutcher et al., 1994). In these two studies (113 subjects total), major adverse effects necessitating discontinuation of the medication included an allergic-type maculopapular rash (seven subjects), laryngospasm (two subjects), orthostatic hypertension (four subjects), and gastrointestinal complaints (three subjects).

NON-TCA ANTIDEPRESSANTS

The antidepressant bupropion (Wellbutrin) has been compared with MPH in a randomized crossover trial that included adolescents (Barrickman et al., 1995). Although both medications resulted in statistically and clinically significant improvement over the baseline measures, there was a trend toward greater improvement with MPH compared to bupropion. It is also possible that this difference was a function of a relatively small dose of bupropion used in the study.

Fluoxetine (Prozac) has also been studied for its effectiveness in ADHD, albeit only in an open trial (Barrickman et al., 1991). About 60% of the 19 subjects age seven to 15 showed significant improvement. A recent trial in eight male adolescents with comorbid CD and substance use disorder, who remained or became depressed after one month or more of abstinence from abused substances during residential treatment for the disorder, found benefit with a fixed dose of 20 mg of fluoxetine (Riggs et al., 1997). These findings support the need for further studies comparing bupropion and fluoxetine to placebo or other medications in adolescents with disruptive behavior disorders.

Dosing

The dose of bupropion in the Barrickman et al. (1995) study was 1.5 mg/kg/day in the first week and 2 mg/kg/day in the second week. The final titrated dose was 3.3 ± 1.2 (range, 1.4 to 5.7) mg/kg/day. The first dose was given in the morning, the second dose at four p.m.; a third dose was added, if needed, at noon. The average dose of fluoxetine in the Barrickman et al. (1991) study was 27 mg/day (range, 20 to 60 mg/day).

Side Effects and Adverse Effects; Medical Monitoring

Bupropion is associated with an increased incidence of seizures (0.4%) that may exceed that of other marketed antidepressants by as much as fourfold. Weight loss, excitement, psychosis, and maculopapular lesions have been reported in adults (Barrickman et al., 1995). Exacerbation of tics (Spencer et al., 1993) and skin rashes may be of particular concern in children and adolescents.

ALPHA-2 ADRENERGIC AGONISTS

Clonidine, an alpha-2 adrenergic antihypertensive medication that has been used in the treatment of Tourette's syndrome, has also been studied in the treatment of ADHD. As of 10 years ago, the only controlled study of clonidine in the treatment of ADHD was done in latency-age children. It found clonidine to be a safe and effective medication for at least some children with ADHD (Hunt, Minderaa, and Cohen, 1985).

In the past decade, there has been one retrospective chart review (Steingard et al., 1993) and one double-blind placebo-controlled study (Singer et al., 1995) of clonidine in ADHD that included adolescents. Whereas the retrospective study reported that ADHD symptoms responded to clonidine especially in the presence of tics, the double-blind study found that clonidine did not differ significantly from placebo in reducing either ADHD symptoms or tics. With studies of efficacy of clonidine in ADHD with or without Tourette's syndrome reporting conflicting findings, the use of clonidine in ADHD remains controversial.

Guanfacine (Tenex) is an alpha-2 noradrenergic agonist similar to clonidine. It is said to be longer acting, more receptor-specific, and less sedating than clonidine. Two open studies of guanfacine in ADHD have been published. Hunt, Arnsten, and Asbell (1995) found guanfacine to reduce hyperactive behaviors and enable attentional activity with minimal side effects. Chappell et al. (1995), studying comorbid ADHD and Tourette's syndrome, found significant improvement in attention as well as decrease in the severity of motor and phonic tics.

Pharmacoepidemiologic studies indicate alpha agonists are being prescribed for CD and aggressive symptoms (Stoewe et al., 1995; Connor et al., 1998). An open trial of clonidine in 17 subjects age five to 15 who all had either CD or ODD reported that clonidine decreased aggression (Kemph et al., 1993). Without controlled trials, however, the efficacy of clonidine or guanfacine for this purpose is unknown.

Dosing

The mean optimal dose of clonidine in the Steingard et al. (1993) study was 0.19 ± 0.12 mg/day (range, 0.025 to 0.6 mg/day). Clonidine may be dosed three or four times a day and is usually started at a dose of 0.05 mg once or twice a day and increased by 0.05 mg every three days. In the Hunt et al. (1995) and Chappell et al. (1995) studies, guanfacine was started at 0.5 mg at bedtime and was titrated upward in 0.5-mg increments every three or four days in two to three divided doses.

Side Effects and Adverse Effects; Medical Monitoring

Both clonidine and guanfacine are primarily antihypertensive medications. Hence, monitoring blood pressure and heart rate during follow-up is essential. Children who present with a baseline pulse rate of less than 60 beats per minute should have cardiac consultation and ECG to determine the etiology of bradycardia and to obtain clearance (Cantwell, Swanson, and Connor, 1997). Sedation is the most frequent and troublesome side effect of clonidine. Worsening or induction of depressive symptoms is also reported. The most common side effects of guanfacine reported in the Chappell et al. (1995) study were fatigue, headache, insomnia, and dizziness usually remitting over three to four days. In another report, out of a cohort of 95 youngsters who received guanfacine in an outpatient neuropharmacology clinic during a 12-month span, five subjects with family risk factors for bipolar disorder developed mental excitedness suggestive of hypomanic episode within three days of starting guanfacine (Horrigan and Barnhill, 1998).

ANTIPSYCHOTICS

In reviewing controlled studies evaluating the safety and efficacy of antipsychotics in the treatment of ADHD, Spencer et al. (1996) found no recent reports of such studies in the literature. Earlier studies of antipsychotics in hyperactive children were confounded by diagnostic uncertainty. With increasing awareness of possible chronic tardive dyskinesia, these medications are rarely used to treat uncomplicated ADHD. However, Campbell et al. (1993) pointed out that children and adolescents are given neuroleptics for a wide variety of symptoms and diagnoses frequently differing from those identified in adults; neuroleptics are most often prescribed in adults demonstrating psychotic symptoms, whereas in children there is more variability in the targeted symptoms (aggression, dyscontrol, etc.). Green (1995) stated that antipsychotic drugs are clinically effective in severely aggressive CD in children and adolescents and pointed out that some are approved for such use in children. However, he cautioned that, in ADHD, antipsychotics should be thought of as third-rank drugs—to be used only when the symptoms are severely disabling.

Severe agitation was the indication for the use of droperidol as prn medication in a child inpatient unit (Joshi et al., 1998). Of 410 consecutive admissions included in this study, 26 received droperidol for severe agitation during hospitalization; 17 of these children had ADHD, CD, or ODD. Use of antipsychotics for such indications, however, remains controversial (Masters, 1998).

Studying mentally retarded children with ADHD and/or CD in a double-blind, placebo-controlled crossover study of thioridazine and methylphenidate, Aman, Marks, Turbott, et al. (1991) reported that, at the doses employed, thioridazine had relatively minor effects, although it was superior to placebo on conduct problems, hyperactivity, and overall improvement as rated by teachers.

There have been recent case reports of risperidone's usefulness in older children and adolescents with hyperactivity and aggression (and possible comorbid mood disorders) who failed other medication trials (Fras and Major, 1995; Schreier, 1998).

Dosing

Doses of droperidol used in the Joshi et al. (1998) report were < 75 lb = 1/4 cc; 75 to 125 lb = 1/2 cc; 125 to 150 lb = 3/4 cc; > 150 lb = 1 cc (1 cc = 2.5 mg). Very large adolescents received larger doses but never more than 2 cc. Doses were repeated after 30 minutes if not effective, but no more than four doses were administered in a 24-hour period. The dose of thioridazine in the Aman et al. (1991) study was 1.75 mg/kg/day. The dose of risperidone for a 16-year-old in the Schreier (1998) paper was initially 1 mg twice a day increased to a maximum of 6 mg/day.

Side Effects and Adverse Effects; Medical Monitoring

In the Joshi et al. (1998) report, two out of the 26 patients developed "mild extrapyramidal symptoms." None had severe dystonic reaction, orthostatic hypotension, or oculogyric crisis. In the Aman et al. (1991) study, thioridazine had no effect on cognitive motor performance and no deleterious effect on IQ performance when the subject's correct answer was reinforced. In the Schreier (1998) report, sedation, weight gain, and maybe anxiety appeared to be troublesome side effects of risperidone. Neuroleptic malignant syndrome is a potentially fatal adverse event that has also been reported in the pediatric age group (Latz and McCracken, 1992; Steingard et al., 1992). Rigidity, hyperthermia, and fluctuating vital signs are seen. When this adverse event is suspected, antipsychotic medication should be stopped and the need for hospitalization evaluated.

191

LITHIUM

A decade ago, the limited data available on lithium in conduct disorders supported the idea that aggression in adolescents could be diminished by lithium treatment, although case reports of aggression worsening with lithium treatment also existed (see Kruesi and Lelio, 1996, for review). Lithium was found to be significantly better than placebo for reducing explosive aggression in 50 CD children age five to 12. Recent reports that include adolescents have added to the mixed picture of some benefit in some teens.

In one study, 80 CD outpatients age six to 15 were assigned to a double-blind trial of lithium, MPH, and placebo (Abikoff and Klein, 1992). MPH produced improvement over placebo, but lithium did not. Another study (Rifkin et al., 1997), of 33 CD inpatients age 12 to 17 who received lithium or placebo double-blind for two weeks, reported that, on several measures of clinical change (Overt Aggression Scale, Behavior Rating Scale, Conners Teacher Rating Scale, Hamilton Rating Scale for Depression), the groups showed no significant differences. Of the patients who completed the study, 8.3% of those receiving placebo (one of 12) versus 21.4% of those receiving lithium (three of 14) were considered responders.

An ongoing study of lithium versus placebo for children and adolescents hospitalized with aggressive CD suggests that it might be unwise to dismiss lithium as a treatment for aggression, as there is much to be clarified about which CD cases are likely to benefit from treatment (Malone et al., 1998). In this report of 28 aggressive-CD subjects age nine to 17 years participating in a double-blind placebo-controlled trial of lithium, classification as affective (explosive) subtype as opposed to predatory (planned) subtype predicted response, irrespective of whether it was drug or placebo response.

Dosing

Malone et al. (1995) applied the lithium test-dose paradigm to the treatment of CD. Sixteen CD patients age eight to 17 had a lithium level drawn 24 hours after a 600-mg loading dose of lithium. Then, using the nomogram of Cooper et al., dose was predicted. Dose predicted ranged from 600 to 1,800 mg per day, and the corresponding steady-state lithium levels were 0.58 to 1.13 mEq/L. However, there are caveats. Malone et al. noted that this technique requires that lithium results be reported with two-decimal-place accuracy and cautioned that many clinical laboratories do not require such accuracy and do not always provide it. Duration of dosing and optimal serum level are considerations that are not completely addressed. Trials with efficacy from lithium appear to run higher serum levels than those that do not. For example, Campbell et al. (1995) noted positive efficacy with a mean serum level of 1.12 mEq/L, whereas the Rifkin et al. (1997) negative trial had a mean serum of 0.79 mEq/L. This impression is confounded by the difference in age range and duration of the two trials. Nonetheless, if the benefit of higher lithium level replicates in adolescents, it would go against the conventional wisdom that a trial with serum levels anywhere between 0.6 and 1.2 mEq/L is adequate.

Side Effects and Adverse Effects; Medical Monitoring

Potential side effects of lithium administration have been described in several studies. Most of these untoward effects diminish or disappear within the first two weeks of administration. Fine tremor, polydipsia, polyuria, nausea, malaise, diarrhea, headache, sedation, weight gain, anorexia, exacerbation of acne, hypothyroidism, hair loss, and leukocytosis are some of the side effects associated with lithium usage. Tremor, nausea, and vomiting were the most common side effects in the study of Malone et al. (1995).

ANTICONVULSANTS

Adolescent patients with CD, ODD, or disruptive behavior are receiving anticonvulsants, most often valproic acid or carbamazepine (Stoewe et al., 1995; Donovan et al., 1997; Deltito et al., 1998). Among early controlled trials in pediatric populations, improvement was demonstrated in some studies (Groh, 1976; Puente, 1976) but not others (Conners et al., 1971). In a study (Mattes, 1990) that compared propranolol and carbamazepine, the diagnosis of intermittent explosive disorder appeared to elicit the most positive response with carbamazepine. There was a suggestion that an explosive or affective quality to the aggression predicted response to anticonvulsants.

193

More recent studies using anticonvulsants offer encouragement about the use of valproate and discouraging results regarding the use of carbamazepine. An open trial of valproic acid in 10 CD and ODD adolescents with chronic temper outbursts and mood lability found that all subjects showed clear improvement at five weeks and maintained it during follow-up while taking medication (Donovan et al., 1997). In a methodologically superior study, Steiner (1998) recently completed a study of high-dose (1,000 mg) versus low-dose (125 mg) valproate in 61 adolescent males in a juvenile justice facility, all of whom met criteria for CD and more than half of whom were comorbid for ADHD. The study is remarkable in that controlled psychopharmacological trials in this population are quite rare. Valproate at the high-dose condition resulted in improvement in aggression, hyperarousal, and anger, particularly in the presence of internalizing symptoms like PTSD.

A recent study of carbamazepine in prepubescent children found carbamazepine was not superior to placebo at serum levels of 4.98 to 9.1 mcg/mL (Cueva et al., 1996).

Dosing

For valproate, a dose of 1,000 mg/day was found to be effective in the two studies mentioned earlier (Donovan et al., 1997; Steiner, 1998). In another open trial that included one case each of CD and ODD, a dose of 700 to 900 mg/day resulted in improvement in aggression, anxiety, and mood (Deltito et al., 1998). There was some suggestion that valproate levels of more than 50 mcg/mL were associated with better response (Steiner, 1998).

Side Effects and Adverse Effects; Medical Monitoring

The dose used in these studies were generally well tolerated. Mild sedation, transient nausea, hair loss, and gastrointestinal upset were reported by a few patients (Donovan et al., 1997; Deltito et al., 1998). Monitoring serum valproic acid level, liver function tests, and complete blood counts are recommended one week after each dose increase and at regular six-month intervals.

Weight gain has been reported in adolescent girls receiving valproate (Garland and Behr, 1996). Isojarvi et al. (1993) reported that 80% of the women who received valproate for treatment of epilepsy before age 20 developed polycystic ovaries or hyperandrogenism. However, epilepsy itself has been associated with reproductive/endocrine disorders (Bilo et al., 1988), thereby raising the possibility that the abnormalities reported in the Isojarvi et al. (1993) study were the result of neurotransmitter changes in epilepsy and not of valproate treatment. As the hormonal effects of valproic acid have not yet been studied among adolescent girls receiving valproate for nonseizure disorders, potential reproductive problems should be included in discussion of medication choices with families (Geller, 1998).

BETA-ADRENERGIC ANTAGONISTS

Although beta-blockers were first reportedly used for disruptive behavior in adults in the 1970s, as of 1993 there appear to be fewer than 30 cases of adolescents treated with beta-blockers in the literature (Connor, 1993). Moreover, many of the reports involve concomitant administration of other drugs. Therefore, the role of beta-blockers in treatment of CD, ODD, or ADHD remains a matter of speculation. However, a recent study of placebo versus beta-blocker (pindolol) augmentation of selective serotonin reuptake inhibitors (SSRIs) in adults with depression found that those who were more reward-dependent, less harm-avoidant, and more novelty-seeking were more likely to benefit from the combination (Tome et al., 1997). As these are personality characteristics often associated with CD, one wonders if the combination of SSRIs and beta-blockers may be useful in the treatment of CD or CD comorbid with depression.

Dose

The dose range of propranolol reported in the review by Connor (1993) was 20 to 300 mg/day for adolescents. For pindolol, Tome et al. (1997) used a dose of 2.5 mg three times a day in adults.

Side Effects and Adverse Effects; Medical Monitoring

Most of the beta-blockers (propranolol, pindolol, nadolol, metoprolol) are nonselective and may demonstrate a combination of both beta-

1 and beta-2 receptor side effects. The most common side effects of this class are decreased blood pressure, decreased heart rate, dizziness, nausea/vomiting, weakness, and fatigue. Less commonly reported side effects are mental depression, male impotence, bronchoconstriction, Raynaud's phenomenon, diarrhea, insomnia, and hypoglycemia (due to alteration in carbohydrate metabolism and masking of symptoms associated with low serum glucose).

PLACEBO

Although placebo is not frequently clinically prescribed for CD, placebo does provide a very useful referent for understanding the pharmacological responsiveness of CD. Forty-four (37 male, seven female) CD youth age 9.83 to 17.14 years who were hospitalized for chronic and severe aggression received a two-week single-blind placebo lead-in period as part of a lithium-versus-placebo comparison (Malone et al., 1997). During the two-week placebo baseline period, aggression was measured on a 24-hour basis using the Overt Aggression Scale. Twenty-one subjects did not meet criteria for randomization (baseline responders). Thus, almost half of the subjects, while taking no active medication, benefited from the inpatient milieu/structure and/or placebo. This finding has important treatment and research implications. If medication to treat aggression is initiated immediately upon hospitalization, improvements associated with hospitalization may be attributed inaccurately to pharmacotherapy, resulting in unnecessarily medicating children. In a decade in which managed care reviewers urge rapid initiation of medication, there may be significant use of medication that is unnecessary and potentially harmful.

Approach to Pharmacotherapy

Success of pharmacotherapy in an adolescent and continuation in treatment depends on establishing a treatment contract that includes the adolescent. Most adolescents are brought into treatment by their parents or other caregivers. Expectations of these caregivers need to be addressed in treatment. Involving the parent/caregiver in the treatment requires addressing the behaviors of concern that initially prompted

196

the psychiatric consultation. The Conners Teachers Rating Scale and the Conners Parents Rating Scale are the most commonly used measures for inattention and hyperactivity. Adolescents are frequently able to enter into a contract to reduce problems with anger and with concentrating on academic tasks and to improve relations with parents. Self-report measures such as the Conners–Wells Self Report Scale can be useful in engaging the adolescent in pharmacotherapy.

One emerging trend in symptom assessment is a more sophisticated appreciation of aggression and its measurement (Vitiello et al., 1990; Kruesi et al., 1994). Sources of difficulty include definition of aggression and of the subtypes (e.g., reactive [affective, impulsive] vs. proactive or predatory); choices between frequency and severity ratings; low frequencies of certain types of aggressive acts, particularly severe physical aggression; weighting of different specific behaviors; information source; lack of empirical validation for many measures of aggression; and ethical concerns. Although differing terms are used, there is beginning to be a consensus that subtype distinctions regarding aggression are important for thinking about the future of pharmacological treatment.

Operationalizing the definition of aggression—or determining the target behaviors of aggression to be measured in a medication trial—is important and often needs to be case-specific. However, preexistent rating scales can be employed and/or modified to fit a particular case. One useful instrument is the Modified Overt Aggression Scale (Kay, Wolkenfield, and Murrill, 1988), a severity-oriented instrument with four subscales: Verbal Aggression, Aggression Against Property, Autoaggression (self-mutilation and suicide attempts), and Physical Aggression Directed Toward Others. Differentiating between types of aggression can be pertinent in medication trials. The Predatory (planned)–Affective (explosive) index of Vitiello et al. (1990) has been shown to differentiate treatment responders from nonresponders, regardless of agent used. Treatment response was associated with a more affective and less predatory subtype of aggression (Malone et al., 1998).

Determining the base frequency of the aggressive behavior(s) is an often neglected but very informative part of the treatment process. It is not uncommon to see a patient whose consultation has been precipitated by a particularly severe aggressive outburst that caused physical injury. Yet, if the severe episodes occur only every three to four months, then trials of sufficient duration to examine the effect of medication

197

will be quite long. Often, however, if the day-to-day, more minor outbursts are not ameliorated, then a trial will be abandoned far earlier. As Gardner and Cowdry's (1986) trial showed, a medication such as carbamazepine may reduce the severe episodes but not touch the more frequent but less severe aggressive behavior.

In the case of adolescent ADHD with no comorbidities other than ODD or CD, psychostimulants are the first choice. MPH is the only stimulant that has been studied exclusively in adolescents. If MPH is found to be too short-acting or if rebound symptoms are a problem despite multiple dosing, amphetamine preparations (e.g., Adderall) may be tried, as they have a longer half-life and typically have longer lasting clinical effects. Emergence of tics after initiation of therapy with stimulants, or worsening of preexisting tics, may be managed either by reducing the dose or by substituting TCAs. In a recent study comparing clonidine and desipramine versus placebo in children with comorbid ADHD and tic disorder, desipramine was found to be superior to clonidine and placebo in reduction of ADHD symptoms as well as tic symptoms (Singer et al., 1995). Up to 50% of adolescents may show less than moderate response even after maximizing stimulant dosage. Second-line medications include TCAs, bupropion (Wellbutrin), and alpha agonists (clonidine and guanfacine). The evidence for TCAs is probably the most compelling at this time. However, if reliable storage and administration of medications are in question or if there are concerns of suicidality, one of the other agents should be chosen. Bupropion may be tried if there are no risk factors for the development of seizures or tics; guanfacine may be tried if there is family history or previous occurrence of tics.

When CD or ODD is the primary diagnosis, the decision to use medication may depend on the presence and type of aggression as well as comorbidities (Kruesi and Lelio, 1996). In addition to nonpharmacological interventions (Dulcan, 1997), the use of medications should be discussed with the adolescent and the parent.

1. If there are comorbid diagnoses for which pharmacological treatment is beneficial, such comorbidities should be treated (e.g., MPH for ADHD; mood stabilizers for bipolar disorder).
2. Immediate dangerousness may require neuroleptic medications.
3. For explosive or affective aggression, lithium or valproate may be tried.

4. For PTSD-like symptoms, valproate, alpha agonist, or beta-blocker may be tried.

5. If initial trials are unsuccessful or if none of the above conditions is fulfilled, empirical trials of mood stabilizers, alpha agonists, beta-blockers, or neuroleptics may be tried after discussion with the patient and parent.

COMBINATION TREATMENT

Combination treatment is an emerging trend in pediatric psychophar-macology (Wilens et al., 1995). In a study of combined pharmacother-apy (CPT) with two or more psychotropic medications in residential treatment centers, Connor et al. (1997) reported that 60% of the children and adolescents in these facilities had a history of CPT. Aggression was found to be significantly associated with CPT. In a study of prescribing practices of outpatient child psychiatrists, Kaplan, Simms, and Busner (1994) found that 11% of the medicated sample in New York and 22% of the medicated sample in Ohio received more than one psychopharma-cological agent. There are few trials of CPT in child psychiatric disorders (Carlson et al., 1995) and none specifically in adolescents. In a retrospective chart review discussed earlier, Wilens, Biederman, Geist, et al. (1993) reported the use of CPT in adolescents and children with ADHD and other comorbid disorders.

The question of adding another medication to the first arises when (a) there is partial response to a single agent and potential for additive or synergistic effects; (b) use of another agent may lower the dose and hence the side effects of the first; (c) two separately conceptualized symptom clusters with different purported medication responses coexist; and (d) treatment of adverse effects of the first medication is required (Wilens et al., 1995).

After optimizing the dose of stimulants to adequately control ADHD symptoms, there is a widespread practice of adding a single bedtime dose of clonidine if sleep problems persist. The initial scare after the 1995 broadcast report of sudden deaths in three children taking a combination of MPH and clonidine diminished (Popper, 1995). However, there have been renewed concerns after recent case reports of cardiovascular problems in children taking the combination (Cantwell et al., 1997). The combination remains controversial despite estimated wide use (Johnston, Witkovsky, and Fruehling, 1995).

199

RECOMMENDED DURATION OF TREATMENT

This is an unsettled question. It is reasonable to note that the first pediatric long-term pharmacological trial of stimulants was published only in 1997 (Gillberg et al., 1997) despite the fact that stimulants have been in use for youth for 50 years and have had FDA approval for pediatric usage. In the authors' experience, consumers are apt to vote with their feet (i.e., cease taking medication) when medications are not effective or if side effects are problematic. However, patient discontinuation/noncompliance in spite of overall benefit does occur. A recent psychopharmacoepidemiologic study sheds some disquieting light on the question of treatment duration and effectiveness. In a study of outpatient prescriptions at community mental health centers for youth, fewer than 25% of the youth prescribed antidepressants, antimanics, or neuroleptics as inpatients continued taking them for six months or more while outpatients (Safer, 1997). In contrast, 59% of youth prescribed stimulants were still receiving them six months later. Unfortunately, the possible confound of greater likelihood of stimulant prescription for prepubertal youth as opposed to adolescents cannot be ruled out.

Research/Issues for the Next 10 Years

Given the dramatic increases in prescriptions, a great deal of research is needed to address psychopharmacological use in adolescents (Olfson et al., 1998). Conditions like CD, which have the great burdens of societal cost and family suffering (Kruesi and Astrachan, 1995), need to be prioritized in pharmacotherapeutic investigations. There is an array of issues that warrant research:

1.   Dose response and dosage duration in adolescents need to be worked out—even for commonly used drugs (e.g., Klorman et al., 1990, argued for longer follow-up in order to more clearly delineate stimulant effectiveness) or for lithium (i.e., if an adolescent does not respond adequately to a lower dose/serum level [e.g., the "usual" range, 0.6 to 1.2 mEq/L], how long does one persist, and how high a serum level should be tried?).

2. Comorbidity with ADHD, CD, or ODD appears to be the rule rather than the exception in clinical populations; thus, we need to examine comorbid cases in order to arrive at relevant pharmacological knowledge. For example, the trial by Steiner (1998) of valproate in CD identified PTSD comorbidity as a relevant predictor of medication response. There are almost no data on pharmacological treatment of PTSD in adolescents, yet it appears to be a frequent occurrence within foster care populations (Stoewe and Kruesi, 1997). Clearly, this is a comorbidity of relevance to juvenile justice and foster care populations.

3. More research is needed into the efficacy, effectiveness, safety, dosing, and adverse effects of newer agents that are beginning to see significant clinical use (e.g., guanfacine, bupropion, risperidone, olanzapine). Safety issues and adverse events, such as the report of hypomanic switch with guanfacine and the risk factors for this adverse effect, warrant scrutiny.

4. The reported rate of response of adolescent ADHD to TCAs in the currently available studies is higher than what is usual with stimulants. The study was small, but the results were all the more surprising considering that the cases studied had previously failed other medication trials and were likely more severe cases. Replication of these findings and the factors that might play a role in TCA response need to be clarified.

5. Medication trials continue to be done predominantly on boys. Studies including sufficiently large numbers of girls are necessary to draw conclusions about efficacy and side effects specific to adolescent females.

6. Systematic studies of combination treatment is yet another area in which not much has been done. CPT or the use of multiple medications has been increasingly discussed in the pediatric psychopharmacological literature (Wilens et al., 1995). However, the practice remains poorly studied (Connor et al., 1998).

How are these six issues to be addressed? Besides traditional efficacy studies, other methods like pharmacoepidemiology need to be exploited as well. Pharmacoepidemiologic data are particularly important in children and adolescents, and they are needed immediately for public health reasons (Vitiello and Hoagwood, 1997). There is agreement that more studies of pediatric psychopharmacological prescribing practices are desperately needed in the face of increased prescription of medications that are not specifically labeled for pediatric use and the efficacy and safety of which in youth are at best underdocumented, if not unknown (Jensen et al., 1994; Gadow, 1997; Kaplan, 1997; Safer, 1997; Vitiello and Hoagwood, 1997; Connor et al., 1998).

REFERENCES

Abikoff, H. & Klein, R. G. (1992), Attention-deficit hyperactivity and conduct disorder: Comorbidity and implications for treatment. *J. Consulting and Clin. Psychol.*, 60:881–892.

Aman, M. G., Marks, R. E., Turbott, S. H., et al. (1991), Methylphenidate and thioridazine in the treatment of intellectually subaverage children. *J. Am. Acad. Child Adolesc. Psychiat.*, 30:816-824.

American Psychiatric Association (1994), *Diagnostic and Statistical Manual of Mental Disorders* (4th ed.). Washington, DC: APA.

Bagley, C., Bolitho, F. & Bertrand, L. (1995), Mental health profiles, suicidal behavior, and community sexual assault in 212 Canadian adolescents. *Crisis*, 16:126–131.

Barkley, R. A., Anastopoulos, A. D., Guevremont, D. C. & Fletcher, K. E. (1991), Adolescents with ADHD: Patterns of behavioral adjustment, academic functioning and treatment utilization. *J. Amer. Acad. Child Adolesc. Psychiat.*, 30:752–761.

——— Fischer, M., Edelbrock, C. S. & Smallish, L. (1990), The adolescent outcome of hyperactive children diagnosed by research criteria: I. An 8-year follow-up study. *J. Amer. Acad. Child Adolesc. Psychiat.*, 29:546–557.

——— Murphy, K. R. & Kwasnik, D. (1996), Motor vehicle driving competencies and risks in teens and young adults with attention deficit hyperactivity disorder. *Pediatrics*, 98(6 Pt 1):1089–1095.

Barrickman, L., Noyes, R., Kuperman, S., Schumacher, E. & Verda, M. (1991), Treatment of ADHD with fluoxetine: A preliminary trial. *J. Amer. Acad. Child Adolesc. Psychiat.*, 30:762–767.

——— L. L., Perry, P. J., Allen, A. J., Kuperman, S., Arndt, S. V., Herrmann, K. J. & Schumacher, E. (1995), Bupropion versus Methylphenidate in the treatment of attention deficit hyperactivity disorder. *J. Amer. Acad. Child Adolesc. Psychiat.*, 34:649–657.

Biederman, J., Baldessarini, R., Wright, V., Knee, D. & Harmatz, J. (1989), A double-blind placebo-controlled study of desipramine in the treatment of attention deficit disorder: I. Efficacy. *J. Amer. Acad. Child Adolesc. Psychiat.*, 28:777–784.

————— Faraone, S., Mick, E., et al. (1996), Attention deficit hyperactivity disorder and juvenile mania: An overlooked comorbidity? *J. Amer. Acad. Child Adolesc. Psychiat.,* 35:997–1008.

————— Faraone, S. V., Taylor, A., Sienna, M., Williamdon, S. & Fine, C. (1998), Diagnostic continuity between child and adolescent ADHD: Findings from a longitudinal clinical sample. *J. Amer. Acad. Child Adolesc. Psychiat.,* 37:305–313.

————— Newcorn, J. & Sprich, S. (1991), Comorbidity of attention deficit hyperactivity disorder with conduct, depressive, anxiety, and other disorders. *Amer. J. Psychiat.,* 148:564–577.

————— Wilens, T., Mick, E., Faraone, S. V., Weber, W., Curtis, S., Thornell, A., Pfister, K., Jetton, J. G. & Soriano, J. (1997), Is ADHD a risk factor for psychoactive substance use disorders? Findings from a four-year prospective follow-up study. *J. Amer. Acad. Child Adolesc. Psychiat.,* 36:21–29.

Bilo, L., Melo, R., Nappi, C., et al. (1988), Reproductive endocrine disorders in women with primary generalized epilepsy. *Epilepsia,* 29:612–613.

Bird, H. R., Canino, G., Rubio-Stipec, M., Gould, M. S., Ribera, J., Sesman, M., Woodbury, M., Huertas-Goldman, S., Pagan, A., Sanchez-Lacay, A. & Moscoso, M. (1988), Estimates of the prevalence of childhood maladjustment in a community survey in Puerto Rico: The use of combined measures. *Arch. Gen. Psychiat.,* 45:1120–1126.

Boulos, C., Kutcher, S., Marton, P., et al. (1991), Response to desipramine treatment in adolescent major depression. *Psychopharmacol. Bull.,* 27:59–65.

Boyle, M. H., Offord, D. R., Racine, Y., Szatmari, P., Fleming, J. E. & Sanford, M. (1996), Identifying thresholds for classifying childhood psychiatric disorder: Issues and prospects. *J. Amer. Acad. Child Adolesc. Psychiat.,* 35:1440–1448.

Brown, R. T. & Sexon, S. B. (1988), A controlled trial of methylphenidate in black adolescents. *Clin. Pediatrics,* 27(2):74–81.

————— & —————. (1989), Effects of methylphenidate on cardiovascular responses in attention deficit hyperactivity disordered adolescents. *J. Adolesc. Health Care,* 10:179–183.

Campbell, M., Adams, P. B., Small, A. M., et al. (1995), Lithium in hospitalized aggressive children with conduct disorder: A double blind and placebo controlled study. *J. Amer. Acad. Child Adolesc. Psychiat.,* 34:445–453.

———— Gonzalez, N., Ernst, M., Silva, R. & Werry, J. (1993), Antipsychotics (neuroleptics). In: *Practitioners Guide to Psychoactive Drugs for Children and Adolescents*, ed. J. Werry and M. Aman. New York, Plenum Press, pp. 269–296.

Cantwell, D. P., Swanson, J. & Connor, D. F. (1997), Case study: Adverse response to clonidine. *J. Amer. Acad. Child Adolesc. Psychiat.*, 36:539–544.

Carlson, G. A., Rapaport, M. D., Kelly, K. L. & Pataki, C. S. (1995), Methylphenidate and desipramine in hospitalized children with comorbid behavior and mood disorder. *J. Child Adolesc. Psychopharmacol.*, 5:191–204.

Chappell, P. B., Riddle, M. A., Scahill, L., Lynch, K. A., Schultz, E., Arnsten, A., Leckman, J. F. & Cohen, D. J. (1995), Guanfacine treatment of comorbid attention deficit hyperactivity disorder and Tourette's Syndrome: Preliminary clinical experience. *J. Amer. Acad. Child Adolesc. Psychiat.*, 34:1140–1146.

Cohen, P., Cohen, J. & Kasen, S. (1993), An epidemiological study of disorders in late childhood and adolescence, I: Age- and gender-specific prevalence. *J. Child Psychol. Psychiat.*, 34:851–867.

Comings, D. E. & Comings, B. G. (1987), A controlled study of Tourette's Syndrome, I: Attention deficit disorder, learning disorder and school problems. *Am. J. Hum. Genet.*, 41:701–741.

Conners, C. K., Kramer, R., Rothschild, G. H., et al. (1971), Treatment of young delinquent boys with diphenylhydantoin sodium and methylphenidate. *Arch. Gen. Psychiat.*, 24:156–160.

Connor, D. (1993), Beta-blockers for aggression: A review of the pediatric experience. *J. Child Adolesc. Psychopharmacol.*, 3:99–114.

Connor, D. F., Ozbayrak, K. R., Harrison, R. J. & Melloni, R. H. (1998), Prevalence and patterns of psychotropic and anticonvulsant medication use in children and adolescents referred to residential treatment. *J. Child Adolesc. Psychopharmacol.*, 8:27–38.

———— ———— Kusiak, K. A., et al. (1997), Combined pharmacotherapy in children and adolescents in a residential treatment center. *J. Amer. Acad. Child Adolesc. Psychiat.*, 36:248–254.

Cueva, J. E., Overall, J. E., Small, A. M., Armenteros, J. L., Perry, R. & Campbell, M. (1996), Carbamazepine in aggressive children with conduct disorder: A double-blind and placebo-controlled study. *J. Amer. Acad. Child Adolesc. Psychiat.*, 35:480–490.

Deltito, J. A., Levitan, J., Damore, J., Hajal, F. & Zambenedetti, M. (1998), Naturalistic experience with the use of divalproex sodium on an in-patient unit for adolescent psychiatric patients. *Acta. Pschiatr. Scand.*, 97:236–240.

Donovan, S. J., Susser, E. S., Nunes, E. V., Stewart, J. W., Quitkin, F. M. & Klein, D. F. (1997), Divalproex treatment of disruptive adolescents: A report of 10 cases. *J. Clin. Psychiat.*, 58:12–5.

Dulcan, M. (1997), Practice parameters for the assessment and treatment of children, adolescents, and adults with attention-deficit hyperactivity disorder. *J. Amer. Acad. Child Adolesc. Psychiat.*, 36(10 suppl):85S–121S.

Efron, D., Jarman, F. & Barker, M. (1997), Side effects of methylphenidate and dextroamphetamine in children with attention deficit hyperactivity disorder: A double-blind, crossover trial. *Pediatrics*, 100:662–666.

Elliott, G. R. & Popper, C. W. (1990/1991), Tricyclic antidepressants: The QT interval and other cardiovascular parameters [editorial]. *J. Child Adolesc. Psychopharmacol.*, 1:187–189.

Evans, S. E. & Pelham, W. E. (1991), Psychostimulant effects on academic and behavioral measures for ADHD junior high school students in a lecture format classroom. *J. Abnormal Child Psychology*, 19:537–552.

Fras, I. & Major, L. F. (1995), Clinical experience with risperidone [letter]. *J. Amer. Acad. Child Adolesc. Psychiat.*, 34:833.

Gadow, K. D. (1997), An overview of three decades of research in pediatric pharmacoepidemiology. *J. Child Adolesc. Psychopharmacol.*, 7:219–236.

Gardner, D. L. & Cowdry, R. W. (1986), Positive effects of carbamazepine on behavioral dyscontrol in borderline personality disorder, *Am. J. Psychiat.*, 143(4):519–522.

Garland, E. J. & Behr, R. (1996), Hormonal effects of valproic acid? *J. Amer. Acad. Child Adolesc. Psychiat.*, 35:1424–1425.

Gastfriend, D. R., Biederman, J. & Jellinek, M. S. (1985), Desipramine in the treatment of attention deficit disorder in adolescents. *Psychopharmacol. Bull.*, 21:144–145.

Geller, B. (1998), Valproate and polycystic ovaries: Dr. Geller replies. *J. Amer. Acad. Child Adolesc. Psychiat.*, 37:9–10.

Gillberg, C., Melander, H., von Knorrring, A., et al. (1997), Long-term stimulant treatment of children with attention-deficit hyperactivity disorder symptoms. *Arch. Gen. Psychiat.*, 54:857–864.

Green, W. H. (1995), *Child and Adolescent Clinical Psychopharmacology. 2nd Edition*, Baltimore: Williams & Wilkins.

Groh, C. (1976), The Psychotropic effect of tegretol in non-epileptic children, with particular reference to the drug's indications. In: *Epileptic Seizures-Behavior-Pain*, ed. B. W. Bern, H. Huber, pp. 259–263.

Hendren, R. L., Hodde-Vargas, J. E., Vargas, L. A., Orrison, W. W. & Dell, L. (1991), Magnetic resonance imaging of severely disturbed children—a preliminary study. *J. Amer. Acad. Child Adolesc. Psychiat.*, 30:466–470.

Hill, J. C. & Schoener, E. P. (1996), Age-dependent decline of attention deficit hyperactivity disorder. *Amer. J. of Psychiat.*, 153:1143–1146.

Horrigan, J. P. & Barnhill, L. J. (1998), Does guanfacine trigger mania in children? *J. Child and Adolesc. Psychopharmacol.*, 8:149–150.

Hunt, R. D., Arnsten, A. F. & Asbell, M. D. (1995), An open trial of guanfacine in the treatment of attention deficit hyperactivity disorder. *J. Amer. Acad. Child. Adolesc. Psychiatry,* 34:50–54.

———— Minderaa, R. B. & Cohen, D. J. (1985), Clonidine benefits children with attention deficit disorder and hyperactivity: Report of a double-blind placebo crossover therapeutic trial. *J. Amer. Acad. Child Psychiat.,* 24:617–629.

Isojarvi, J. I. T., Laatikainen, T. J., Pakarinen, A. J., et al. (1993), Polycystic ovaries and hyperandrogenism in women taking valproate for epilepsy. *N. Engl. J. Med.*, 329:1383–1388.

Jensen, P. S., Vitiello, B., Leonard, H. & Laughren, T. P. (1994), Design and methodology issues for clinical treatment trials in children and adolescents. Child and adolescent psychopharmacology: Expanding the research base. *Psychopharmacol. Bull.*, 30(1):3–8.

Johnston, H. F., Witkovsky, M. T. & Fruehling, J. (1995), The clonidine scare. *Just the Facts,* 2(3). (University of Wisconsin Child Psychopharmacology Information Service.)

Joshi, P. T., Hamel, L., Joshi, A. R. T. & Capozzoli, J. A. (1998), Use of droperidol in hospitalized children. *J. Amer. Acad. Child Adolesc. Psychiat.,* 37:228–230.

Kaplan, S. L. (1997), Pediatric psychopharmacoepidemiology: An introduction. *J. Child Adolesc. Psychopharmacol.*, 7:215–218.

———— & Busner, J. (1997), Prescribing practices of inpatient child psychiatrists under three auspices of care. *J. Child Adolesc. Psychopharmacol.*, 7:275–286.

———— ———— Kupeitz, S., et al. (1990), Effects of methylphenidate on adolescents with aggressive conduct disorder and ADDH: A preliminary report. *J. Amer. Acad. Child Adolesc. Psychiat.*, 29:274–281.

———— Simms, R. M. & Busner, J. (1994), Prescribing practices of outpatient child psychiatrists. *J. Amer. Acad. Child Adolesc. Psychiat.*, 33:35–44.

Kay, S. R., Wolkenfield, F. & Murrill, L. M. (1988), Profiles of aggression among psychiatric patients I. Nature and Prevalence. *J. Nervous and Mental Disease,* 176:539–546.

Kemph, J. P., DeVane, C. L., Levin, G. M., et al. (1993), Treatment of aggressive children with clonidine: Results of an open pilot study. *J. Amer. Acad. Child Adolesc. Psychiat.*, 32:577–581.

Klein, R. G., Abikoff, H., Klass, E., et al. (1997), Clinical efficacy of methylphenidate in conduct disorder with or without attention deficit hyperactivity disorder. *Arch. Gen. Psychiat.*, 54:1073–1080.

Klorman, R., Brumaghim, J. T., Fitzpatrick, P. A. & Borgstedt, A. D. (1990), Clinical effects of a controlled trial of methylphenidate on adolescents with attention deficit disorder. *J. Amer. Acad. Child Adolesc. Psychiat.*, 29:702–709.

———— Coons, H. W. & Borgstedt, A. D. (1987), Effects of methylphenidate on adolescents with childhood history of attention deficit disorder, I: Clinical findings. *J. Amer. Acad. Child Adolesc. Psychiat.*, 26:363–367.

Kruesi, M. J. P. & Astrachan, B. M. (1995), Comments on the report card from a services research perspective. *Arch. Gen. Psychiat.*, 52:727–728.

———— Hibbs, E. D., Hamburger, S. D., Rapoport, J. L., Keysor, C. S. & Elia, J. (1994), Measurement of aggression in children with disruptive behavior disorders. *J. Offender Rehabilitation*, 21: 159–172.

———— & Lelio, D. F. (1996), Disorders of Conduct and Behavior. In: *Diagnosis and Psychopharmacology of Childhood and Adolescent Disorders, Second Edition,* ed. J. Weiner. New York: Wiley, pp. 401–447.

Kutcher, S., Boulos, C., Ward, B., et al. (1994), Response to desipramine treatment of adolescent depression: A fixed dose, placebo-controlled trial. *J. Amer. Acad. Child Adolesc. Psychiat.*, 33:686–694.

Latz, J. R. & McCracken, J. T. (1992), Neuroleptic malignant syndrome in children and adolescents: Two case reports and a warning. *J. Child Adolesc. Psychopharmacol.*, 2:123–129.

Malone, R. P., Bennett, D. S., Luebbert, J. F., et al. (1998), Aggression classification and treatment response, *Psychopharmacol. Bull.,* 34(1):41–45.

———— Delaney, M. A., Luebbert, J. F., et al. (1995), The lithium test dose prediction method in aggressive children. *Psychopharmacol. Bull.,* 31:379–382.

———— Luebbert, J. F., Delaney, M. A., et al. (1997), Nonpharmacological response in hospitalized children with conduct disorder. *J. Amer. Acad. Child Adolesc. Psychiat.,* 36:242–247.

Masters, K. (1998), Droperidol in hospitalized children (letter). *J. Amer. Acad. Child Adolesc. Psychiat.,* 37(8).

Mattes, J. (1990), Comparative effectiveness of carbamazepine and propranolol for rage outbursts. *J. Neuropsychiat. Neurosc.,* 2:159–164.

McLeer, S. V., Callaghan, M. & Henry, D. (1994), Psychiatric disorders in sexually abused children. *J. Amer. Acad. Child Adoesc. Psychiat.,* 33:313–319.

Myers, W., Scott, K., Burgess, A. W. & Burgess, A. G. (1995), Psychopathology, biopsychosocial factors, crime characteristics, and classification of 25 homicidal youths. *J. Amer. Acad. Child Adolesc. Psychiat.,* 34(11):1483–1489.

Nada-Raja, S., Langley, J. D., McGee, R., Williams, S. M., Begg, D. J. & Reeder, A. I. (1997), Inattentive and hyperactive behaviors and driving offenses in adolescence *J. Amer. Acad. Child Adolesc. Psychiat.,* 36:515–522.

Olfson, M., Marcus, S. C., Pincus, H. A., Zito, J. M., Thompson, J. W. & Zarin, D. A. (1998), Antidepressant prescribing practices of outpatient psychiatrists. *Arch. Gen. Psychiat.,* 55:310–316.

Pelham, W. E., Vodde-Hamilton, M., Murphy, D. A., Greenstein, J. & Vallano, G. (1991), The effects of methylphenidate on ADHD adolescents in recreational, peer group and classroom settings. *J. Clin. Child Psychol.,* 20:293–300.

Peterson, B. S. (1995), Neuroimaging in child and adolescent neuropsychiatric disorders. *J. Amer. Acad. Child Adolesc. Psychiat.,* 34: 1560–1576.

Popper, C. W. (1995), Combining methylphenidate and clonidine: Pharmacological questions and news reports about sudden death. *J. Child Adolesc. Psychopharmacol.,* 5:157–166.

Puente, R. (1976), The use of carbamazepine in the treatment of behavioral disorders in children. In: *Epileptic Seizures-Behavior-Pain*, ed. B. W. Bern, H. Huber, pp. 259–263.

Rapoport, J. L. & Kruesi, M. J. P. (1984), Organic Therapies (Child Psychiatry). In: *Comprehensive Text Book of Psychiatry/IV*, ed. H. Kaplan & B. Sadock. Baltimore: Williams and Wilkins, pp. 1793–1798.

Rey, J. M. (1993), Oppositional defiant disorder. *Amer. J. Psychiat.*, 150:1769–1778.

Rifkin, A., Karajgi, B., Dicker, R., et al. (1997), Lithium treatment of conduct disorder in adolescents. *Am. J. Psychiat.*, 154(4):554–555.

Riggs, P. D., Mikulich, S. K., Caffman, L. M. & Crowley, T. J. (1997), Fluoxetine in drug-dependent delinquents with major depression: An open trial. *J. Child Adolesc. Psychopharmacol.*, 7:87–95.

———— Thompson, L. L., Mikulich, S. K., Whitmore, E. A. & Crowley, T. J. (1996), An open trial of pemoline in drug-dependent delinquents with attention-deficit hyperactivity disorder. *J. Amer. Acad. Child Adolesc. Psychiat.*, 35:1018–1024.

Safer, D. J. (1997), Changing patterns of psychotropic medications prescribed by child psychiatrists in the 1990's. *J. Child Adolesc. Psychopharmacol.*, 7:267–274.

———— Zito, J. M. & Fine, E. M. (1996), Increased methylphenidate usage for attention deficit disorder in the 1990's. *Pediatrics*, 98:1084–1088.

Schreier, H. A. (1998), Risperidone in young children with mood disorders and aggressive behavior. *J. Child Adolesc. Psychopharmacol.*, 8(1):49–59.

Semrud-Clikeman, M. & Hynd, G. W. (1990), Right hemispheric dysfunction in non-verbal learning disabilities: Social, academic and adaptive functioning in adults and children. *Psychol. Bull.*, 107:196–209.

Singer, H. S., Brown, J., Quaskey, S., Rosenberg, L. A., Mellits, E. D. & Denckla, M. B. (1995), The treatment of attention deficit hyperactivity disorder in Tourette's syndrome: A double-blind placebo-controlled study with clonidine and desipramine. *Pediatrics*, 95:74–81.

Smith, B. H., Pelham, W. E., Evans, S., Gnagy, E., et al. (1998), Dosage effects of methylphenidate on the social behavior of adolescents diagnosed with attention-deficit hyperactivity disorder. *Exp. Clin. Psychopharmacol.*, 6:187–204.

———— ———— Gnagy, E. & Yudell, R. S. (1998), Equivalent effects of stimulant treatment for attention deficit hyperactivity disorder

209

during childhood and adolescence. *J. Amer. Acad. Child Adolesc. Psychiat.,* 37:314–321.

Spencer, T., Biederman, J., Steingard, R. & Wilens, T. (1993), Bupropion exacerbates tics in children with attention deficit hyperactivity disorder and tic disorder or Tourette's Syndrome. *J. Amer. Acad. Child Adolesc. Psychiat.,* 32:211–214.

——————— Wilens, T., et al. (1995), ADHD and thyroid abnormalities: A research note. *J. Child Psychol. Psychiat.,* 36:879–885.

——— ——— ——— Harding, M., O'Donnell, D. & Griffin, S. (1996), Pharmacotherapy of attention deficit disorder across the life cycle. *J. Amer. Acad. Child Adolesc. Psychiat.,* 35(4):409–432.

Steiner, H. (1998), Valproate and related compounds in the treatment of conduct disorder. Presented at the 45th annual meeting of the American Academy of Child and Adolescent Psychiatry, Anaheim.

Steingard, R., Biederman, J., Spencer, T., Wilens, T. & Gonzalez, A. (1993), Comparison of clonidine response in the treatment of attention-deficit hyperactivity disorder with and without comorbid tic disorders. *J. Amer. Acad. Child Adolesc. Psychiat.,* 32:350–353.

——— Khan, A., Gonzalez, A. & Herzog, D. B. (1992), Neuroleptic malignant syndrome: Review of experience with children and adolescents. *J. Child and Adolesc. Psychopharmacol.,* 2:183–198.

Stoewe, J. K. & Kruesi, M. J. P. (1997), Pharmacoepidemiology of aggressive/affective disorders. Presented at 44th annual meeting of the American Academy of Child and Adolescent Psychiatry, Toronto.

——— ——— & Lelio, D. F. (1995), Psychopharmacology of aggressive states and features of conduct disorder. *Child and Adolescent Psychiatry Clinics of North America.* Philadelphia: W.B. Saunders Co., pp. 359–379.

Swanson, J. M., Wigal, S. & Greenhill, L. L., et al. (1998), Analog classroom assessment of Adderall in children with ADHD. *J. Amer. Acad. Child Adolesc. Psychiat.,* 37:519–526.

Tome, M. B., Cloninger, C. R., Watson, J. P. & Isaac, M. T. (1997), Seroternergic auto receptor blockade in the reduction of antidepressant latency: Personality variables and response to paroxetine and pindolol. *J. Affect. Disord.,* 44(2–3):101–109.

Varley, C. K. (1983), Effects of methylphenidate on adolescents with attention deficit disorder. *J. Amer. Acad. Child Adolesc. Psychiat.,* 22:351–354.

Vitaro, F., Gendreau, P. L., Tremblay, R. & Oligny, P. (1998), Reactive and proactive aggression differentially predict later conduct problems. *J. Child Psychol. Psychiat.,* 39:377–385.

Vitiello, B., Behar, D., Hunt, J., Stoff, D. & Ricciuti, A. (1990), Subtyping aggression in children and adolescents. *J. Neuropsychiat.*, 2:189–192.

Vitiello, B. & Hoagwood, K. (1997), Pediatric pharmacoepidemiology: Clinical applications and research priorities in children's mental health. *J. Child Adolesc. Psychopharmacol.*, 7:287–290.

Weinberg, N. Z., Rahdert, E., Colliver, J. D. & Glantz, M. D. (1998), Adolescent substance abuse: A review of the past 10 years. *J. Amer. Acad. Child Adolesc. Psychiat.*, 37:252–261.

Weiss, R. E., Stein, M. A., Trommer, B. & Reftoff, S. (1993), Attention-deficit hyperactivity disorder and thyroid function. *J. Pediatr,* 123:539–545.

Wender, E. W. (1995), Attention deficit hyperactivity disorders in adolescence. *Developmental and Behavioral Pediatrics,* 16(3): 192–195.

Wilens, T. & Biederman, J. (1992), Stimulants. *Child and Adolescent Psychiatric Clinics of North America,* March: 204–207.

———— ———— Baldessarini, R. J., Puopolo, P. R. & Flood, J. G. (1993), Electrocardiographic effects of Desipramine and 2-hydroxydesipramine in children, adolescents, and adults treated with Desipramine. *J. Amer. Acad. Child Adolesc. Psychiat.*, 32:798–804.

———— ———— Geist, D. E., Steingard, R. & Spencer, T. (1993), Nortriptyline in the treatment of ADHD: A chart review of 58 cases. *J. Amer. Acad. Child Adolesc. Psychiat.*, 32:343–349.

Wilens, T. E., Spencer, T., Biederman, J., et al. (1995), Combined pharmacotherapy: An emerging trend in pediatric psychopharmacology. *J. Amer. Acad. Child Adolesc. Psychiat.,* 34:110–112.

211

13 PHARMACOLOGIC TREATMENT OF AFFECTIVE DISORDERS IN ADOLESCENTS

DWIGHT V. WOLF AND KAREN DINEEN WAGNER

Major Depression

Early views of depression in children and adolescents were characterized by skepticism that the disorder could occur so early. As clinical knowledge has grown, it has been shown that depressive disorders in children and adolescents do occur and that they can be diagnosed in a standardized fashion with predictive validity (Carlson and Cantwell, 1982; Kovacs et al., 1984). Although early theories suggested that children and adolescents may often experience a "masked" form of depression with predominantly behavioral symptoms, more recent studies have shown significant symptomatic similarities with adult depression (Kovacs, 1996). Major depression in adolescents is defined using DSM–IV (American Psychiatric Association, 1994b) criteria of at least a two-week duration of depressed or irritable mood and/or diminished interest, along with at least four of the following symptoms: weight or appetite change, sleep disturbance, fatigue or loss of energy, psychomotor retardation or agitation, diminished concentration, feelings of worthlessness or guilt, and suicidal ideation, attempt, or plan.

Major depression has been shown to occur with a point prevalence of 2% to 8% in adolescents (Kashani et al., 1987; Roberts, Lewinsohn, and Seeley, 1995) and with a lifetime prevalence of 15% to 20% (Lewinsohn et al., 1993; Kessler et al., 1994). Of particular significance is the observation that about 50% of adult depressed patients reported a first depressive episode before age 20 (Burke et al., 1991)—emphasizing the importance of appropriate diagnosis and treatment in the adolescent age group.

The gender ratio of major depression is the same for boys and girls until puberty, when the female-to-male ratio approaches 2:1 as observed in the adult population (Lewinsohn et al., 1994). Secular increases have also been observed, with depression becoming more common and the age of onset of first episodes being younger in individuals born in the latter portion of the 20th century (Ryan et al., 1992).

CLINICAL PRESENTATION

The diagnosis of depression in adolescents is made on clinical presentation and history. It is important that both the parents and adolescents are interviewed individually in order to allow them to describe the problems and to freely express their concerns. Given the high risk of depression in the offspring of depressed parents (Wickramaratne and Weissman, 1998), a family history of affective disorders should be explored. The clinician should also be aware that concurrent depression in a parent may contribute to either underreporting or overreporting symptoms in the child (Weller and Weller, 1990). Other useful sources of information may include extended family members, teachers, other school staff, and school records, including the adolescent's grade reports. The issue of confidentiality should be discussed early in the interview. The adolescent may be reassured that the information gathered will be treated as confidential, with breach of confidentiality indicated only regarding issues of safety and, in particular, suicidality.

Clinical observation of a depressed adolescent may reveal a dysphoric or irritable mood. Unlike their parents, adolescents are often unaware of the extent of their irritability. Loss of interest may be reflected in fewer activities and isolation from peers. Poor concentration often leads to a decline in school performance. Of note, anhedonia, weight change, hopelessness, hypersomnia, and substance abuse are more commonly reported in depressed adolescents as compared to depressed children (Ryan et al., 1987). Such adolescents' self-esteem is often low, and they may be highly self-critical. Hopelessness may lead to suicidal actions.

Rating scales may be useful to quantify the adolescent's baseline level of depression and to monitor treatment efficacy. The Childhood Depression Rating Scale–Revised (Poznanski et al., 1984) is a clinician-administered instrument that uses information obtained from the adolescent and parent. The Childhood Depression Inventory (Kovacs, 1981) is a 27-item self-report scale.

The differential diagnosis for major depression in adolescents includes medical conditions such as infections (e.g., encephalitis, pneumonia, AIDS), neurological disorders (e.g., seizure disorders, multiple sclerosis), and endocrine abnormalities (e.g., hypothyroidism, hypopituitarism, Cushing's disease). Medications such as antihypertensives, anticonvulsants, and oral contraceptives have been associated with depression. Recently, Norplant®, an increasingly popular contraceptive for adolescents, has been linked to depression (Wagner and Berenson, 1994; Wagner, 1996). Substance abuse including alcohol abuse and withdrawal reactions from cocaine or amphetamines may also present with symptoms mimicking those of major depression (Wise and Rundell, 1988). Psychiatric disorders may also present with symptoms similar to those of major depression. Adjustment disorder with depressed mood should be considered in the presence of an identifiable stressor with resultant symptoms that are below threshold in number to meet criteria for major depression and the duration of which is less than six months. Dysthymia should also be in the differential for major depression. The clinician should keep in mind that dysthymia coexists with major depression, ("double depression") in about 30% of cases (Kovacs, 1996). Bipolar disorder should also be considered, particularly if a family history of bipolar disorder is elicited. A switch rate from unipolar depression to bipolar illness has been reported in adolescents and young adults to be 20% to 30% of cases (Kovacs, 1996). Other nonaffective psychiatric illnesses may present with a depressed mood, including anxiety disorders such as separation anxiety disorder, generalized anxiety disorder, and posttraumatic stress disorder. Psychotic illnesses may also present with depressive symptoms.

Studies have shown consistently high rates of comorbid psychiatric disorders in depressed children and adolescents. The comorbidity rate in children and adolescents with depression has been reported to be 80% to 95% (Kovacs, 1996). The most common comorbid disorders in adolescents with depression are anxiety disorders (Biederman et al., 1995; Kovacs, 1996), with rates ranging from 40% to 50% (Kovacs, 1996). Separation anxiety appears to be the most common comorbid disorder among depressed adolescents and children (Kovacs et al., 1989). Other common comorbid diagnoses include dysthymia, which occurs in about 30% of cases (Kovacs, 1996), conduct disorder and oppositional defiant disorder, which occur in 21% to 83% of cases, and attention deficit/hyperactivity disorder (ADHD), which occurs in 0% to 57% of cases (Angold and Costello, 1993). Substance abuse frequently cooccurs with depression.

Adolescents with major depression are at risk for impairment in school performance and interpersonal relationships (Arsanow, Carlson, and Guthrie, 1987), which may interfere with achievement of appropriate developmental tasks. Suicidal behavior is a common sequela (Kovacs, Goldston, and Gatsonis, 1993). A 10-year follow-up of depressed child and adolescent outpatients found that 4.4% committed suicide (Rao et al., 1993). Mood disorder, prior suicide attempt, and substance abuse are the major risk factors for adolescent suicide (Shaffer et al., 1996). Follow-up studies of depressed children and adolescents have shown a high relapse rate: 59% in outpatients (McCauley et al., 1993) and 61% in inpatients (Emslie et al., 1997). Continuity between adolescent depression and adult depression has been reported (Rao et al., 1995). It is postulated that early treatment may prevent or lessen the adverse developmental effects of childhood and adolescent depression (Goodyer et al., 1997).

PHARMACOLOGIC AGENTS

The major types of antidepressants for the treatment of adolescent depression will be reviewed and then followed by a recommended treatment approach.

Tricyclic Antidepressants

To date, there have been six double-blind placebo-controlled studies of tricyclic antidepressants (TCAs) in adolescents. No significant differences have been found between TCA and placebo response in any of these studies (Puig-Antich et al., 1987; Geller et al., 1990; Geller et al., 1992; Tancer et al., 1992; Kutcher et al., 1994; Birmaher et al., 1998). Putative reasons for the lack of demonstrable clinical efficacy of the TCAs include the relatively small number of studies (Geller et al., 1992; Geller et al., 1996), neurobiologic differences between children and adults, a more severe and treatment-resistant depression in children and adolescents, and environmental factors (Geller et al., 1996). Several open trials have shown a positive response rate of 60% to 80%

(Puig-Antich et al., 1979; Preskorn, Weller, and Weller, 1982; Geller et al., 1986).

Although there are no controlled data to support the preferential use of any TCA, imipramine has historically been the most widely used TCA in adolescents. TCAs should be administered beginning with small dosages, with a gradual titration upward. A general guideline includes initiation of dosage at 0.5 mg/kg with dosage increases of 0.5 mg/kg up to a range of 2.5 to 5 mg/kg. A nortriptyline dosage schedule developed by Geller et al. (1985) and Geller and Carr (1988) recommends a single starting dose for adolescents of 50 mg. Medication dosage should be within the therapeutic blood level for the TCA selected. Maximal blood levels within the therapeutic range should be achieved before considering the patient a TCA nonresponder.

Common side effects of TCAs are sedation, dry mouth, cavities, blurred vision, constipation, and mild tachycardia. Uncommon and more concerning is the risk of exacerbation of tics, potentiation of mania, rash, hypertension, seizures, and heart block. At least six sudden deaths have been reported in children taking desipramine. One case involved a 12-year-old who was taking desipramine for ADHD (Riddle, Geller, and Ryan, 1993). The cardiotoxic effects of TCAs should be monitored by the use of electrocardiograms (ECGs) both at baseline and with dosage increases. Although a conservative approach may warrant obtaining a repeat ECG with each dosage increase, a more practical guideline has been proposed by Elliot and Popper (1990/1991): Obtain ECG, pulse rate, and blood pressure at baseline, at a dose of 3 mg/kg per day, and at a final dose of no more than 5 mg/kg per day. Parameters suggested for children over age 10 include pulse under 100 beats per minute, systolic blood pressure maximum of 140 mm Hg, diastolic blood pressure maximum of 85 mm Hg, PR interval less than or equal to 200 milliseconds, QRS interval widening to no greater than 30% over baseline, and QTC interval less than 460 milliseconds (Kye et al., 1996). Before initiating a TCA, a complete blood count, blood chemistry profile, thyroid-function test, and urinalysis should be obtained. These should be repeated on an annual basis, with the exception of the thyroid-function test.

Selective Serotonin Reuptake Inhibitors

Two placebo-controlled double-blind studies have demonstrated the efficacy of selective serotonin reuptake inhibitors (SSRIs) in the treatment of adolescent depression. In one study (Emslie et al., 1997), 96 child and adolescent outpatients (aged seven to 17) with major depression were randomized to fluoxetine 20 mg or placebo in an eight-week trial. An intent-to-treat analysis found a significantly superior response rate for the fluoxetine group (56%) compared to the placebo group (33%) on clinical global improvement. No differences were shown between the response rate of children compared to adolescents. Side effects were minimal—with discontinuation of medication in four patients treated with fluoxetine and one treated with placebo. Of the patients who discontinued fluoxetine, three developed mania and one developed a rash. The results of this study provide a significant advance for the treatment of depressed adolescents, as an earlier controlled study of a smaller number of adolescents ($N = 40$) failed to demonstrate a statistically significant difference between fluoxetine and placebo response rates (Simeon et al., 1990). Previous open trials with fluoxetine reported response rates ranging from 64% to 71% in adolescents (Joshi et al., 1989; Boulos et al., 1992).

A large-scale multisite double-blind placebo-controlled study of paroxetine and imipramine for the treatment of adolescent depression has been reported (Keller et al., 1998). Two hundred seventy-five 12- to 19-year-old outpatients with major depression were randomized to paroxetine, imipramine, or placebo for an eight-week trial. Paroxetine dosages were titrated up to a maximum of 40 mg ($M = 28.0$ mg) and impiramine to a maximum of 300 mg daily ($M = 205.8$ mg). Response to paroxetine was statistically superior to response to imipramine and placebo on measures of affect, global improvement, and remission of depressive symptoms. There were no significant differences between imipramine and placebo on any measure.

The most frequently reported adverse events were headaches in the paroxetine (34%) and placebo (39%) groups and dizziness in the imipramine group (47%). Thirty-two percent of the imipramine patients withdrew for an adverse event—which was significantly higher than the percentage of paroxetine patients who withdrew. The imipramine group had significantly more cardiovascular adverse events (e.g., tachycardia, postural hypotension, ECG abnormalities including QT prolongation) than the paroxetine group had (Wagner et al., 1998). A previous open trial and small controlled study also showed the efficacy of paroxetine in treating depressed children and adolescents, and minimal side effects were noted (Rey-Sanchez and Gutierrez-Casares, 1997).

The efficacy of sertraline in the treatment of depressed adolescents has been investigated in a multisite open 10-week trial with a 12-week continuation phase for responders (Ambrosini et al., 1999). Fifty-three adolescent outpatients with a diagnosis of major depression were administered sertraline 50 to 200 mg daily. The mean sertraline dosages at six and 10 weeks were 93.3 mg and 127.2 mg, respectively. At six weeks, 65% of adolescents showed significant clinical improvement of depression. Of note, by 10 weeks, 84% showed a showed a significant positive response. Improvement was maintained over the 12-week continuation phase. Sertraline was well tolerated; the most frequent side effects were insomnia, headache, nausea, and dizziness. No patient developed manic symptoms. One patient discontinued because of akathisia. In an open study of 13 depressed adolescent inpatients who received sertraline (mean dosage = 110 mg) and who were followed as outpatients, significant improvement of depression was reported, although one patient developed mania (McConville et al., 1996).

Before initiating SSRIs, a complete blood count, blood chemistry profile, thyroid-function test, and urinalysis should be obtained. These should be repeated on an annual basis, with the exception of thyroid-function test. Adolescent females should have a urine or serum pregnancy test before initiating any SSRI.

Treatment with SSRIs should begin at a low dose, with gradual titration upward to minimize the potential for side effects such as irritability, gastrointestinal symptoms, and insomnia. Fluoxetine dosage should begin at 5 to 10 mg per day, although side effects may be prevented by beginning with 5 mg per day. A dosage increase of 10 mg every four weeks as clinically indicated is a reasonable strategy. Dosage range for fluoxetine is generally 5 to 40 mg per day. Dosages greater than 20 mg per day can be administered on a divided schedule to lessen the possibility of side effects. Due to its long half-life, fluoxetine may also be administered on an every-other-day basis, if needed, to reduce side effects. Jain et al. (1992) found no additional benefit from dosages greater than 40 mg in the treatment of depressed adolescents. Recommended dosage at treatment initiation of sertraline is 25 to 50 mg per day, with gradual dosage increases in 50-mg increments every four weeks as clinically indicated. Typical therapeutic doses range from 25 to 200 mg per day. As with fluoxetine, a divided-dose regimen may prove useful in reducing the possibility of side effects. Paroxetine therapy may be instituted at 5 to 10 mg per day, with gradual titration by 10 mg every four weeks as clinically indicated. Typical therapeutic dosages of paroxetine range from 5 to 40 mg per day.

SSRIs tend to be well tolerated in adolescents. Common side effects include gastrointestinal symptoms, headache, anxiety, nervousness, insomnia, weight loss, increased sweating, and akathisia. Some children may exhibit behavioral activation with resultant symptoms of motor restlessness, social disinhibition, or subjective excitation. Dosage reduction may resolve these symptoms. Several reports of induction of mania or hypomania in children and adolescents treated with SSRIs have been reported (Jain et al., 1992; McConville et al., 1996; Emslie et al., 1997; Mandoki et al., 1997). When prescribing SSRIs to an adolescent with a family history of bipolar disorder, the adolescent should be monitored for possible emergence of manic symptoms. A major advantage of the SSRIs is their safety in overdose (Barbey and Roose, 1998). The clinician should be aware that the SSRIs do inhibit the activity of human cytochrome P450 enzymes, which are responsible for the oxidative metabolism of many drugs (Greenblatt et al., 1998). In particular, they can increase TCA plasma concentrations to potentially toxic levels. Fluvoxamine is a highly potent inhibitor of P450 and can reduce clearance of clozapine, tacrine, and chloroguanide (Hiemke et al., 1994; Jeppesen et al., 1996; Becquemont et al., 1997; Jeppesen, Rasmussen, and Brosen, 1997). Other potential SSRI interactions occur with warfarin, phenytoin, tolbutamide, diazepam, alprazolam, and carbamazepine (Greenblatt et al., 1998). SSRIs plus nefazadone may lead to an increased serum level of a nefazadone metabolite, which has been associated with dysphoric agitation (Schatzberg et al., 1997).

Monamine Oxidase Inhibitors

There have been no controlled studies of the use of monamine oxidase inhibitors (MAOIs) for the treatment of adolescent depression. Although one study reported a good response rate (74%) in 23 adolescents treated with MAOIs (Ryan et al., 1988), the risk of hypertensive crisis and the need for strict dietary compliance limit their use in this age group.

Newer Antidepressants

To date, the following newer antidepressants have received little systematic investigation in adolescents.

Venlafaxine. One double-blind placebo-controlled study of venlafax-ine in 33 outpatients age eight to 17 with major depression has been reported (Mandoki et al., 1997). Adolescents were randomized to either a venlafaxine-plus-psychotherapy group or a placebo-plus-psychother-apy group for a six-week trial. Venlafaxine doses in adolescents ranged from 25 to 75 mg per day. Both groups were noted to improve, and there were no significant differences between them. Venlafaxine was well tolerated by the adolescents, and side effects were limited primarily to nausea and increased appetite. One child in the venlafaxine group developed manic symptoms.

Nefazodone. There have been no controlled studies of nefazodone in the treatment of adolescent depression. An open study of 26 depressed child and adolescent outpatients age seven to 17 who received nefazo-done 100 to 200 mg per day showed improvement in depression. No serious side effects or ECG changes were found (Magnus et al., 1997).

Mirtazapine. There have been no studies reported of mirtazapine for adolescent depression.

Augmentation Strategies

Few controlled-study data are available about the treatment of refrac-tory depression in adolescents. Positive findings have been reported for the use of lithium augmentation of TCAs for adolescent depression (Ryan et al., 1988). In addition to lithium, augmentation strategies that have been used for adults include pindolol, thyroid, stimulants, and buspirone, as well as SSRI–TCA combinations (Nelson, 1998). Al-though these may be useful for treatment of refractory adolescent depression, they remain to be investigated. With SSRI–TCA combina-tions, it is important to monitor TCA levels, as the SSRIs, especially paroxetine and fluoxetine, can significantly raise them (Nelson et al., 1991; Brosen et al., 1993; Preskorn et al., 1994).

Treatment Recommendations

As the SSRIs have the most data available to support their efficacy and safety in adolescent depression, they are proposed as the first-line treatment. Given that there may be differential effects in the efficacy of one SSRI compared to another in treating adult depression (Apter,

Thase, and Birkett, 1986; Brown and Harrison, 1992), it is reasonable to consider switching from one SSRI to another if a given SSRI at maximal tolerable doses is ineffective.

If the adolescent fails to respond to any SSRI, then switching to a different class of antidepressant is recommended. At present, no data support the use of one agent over another. Therefore, whether the clinician chooses a TCA, nefazodone, or venlafaxine should be based on clinical experience. Other factors to consider for a given adolescent are medication side effects, medical conditions, previous medication trials, comorbid psychiatric conditions, and familial history of a positive response to a particular antidepressant.

The question remains as to whether to continue with monotherapy or to consider augmentation for an adolescent who does not respond to initial monotherapy. If an adolescent has a partial response to an SSRI, augmentation may be a useful strategy.

As additional controlled studies are completed with depressed adolescents, there will be more information available to determine the order of antidepressant selection. As major depression has a high recurrence rate, it is recommended that pharmacologic treatment continue for a minimum of six months after achieving resolution of symptoms. Medication discontinuation should be accomplished gradually, with a slow, stepwise reduction in dosage over a two- to three-month period. The clinician should carefully monitor the adolescent for withdrawal syndromes and reemergence of depressive symptoms.

Dysthymic Disorder

Dysthymic disorder in adolescents is defined using *DSM–IV* criteria by a predominantly depressed or irritable mood of at least one year's duration (no more than two months symptom-free) with two or more of the following: appetite changes, sleep difficulties, reduced energy, decreased self-esteem, poor concentration or difficulty with decision making, and hopelessness. The incidence of dysthymia in adolescents is estimated to be 3.4% (Garrison et al., 1997).

CLINICAL PRESENTATION

The diagnosis of dysthymia, like that of depression, is made on clinical presentation and history. The approach to the evaluation is similar to that for depression. Care should be taken in exploring the chronology of the disorder and in screening for other disorders, such as major depression. The differential diagnosis for dysthymia mirrors that of major depression and includes medical conditions, neurological disorders, endocrine abnormalities, medication side effects, substance abuse, and psychiatric disorders.

The median duration of dysthymic disorder in children and adolescents has been reported to be 3.9 years. Comorbid externalizing disorders have been found to prolong the course of dysthymia by 2.5 years (Kovacs et al., 1997). Compared to youth with major depressive disorder, adolescents with dysthymic disorder have more social impairment and more comorbid externalizing (Shain et al., 1991; Ferro et al., 1994). Adolescents who have recovered from dysthymia were found to have significant psychosocial difficulties, including low peer support, high self-consciousness, and behavior problems (Klein, Lewinsohn, and Seeley, 1997).

PHARMACOLOGIC AGENTS

There have been no studies examining the pharmacologic treatment of adolescent dysthymia. Studies of adults with dysthymia have shown clinical efficacy of SSRIs, TCAs, and MAOIs at comparable dosages to those used in treating major depression (Thase et al., 1996; Kocsis et al., 1997). In the absence of adolescent studies, it is recommended that the same pharmacologic treatment approach be used as for adolescent major depression.

Bipolar Disorder

Although Kraepelin (1921) noted the occurrence of mania in childhood, it was not until the 1990s that the existence of childhood mania was generally accepted. Unlike the presentation of bipolar disorder in children, that in adolescents is similar to that in adults. Bipolar disorder in adolescents is defined using *DSM–IV* criteria of a manic episode with at least one week (unless hospitalized) of an elevated, expansive, or irritable mood. Three additional symptoms (four symptoms for irritable mood) are required, including grandiosity, decreased sleep, pressured speech, flight of ideas, distractibility, increase in goal-directed activity, and excessive risk-taking. These symptoms must be of sufficient severity to cause significant impairment in functioning or to require hospitalization. Although not a diagnostic criterion, mood-congruent psychotic symptoms are often found with adolescent bipolar disorder (Carlson and Strober, 1978; McGlashan, 1988; Carlson, Fennig, and Bromet, 1994).

The lifetime prevalence of adolescent bipolar disorder is estimated as 0.94% to 0.99%, with a one-year incidence rate of 0.13% (Lewinsohn et al., 1995). These estimates may be low, as it is believed that adolescent bipolar disorder is underdiagnosed (Weller et al., 1986; Isaac, 1995; Wozniak et al., 1995). As with major depression, a secular trend has been noted in bipolar illness, with earlier age of onset associated with successively later birth year (Rice et al., 1987). As 20% of adults with bipolar disorder experience their first episode in adolescence (American Academy of Child and Adolescent Psychiatry [AACAP], 1997), it is important to recognize and treat this disorder in adolescents.

CLINICAL PRESENTATION

The diagnosis of bipolar disorder is made on the basis of clinical presentation and history obtained from the adolescent and parents in individual interviews. Other useful sources of information may include extended family members, teachers, other school staff, and grade reports. It is important to be attentive to family history, as parents may have undiagnosed bipolar disorder, which may contribute to minimization or failure to recognize the significance of their adolescent's symptoms (Geller, 1996; Geller and Luby, 1997).

Clinical examination of adolescents with mania may reveal an elated, euphoric, or irritable affect. Irritability, rather than elation, is a more common presentation for adolescents (Bowring and Kovacs, 1992; Wozniak et al., 1995). The adolescent is often "intrusive," which may be described by parents as the adolescent's being "in my face." Adolescents often have little insight into their intrusiveness. Racing thoughts and distractibility contribute to poor school performance. With relatively little need for sleep, the adolescent is often energized and involved in many seemingly random activities. Adolescents may engage in increased sexual activity and substance abuse. The clinician should also be aware that cycling among mania, euthymia, and depression may occur at a much higher rate than in adult bipolar illness, with continuous brief episodes possibly occurring in a majority of cases (Geller et al., 1995).

The Mania Rating Scale (Young et al., 1978) may be useful in quantifying the adolescent's level of mania and in monitoring treatment efficacy. This scale is an 11-item clinician-administered instrument.

The differential diagnosis of bipolar disorder includes conditions such as endocrine abnormalities, neurological disorders, and infectious diseases. Psychiatric disorders in the differential include ADHD, conduct disorder, oppositional defiant disorder, schizophrenia, and substance abuse (Weller, Weller, and Fristad, 1995; Geller and Luby, 1997).

Comorbid conditions with adolescent bipolar disorder include conduct disorder (Kovacs and Pollock, 1995), ADHD (Koehler-Troy, Strober, and Melanbaum, 1986; Lewinsohn et al., 1994; Wozniak and Biederman, 1996), anxiety disorders (Geller et al., 1995; Geller and Luby, 1997), and substance abuse (Strober et al., 1995).

A prospective, five-year follow-up study of adolescents with bipolar disorder found that, although the recovery rate was 96%, there was a 46% relapse rate, and 20% attempted suicide (Strober et al., 1995). Comorbid conduct disorder (Kovacs and Pollock, 1995) and ADHD (Wozniak et al., 1995) may worsen the course of adolescent bipolar disorder. The rate of switching from depression to mania has been reported in about 20% of adolescent cases (Strober and Carlson, 1982).

PHARMACOLOGIC AGENTS

The major mood stabilizers for the treatment of adolescent bipolar disorder will be reviewed and then followed by a recommended treatment approach.

Lithium Carbonate

There is one double-blind placebo-controlled study of lithium treatment for adolescent bipolar disorder. Twenty-five 12- to 18-year-old outpatients with diagnoses of bipolar disorder and substance dependence were randomized to lithium ($n = 13$) or placebo ($n = 12$) for a six-week trial. There was a significantly greater response to lithium (46.2%) than to placebo (8.3%). The mean lithium level for treatment response was 0.9 mEq/L (Geller et al., 1998). Side effects of polydipsia and polyuria occurred significantly more in the lithium group than in the placebo group. Previous open studies of lithium treatment for 59 children and adolescents (DeLong and Aldershof, 1987) and 50 adolescents (Strober et al., 1988) showed response rates of 66% and 68%, respectively.

Before initiating lithium therapy, a medical history should be obtained regarding renal, cardiac, or thyroid disease. Renal disease may constitute a relative contraindication to lithium therapy, but individuals with stable renal disease may be treated with lithium safely with frequent monitoring of lithium level and renal function. Lithium may affect cardiac function, may produce ECG changes, and should be used cautiously in an adolescent with cardiovascular disease (Botteron and Geller, 1995). Adolescents should be cautioned to avoid nonsteroidal antiinflammatory drugs (NSAIDs), as they may produce toxic lithium levels by interfering with renal excretion (Jefferson, Greist, and Baudhiun, 1981). Likewise, the clinician should explore the use of diuretic therapy and low-salt diets, as these can also affect lithium level. Adolescent females should be evaluated for pregnancy before initiating lithium therapy. Although the risk of teratogenic effects, in particular Ebstein's anomaly, may have been initially overestimated (Jacobson et al., 1992), it is recommended that lithium be avoided during pregnancy, particularly in the first trimester (Green, 1995).

Baseline laboratory studies should include a complete blood count with differential, as lithium may cause neutropenia. Electrolytes, creatinine, creatinine clearance, blood urea nitrogen, and urine osmolality should be obtained to evaluate renal function. Thyroid-function tests with baseline measurement of thyroid-stimulating hormone should be obtained, as lithium may interfere with thyroid function. Adolescent females should have a urine or serum pregnancy test before lithium initiation. When clinically indicated, an ECG should be obtained. Lithium level, urinalysis, thyroid function, and renal function should be monitored at three- to six-month intervals (Rosenberg, Holttum, and Gershon, 1994).

Lithium levels required for the treatment of acute mania range from 0.6 to 1.2 mEq/L (Viesselman et al., 1993). One approach to initiating lithium therapy is to choose a reasonable starting dose and follow serial lithium levels over time. Lithium levels should always be obtained 12 hours following the last dose (AACAP, 1997). Weller et al. (1986) has developed a lithium initiation protocol with dosages based on body weight (about 25 to 30 mg/kg per day). However, the possibility that some patients, perhaps slow metabolizers of lithium, will develop levels greater than 1.4 mEq/L has led some clinicians to recommend caution if this protocol is followed (Fetner and Geller, 1992; AACAP, 1997). Others have recommended a pharmacokinetic approach to lithium initiation. In this protocol, a single 600-mg test dose is given, serum lithium level is drawn at 24 hours, and, based on the level, a corresponding dosage to achieve therapeutic level is read from a table (Cooper, Bergner, & Simpson, 1973; Fetner and Geller, 1992). In general, starting dosages for lithium range from 300 to 900 mg per day on a two- or three-times-a-day schedule. Maintenance levels for lithium are generally lower than those required in the acute phase. Based on adult data (APA, 1994), maintenance levels are generally between 0.6 and 0.8 mEq/L.

Although lithium is well tolerated by adolescents, a number of side effects may occur. Common side effects include nausea, tremor, polyuria, polydipsia, fatigue, and weight gain. Enuresis may be noted in some patients. In general, these side effects may not require discontinuation of the medication, although they may contribute to noncompliance. Likewise, the exacerbation of acne may also interfere with compliance in this age group. A dermatology consultation may prove helpful, as lithium-induced acne is usually responsive to treatment.

Renal effects include polyuria and polydipsia. Active adolescents may be particularly prone to dehydration, and education of families and patients is essential regarding this issue. Lithium should be stopped and the physician contacted should dehydration occur (Botteron and Geller, 1995). Structural changes in the kidney have been noted in adults on long-term lithium therapy (Gelenberg and Schoonover, 1991), and, although potential renal damage in children and adolescents is thought to be rare (Khandelwal, Varma, and Murthy, 1984), renal function should be assessed every six months (Fetner and Geller, 1992).

Lithium may affect the cardiovascular system with effects on cardiac conduction and ECG changes. Some reversible cardiac-conduction abnormalities have been reported in children (Campbell et al., 1972). Baseline ECGs should be obtained with follow-up ECGs as clinically indicated.

Lithium may affect the thyroid, and studies have shown rates of hypothyroidism to be 5% to 15% in adults treated with lithium for longer than six months (Vestergaard, 1983). Thyroid-function tests should be repeated on a six-month basis. Lithium-induced hypothyroidism should be treated with replacement therapy (Botteron and Geller, 1995; AACAP, 1997).

Neurological symptoms may also occur. Headaches, tremor weakness, and cognitive blunting may occur rarely in children (Lazarus et al., 1981) but, in some cases, may be of sufficient severity to warrant medication discontinuation (Geller et al., 1994).

Medication interactions may occur with lithium. Neuroleptic medications, though frequently combined with lithium, may be more likely to cause neuroleptic malignant syndrome when used in combination (Green, 1995). Several medications may cause elevations in lithium levels. These include thiazide diuretics, NSAIDs, carbamazepine, and tetracycline (Botteron and Geller, 1995; AACAP, 1997).

Valproic Acid

There are no double-blind placebo-controlled studies of valproic acid in the treatment of adolescent bipolar disorder. An open trial of 15 outpatients (age 15 to 20) with mania who were treated with valproate 750 to 2,000 mg per day for seven weeks showed moderate to marked improvement in 12 patients and some improvement in one patient (Papatheodorou et al., 1994). Few side effects were found.

Before initiating valproate therapy, coagulation studies, complete blood count with differential, and baseline liver-function studies should be obtained. Adolescent females should have a urine or serum pregnancy test. As fatal hepatotoxicity has been reported, baseline laboratory studies should be repeated on a three- to six-month basis along with checks of valproate serum levels (Weller, Weller, and Svadjian, 1996; AACAP, 1997).

Therapeutic serum levels for the treatment of mania have not been established. Recommended starting dosages range from 100 to 250 mg twice daily, with gradual adjustments in dosage to achieve serum levels of 50 to 100 mg/L (Botteron and Geller, 1995; Weller et al., 1996). If the patient is tolerating the medication, it may be necessary to increase serum levels up to 120 mg/L to achieve a positive response.

Although valproate is generally well tolerated, common side effects include rash, tremor, and gastrointestinal symptoms. Sedation may occur but is more common at initiation of therapy and is usually transient. Alopecia has been noted (APA, 1994) and may prove problematic with compliance in adolescents. More severe side effects include fatal hepatotoxicity, aplastic anemia, coagulopathies, and thrombocytopenia. Valproate may be associated with the risk of neural-tube defects in the first trimester (PDR, 1998). These risks should be discussed with female patients. A study of women with epilepsy who were begun on valproate before age 20 demonstrated an 80% prevalence of polycystic ovaries and hyperandrogenism (Isojarvi et al., 1993). The relevance of these findings for adolescents with bipolar disorder is debated; the adolescents and parents, however, should be informed about these issues.

Carbamazepine

There are no double-blind placebo-controlled studies of carbamazepine in the treatment of adolescent bipolar disorder. One report described a series of 19 treatment-resistant bipolar adolescents who were treated with a combination of lithium and carbamazepine with positive response (Garfinkel et al., 1985).

Before initiating carbamazepine therapy, adolescents should undergo baseline laboratory studies with liver-function tests, complete blood count with differential, and thyroid-function tests. Adolescent females should have a serum or urine pregnancy test. As carbamazepine may cause bone-marrow suppression, biweekly blood counts should be obtained for the first three months of treatment (Weller et al., 1996). Upon achieving a therapeutic level, blood counts, liver-function tests, and carbamazepine level should be obtained every three to six months (Rosenberg et al., 1994). Families should be educated regarding symptoms of agranulocytosis, including bruising and fever. If bone-marrow suppression occurs, the medication should be discontinued.

Carbamazepine therapy in adolescents may begin with dosages of 200 mg twice daily or 15 to 30 mg/kg. Levels should be monitored carefully, and dosages may be increased every fourth day as tolerated (Weller et al., 1996). A two- or three-times-a-day dosage schedule is recommended. As carbamazepine causes autoinduction of hepatic enzymes, a decrease in carbamazepine blood levels may be observed frequently despite stable dosages and good compliance (AACAP, 1997). As therapeutic serum levels for the treatment of adolescent mania have not been established, the recommended range is that used for treating seizure disorders, or 8 to 12 mEq/L (McElroy and Keck, 1995).

Carbamazepine has a number of potential side effects, including sedation, dizziness, nausea, and vomiting. Neutropenia and agranulocytosis may occur and may require medication discontinuation. Cases of hepatitis have also been documented, and hepatic function should be carefully monitored. Rashes may occur in 10% to 15% of patients and may require medication discontinuation. Carbamazepine has also occasionally been associated with hypothyroidism and the syndrome of inappropriate secretion of antidiuretic hormone (Botteron and Geller, 1995).

Gabapentin

There have been no controlled studies of gabapentin for the treatment of adolescent bipolar disorder. In a retrospective study, 18 adolescents with bipolar disorder who had failed previous medication trials or were not able to tolerate the medication were administered gabapentin as the single stabilizing agent. Doses of gabapentin ranged from 900 to 2,400 mg per day. All patients who remained on gabapentin showed cessation of cycling, and six patients demonstrated improved mood. Improved appetite and weight gain were reported side effects. Two adolescents discontinued gabapentin, in one case because of sedation and in the other because of rapid mood swings and irritability with methylphenidate (Ryback, Brodsky, and Munasifi, 1997).

Treatment Recommendations

Few data substantiate the selection of one mood stabilizer over another in the treatment of adolescent depression. Lithium is the only medication that has been studied in a controlled fashion; however, the sample size was small.

Whether to select lithium or valproic acid as the first-line treatment should be based on clinical experience and potential side effects for a given patient. For example, in a substance-abusing patient, the renal metabolism of lithium may be preferred over the hepatic metabolism of valproic acid. Or, an adolescent who plays a musical instrument may not be able to tolerate a lithium-induced tremor, so valproic acid may be the optimal choice.

There is some evidence that, in the case of mixed mania or rapid-cycling mania in adults, valproic acid is more effective than lithium (McElroy et al., 1988; Calabrese and Delucchi, 1989). It may be reasonable to select valproic acid initially for adolescents with this clinical presentation.

There are no controlled-study data regarding the issue of monotherapy or augmentation strategies for adolescent bipolar disorder. Monotherapy has the advantages of lack of drug interactions and greater compliance in adolescents. Initiation of a trial of either lithium or valproic acid, followed by the other agent in the case of treatment nonresponse, is reasonable. Given the scarcity of information about use of carbamazepine for adolescent mania, this treatment should be considered third-line. Gabapentin may prove to be a useful treatment, but there is little clinical or research experience using gabapentin for the treatment of adolescent bipolar disorder.

With regard to augmentation strategies, lithium plus an anticonvulsant has been reported to have a positive response for adolescents with bipolar disorder (Himmelhoch and Garfinkel, 1986). In an open study of 11 adolescent patients with mania who failed to respond to lithium, the combination of lithium, valproate, and neuroleptic produced at least a moderate response in nine patients. No significant side effects were noted (West et al., 1994). A reasonable augmentation strategy for adolescent bipolar disorder is lithium plus valproic acid, followed by lithium plus carbamazepine in the case of treatment nonresponse.

With increased research interest in the treatment of adolescent bipolar disorder, more information will become available to guide medication selection and maintenance. In an 18-month prospective study of 37 adolescents with bipolar disorder, the rate of relapse in patients who discontinued lithium was three times higher than that in those who continued lithium (Strober et al., 1990). Given the high relapse rate, it is recommended that medication be continued for at least one year after symptom resolution. Medication discontinuation should be done gradually, over the course of at least three months. In adults with bipolar disorder, long-term maintenance on mood stabilizers is advised (Post et al., 1992). However, for adolescents, there is insufficient information available to recommend prolonged maintenance therapy for an adolescent with one manic episode, especially as little is known about long-term side effects of mood stabilizers for young adolescents. In the case of adolescents with a second episode of illness, consideration should be given to long-term maintenance therapy.

REFERENCES

Ambrosini, P. J., Wagner, K. D., Biederman, J., et al. (1999), Multicenter open-label sertraline study in adolescent outpatients with major depression. *J. Amer. Acad. Child Adolesc. Psychiat.*, 38(5), 566–572.

American Academy of Child and Adolescent Psychiatry (1997), Practice parameters for the assessment and treatment of children and adolescents with bipolar disorder. *J. Amer. Acad. Child & Adolesc. Psychiat.*, 36:138–157.

American Psychiatric Association (1994a), American Psychiatric Association practice guideline for the treatment of patients with bipolar disorder. *Amer. J. Psychiat.*, 151 (suppl):1–36.

American Psychiatric Association (1994b), *Diagnostic and Statistical Manual of Mental Disorders, Fourth Edition (DSM-IV).* Washington, DC: APA.

Angold, A. & Costello, E. J. (1993), Depressive comorbidity in children and adolescents: Empirical, theoretical and methodological issues. *Amer. J. Psychiat.*, 150:1779–1791.

Apter, J. T., Thase, M. E. & Birkett, M. (1986), Fluoxetine treatment in depressed patients who failed treatment with sertraline. Presented at the American Society of Clinical Psychopharmacology president's day educational program, Montego Bay, Jamaica.

Arsanow, J. R., Carlson, G. & Guthrie, D. (1987), Coping strategies, self perceptions, hopelessness, and perceived family environments in depressed and suicidal children. *J. Consult & Clin. Psychol.*, 55:361–366.

Barbey, J. T. & Roose, S. P. (1998), SSRI Safety in Overdose. *The J. Clin. Psychiat.*, 59:42–48.

Becquemont, L., Ragueneau, I., LeBot, M. A. et al. (1997), Influence of the CYP1A2 inhibitor fluvoxamine on tacrine pharmacokinetics in humans. *Clin. Pharmacol. Ther.*, 61:619–627.

Biederman, J., Faraone, S., Mick, E. & Lelon, E. (1995), Psychiatric comorbidity among referred juveniles with major depression: Fact or artifact? *J. Amer. Acad. Child & Adolesc. Psychiat.*, 34:579–590.

Birmaher, B., Waterman, G. S., Ryan, N. D., Perel, J., McNabb, J., Ballach, L., Beaudry, M. B., Nasr, F. N., Karambelkar, J., Elterich, G., Quintana, H., Williamson, D. E. & Rao, U. (1998), Randomized, controlled trial of Amitriptyline versus placebo for adolescents with "treatment-resistant" major depression. *J. Amer. Acad. Child & Adolesc. Psychiat.*, 37:527–535.

Botteron, K. N. & Geller, B. (1995), Pharmacologic treatment of childhood and adolescent mania. *Child & Adolesc. Psychiatric Clinics North America*, 4:283–304.

Boulos, C., Kutcher, S., Gardner, D. & Young, E. (1992), An open naturalistic trial of fluoxetine in adolescents and young adults with treatment resistant major depression. *J. Child & Adolesc. Psychopharmacol.*, 2:103–111.

Bowring, M. A. & Kovacs, M. (1992), Difficulties in diagnosing manic disorders among children and adolescents. *J. Amer. Acad. Child & Adolesc. Psychiat.*, 31:611–614.

Brosen, K., Hansen, J. G., Nielson, K. K., et al. (1993), Inhibition by paroxetine of desipramine metabolism in extensive but not in poor metabolizers of sparteine. *Eur. J. Clin. Pharmacol.*, 44:349–355.

Brown, W. A. & Harrison, W. (1992), Are patients who are intolerant to one SSRI intolerant to another? *Psychopharmacol. Bull.*, 28:253–256.

Burke, K. C., Burke, J. D., Rae, D. S. & Regier, D. A. (1991), Comparing age at onset of major depression and other psychiatric disorders by birth cohorts in five U.S. community populations. *Arch. Gen. Psychiat.*, 48:789–795.

Calabrese, J. R. & Delucchi, G. A. (1989), Phenomenology of rapid cycling manic depression and its treatment with valproate. *J. Clin. Psychiat.*, 50:30–34.

Campbell, M., Fish, B., Shapiro, T., Collins, & Poh, C. (1972), Lithium and chlorpromazine: A controlled crossover study of hyperactive severely disturbed children. *J. Autism Child Schizophrenia*, 2:234–263.

Carlson, G. A. & Cantwell, D. P. (1982), Diagnosis of childhood depression: A comparison of the Weinberg and DSM III criteria. *J. Amer. Acad. Child Psychiat.*, 21:247–250.

———— Fennig, S. & Bromet, E. J. (1994), The confusion between bipolar disorder and schizophrenia in youth: Where does it stand in the 1990's? *J. Amer. Acad. Child & Adolesc. Psychiat.*, 33:453–460.

———— & Strober, M. (1978), Manic-depressive illness in early adolescence. A study of clinical and diagnostic characteristics in six cases. *J. Amer. Acad. Child Psychiat.*, 17:138–153.

Cooper, T. B., Bergner, P. E. & Simpson, G. M. (1973), The 24-hour serum lithium level as a prognosticator of dosage requirements. *Amer. J. Psychiat.*, 130:601–603.

DeLong, G. R. & Aldershof, A. L. (1987), Long-term experience with lithium treatment in childhood: Correlation with clinical diagnosis. *J. Amer. Acad. Child & Adolesc. Psychiat.,* 26:389–394.

Elliot, G. R. & Popper, C. W. (1990/1991), Tricyclic Antidepressants: The QT interval and other cardiovascular parameters. *J. Child & Adolesc. Psychopharmacol.,* 1:187–189.

Emslie, G. J., Rush, J., Weinberg, W. A., Kowatch, R. A., Hughes, C. W., Carmody, T. & Rintelmann, J. (1997), A double-blind, randomized, placebo-controlled trial of fluoxetine in children and adolescent with depression. *Arch. Gen. Psychiat.,* 54:1031–1037.

Ferro, T., Carlson, G. A., Grayson, P. & Klein, D. N. (1994), Depressive disorders: Distinctions in children. *J. Amer. Acad. Child & Adolesc. Psychiat.,* 33:664–670.

Fetner, H. H. & Geller, B. (1992), Lithium and tricyclic antidepressants. *Psychiatric Clin. North America,* 15:223–241.

Garfinkel, M., Garfinkel, L., Himmelhoch, J. & McHugh, T. (1985), Lithium carbonate and carbamazepine: An effective treatment for adolescent mania or mixed bipolar patients. *Scientific Proceedings, Annual Meeting of the American Acad. Child & Adolesc. Psychiat.,* pp. 41–42.

Garrison, C. Z., Waller, J. L., Cuffe, S. P., McKeown, R. E., Addy, C. L. & Jackson, K. L. (1997), Incidence of major depressive disorder and dysthymia in young adolescents. *J. Amer. Acad. Child & Adolesc. Psychiat.,* 36:458–465.

Gelenberg, A. J. & Schoonover, S. C. (1991), Bipolar disorder. In: *The Practitioner's Guide to Psychoactive Drugs.* New York: Plenum, pp. 91–124.

Geller, B. (1996), The high prevalence of bipolar parents among prepubertal mood-disordered children necessitates appropriate questions to establish bipolarity. *Current Opinions in Psychiatry,* 9:239–240.

——— & Carr, L. G. (1988), Similarities and differences between adult and pediatric major depressive disorders. In *Depression and Mania,* ed. A. Georgotas & R. Cancro. New York: Elsevier, pp. 565–580.

——— Cooper, T. B., Chestnut, E. C., Anker, J. A., Price, D. T. & Yates, E. (1985), Child and adolescent nortriptyline single dose kinetics predict steady state plasma levels and suggested dose: Preliminary data. *J. Clin. Psychopharmacol.,* 5:154–158.

——— ——— ——— ——— & Schuchter, M. D. (1986), Preliminary data on the relationship between nortriptyline plasma level and response in depressed children. *Amer. J. Psychiat.,* 143:1283–1286.

———— ———— Graham, D., et al. (1990), Double-blind placebo-controlled study of nortriptyline in depressed adolescents using a "fixed plasma level" design. *Psychopharmacol. Bull.*, 26:85–90.

———— ———— ———— et al. (1992), Pharmacokinetically designed double-blind placebo-controlled study of nortriptyline in 6 to 12 year olds with major depressive disorder. *J. Amer. Acad. Child Adolesc. Psychiat.*, 31:34–44.

———— ———— Zimerman, B., et al. (1994), Double-blind placebo controlled study of lithium for depressed children with bipolar family histories. Presented at the Annual Meeting of the Congress of Internationale Neuropharmacologie, Washington, D.C.

———— Luby, J. (1997), Child and adolescent bipolar disorder: A review of the past 10 years. *J. Amer. Acad. Child & Adolesc. Psychiat.*, 36:1168–1176.

———— Sun, K., Zimerman, B., Luby, J., Frazier, J. & Williams, M. (1995), Complex and rapid-cycling in bipolar children and adolescents: A preliminary study. *J. Affect. Disorders,* 34:259–268.

———— Thomas, B., Cooper, M. A., Sun, K., Zimerman, B., Frazier, J., Williams, M. & Heath, J. (1998), Double-blind and placebo controlled study of lithium for adolescent bipolar disorders with secondary substance dependency. *J. Amer. Acad. Child & Adolesc. Psychiat.*, 37:171–178.

Geller, B., Todd, R. D., Luby, J. & Botteron, K. N. (1996), Treatment-resistant depression in children and adolescents. *The Psychiatric Clin. North Amer.*, 19:253–267.

Goodyer, I. M., Herbert, M. B., Tamplin, A., Secher, S. M. & Pearson, J. (1997), Short-term outcome of major depression: II. Life events, family dysfunction, and friendship difficulties as predictors of persistent disorder. *J. Amer. Acad. Child & Adolesc. Psychiat.*, 36: 474–480.

Green, W. H. (1995), *Child and Adolescent Clinical Psychopharmacology.* Baltimore: Williams & Wilkins.

Greenblatt, D. J., von Moltke, L. L, Harmatz, J. S. & Shader, R. I. (1998), Drug interactions with newer antidepressants: Role of human cytochromes #P450. *J. Clinc. Psychiat.*, 59:19–27.

Hiemke, C., Weigmann, H., Härtter, S. et al. (1994), Elevated levels of clozapine in serum after addition of fluvoxamine. *J. Clin. Psychopharmacol.,* 14:279–281.

Himmelhoch, J. M. & Garfinkel, M. E. (1986), Mixed mania: Diagnosis and treatment. *Psychopharmacol. Bull.,* 22:613–620.

Isaac, G. (1995), Is bipolar disorder the most common diagnostic entity in hospitalized adolescents and children? *Adolescence*, 30:273–276.

Isojarvi, J. I. T., Laatikainen, T. J., Pakarinen, A. J., et al. (1993), Polycystic ovaries and hyperandrogenism in women taking valproate for epilepsy. *New Engl. J. Med.*, 329:1383–1388.

Jacobson, S. J., Jones, K., Johnson, K., et al. (1992), Prospective multicentre study of pregnancy outcome after lithium exposure during first trimester. *Lancet*, 339:530–533.

Jain, U., Birmaher, B., Garcia, M., Al-Shabbout, M. & Ryan, N. (1992), Fluoxetine in children and adolescents with mood disorders: A chart review of efficacy and adverse effects. *J. Child & Adolesc. Psychopharmacol.*, 2:259–265.

Jefferson, J. W., Greist, J. H. & Baudhiun, M. (1981), Lithium interactions with other drugs. *J. Clin. Psychopharmacol.*, 1:124–134.

Jeppsen, U., Gram, L. F., Vistisen, K., et al. (1996), Dose-dependent inhibition of CYP1A2, CYP2C19, and CYP2D6 by citalopram, fluoxetine, fluvoxamine and paroxetine. *Eur. J. Clin. Pharmacol.*, 51:73–78.

——— Rasmussen, B. B. & Brosen, K. (1997), Fluvoxamine inhibits the CYP2C19-catalyzed bioactivation of chloroguanide. *Clin. Pharmacol. Ther.*, 62:279–296.

Joshi, P. T., Walkup, J. T., Capozzoli, J. A., Detrinis, R. B. & Coyle J. T. (1989), The use of fluoxetine in the treatment of major depressive disorder in children and adolescents. Presented at the 36th annual meeting of the American Academy of Child and Adolescent Psychiatry, New York.

Kashani, J. H., Beck, N. C., Hoeper, E. W., Fallahi, C., Corcoran, C. M., McAllister, J. A., Rosenberg, T. K. & Reid, J. C. (1987), Psychiatric disorders in a community sample of adolescents. *Amer. J. Psychiat.*, 144:584–589.

Keller, M. B., Ryan, N. D., Birmaher, B., Klein, R. G., Strober, M., Wagner, K. D. & Weller, E. B. (1998), Paroxetine and imipramine in the treatment of adolescent depression. New Research Program Abstracts. Presented at annual meeting of American Psychiatric Association, 123.

Kessler, R. C., McGronagle, K. A., Zhao, S., et al. (1994), Lifetime and 12 month prevalence of DSM-III-R psychiatric disorders in the United States. *Arch. Gen. Psychiat.*, 51:8–19.

Khandelwal, S. K., Varma, V. K. & Murthy, R. S. (1984), Renal function in children receiving long-term lithium prophylaxis. *Amer. J. Psychiat.*, 141:278–279.

Klein, D. N., Lewinsohn, P. M. & Seeley, J. R. (1997), Psychosocial characteristics of adolescents with a past history of dysthymic disorder: Comparison with adolescents with past histories of major depressive and non-affective disorders, and never mentally ill controls. *J. Affect. Disorders,* 42:127–135.

Kocsis, J. H., Zisook, S., Davidson, J., Shelton, R., Yonkers, K., Hellerstein, D. J., Rosenbaum, J. & Hallbreich, U. (1997), Double-blind comparison of sertraline, imipramine and placebo in the treatment of dysthymia—psychosocial outcomes. *Amer. J. Psychiat.,* 154: 390–395.

Koehler-Troy, C., Strober, M. & Melanbaum, R. (1986), Methylphenidate induced mania in a prepubertal child. *J. Clin. Psychiat.,* 47:566–567.

Kovacs, M. (1981), Rating scales to assess depression in school-aged children. *Acta Paedopsychiatry,* 46:305–315.

———— (1996), Presentation and course of major depressive disorder during childhood and later years of the life span. *J. Amer. Acad. Child & Adolesc. Psychiat.,* 35:705–715.

———— Feinberg, T. L., Crouse-Novak, M., Paulauskas, S. L. & Finkelstein, R. (1984), Depressive disorders in childhood: I. A longitudinal prospective study of characteristics and recovery. *Arch. Gen. Psychiat.,* 41:229–237.

———— Gatsonis, C., Paulauskas, S. L. & Richards, C. (1989), Depressive disorders in childhood. IV. A longitudinal study of comorbidity with and risk for anxiety disorders. *Arch. Gen. Psychiat.,* 46:776–782.

———— Goldston, D. & Gatsonis, C. (1993), Suicidal behaviors and childhood onset depressive disorders. *J. Amer. Acad. Child & Adolesc. Psychiat.,* 32:8–20.

———— Obrosky, S., Gatsonis, C. & Richards, C. (1997), First-episode major depressive and dysthymic disorder in childhood: Clinical and sociodemographic factors in recovery. *J. Amer. Acad. Child & Adolesc. Psychiat.,* 36:777–784.

———— & Pollock, M. (1995), Bipolar disorder and comorbid conduct disorder in childhood and adolescence. *J. Amer. Acad. Child & Adolesc. Psychiat.,* 34:715–723.

Kraepelin, E. (1921), *Manic-Depressive Insanity and Paranoia.* Edinburgh: Livingstone.

Kutcher, S., Boulos, C., Ward, B., Marton, P., Simeon, J., Ferguson, H. B., Szalai, J., Katic, M., Roberts, N., Dubois, C. & Reed, K.

(1994), Response to desipramine treatment in adolescent depression: A fixed dose, placebo-controlled trial. *J. Amer. Acad. Child & Adolesc. Psychiat.*, 33:686–694.

Kye, C., Waterman, S., Ryan, N., Birmaher, B., Williamson, B. S., Iyengar, S. & Dachille, S. (1996), A randomized, controlled trial of amitriptyline in the acute treatment of adolescent major depression. *J. Amer. Acad. Child & Adolesc. Psychiat.*, 35:1139–1144.

Lazarus, J. H., John, R., Bennie, E. H., et al. (1981), Lithium therapy and thyroid function: A long-term study. *Psychological Medicine*, 11:85–92.

Lewinsohn, P. M., Clarke, G. N., Seeley, J. R. & Rohde, P. (1994), Major depression in community adolescents: Age at onset, episode duration, and time to recurrence. *J. Amer. Acad. Child & Adolesc. Psychiat.*, 33:809–818.

————— Hops, H., Roberts, R. E., Seeley, J. R. & Andrews, J. A. (1993), Adolescent Psychopathology: I. Prevalence and incidence of depression and other DSM-III-R disorders in high school students. *J. Abnormal Psychology*, 102:133–144.

————— Klein, D. N. & Seeley, J. R. (1995), Bipolar disorders in a community sample of older adolescents: Prevalence, phenomenology, comorbidity, and course. *J. Amer. Acad. Child Adolesc. Psychiat.*, 34:454–463.

Magnus, R. D., Findling, R., Preskorn, S. H., Friesen, S., Marcus, R., Marathe, P. & D'Amico, F. (1997), An open-label pharmacokinetic trial of nefazodone in depressed children and adolescents, Poster No. 110. Presented at NCDEU.

Mandoki, M. W., Tapia, M. R., Tapia, M. A., Summer, G. S. & Parker, J. L. (1997), Venlafaxine in the treatment of children and adolescents with major depression. *Psychopharm. Bull.*, 33:149–154.

McCauley, E., Myers, K., Mitchell, J., Calderon, R., Schloredt, K. & Treder, R. (1993), Depression in young people: Initial presentation and clinical course. *J. Amer. Acad. Child & Adolesc. Psychiat.*, 32:714–722.

McConville, B. J., Minnery, K. L., Sorter, M. T., West, S. A., Friedman, L. M. & Christian, K. (1996), An open study of the effects of sertraline on adolescent major depression. *J. Child & Adolesc. Psychopharmacol.*, 6:41–51.

McElroy, S. L. & Keck Jr., P. E. (1995), Antiepileptic drugs. In: *American Psychiatric Press Textbook of Psychopharmacology*, ed.

A. F. Schatzberg & C. B. Nemeroff. Washington, DC: American Psychiatric Press, p. 686.

—————— —————— & Pope, H. G. et al. (1988), Valproate in the treatment of rapid-cycling bipolar disorder. *J. Clin. Psychopharmacol.*, 8:275–279.

McGlashan, T. H. (1988), Adolescent versus adult onset of mania. *Amer. J. Psychiat.*, 145:221–223.

Nelson, J. C. (1998), Treatment of antidepressant nonresponders: Augmentation or switch? *J. Clin. Psychiat.*, 15:35–41.

—————— Mazuire C. M., Bowers, M. B. Jr, et al. (1991), A preliminary open study of the combination of fluoxetine and desipramine for rapid treatment of major depression. *Arch. Gen. Psychiat.*, 48:303–307.

Papatheodorou, G., Kutcher, S. P., Katic, M. & Szalai, J. P. (1994), The efficacy and safety of divalproex sodium in the treatment of acute mania in adolescents and young adults: An open clinical trial. *J. Clin. Psychopharmacol.*, 15:110–116.

Physician's Desk Reference (1998), 52nd ed, Montvale: Medical Economics.

Post, R. M., Leverich, G. S., Altshuler, L. & Mikalauskas, K. (1992), Lithium-discontinuation-induced refractoriness preliminary observation. *Amer. J. Psychiat.*, 149:1727–1729.

Poznanski, E. O., Grossman, J. A., Buchsbaum, Y., et al. (1984), Preliminary studies of the reliability and validity of the children's depression rating scale. *J. Amer. Acad. Child Psychiat.*, 23:191–197.

Preskorn, S. H., Alderman, J., Chung, M. et al. (1994), Pharmacokinetics of desipramine coadministered with sertraline or fluoxetine. *J. Clin. Psychopharmacol.*, 14:90–98.

—————— Weller, E. B. & Weller, R. A. (1982), Depression in children relationship between plasma imipramine levels and response. *J. Clin. Psychiat.*, 43:450–453.

Puig-Antich, J., Perel, J., Lupatkin, W., et al. (1979), Plasma levels of imipramine (IMI) and desmethylimipramine (DMI) and clinical response to prepubertal major depressive disorder: A preliminary report. *J. Amer. Acad. Child Psychiat.*, 18:616–627.

—————— —————— —————— et al. (1987), Imipramine in prepubertal major depressive disorders. *Arch. Gen. Psychiat.*, 44:81–89.

Rao, U., Ryan, N. D., Birmaher, B., et al. (1995), Unipolar depression in adolescents: Clinical outcome in adulthood. *J. Amer. Acad. Child & Adolesc. Psychiat.*, 34:566–578.

239

————— Weissman, M. M., Martin, J. A. & Hammond, R. W. (1993), Childhood depression and risk of suicide: A preliminary report of a longitudinal study. *J. Amer. Acad. Child & Adolesc. Psychiat.,* 32:21–27.

Rey-Sanchez, F. & Gutierrez-Casares, J. R. (1997), Paroxetine in children with major depressive disorder: An open trial. *J. Amer. Acad. Child & Adolesc. Psychiat.,* 36:1443–1447.

Rice, J., Reich, T., Andreasen, N. C., et al. (1987), The familial transmission of bipolar illness. *Arch. Gen. Psychiat.,* 44:441–447.

Riddle, M. A., Geller, B. & Ryan, N. (1993), Another sudden death in a child treated with desipramine. *J. Amer. Acad. Child & Adolesc. Psychiat.,* 32:792–797.

Roberts, R. E., Lewinsohn, P. M. & Seeley, J. R. (1995), Symptoms of DSM-III-R major depression in adolescence: Evidence from an epidemiological survey. *J. Amer. Acad. Child & Adolesc. Psychiat.,* 34:1608–1617.

Rosenberg, D. R., Holttum, J. & Gershon, S. (1994), *Textbook of Pharmacotherapy for Child and Adolescent Psychiatric Disorders.* New York: Brunner/Mazel.

Ryan, N. D., Puig-Antich, J., Ambrosini, P., et al. (1987), The clinical picture of major depression in children and adolescents. *Arch. Gen. Psychiat.,* 44:854–861.

————— ————— Rabinovich, H., Fried, J., Ambrosini, P., Meyer, V., Torres, D., Dachille, S. & Mazzie, R. (1988), MAOIs in adolescent major depression unresponsive to tricyclic antidepressants. *J. Amer. Acad. Child & Adolesc. Psychiat.,* 27:755–758.

————— Williamson, D. E., Iyengar, S., et al. (1992), A secular increase in child and adolescent onset affective disorder. *J. Amer. Acad. Child & Adolesc. Psychiat.,* 31:600–605.

Ryback, R. S., Brodsky, L. & Munasifi, F. (1997), Gabapentin in bipolar disorder. *J. Neuropsychiat. Clin. Neurosci.,* 2:301.

Schatzberg, A. F., Cole, J. O. & DeBattista, C. (1997), *Manual of Clinical Psychopharmacology, Third Edition.* Washington, DC: American Psychiatric Press.

Shaffer, D., Gould, M. S., Fisher, P. et al. (1996), Psychiatric diagnosis in child and adolescent suicide. *Arch. Gen. Psychiat.,* 53:339–348.

Shain, B. N., King, C. A., Naylor, M. & Alessi, N. (1991), Chronic depression and hospital course in adolescents. *J. Amer. Acad. Child & Adolesc. Psychiat.,* 30:428–433.

Simeon, J. G., Dinicola, V. F., Ferguson, H. B. & Copping, W. (1990), Adolescent depression: A placebo controlled fluoxetine treatment study and follow-up. *Prog. Neuro-psychopharmacol. Biol. Psychiat.,* 14:791–795.

Strober, M. & Carlson, G. (1982), Bipolar illness in adolescents with major depression: Clinical, genetic, and psychopharmacologic predictors in a three to four year prospective follow-up investigation. *Arch. Gen. Psychiat.,* 39:549–555.

———— Morrell, W., Burroughs, J., Lampert, C., Danforth, H. & Freeman, R. (1988), A family study of bipolar I disorder in adolescence: Early onset of symptoms linked to increased familial loading and lithium resistance. *J. Affect. Disorders,* 15:255–268.

———— ———— Lampert, C. & Burroughs (1990), Relapse following discontinuation of lithium maintenance therapy in adolescents with bipolar illness: A naturalistic study. *Amer. J. Psychiat.,* 147(4): 457–461.

———— Schmidt-Lackner, S., Freeman, R., Bower, S., Lampert, C. & DeAntonio, M. (1995), Recovery and relapse in adolescents with bipolar affective illness: A five-year naturalistic, prospective follow-up. *J. Amer. Acad. Child & Adolesc. Psychiat.,* 34:724–731.

Tancer, N. K., Klein, R. G. J., Koplewicz, H. S., et al. (1992), Rate of atypical depression and tricyclic drug response in adolescents {abstract}. *J. Amer. Acad. Child & Adolesc. Psychiat.,* 33:576.

Thase, M. E., Fava, M., Halbreich, U., Kocsis, J. H., Koran, L., Davidson, J., Rosenbaum, J. & Harrison, W. (1996), A placebo-controlled, randomized clinical trial comparing sertraline and imipramine for the treatment of dysthymia. *Arch. Gen. Psychiat.,* 53(9):777–784.

Vestergaard, P. (1983), Clinically important side effects of long-term lithium treatment: A review. *Acta. Psychiat. Scand. (Suppl),* 67:11–36.

Viesselman, J. O., Yaylayan, S., Weller, E. B. & Weller, R. A. (1993), Antidysthymic drugs (antidepressants and antimanics). *Practitioner's Guide to Psychoactive Drugs for Children and Adolescents,* pp. 239–268.

Wagner, K. D. (1996), Major depression and anxiety disorders associated with Norplant. *J. Clin. Psychiat.,* 57:152–157.

———— & Berenson, A. B. (1994), Norplant-associated major depression and panic disorder. *J. Clin. Psychiat.,* 55:478–480.

———— Birmaher, M. D., Carlson, G., Clarke, G., Emslie, G., Geller, B., Keller, M. D., Klein, R., Kutcher, S., Papatheodorou, G., Ryan,

N., Strober, M. & Weller, E. (1998), Safety of paroxetine and imipramine in the treatment of adolescent depression. *New Clin. Drug Evaluators Unit Program Abstracts*, 38:69.

Weller, E. B. & Weller, R. A. (1990), Depressive disorders in children and adolescents. In: *Psychiatric Disorders in Children and Adolescents*, ed. B. Garfinkel, G. Carlson, & E. B. Weller. Philadelphia: Saunders, pp. 3–20, 37–47.

———— ———— & Fristad, M. A. (1995), Bipolar disorder in children: Misdiagnosis, underdiagnosis, and future directions. *J. Amer. Acad. Child & Adolesc. Psychiat.*, 34:709–714.

———— ———— & Svadjian, H. (1996), Mood disorders. In: *Child and Adolescent Psychiatry: A Comprehensive Textbook*, 2nd Edition. ed. M. Lewis. Baltimore, MD: Williams and Wilkins, pp. 650–665.

Weller, R. A., Weller, E. B., Tucker, S. G. & Fristad, M. A. (1986), Mania in prepubertal children: Has it been underdiagnosed? *J. Affect. Disorders,* 11:151–154.

West, S. A., Keck, P. E., McElroy, S. L., Strakowski, S. M., Minnery, K. L., McConville, B. J. & Sorter, M. T. (1994), Open trial of valproate in the treatment of adolescent mania. *J. Child & Adolesc. Psychopharmacol.,* 4:263–267.

Wickramaratne, P. J. & Weissman, M. M. (1998), Onset of psychopathology in offspring by developmental phase and parental depression. *J. Amer. Child & Adolesc. Psychiat.*, 37:933–942.

Wise, M. G. & Rundell, J. R. (1988), *Concise Guide to Consultation Psychiatry*. Washington, DC: American Psychiatric Press.

Wozniak, J. & Biederman, J. (1996), A pharmacological approach to the quagmire of comorbidity in juvenile mania. *J. Amer. Acad. Child & Adolesc. Psychiat.,* 35:826–828.

———— ———— Kiely, K., Ablon, J. S., Faraone, S. V., Mundy, E. & Mennin, D. (1995), Mania-like symptoms suggestive of childhood-onset bipolar disorder in clinically referred children. *J. Amer. Acad. Child & Adolesc. Psychiat.,* 34:867–876.

Young, R. C., Biggs, J. T., Ziegler, V. E. & Meyer, D. A. (1978), A rating scale for mania: Reliability, validity, and sensitivity. *Br. J. Psychiat.,* 133:434.

14 PHARMACOLOGIC TREATMENT OF ANXIETY DISORDERS IN ADOLESCENTS

ROBINDER K. BHANGOO AND MARK A. RIDDLE

Until recently, most research and clinical practice in the area of pharmacological treatment of anxiety disorders in children and adolescents focused on tricyclics and benzodiazepines. Results were inconsistent, and few studies were controlled. Results, though, were sufficiently promising to support the alleviation of anxiety symptoms with pharmacological treatment in some children. Since the recent introduction of selective serotonin reuptake inhibitors (SSRIs) and buspirone in the United States, this situation has begun to change. For the first time, large controlled studies of the safety and efficacy of SSRIs and buspirone in children and adolescents with anxiety disorders are in progress. Soon, research data will be available to guide clinical practice.

Classification/Nosology

Currently, in the *Diagnostic and Statistical Manual of Mental Disorders, Fourth Edition* (*DSM–IV*; American Psychiatric Association [APA], 1994), there are 10 anxiety disorders (if selective mutism is included). When considering the various disorders, we have tried to describe the core symptoms of a disorder with a simple word or phrase. Using this approach, each of the 10 disorders can be classified under one of five categories: "fears," "worries," "physical symptoms," "excessive response to stress," and obsessions-compulsions. This chapter will not focus on obsessive-compulsive disorder (OCD). Although there is a high rate of comorbidity of OCD with other anxiety disorders, and there is an increased rate of anxiety disorders in first-degree relatives of OCD probands (Gerald Nestadt, M.D., personal communication, January 1999), OCD may also be viewed as a "neuropsychiatric" disorder. As such, OCD may be grouped with tic disorders (Pauls et al., 1995) as well as with the other anxiety disorders.

The fears category could describe several disorders, including separation anxiety ("fear of aloneness or loss"), specific phobias ("fear of danger"), social phobia ("fear of humiliation"; also called avoidant disorder in earlier editions of *DSM*), selective mutism ("fear of humiliation"), and agoraphobia ("fear of the marketplace"). The worries category would include generalized anxiety disorder (GAD). GAD, which, when applied to children, was called overanxious disorder in *DSM–III* and *DSM–III–R*, is manifested by excessive worry or apprehensive expectation that the youngster finds difficult to control. The physical-symptoms category includes panic disorder, although physical symptoms such as "butterflies in the stomach" or sweaty palms can occur in any of the anxiety disorders. The excessive-response-to-stress category includes both acute stress disorder and posttraumatic stress disorder (PTSD). Overall, the most common presenting symptoms in children and adolescents are worries, fears, and physical symptoms, although true panic attacks are relatively rare in adolescents.

Family and clinical studies have revealed that anxiety symptoms from several different *DSM* anxiety disorders may present together (Kashani and Orvaschel, 1990). It also has been shown that the anxiety disorders appear to evolve over a lifetime—with different disorders having different age ranges in which they most commonly present (Anderson et al., 1987; Francis, Last, and Strauss, 1987; Bell-Dolan, Last, and Strauss, 1990; Kashani and Orvaschel, 1990; Bernstein and Borchardt, 1991; Last et al., 1992; Schneier et al., 1992; Strauss and Last, 1993). These observations have led to speculation that the multiple expressions of "anxiety" could be caused by only one vulnerability (or a few) in an individual. In other words, the presentation of anxiety in an adolescent with this vulnerability could include several anxiety disorders, either during one episode or across a lifetime.

Epidemiology

A number of epidemiological studies show that anxiety disorders are common in adolescents (Bird et al., 1988; Kashani and Orvaschel, 1988, 1990; Regier et al., 1988; McGee et al., 1990; Whitaker et al.,

1990). The question of just how common these disorders are can be addressed by examining the definition of disorder. If the diagnosis of disorder simply requires symptom expression, but no signs of functional impairment, then the prevalence rates would be high. The lowest prevalence rates would be seen if a diagnosis could be made only if symptoms needed to be seen along with "clinically significant" impairment and/ or distress. Rates between these two would be seen if a diagnosis required symptoms along with "some" evidence of impairment and/or distress. Thus, the reported prevalence of anxiety disorders in children and adolescents must be examined carefully with regard to stringency of diagnostic criteria. Considering that *DSM–IV* was the first edition of the *DSM* to require functional impairment to make a psychiatric diagnosis (APA, 1994), studies done using previous editions might reflect higher prevalence rates of disorders than studies done more recently.

In a comprehensive review of 16 methodologically sound epidemiological studies of anxiety in children and adolescents, Costello and Angold (1995) found rates of all anxiety disorders combined to range from 5.7% to 17.7% across the studies, with half of the studies having combined rates above 10%. When studying the rates as a function of the mean age of subjects, Costello and Angold found that there was a nonsignificant trend for a slight rise in prevalence rates as age increased. Based on the data reviewed, anxiety disorders appear to be common in the adolescent population. When even the lowest prevalence rate (6%) measured in these studies is considered, anxiety disorders join attention-deficit hyperactivity disorder (ADHD), with a prevalence rate of 3% to 5% (APA, 1994), as a public health concern. However, in contrast to ADHD, anxiety disorders often present as a "silent epidemic." As anxiety disorders manifest more as internalized symptoms as compared to the externalizing behavioral symptoms of ADHD, it is not surprising that children with anxiety are not usually brought to clinical attention. In fact, in their review, Costello and Angold noted that anxiety disorders, in contrast to other psychiatric disorders, are more often revealed by children rather than their parents.

Developmental Issues

Presentation of anxiety appears to evolve over a lifetime, with certain diagnoses being more common at different points in the life cycle. In their study of a large clinical sample, Last et al. (1992) found that the age of symptom onset varied with type of anxiety disorder. They found mean ages of symptom onset as follows: 7.5 years for separation anxiety, 8.4 years for simple (or specific) phobia, 10.8 years for overanxious disorder, and 11.3 years for social phobia.

In a study assessing children from a community sample in three age groups (ages 8, 12, and 17), Kashani and Orvaschel (1990) found similar trends in anxiety diagnoses across the age groups. There was an inverse correlation between the rates of "fear of separation," "fear of strangers," and age. On the other hand, rates of "anxiety of past imperfections," "fear of social situations," "worrying a lot," and "worrying what others think of me" rose with age. These data suggest that fear of separation and strangers decreases as children enter adolescence. They also show that interpersonal concerns, social anxiety, and concerns about personal adequacy all increase as children progress through adolescence (Kashani and Orvaschel, 1990).

Similar findings were reported by Francis et al. (1987), who evaluated 45 children and adolescents with separation anxiety disorder. They found that younger children reported more symptoms of separation anxiety than did adolescents. Anderson et al. (1987) also found that the most frequently occurring anxiety disorder in preadolescents was separation anxiety disorder, whereas Schneier et al. (1992) and Strauss and Last (1993) found that social phobia had age of onset in early to middle adolescence. Bell-Dolan et al. (1990) found that more adolescents than preadolescents endorsed fears of public speaking, blushing, excessive worry about past behavior, and self-consciousness.

These studies contribute to the formulation of a developmental path of anxiety disorders—with separation anxiety occurring more often in prepubertal children and social phobia occurring more often in adolescents. When a child is young and totally dependent on his or her caregivers for safety and sustenance, losing these caregivers presents a serious threat to survival. Separation from these caregivers and fear of loss or separation would be problems of this developmental period. As a child matures, motor and cognitive development unfolds, allowing the child to become mobile and accessible to aspects in his or her environment that could threaten existence, such as animals or heights. Phobias centered around these dangers are also a problem of the young child. Further development in cognition and language skills allows the child to interact with others, and social development creates the importance of noncaregivers in the child's life. Social fears then become more prevalent. As skills continue to develop, mastery and pride in performance take on more importance. Adequacy fears and performance anxieties can appear only in the child who has developed to this point. As the child continues to grow and participate in the world outside the home and is exposed to public places, fear of the new stimuli may develop. The anxiety-prone child may consider these public places as threatening. These same places might not have been considered frightening to the same child at a younger age, when he or she was cognitively unable to appreciate the social significance of public places and unable to experience any place outside the home without the protective enfolding of caregivers. The studies outlined are consistent with these observations. They support the idea that anxiety disorders present differently at different developmental stages. However, these studies were cross-sectional and not longitudinal; therefore, we cannot be sure of the progression of anxiety disorders in an individual youngster through his or her lifetime. For example, longitudinal studies are needed to see if separation anxiety predisposes an individual to other anxiety disorders.

Focusing on impairment within a developmental perspective, Kashani and Orvaschel (1990) compared anxious subjects to nonanxious subjects in varying age groups. As compared to the nonanxious controls, the younger age group with anxiety had better peer relationships than the adolescent age group. Also, the nonanxious groups did not differ with regard to difficulties in family functioning, but the anxious adolescents' rates of family difficulties were significantly higher than those of the younger age group. These findings indicate a need to examine the relation among anxiety, developmental stage, and social functioning. Further studies are needed, particularly longitudinal studies, in order to follow the course of anxiety disorders through childhood and adolescence and into adulthood—assessing clinical symptoms as well as functional impairment over time.

Comorbidity

With regard to psychopharmacology, comorbidity plays a role in the formulation of a treatment plan for a youngster who presents with an anxiety disorder. If the patient presents with a comorbid diagnosis, the treatment plan would vary depending on whether the comorbid disorder would respond to the same agent used to treat the anxiety disorder, whether it would respond to a different class of medication, or whether it would not respond to medication at all. For example, a patient presenting with an anxiety disorder and depression might be treated with a single medication, whereas a patient with an anxiety disorder and ADHD might be treated with two medications, and an adolescent with an anxiety disorder and oppositional defiant disorder might be treated with a single medication but might also need a behavioral plan.

Epidemiological studies show a high rate of comorbidity between anxiety disorders and other psychiatric disorders, especially depressive disorders. Several studies have examined these rates. Kashani and Orvaschel (1990) found that about 36% of their sample with anxiety disorders met criteria for two or more anxiety diagnoses. When compared to nonanxious controls, the 17-year-old anxious adolescents had significantly poorer peer relationships and more behavioral problems, mood problems, somatic complaints, school difficulties, and poor self-concepts. Kashani and Orvaschel (1988) found a high comorbidity rate between anxiety and depression; 69% of adolescents with an anxiety disorder associated with functional impairment also had a major depression. McGee et al. (1990) found that, in the adolescents who had an anxiety disorder, about 15% had two or more anxiety disorders, 12% had a concurrent depressive disorder, 6% had a disorder in the conduct/oppositional realm, and 4% had ADHD. Bird et al. (1988) used a weighting process to correct for bias and found that about 17% of the anxious children and adolescents had an affective disorder, 39% had a conduct/oppositional disorder, and 21% had ADHD. It should be noted that this study consisted of both children and adolescents.

It has been reported that children and adolescents with concurrent anxiety and depressive disorders have increased severity of anxiety (Strauss et al., 1988; Bernstein, 1991) and depressive symptoms (Bernstein, 1991; Mitchell et al., 1988) compared with children without comorbidity (Bernstein and Borchardt, 1991).

Diagnostic Assessment

One of the first problems with diagnosis of anxiety disorders in adolescents is identifying the youngster who needs treatment. In contrast to adults—who generally request help for themselves when suffering from excessive worries, fears, or physical symptoms of anxiety—children are brought to the clinician by their parents, who may be concerned about "behavioral problems" and unaware of their child's anxiety symptoms. As part of their anxiety disorder, adolescents may have a fear of humiliation or failure that would prevent them from revealing their anxiety symptoms to their parents. Unless the symptoms manifest in an externalized form, such as refusal to go to school, the disorder may go undetected while the child experiences symptoms. Education as to warning signs may alert parents and teachers of children and adolescents at risk—increasing their referral for evaluation.

Thorough evaluation requires an assessment of the adolescent and the parents. Assessment of the adolescent will be outlined initially; next, recommendations for a parental assessment are made. After completing the evaluation, the clinician should obtain an understanding of the thoughts, feelings, and behaviors of the adolescent as well as an idea of how his or her life has been affected both in school and in social settings. Evaluating the adolescent cognitively includes exploring his or her worries or thoughts, and a successful interview with the adolescent allows the clinician to understand the amount of distress or negativity the adolescent is experiencing. Behavioral changes witnessed in adolescents with anxiety disorders include avoidance of certain situations and/or clinging to caregivers due to a fear of separating. To assess the degree of impairment due to an anxiety disorder, academic performance and interpersonal relationships are evaluated. Much information about an adolescent's interpersonal relationships can be obtained by examining behavioral patterns.

The American Academy of Child and Adolescent Psychiatry's "Practice Parameters for the Assessment and Treatment of Children and Adolescents with Anxiety Disorders" (Bernstein and Shaw, 1997) outlines a comprehensive approach to evaluating anxiety symptoms. Evaluation of the youngster includes a history of the onset and development of the anxiety symptoms, with associated stressors, along with the patient's medical, school, social and family history, and a mental status examination. Special attention to the specifics of the anxiety helps to differentiate among the various anxiety disorders. Key points to look for include whether the anxiety is stimulus-specific, spontaneous, or anticipatory and if avoidant behavior is present. Developmental history from infancy and early childhood—including information on temperament, ability to soothe self or be soothed, quality of attachment, adaptability, stranger and separation responses, and childhood fears—all help to form a longitudinal picture of the child. When obtaining medical history, one should inquire about number of visits to physician or emergency room for symptoms that could be somatic components of anxiety. Medications can induce anxiety, so a medication history may reveal a source of symptoms. School history, including the adolescent's pattern of attendance, and social history, covering any environmental stressors, are also important. Relevant topics in the social history include the degree of involvement with the peer group and social competence.

In addition to the interview of the child, specific instruments may be used to elicit further information. If given from a variety of perspectives (i.e., self-report, clinician report, parent report), a more accurate assessment may be made. Self-reports are especially useful as children and adolescents may be more comfortable putting their concerns on paper in private rather than speaking them aloud. Three self-report instruments available include the Revised Children's Manifest Anxiety Scale (RC–MAS; Reynolds and Richmond, 1978); the Multidimensional Anxiety Scale for Children (March et al., 1997), and the Screen for Child Anxiety Related Emotional Disorders (Birmaher et al., 1997).

Current practice is to have a portion of the evaluation include an interview with the adolescent alone, usually after meeting with the parents and patient together. In addition to providing a safe forum for the adolescent to express his or her feelings and concerns, this practice allows clinicians to obtain a more accurate assessment of the adolescent's symptoms. Studies have shown that parents often report fewer anxiety symptoms as compared to those reported by the adolescent. McGee et al. (1990) obtained information about psychiatric symptoms by clinician interviews of adolescents and questionnaires completed by their parents. The results were that parents confirmed only one third of the adolescent-reported anxiety-depressive disorders. In Kashani and Orvaschel's (1990) study of anxiety across three age groups, both children and parents were interviewed separately by structured interviews. Data from the children's interviews revealed rates of symptoms described previously in this chapter. Data from the parents' interviews revealed similar findings across the age groups; however, all the reported rates were lower. This is consistent with findings of another study (Weissman et al., 1987) in which parents reported fewer internalizing disorders in their children as compared to those reported by the children themselves.

Assessment of the parents is important as well—in order to be aware of any treated or untreated psychopathology. Family history should be examined for anxiety and other psychiatric disorders but should also be examined for any medical conditions that may present as anxiety (e.g., hyperthyroidism). It is important to assess parental response to an adolescent's illness, parental coping mechanisms, and parental interactions with the adolescent. Parents can be accommodating, punitive, or enabling, and each response would have different effects on the child. Family interactions, by report and observation, should be examined for dysfunctional patterns.

Anxiety disorders can be associated with many somatic symptoms, including tachycardia, palpitations, pounding heart, hyperventilation, sensations of shortness of breath or smothering, feeling of choking, chest pain or discomfort, diaphoresis, trembling or shaking, nausea or abdominal distress, dizziness, unsteady gait, light-headedness or faintness, numbness or tingling sensations, and chills or hot flashes (APA, 1994). Several medical conditions may mimic anxiety disorders—including hyperthyroidism, hyperparathyroidism, vestibular dysfunction, cardiac arrhythmias, caffeinism, pheochromocytoma, and seizure disorders (APA, 1994) as well as migraines, central nervous system disorders, and hypoglycemia (Bernstein and Shaw, 1997). An appropriate initial assessment including a medical interview, physical examination, and laboratory data assists in detecting a medical condition that may cause anxiety symptoms. A comprehensive (but not mandatory) laboratory evaluation would include electrolytes, glucose, thyroid-function tests, calcium, urine toxicology screen, and electrocardiogram (ECG).

Other psychiatric diagnoses can present with symptoms appearing as an anxiety disorder—including adjustment disorder, ADHD, substance use disorders, eating disorders, somatoform disorders, reactive attachment disorders, pervasive developmental disorders, schizophrenia, and sleep terror disorder (Bernstein and Shaw, 1997). As there is a reported comorbidity of anxiety and depression in adolescents (Bird et al., 1988; Kashani and Orvaschel, 1988; McGee et al., 1990), evaluation for mood disorders may detect a depression overshadowed by the anxiety symptoms. When a specific type of anxiety disorder has been diagnosed, patients evaluated for other anxiety disorders may reveal additional diagnoses, as there is a high frequency of anxious adolescents having more than one anxiety disorder (Kashani and Orvaschel, 1990; McGee et al., 1990).

Treatment

Treatment begins with the feedback session following the initial evaluation, when the clinician's conclusions and recommendations are presented to the adolescent and parents. Frequently, the anxiety disorder can be understood from the perspective of a disease or illness vulnerability. However, as with any illness, stress and environmental factors may exacerbate the symptoms; self-esteem can be affected, and learned behaviors can develop. Therefore, treatment may include medication for the illness vulnerability; cognitive-behavioral therapy for the learned components and to train the adolescent to cope with the vulnerability; and parent behavioral management training and individual psychotherapy to provide support, guidance, and identification of conflicts. Parents can help their adolescents by encouraging participation in cognitive-behavioral therapy, even though it may require exposing the adolescent to distressing anxiety symptoms. Education regarding the cause of anxiety and expected outcomes of treatment can help parents with their concerns.

The use of psychotropics in children and adolescents has not been extensively studied. There is a lack of controlled trials assessing the safety and efficacy of these medications in pediatric anxiety disorders. The available data are reviewed here, followed by recommendations for pharmacological treatment of adolescents, with the caveat that subjects in these studies usually included prepubertal children. This is a limitation in the information available, in that we do not have a clear understanding of the effects of development and maturation on the safety, efficacy, and metabolic disposition of psychopharmacologic agents. Therefore, it has not been established that results seen in children are generalizable to adolescents. This is an area deserving further study.

There are four major groups of medications available to treat anxiety disorders, although there are no FDA indications for any of them in adolescents. The four groups are the benzodiazepines, the tricyclics, buspirone, and the SSRIs. There have been no consistent results from controlled trials for any group. The SSRIs are under active investigation for treatment of generalized anxiety disorder, social phobia, separation anxiety disorder, and PTSD.

Beta-blockers have been used to treat performance anxiety in adults, but studies in adults have not shown significant results (Riddle et al., in press). Data are not extensive in children and adolescents and are in the area of aggressive dyscontrol. There are no placebo-controlled studies of beta-blockers in treatment of pediatric anxiety disorders, but there is one open-label study of 11 children with PTSD whose symptoms showed some improvement when treated with propranolol (Famularo, Kinscherff, and Fenton, 1988). There is another report that propranolol relieved symptoms in 13 of 14 children with hyperventilation syndrome (Joorabchi, 1977).

BENZODIAZEPINES

In adults, benzodiazepines are indicated for generalized anxiety disorder, panic disorder, and alcohol withdrawal. In children and adolescents, however, benzodiazepines are used to treat seizures, night terrors, somnambulism, and debilitating muscle tension (Coffey, 1993), owing to their anticonvulsant, muscle-relaxant, and hypnotic effects (Dantzer, 1985). Although indication for use in adolescents has not been established, benzodiazepines may be helpful in treating anxiety disorders such as overanxious disorder of childhood, social phobia, separation anxiety disorder, and panic disorder as well as other situations of acute anxiety (Coffey, 1993).

Review of Published Studies

Biederman (1987) reported three cases of prepubertal children with diagnoses of separation anxiety disorder, overanxious disorder of childhood, and childhood avoidant disorder—all with physical symptoms similar to those seen in adult panic disorder. These children were treated with clonazepam 0.5 to 3 mg per day. All children were reported to have improved with minimal side effects and maintenance of improvement on follow-up ranging from five months to three years.

In an open trial of four adolescents with panic disorder, Kutcher and Mackenzie (1988) noted an improvement using clonazepam 0.5 mg twice a day. Specifically, they noted a decrease of about 80% in Hamilton Anxiety Rating Scale (HARS) scores after two weeks of treatment. The average frequency of panic attacks decreased about 90%. They also observed that somatic symptoms of anxiety improved more rapidly than psychological symptoms of anxiety (Kutcher and MacKenzie, 1988).

253

In an open clinical trial assessing alprazolam in children and adolescents age seven to 17 with overanxious and avoidant disorders, Siméon and Ferguson (1987) found significant global improvements on clinician, parent, and teacher ratings. The study, which used a placebo–drug–placebo design, demonstrated significant improvements in anxiety symptoms measured on clinician-rated global severity scales, Conners parent questionnaires and Conners Teacher Questionnaires. Most of the improvements noted during the drug-treatment phase were continued through the posttreatment placebo phase.

In a double-blind crossover trial comparing clonazepam to placebo in 15 children age seven to 13, nine children had a moderate to marked improvement on as much as 2 mg per day of clonazepam, but statistical comparisons failed to show significance in favor of clonazepam (Graae et al., 1994).

The efficacies of alprazolam and imipramine were compared in two studies by Bernstein, Garfinkel, and Borchardt (1990) in children and adolescents with school refusal. The open-label study assessed 17 school refusers age nine to 17 with varying diagnoses. Unfortunately, none of the subjects had an anxiety disorder without a comorbid mood disorder. Sixty-five percent had both depressive and anxiety disorders, 23% had depression only, and 12% did not meet criteria for a *DSM–III* diagnosis but had symptoms of depression and anxiety. Standard doses of alprazolam and imipramine were used; all blood levels were in the therapeutic range. Each subject was also included in a multimodal treatment program that included a school-reentry program and psychotherapy. Sixty-seven percent of each group were rated moderately or markedly improved after about eight weeks of treatment, and about 50% of each group returned to school (Bernstein et al., 1990).

The eight-week, double-blind, placebo-controlled study assessing alprazolam and imipramine in school refusers included 24 children and adolescents not included in the open trial (Bernstein et al., 1990). The subjects, seven to 18 years old, received standard doses of alprazolam, imipramine, or placebo. At eight weeks, significant differences were seen in scores on the Anxiety Rating for Children scale. The alprazolam group showed the most improvement, and the placebo group showed the least improvement. Statistically significant differences were not seen in the other rating scales, but similar trends were noted. The differences seen may have been due to differences in the baseline scores among the three groups. In these studies, it appeared that eight weeks of treatment with medication were needed to reveal improvements in anxiety and depressive symptoms (Bernstein et al., 1990).

Siméon et al. (1992) conducted a double-blind placebo-controlled study of alprazolam in 30 children age eight to 17 with overanxious disorder or avoidant disorder. Statistically significant group differences were not seen, but alprazolam appeared to be more efficacious than placebo, with 88% improvement on alprazolam versus 62% improvement on placebo.

A double-blind placebo-controlled study of clonazepam in adolescents with panic disorder showed benefit with active medication on measures of generalized anxiety, frequency of panic attacks, and school and social disability (Kutcher and Reiter, personal communication, 1996).

Thirteen pediatric oncology patients age seven to 16 awaiting bone-marrow aspirations and spinal taps were treated in an open-label study of alprazolam at low doses (0.125 to 1.0 mg) and were shown to have a decrease in anticipatory and acute situational anxiety (Pfefferbaum, Overall, et al., 1987).

Side Effects

When starting an adolescent on a benzodiazepine, one should warn patients and parents of potential side effects, the most common being drowsiness and sedation. Other adverse effects noted in the studies reviewed here are headaches, incoordination, irritability, diplopia, tremor, depression, dysphoria, and behavioral disinhibition (Biederman 1987, 1991; Siméon and Ferguson, 1987; Bernstein et al., 1990; Kutcher et al., 1992; Graae et al., 1994).

Behavioral disinhibition has been described in children and adolescents treated with benzodiazepines. It consists of irritable, aggressive, and impulsive behavior (Siméon and Ferguson, 1987; Graae et al., 1994). Reiter and Kutcher (1991) reported two cases of adolescents treated with benzodiazepines who developed disinhibition with some "hypomanic" features that resolved with discontinuation of the medications. Siméon et al. (1992) found a significant increase in beta activity in bilateral hemispheres on electroencephalograms done during alprazolam treatment, but this has not been established as an etiology for benzodiazepine-induced disinhibition. The "neuroleptic" etiology of disinhibition is suggested by a report of three children with structural brain damage who were disinhibited on clonazepam (Commander, Green, and Prendergast, 1991).

There is concern about benzodiazepines' potential negative cognitive effects beyond those due to sedation. However, Siméon and Ferguson (1987) and Siméon et al. (1992) did not show any decline in functioning on cognitive measures when subjects were treated with alprazolam, and teacher reports did not show any decline in academic functioning during the treatment period. Two cases in which children developed psychotic symptoms while on benzodiazepines were reported (Pfefferbaum, Butler, et al., 1987), and the patients' symptoms resolved with discontinuation of the medication.

A risk of benzodiazepines is the development of tolerance, dependence, and abuse, which, although insufficiently studied in children and adolescents, has been extensively documented in adults (Salzman, 1989). The incidence of adolescent self-medication with benzodiazepines was reported by Pederson and Lavik (1991) in a longitudinal study of more than 1,000 adolescents in Sweden. In the group surveyed, 10% reported using anxiolytics and/or hypnotics in the past year, the majority for alleviating stress, depression, or sleep disorders. A smaller percentage reported taking the drugs for intoxication and obtained the drugs from peers and illegal sources (Pederson and Lavik, 1991). Although there are no reports of adolescent fatalities with overdose of benzodiazepines alone (Kutcher et al., 1992), depressant effects on the central nervous system and absorption rate of the benzodiazepines are potentiated by alcohol (Rall, 1990).

Clinical Practice

Considering the potential for abuse and dependence, Coffey (1993) has recommended that benzodiazepines be used only when other medication and psychosocial treatments have failed and that duration of treatment be brief. Benzodiazepines, though, can be helpful in certain clinical situations, such as for decreasing anxiety before medical procedures. Due to their rapid anxiolytic effects, benzodiazepines can also be used to acutely decrease anxiety while awaiting the onset of effects of an alternative medication, such as an SSRI.

The benzodiazepines most commonly studied and used in clinical practice have been clonazepam, lorazepam, and alprazolam. The major difference between these medications is in the half-lives, with clonazepam having the longest duration and lorazepam and alprazolam having the shortest. Clonazepam is simpler to administrate if anxiety reduction is required throughout the day. If there is a concern about side effects, lorazepam and alprazolam might be better choices.

Dosing should be considered carefully, as, in general, benzodiazepines are absorbed and metabolized more rapidly in children than in adults (Siméon, 1993). There are no pharmacokinetic data in adolescents, but it is believed that adolescents have a slower metabolism than children (Coffey, 1993). Thus, doses need to be adjusted accordingly. On discontinuation of benzodiazepines, adolescents can develop rebound anxiety, recurrence of anxiety symptoms, insomnia, muscle tension, and, rarely, seizures (Coffey, 1993). Slowly tapering off the medication can decrease the likelihood of these symptoms. Recommendations for tapering have been to reduce the dose no more than 25% of the maintenance dose every three to five days (Kutcher et al., 1992). Sugai (1993) found that reduction of clonazepam by less than 0.04 mg/kg per week was a safe tapering schedule.

TRICYCLIC ANTIDEPRESSANTS

Tricyclic antidepressants (TCAs) were among the first medications studied for the treatment of anxiety disorders in children and adolescents. Although TCAs have been the drugs most systematically studied for pediatric anxiety, results have not been consistent. Use of TCAs in treating school refusal and separation anxiety has not consistently proved to be efficacious. The one TCA that has been shown to decrease "anxiety" symptoms has been clomipramine in treatment of OCD.

Review of Published Studies

A school-refusal treatment study showed evidence of decreased anxiety symptoms and success in returning to school with imipramine as compared to placebo (Gittleman-Klein and Klein, 1971, 1973). These results, though, were not replicated in a study of clomipramine and school refusers—in which a positive effect with clomipramine was not shown (Berney, 1981). An interesting finding from that study was that, when compared to preadolescents, adolescents demonstrated a quicker short-term therapeutic response to clomipramine in measures of overall severity, depression, and separation anxiety (Berney, 1981). Two decades after their initial study, in a trial of imipramine versus placebo for children with separation anxiety disorder, Klein, Koplewicz, and Kanner (1992) were not able to show significant differences between these two treatments.

Side Effects

The TCAs have a number of associated adverse effects that in many cases limit their ability to be used as continued treatment. Many of these effects may be attributed to the anticholinergic effects of the TCAs—including dry mouth, blurred vision, orthostatic changes and dizziness, constipation, urinary retention, sedation, and weight gain (Biederman, 1990; Kutcher et al., 1992). More potentially serious side effects are related to the TCAs cardiac effects. More specifically, the TCAs have been associated with changes in blood pressure, pulse and conduction defects (Biederman, 1990). Sinus tachycardia appears to be the most common side effect (Kutcher et al., 1992) and sustained tachycardia of 130 bpm or greater in adolescents warrants medication change or further investigation, such as an echocardiogram to measure cardiac output and ventricular function (Biederman, 1990). Other effects, such as a widening of the PR interval and QRS complex, have occurred (Kutcher et al., 1992), and reported values of concern are: PR interval > 200 msec (indicating block) and QRS > 120 msec (indicating right bundle-branch block) (Bierderman, 1990). These values should alert the clinician to solicit consultation from medical staff. There appears to be a greater sensitivity to cardiac effects in children and adolescents versus adults and any premorbid conduction abnormalities should act as contraindications for the use of TCAs (Kutcher et al., 1992). TCAs are toxic in overdose secondary to cardiotoxicity (primarily), reduced seizure threshold and central nervous system depression (Kutcher et al., 1992). If concerned about an adolescent's suicidal risk or impulsivity, the TCAs should be avoided.

Clinical Practice

Due to the potential for side effects and lethality, along with the need for monitoring of blood levels and ECG's, the TCAs do not constitute a first line treatment of anxiety disorders. Commonly used

TCAs include nortriptyline, imipramine and clomipramine. Nortripty-line and imipramine are often used with children with an anxiety disorder occurring alone or comorbid with depression, ADHD or enuresis. Clomipramine mainly has been used in adolescents with OCD.

Dosing guidelines are to start at 10 to 25 mg per day and titrate slowly, increasing by 20% to 30% every four to five days. When an effective dose is achieved, or if the dose reaches 3 mg/kg per day, a serum TCA level and an ECG should be checked (Biederman, 1990; Kutcher et al., 1992). On discontinuation of TCAs, the dose should be slowly tapered at a rate of 20% to 25% weekly, as there have been reports of a TCA withdrawal syndrome (Kutcher et al., 1992). Symptoms of withdrawal appear to be related to an increase in cholinergic functioning, with effects such as perspiration, malaise, restlessness, irritability, insomnia, and vivid dreams (Kutcher et al., 1992). Nausea, vomiting, and diarrhea may also occur and can be severe (Biederman, 1990; Kutcher et al., 1992).

BUSPIRONE

The 5-HT1A presynaptic receptor is part of a negative feedback loop that causes a decrease in the release of serotonin when concentrations of the neurotransmitter rises in the synapse. Buspirone, a 5-HTIA agonist, acts to stimulate this receptor and thus decrease the outflow of serotonin as well as to bind to the postsynaptic neuron and to decrease serotonin's action by blocking the receptor (Pfeffer, Jiang, and Domeshek, 1997). It is unclear how decreasing the effects of serotonin exerts an anxiolytic effect, but buspirone has been compared to classical benzodiazepines with regard to its ability to decrease anxiety, with less side effects of drowsiness, dependence, and incoordination (Ansseau et al., 1990). It has been postulated that the lack of sedation is due to buspirone's ability to increase the firing of noradrenergic cells in the locus ceruleus and dopaminergic cells in the substantia nigra-compacta (Eison and Temple, 1986; Zwier and Rao, 1994). The absence of addictive properties makes buspirone an especially attractive option for treatment of anxiety disorders. The data supporting its efficacy, however, are limited.

Review of Published Studies

Kranzler (1988) reported the case of a 13-year-old boy with overanxious disorder who was treated with buspirone after a trial of desipramine had to be stopped because of side effects. On a dose of 5 mg twice per day, he had a decrease in his anxiety symptoms, a drop in his HARS scores, and improved behavior after about four weeks. He could not tolerate a dose of 15 mg per day due to daytime sedation (Kranzler, 1988). Adolescents with overanxious disorder without panic attacks had similar improvements, as measured by HARS scores, when treated with buspirone in doses ranging from 15 to 30 mg (Kutcher et al., 1992). Zwier and Rao (1994) described a 16-year-old male with social phobia and schizotypal personality disorder who was treated with as much as 20 mg of buspirone per day. Although he did not have a formal thought disorder, he presented with odd thoughts and had ratings in the "moderately severe" range on the Anxiety, Tension, and Unusual Thought Content scales of the Brief Psychiatric Rating Scale (BPRS). After less than two weeks of treatment with buspirone, the patient described a decrease in anxiety symptoms; over the next year, improvement was maintained, and the patient also enjoyed increased social interactions. One year after initial treatment, a repeat administration of the BPRS showed a score in the "mild" range for tension, and there were no symptoms of anxiety or unusual thoughts (Zwier and Rao, 1994). In an open-label study of buspirone in 25 prepubertal children who were hospitalized with aggressive behavior and anxiety symptoms, buspirone was titrated to doses up to 50 mg per day (Pfeffer et al., 1997). In the 75% of patients who completed the study, there was significant improvement noted in depression and anxiety rating scale scores and in assessment of clinical global functioning, as well as in the quality and amount of the aggressive behavior. Overall, the children spent 86% less time in seclusion or physical restraints and had a 52% decrease in Children's Depression Inventory scores (Pfeffer et al., 1997). In an open-label study not specific for anxiety disorders, Siméon et al. (1994) found widespread improvements in symptoms of anxiety, depression, and behavioral problems in 15 children treated with buspirone (average daily dose, 19 mg). Although buspirone is often compared to the benzodiazepines, there are few data comparing these two medications in adolescents. Using a double-blind design, Ansseau et al. (1990) compared the efficacy of buspirone and oxazepam in 26 adults age 19 to 54. Initially, significant differences were noted; specifically, oxazepam caused a greater reduction in anxiety symptoms in the first four weeks. This trend, however, was not continued through the whole study; no significant differences were noted between the two groups (Ansseau et al., 1990).

Side Effects

The appeal of buspirone seems to reside in its minimal side effect profile and lack of addiction potential. The literature supports these claims; adverse reactions are mild and are commonly limited to gastrointestinal discomfort and nausea, sedation, headaches, and nighttime sleep disturbances (Kutcher et al., 1992; Siméon et al., 1994; Pfeffer et al., 1997). There is no evidence of a withdrawal syndrome emerging even after continued use (Rakel, 1990), and data support the decreased risk of addiction (Murphy, Owen, and Tyrer, 1989). However, Pfeffer et al. (1997) reported that 25% of their patients had to discontinue buspirone due to the emergence of activation, impulsivity, and manic-like symptoms. This makes one consider a family or personal history of bipolar disorder a possible contraindication for buspirone (Pfeffer et al., 1997).

Clinical Practice

The minimal side effects and lack of addictive potential make buspirone an attractive choice for treating adolescents with anxiety disorders. However, clinical experience suggests that buspirone may be less potent in decreasing anxiety symptoms than other anxiolytics are. Dosing guidelines for buspirone include beginning at 5 mg three times a day and continued titration of the thrice-daily dosing by doubling the total daily dose every two weeks to a maximum daily dose of 60 mg (Riddle et al., in press). A multisite, double-blind, placebo-controlled study is underway to assess buspirone's efficacy in treatment of anxiety disorders.

SELECTIVE SEROTONIN REUPTAKE INHIBITORS

Since their introduction about 10 years ago, SSRIs have been shown to be efficacious in treatment of depression, OCD, social phobia, panic disorder, and PTSD in adults (Birmaher et al., 1994). Literature regarding children and adolescents is not as extensive. However, a low side effect profile and apparent safety in overdose make the SSRIs a desirable option for treatment of anxiety disorders. This is a growing area of research, and data already published in reports presented show promise.

Review of Published Studies

Manassis and Bradley (1994) reported the treatment of five children age five to 11 with varying anxiety disorders who were treated with fluoxetine at doses up to 20 mg per day. All children had improvements in anxiety symptoms according to self-report, parent ratings, and RC–MAS results within six weeks (Manassis and Bradley, 1994). Black and Uhde (1994) conducted a double-blind, placebo-controlled study of fluoxetine in the treatment of elective mutism. The 15 subjects were six to 12 years old. There were significant improvements in the fluoxetine group on symptoms of anxiey, mutism, and social anxiety using ratings by parents, clinicians, and teachers (Black and Uhde, 1994), although most of the children continued with symptoms by the end of the study. A retrospective review of charts of 21 outpatient children and adolescents age 11 to 17 with follow-up assessment by treating nurses and patients' mothers was done to assess the efficacy of fluoxetine for anxiety disorders such as overanxious disorder, social phobia, and separation anxiety disorder (Birmaher et al., 1994). Eighty-one percent of the patients showed moderate to marked improvement on mean doses of 26 mg per day (range, 10 to 60 mg per day). The results were mostly seen within six to eight weeks of treatment. It should be noted that, after controlling for depressive scores, there was still a significant improvement in anxiety symptoms. This argues for fluoxetine's direct anxiolytic effect—as opposed to the improvement in anxiety symptoms being a secondary action of antidepressant effects (Birmaher et al., 1994).

In an open trial of fluoxetine in treatment of selective mutism, 21 children age five to 14 were given fluoxetine (mean daily doses of 28 mg) over nine weeks. Seventy-six percent of the children displayed significant improvement in symptoms of social anxiety (Dummit et al., 1996).

In an open-label trial of 16 youngsters age nine to 18 years, Fairbanks et al. (1997) studied fluoxetine treatment of mixed anxiety disorders. Significant improvements were seen in parent reports, clinician reports, and self-reports. The mean dose for adolescents was 40 mg per day, and mean length of time for treatment response was five weeks. It seemed that, compared to subjects with multiple anxiety diagnoses, subjects with only one anxiety disorder responded to lower doses (Fairbanks et al., 1997).

Side Effects

Most adolescents treated with SSRIs do not experience clinically meaningful side effects. Side effects that do occur involve the central nervous system and the gastrointestinal tract. In general, gastrointestinal side effects are milder in children and adolescents than in adults.

Side effects reported from the use of fluoxetine indicate a dose-dependent activating effect—producing insomnia and behavioral and motoric changes (Riddle et al., 1992). In their study of 10 patients treated with fluoxetine, usually 20 mg per day, Riddle et al. (1990) observed that 40% of the children experienced agitation and activation. Using higher doses of fluoxetine, Apter et al. (1994) saw a 40% rate of hyperactivity and agitation in study patients. There have been other reports of bizarre behavior on fluoxetine 20 mg per day that remitted after reduction of the dose to 15 mg per day (Manassis and Bradley, 1994) and reports of dermatitis (Apter et al., 1994; Manassis and Bradley, 1994). Youngsters taking sertraline for treatment of OCD reported mild to moderate side effects—mostly insomnia, nausea, agitation, and tremor (March et al., 1998).

Clinical Practice

Most published studies have been open studies done with fluoxetine in the treatment of various anxiety disorders such as social phobia, separation anxiety, overanxious disorder, OCD, and elective mutism. Double-blind, placebo-controlled studies are underway to assess the anxiolytic effects of other SSRIs, such as fluvoxamine, in treatment of anxiety disorders. Paroxetine and fluoxetine are being studied for the treatment of OCD. Results from these studies will be needed to determine the safety and efficacy of the medications for adolescents with anxiety.

Recommendations for dosing SSRIs include beginning at a low dose, such as 5 to 10 mg per day for fluoxetine, and titrating the dose slowly in response to absence of therapeutic response. If medication is tolerated and improvement is not noted, then further increases in the doses should be made, with careful monitoring of the patient for signs of activation, agitation, or impulsiveness.

The low side effect profile, lack of need for blood levels, and safety in overdose make the SSRIs a probable first-line therapy for treatment

263

of anxiety disorders. Longitudinal studies are lacking and are needed to determine the long-term safety and efficacy of the SSRIs in adolescents.

Issues for the Next Ten Years

In order to further advances in the diagnosis and treatment of anxiety disorders in adolescents, there must be a continuation in the recent growth of research in this population. Diagnostic clarity across age groups, as provided by developmentally consistent diagnostic criteria, will assist in accurately assessing, describing, and categorizing an adolescent's symptoms and disorders. Not only will this increase our understanding of the disease process in anxiety disorders, it will help us to identify possible deterrents to a child's normal development. In examining the developmental issues, it appears that puberty provides a vulnerable period that is followed by increased emergence of some psychiatric symptoms. More investigation is required to explore the psychosexual changes that may be contributing to this phenomenon. Longitudinal and follow-up studies would be helpful in tracking the course of these illnesses.

In regards to pharmacological treatments, there is a need for more controlled studies of medications—with sufficient sample size, dosage of medication, and duration of treatment. The safety and efficacy of these medications should be examined further given the hesitation of parents to expose their children to potential side effects. Follow-up or longitudinal studies would be helpful to monitor for long-term side effects, especially with the newer agents. Pharmacokinetic studies can provide information on the metabolism and absorption of these medications, with special attention to possible trends in pharmacokinetics through the stages of puberty and adolescence. Finally, studies monitoring the use of medications in combination with psychosocial interventions could be used to strengthen treatment plan outcomes for anxious adolescents.

REFERENCES

American Psychiatric Association (1994), *Diagnostic and Statistical Manual of Mental Disorders (4th ed.).* Washington, DC: APA.

264

Anderson, J. C., Williams, S., McGee, R. & Silva, P. A. (1987), *DSM-III* disorders in preadolescent children: Prevalence in a large sample from the general population. *Arch. Gen. Psychiat.,* 44:69–76.

Ansseau, M., Papart, P., Gerard, M. A., von Frenckell, R. & Franck, G. (1990), Controlled comparison of buspirone and oxazepam in generalized anxiety. *Neuropsychobiology,* 24(2):74–78.

Apter, A., Ratzoni, G., King, R. A., Weizman, A., Iancu, I., Binder, M. & Riddle, M. A. (1994), Fluvoxamine open-label treatment of adolescent inpatients with obsessive-compulsive disorder or depression. *J. Amer. Acad. Child Adolesc. Psychiat.,* 33:342–348.

Bell-Dolan, D. J., Last, C. G. & Strauss, C. C. (1990), Symptoms of anxiety disorders in normal children. *J. Amer. Acad. Child Adolesc. Psychiat.,* 29:759–765.

Berney, T. (1981), School phobia: A therapeutic trial with clomipramine and short term outcome. *Brit. J. Psychiat.,* 138:110–118.

Bernstein, G. A. (1991), Comorbidity and severity of anxiety and depressive disorders in a clinic sample. *J. Amer. Acad. Child Adolesc. Psychiat.,* 30:43–50.

——— & Borchardt, C. M. (1991), Anxiety disorders of childhood and adolescence: A critical review. *J. Amer. Acad. Child Adolesc. Psychiat.,* 30:519–532.

——— Garfinkel, B. D. & Borchardt, C. M. (1990), Comparative studies of pharmacotherapy for school refusal. *J. Amer. Acad. Child Adolesc. Psychiat.,* 29:773–781.

——— & Shaw, K. (principal authors) (1997), Practice parameters for the assessment and treatment of children and adolescents with anxiety disorders. *J. Amer. Acad Child Adolesc. Psychiat.,* 36 (10 Suppl): 69S–84S.

Biederman, J. (1987), Clonazepam in the treatment of prepubertal children with panic-like symptoms. *J. Clin. Psychiat.,* 48(10):38–41.

——— (1990), The diagnosis and treatment of adolescent anxiety disorders. *J. Clin. Psychiat.,* 51(5):20–26.

——— (1991), Psychopharmacology. In: *Textbook of Child and Adolescent Psychiatry,* ed. J. M. Wiener. Washington, DC: American Psychiatric Press, pp. 545–570.

Bird, H. R., Canino, G., Rubio-Stipec, M., Gould, M. S., Ribera, J., Sesman, M., Woodbury, M., Huertas-Goldman, S., Pagan, A., Sanchez-Lacay, A. & Moscoso, M. (1988), Estimates of the prevalence of childhood maladjustment in a community survey in Puerto Rico. *Arch. Gen. Psychiat.,* 45:1120–1126.

Birmaher, B., Khetarpal, S., Brent, D., Cully, M., Balach, L., Kaufman, J. & McKenzie, Neer. S. (1997), The screen for child anxiety related emotional disorders (SCARED): Scale construction and psychometric characteristics. *J. Amer. Acad. Child Adolesc. Psychiat.*, 36:545–553.

———— Waterman, G. S., Ryan, N., Cully, M., Balach, L., Ingram, J. & Brodsky, M. (1994), Fluoxetine for childhood anxiety disorders. *J. Amer. Acad. Child Adolesc. Psychiat.*, 33:993–999.

Black, B. & Uhde, T. W. (1994), Treatment of elective mutism with fluoxetine: A double-blind., placebo-controlled study. *J. Amer. Acad. Child Adolesc. Psychiat.*, 33:1000–1006.

Coffey, B. J. (1993), Review and update: Benzodiazepines in childhood and adolescence. *Psychiatric Annals*, 23:332–339.

Commander, M., Green, S. H. & Prendergast, M. (1991), Behavioural disturbances in children treated with clonazepam. *Dev. Med. Child Neurol.*, 33:362–363.

Costello, E. J. & Angold, A. (1995), Epidemiology. In: *Anxiety Disorders in Children and Adolescents*, ed. J. S. March. New York: The Guilford Press, pp. 109–124.

Dantzer, R. (1985), Benzodiazepines and the limbic system. In: *Psychopharmacology of the Limbic System*, ed. M. Trimble & E. Zarifiam. Oxford: Oxford University Press, pp. 148–163.

Dummit, E. S., Klein, R. G., Tancer, N. K., Asche, B. & Martin, J. (1996), Fluoxetine treatment of children with selective mutism: An open trial. *J. Amer. Acad. Child Adolesc. Psychiat.*, 35:615–621.

Eison, A. S. & Temple, D. L. (1986), Buspirone: Review of its pharmacology and current perspectives on its mechanism of action. *Amer. J. Med.*, 80(suppl 3B):1–9.

Fairbanks, J. M., Pine, D. S., Tancer, N. K., Dummit, E. S., Kentgen, L. M., Martin, J., Asche, B. K. & Klein, R. G. (1997), Open fluoxetine treatment of mixed anxiety disorders in children and adolescents. *J. Child & Adolesc. Psychopharm.*, 7:17–29.

Famularo, R., Kinscherff, R. & Fenton, T. (1988), Propranolol treatment for childhood posttraumatic stress disorder, acute type: A pilot study. *Amer. J. Diseases Children*, 142:1244–1247.

Francis, G., Last, C. G. & Strauss, C. C. (1987), Expression of separation anxiety disorder: The roles of age and gender. *Child Psychiat. Human Dev.*, 18:82–89.

Gittleman-Klein, R. & Klein, D. (1971), Controlled imipramine treatment of school phobia. *Arch. Gen. Psychiat.*, 25:204–207.

—— & —— (1973), School phobia: Diagnostic considerations in the light of imipramine effects. *J. Nerv. Ment. Dis.,* 156:199–215.

Graae, F., Milner J., Rizzotto L. & Klein, R. G. (1994), Clonazepam in childhood anxiety disorders. *J. Amer. Acad. Child Adolesc. Psychiat.,* 33:372–376.

Joorabchi, B. (1977), Expressions of the hyperventilation syndrome in childhood: Studies in the management, including an evaluation of the effectiveness of propranolol. *Clin. Ped. (Phila.),* 16:1110–1115.

Kashani, J. H. & Orvaschel, H. (1988), Anxiety disorders in mid-adolescence: A community sample. *Amer. J. Psychiat.,* 145:960–964.

Kashani, J. H. & Orvaschel, H. (1990), A community study of anxiety in children and adolescents. *Amer. J. Psychiat.,* 147:313–318.

Klein, R. G., Koplewicz, H. S. & Kanner, A. (1992), Imipramine treatment of children with separation anxiety disorder. *J. Amer. Acad. Child Adolesc. Psychiat.,* 31:21–28.

Kranzler, H. R. (1988), Use of buspirone in an adolescent with overanxious disorder. *J. Amer. Acad. Child Adolesc. Psychiat.,* 27:789–790.

Kutcher, S. P. & Mackenzie, S. (1988), Successful clonazepam treatment of adolescents with panic disorder. *J. Clin. Psychompharmacol.,* 8:299–301.

—— Reiter, S., Gardner, D. M. & Klein, R. G. (1992), The pharmacotherapy of anxiety disorders in children and adolescents. *Ped. Psychopharmacol.,* 15:41–67.

Last, C. G., Perrin, S., Hersen, M. & Kazdin, A. E. (1992), DSM-III-R anxiety disorder in children: Sociodemographic and clinical characteristics. *J. Amer. Acad. Child Adolesc. Psychiat.,* 31:1070–1076.

Manassis, K. & Bradley, S. (1994), Fluoxetine in anxiety disorders. *J. Amer. Acad. Child Adolesc. Psychiat.,* 33:761–762.

March, J. S., Biederman, J., Wolkow, R., et al. (1998), Sertraline in children and adolescents with obsessive-compulsive disorder. *J. Amer. Med. Assn.,* 280:1752–1756.

—— Parker, J. D. A., Sullivan, K., Stallings, P. & Conners, C. K. (1997), The multidimensional anxiety scale for children (MASC): Factor structure, reliability and validity. *J. Amer. Acad. Child Adolesc. Psychiat.,* 36:554–565.

McGee, R., Feehan, M., Williams, S., Partridge, F., Silva, P. A. & Kelly, J. (1990), *DSM-III* disorders in a large sample of adolescents. *J. Amer. Acad. Child Adolesc. Psychiat.,* 29:611–619.

Mitchell, J., McCauley, E., Burke, P. M. & Moss, S. J. (1988), Phenomenology of depression in children and adolescents. *J. Amer. Acad. Child Adolesc. Psychiat.,* 27:12–20.

Murphy, S. M., Owen, R. & Tyrer, P. (1989), Comparative assessment of efficacy and withdrawal symptoms after six and twelve weeks' treatment with diazepam or buspirone [see comments]. *Br. J. Psychiat.,* 154:529–534.

Pauls, D. L., Alsobrook, J. P., Goodman, W., Rasmussen, S. & Leckman, J. F. (1995), A family study of obsessive-compulsive disorder. *Amer. J. Psychiat.,* 152:72–75.

Pederson, W. & Lavik, N. J. (1991), Adolescents and benzodiazepines: Prescribed use, self-medication and intoxication. *Acta. Psychiat. Scand.,* 84:94–98.

Pfeffer, C. R., Jiang, H. & Domeshek, L. J. (1997), Buspirone treatment of psychiatrically hospitalized prepubertal children with symptoms of anxiety and moderately severe aggression. *J. Child & Adolesc. Psychopharmacol.,* 7:145–155.

Pfefferbaum, B., Butler, P. M., Mullins, D. & Copeland, D. R. (1987), Two cases of benzodiazepine toxicity in children. *J. Clin. Psychiat.,* 48:450–452.

——— Overall, J. E., Baron, H. A., Frankel, L. S., Sullivan, M. R. & Johnson, K. (1987), Alprazolam in the treatment of anticipatory and acute situational anxiety in children with cancer. *J. Amer. Acad. Child Adolesc. Psychiat.,* 26:532–535.

Rakel, R. E. (1990), Long-term buspirone therapy for chronic anxiety: A multicenter international study to determine safety. *South Med. J.,* 83:194–198.

Rall, T. W. (1990), Hypnotics and sedatives: Ethanol. In: *Goodman and Gilman's The Pharmacological Basis of Therapeutics, 8th ed,* ed. Gilman, A. F., Rall, T. W., Nies, A. S. & Taylor, P. New York: Pergamon Press, pp. 345–382.

Regier, D. A., Boyd, J. H., Burke, J. D., Rae, D. S., Myers, J. K., Kramer, M., Robins, L. N., George, L. K., Karno, M. & Locke, B. Z. (1988), One-month prevalence of mental disorders in the United States. *Arch. Gen. Psychiat.,* 45:977–986.

Reiter, S. & Kutcher, S. P. (1991), Disinhibition and anger outbursts in adolescents treated with clonazepam. *J. Clin. Psychompharmacol.,* 11(4):268.

Reynolds, C. R. & Richmond, B. O. (1978), What I think and feel: a revised measure of children's manifest anxiety. *J. Abnorm. Child Psychol.,* 6:271–280.

Riddle, M. A., Bernstein, G., Cook, E., Leonard, H., March, J. S. & Swanson, J. (in press), Anxiolytics, Adrenergics and Naltrexone. *J. Amer. Acad. Child Adolesc. Psychiat.*

―――― Hardin, M. T., King, R., Scahill, L. & Woolston, J. L. (1990), Fluoxetine treatment of children and adolescents with Tourette's and obsessive compulsive disorders: Preliminary clinical experience. *J. Amer. Acad. Child Adolesc. Psychiat.*, 29:45–48.

―――― Scahill, L., King, R. A. et al. (1992), Double-blind crossover trial of fluoxetine and placebo in children and adolescents with obsessive-compulsive disorder. *J. Amer. Acad. Child Adolesc. Psychiat.*, 31:1062–1069.

Salzman, C. (1989), Treatment with antianxiety agents. In: *Treatments of Psychiatric Disorders: A Task Force Report of the American Psychiatric Association., Vol 3.* Washington, DC: APA, p. 2036.

Schneier, F. R., Johnson, J., Hornig, C. D., Liebowitz, M. R. & Weissman, M. M. (1992), Social phobia: Comorbidity in an epidemiologic sample. *Arch. Gen. Psychiat.*, 49:282–288.

Siméon, J. G. (1993), Use of anxiolytics in children. *L'Encéphale*, XIX:71–74.

―――― Ferguson, H. B. (1987), Alprazolam effects in children with anxiety disorders. *Can. J. Psychiat.*, 32:570–574.

―――― ―――― Knott, V., Roberts, N., Gauthier, B., Dubois, C. & Wiggins, D. (1992), Clinical, cognitive, and neurophysiological effects of alprazolam in children and adolescents with overanxious and avoidant disorders. *J. Amer. Acad. Child Adolesc. Psychiat.*, 31:29–33.

―――― Knott, V. J., Dubois, C., Wiggins, D., Geraets, I., Thatte, S. & Miller, W. (1994), Buspirone therapy of mixed anxiety disorders in childhood and adolescence: A pilot study. *J. Child Adolesc. Psychopharmacol.*, 4:159–170.

Strauss, C. C. & Last, C. G. (1993), Social and simple phobias in children. *J. Anx. Disord.*, 7:141–152.

―――― ―――― Hersen, M. & Kazchin, A. E. (1988), Association between anxiety and depression in children and adolescents with anxiety disorder. *J. Abnorm. Child Psychol.*, 16:57–68.

Sugai, K. (1993), Seizures with clonazepam: Discontinuation and suggestions for safe discontinuation rates in children. *Epilepsia*, 34:1089–1097.

Weissman, M. M., Wickramaratne, P., Warner, V., et al. (1987), Assessing psychiatric disorders in children. *Arch. Gen. Psych.*, 44:747–753.

269

Whitaker, A., Johnson, J., Shaffer, D., Rapoport, J. L., Kalikow, K., Walsh, T., Davies, M., Braiman, S. & Dolinsky, A. (1990), Uncommon troubles in young people. *Arch. Gen. Psychiat.,* 47:487–496.

Zwier, K. J. & Rao, U. (1994), Buspirone use in an adolescent with social phobia and mixed personality disorder (cluster A type). *J. Amer. Acad. Child Adolesc. Psychiat.,* 33:1007–1011.

15 PHARMACOLOGIC TREATMENT OF PSYCHOSIS AND PERVASIVE DEVELOPMENTAL DISORDERS IN ADOLESCENTS

ILEANA BERNAL-SCHNATTER AND ROBERT L. HENDREN

A tremendous increase in the psychotropic pharmacological agents available for the treatment of psychotic disorders and pervasive developmental disorders (PDD) took place in the past 10 years. The advent of atypical antipsychotics opened the prospect of treating adolescents with psychiatric disorders with fewer adverse effects, thereby improving compliance and decreasing the risk for tardive dyskinesia. The likelihood of targeting both positive and negative symptoms of schizophrenia spectrum disorders with the newer antipsychotics is another great advancement. Selective serotonin reuptake inhibitors (SSRIs) have also been introduced to our armamentarium for treating adolescents in recent years. SSRIs may be useful in managing aggressive and perseverative behaviors often associated with PDD.

Problems exist, however, in using these medications. Despite the widespread use of many of these newer agents in adolescents, there continues to be a lack of FDA-approved psychotropic drugs for this age group. There are currently no FDA-approved drugs specific for the treatment of PDD. Another problem is the relative lack of double-blind controlled studies demonstrating the efficacy of these medications in this population. This dearth of information forces clinicians to extrapolate dosages for their young patients from the existing adult literature.

Clearly, the state of the art in adolescent psychopharmacology in the treatment of PDD and psychosis is in an early stage. Despite this, in the face of severely incapacitating illness, we are often compelled to treat with newer and less understood pharmacological agents in the hopes that these youngsters will be able to live to their fullest potentials.

Classification

The *Diagnostic and Statistical Manual of Mental Disorders, Fourth Edition* (*DSM–IV*; American Psychiatric Association, 1994) places autistic disorder, Rett's disorder, childhood disintegrative disorder, Asperger's disorder and pervasive developmental disorder not otherwise specified (PDD–NOS) all under the rubric of pervasive developmental disorders. These disorders share similar patterns of impaired social interactions and language as well as restricted repetitive and stereotyped behaviors, interests, and activities.

Rett's disorder differs from autism in that it has been identified only in girls, who, after two years of normal development, experience deceleration of head growth, loss of purposeful hand movements, and poorly coordinated gait and trunk movements. In Asperger's disorder, there are no clinically significant language or cognitive delays. Childhood disintegrative disorder (Heller's syndrome) has at least a two-year period of normal development before onset. The diagnosis of PDD–NOS is applied to a heterogeneous group of youngsters who have symptoms of the PDD diagnostic category but who do not fully meet the criteria for any of the specific disorders.

Asperger's disorder has been a controversial addition to *DSM–IV*. Some experts identify Asperger's disorder as a form of high-functioning autism, whereas others think it is more of a PDD spectrum disorder. Although investigators agree that, at least at present, Asperger's disorder does appear to represent a distinct diagnostic entity, it is difficult to define what distinguishes it from PDD–NOS. Gillberg (1995) has established useful criteria for Asperger's disorder that include social impairment, narrow range of interests, repetitive routines, speech and language peculiarities, nonverbal communication problems, and motor clumsiness.

Psychotic symptoms among adolescents can occur among a wide range of psychiatric disorders such as schizophrenia, affective disorders with psychotic features, substance-induced psychotic states, and dissociative disorders. In *DSM–IV*, the term psychosis refers to symptoms that may include hallucinations, delusions, disorganized speech, and/ or grossly disorganized behaviors. Although treating the underlying etiology of the psychosis is the most important part of treatment, the psychotic features must also be addressed, necessitating the use of antipsychotic medications.

Epidemiology

Evolving diagnostic conceptualizations of autism and schizophrenia as being distinct clinical entities rather than generalized under the broad category of childhood schizophrenia have made it challenging for investigators to keep current in the epidemiological identification of these disorders. Nevertheless, existing data indicate that autistic disorder is at least 1.4 times more common than schizophrenia in the childhood population (Kolvin, 1971; Burd and Kerbeshian, 1987).

Although statistics vary due to diverse population samples and criteria, autism is believed to have a prevalence of four per 10,000 (Ritvo et al., 1989). Diagnostic agreement as to what constitutes PDD–NOS and Asperger's syndrome is a problem in epidemiologic studies, resulting in prevalence ratios ranging from five to 20 per 10,000, depending on the study. Childhood disintegrative disorder and Rett's syndrome are thought to be quite rare. The male-to-female autism ratio is about 4:1, with females exhibiting more severe forms of the illness (Tsai and Ghazivddin, 1997; Volkmar, Szatmari, and Sparrow, 1993). The majority of autistic individuals present with IQs in the retarded range of intellectual functioning (Rutter, 1978). Autism is currently believed to have an even distribution among socioeconomic groups.

There are fewer epidemiological data for early-onset schizophrenia, but the adolescent prevalence is thought to be about one per 1,000 (Werry, 1991). The male-to-female ratio is about 2:1 (Green et al., 1984). Intellectual functioning tends to be in the average to low-average range. Lower socioeconomic groups demonstrate a higher prevalence of schizophrenia. Examining psychotic disorders in general, one study of a community-based sample found psychosis present in one per 100 adolescents (Evans and Acton, 1972); an adolescent inpatient study found psychosis in five per 100 inpatients (Steinberg, 1985).

Assessment

The purpose of assessment is primarily twofold—to identify the cause of the illness and to assess the impact of the illness on the child.

In obtaining the chief complaint and history of present illness, we try to ascertain the progression of the illness and what current symptomatology needs to be addressed. Perinatal, developmental, family, medical, and social histories are essential in determining the etiology, as are the assessment of the young person's ability to function academically, socially, and in other settings throughout development. Through the assessment, we hope to establish a diagnosis, identify the most beneficial course of treatment, and determine the prognosis in order to predict the youngster's future needs.

When assessing for PDD, it is essential to focus on language, social relatedness, interests, and activities. One must know if there were any developmental delays or any periods of deterioration in previously acquired skills. PDD also has a high rate of associated perinatal trauma. The medical evaluation includes a physical examination as well as a metabolic, neurologic, and genetic evaluation. Genetic disorders that have been associated with PDD are fragile X syndrome (Bloomquist et al., 1985), tuberous sclerosis, and neurofibromatosis. Congenital disorders such as rubella (Chess, 1997) and metabolic disorders such as phenylketonuria have been identified. Neurological abnormalities are found commonly, making a neurological examination including an electroencephalogram (EEG) and in some cases a CT scan or MRI essential.

Primary speech pathology and primary hearing pathology must be ruled out, as they may resemble PDD. Psychological testing to assess adaptive and academic functioning is useful, as is IQ testing, because a high proportion of these youth are mentally retarded. Rating scales and questionnaires are also helpful, such as the Childhood Autism Rating Scale, the Children's Atypical Development Scale, and the Asperger's Syndrome Diagnostic Interview.

The assessment of psychotic symptoms can be challenging, as the etiologies are manifold. The history helps differentiate a primary psychotic disorder, such as schizophrenia, from a secondary psychotic disorder, such as dissociative disorders, mood disorders with psychotic features, and organic psychotic conditions. Again, the cause of the illness will dictate the course of action. A thorough physical examination of the youngster is required, especially for the first episode of psychotic symptoms. The youngster needs a neurological evaluation that may include an EEG and CT scan or MRI. She also should have metabolic, endocrine, infectious diseases, and drug screening. A psychological test battery should be requested and should include IQ and adaptive and academic functioning. Projective testing may add useful information when psychotic symptoms are subtle. Speech and language disorders can be confused with psychotic symptoms and should be considered. Rating scales such as the Formal Thought Disorder Rating Scale can be of help (Caplan et al., 1989).

Developmental Issues

Development in youngsters with PDD is characterized by delays and regressions with differing clinical course and outcome depending on the specific syndrome manifested. Autistic preschoolers manifest disturbances in social relatedness and language and uneven cognitive development. School brings increasing demands that require greater adaptive skills. The autistic child's challenged coping abilities may result in self-stimulatory and self-injurious behaviors. During this period, some children are able to attain modest language ability as well as limited attachments and relatedness. During adolescence, a few youths experience significant developmental deterioration, whereas the majority make progress in their development (Kobayashi, Murata, and Yoshinaga, 1992).

In order to distinguish psychotic process (i.e., hallucinations, delusions, thought disorders) from normal childhood and adolescent development, an understanding of development is essential. In preschoolers, the presence of tactile and visual hallucinations is common with stress. Delusions and thought disorders are difficult to assess due to the degree of cognitive and language development present at this stage, when magical thinking and illogical thoughts may be normal. Hallucinations, delusions, and thought disorders are more indicative of a psychotic disorder in school-age children. By adolescence, psychotic illness is generally similar to adult pathology (Volkmar, 1996).

Differential Diagnosis

The differential diagnosis for PDD consists of mental retardation, schizophrenia, developmental language disorders, Landau-Kleffner's syndrome, attention deficit hyperactivity disorder (ADHD), selective mutism, reactive attachment disorder, and schizotypal disorder. Mental retardation is distinguished from PDD in that it exhibits uniform deficits in intellectual functioning, whereas IQ deficits are unevenly distributed in PDD. Social, verbal, and nonverbal skills parallel mental age in mental retardation and can usually be differentiated from PDD using adaptive-functioning assessments such as the Vineland Adaptive Functioning Scale. Children with severe and profound mental retardation can also exhibit a lack of communication skills, stereotypies, self-injurious behaviors, and impaired social interactions and may require more extensive evaluation of language and social skills in order to distinguish between the two (Campbell and Shay, 1995).

Although children with either schizophrenia or PDD can exhibit poor social interactions, perseverative speech, and aggressive behaviors, there are significant differences. With schizophrenia, adolescents generally have IQs in the normal range and grossly normal early development. Hallucinations and delusions are very rare in PDD, and 80% of youngsters with autism are mentally retarded (Rutter, 1978), whereas those with Asperger's disorder have much higher verbal than performance skills, leading some to refer to this as a nonverbal learning disability.

Developmental language disorders also need to be ruled out when considering a diagnosis of PDD (Bartak, Rutter, and Cox, 1995). Children with development language disorder can exhibit impairments in comprehensive and or expressive speech. They have lower verbal than performance IQ scores and developmental speech delays. By adolescence, these delays are much less pronounced, and the adolescents display relatively normal social interactions, activities, and interests (Cantwell et al., 1989).

Landau-Kleffner's syndrome is characterized by seizures and receptive aphasia followed by expressive language impairments after a period of normal development. Landau-Kleffner's syndrome is distinguished from childhood disintegrative disorder in that youngsters with Landau-Kleffner's syndrome do not exhibit declines in their intellectual functioning but do retain nonverbal communication as well as social relatedness (Stefanatos, Grover, and Geller, 1995).

Children with reactive attachment disorder can exhibit either indiscriminate sociability or inhibited social interactions due to grossly inadequate childrearing. These children tend to respond to warm, nurturing environments. Although children with PDD may also respond to a supportive adult, they generally have warm, responsive caretakers.

Whereas similar features of impulsivity and hyperactivity may be present in children with ADHD and PDD, impairments in language, interests, and social interactions are not usually found in children with ADHD. Development and intellectual functioning are generally intact in children with ADHD.

Other disorders that should be considered in the differential diagnosis of PDD are selective mutism, which is present only in certain social situations, and schizotypal personality disorder. Children with schizotypal personality exhibit odd or eccentric speech and behavior but lack other difficulties associated with PDD.

Psychopathology in adolescents is similar in presentation to that found in adults and therefore is easier to classify in contrast to presentation in children. Diagnosing adolescents with psychotic symptoms includes the differential diagnosis of mood disorders, organic disorders, primary psychotic disorders (schizophrenia spectrum disorders) and nonpsychotic disorders that may manifest psychotic-like symptoms including dissociative disorders, personality disorders, and obsessive-compulsive disorder (McClellan et al., 1997). There is theoretical discussion about a small group of children classified as having "multidimensionally impaired disorder" (Kumra, Jacobsen, Lenane, Zahn, et al., 1998). These children are characterized by poor reality-testing with brief episodes of hallucinations and delusions under stress, mood lability, poor socialization, cognitive impairments, and absence of thought disorder. In contrast to children with very early onset schizophrenia this group does not appear to progress to schizophrenia but may develop other disorders with transient psychotic symptoms.

Affective disorders with commonly associated psychotic features include major depressive disorder and bipolar disorder. Recently, a group of children with a relatively rapid onset of ADHD and affective instability was identified. Many investigators theorize that these symptoms may represent an early form of bipolar disorder. Research in this area is still in its early stages (Biederman et al., 1998).

Organic disorders presenting with psychotic symptoms include seizures, delirium, substance-induced psychosis, brain lesions, infections, and metabolic or neurodegenerative encephalopathies. This highlights the point that psychotic symptoms warrant a thorough medical evaluation.

Primary psychotic disorders are schizophrenia, schizoaffective disorder, schizophreniform disorder, and delusional disorder. Generally, these disorders in adolescence have the same presentation, course, and prognosis as in adults.

Transient psychotic symptoms have been observed in dissociative disorder and borderline personality disorder. Obsessions in youth with obsessive-compulsive disorder can be so severe that they are indistinguishable from delusions. In fact, it is not uncommon to find a teenager misdiagnosed with obsessive-compulsive disorder demonstrating a symptomatic progression to a clearer presentation of schizophrenia.

Comorbidity

Diagnosing comorbid illness in autism can be challenging, particularly in the more seriously ill youngster, who lacks any communication skills. Comorbidity studies have suggested an increased incidence of Tourette's disorder (Commings and Commings, 1991), affective disorders (Ghazinddin and Tsai, 1991; Kerbeshian and Burd, 1996), and obsessive-compulsive disorder in children with autism. The possibility of comorbidity associated with autism is essential to keep in mind to identify potentially useful pharmacological interventions.

Asperger's disorder is commonly associated with Tourette's disorder, obsessive-compulsive disorder, and affective disorder. Due to their high rate of cooccurrence, there has been speculation about similar genetic etiologies in these illnesses.

Comorbidity in schizophrenic youth highlights the importance of augmentation strategies in treating these patients. Schizophrenia is associated with major depressive disorder, panic disorder, and substance abuse.

Biochemical Correlates

There have not been any established neurotransmitter abnormalities identified in the etiology of autism, but several possible links have been investigated. Serotonin is the most studied neurotransmitter in autism, and there are three interesting findings. The first is that about one third of patients with autism exhibit hyperserotonemia (Anderson et al., 1987). Second, although half of mentally retarded individuals are hyperserotonemic, hyperserotonemia is also found in nonmentally retarded people with autism; this information may someday be useful in identifying autistic subtypes (Tsai and Ghazinddin, 1997). A third correlate has been the identification of hyperserotonemia in first-degree relatives of hyperserotonemic autistic probands, implicating a possible genetic vulnerability to autism (Cook, Leventhal, and Freedman, 1998).

Hyperdopaminergic activity is thought to be associated with increased motor activity and stereotypic movements. Homovanillic acid, a dopamine metabolite, is found in higher concentration in the cerebrospinal fluid of severely affected autistic children with autism (Gillberg and Stendsen, 1987).

Due to behavioral parallels of decreased pain sensitivity and social withdrawal observed in opioid addiction and in autism, the opioid system has also been studied. Findings demonstrate both increased and decreased cerebrospinal-fluid beta-endorphin levels in autism, making any correlation with autism difficult to ascertain at this time (Ross, Klykylo, and Hitzemann, 1987; Gillberg et al., 1990).

Biochemical studies have not identified any single neurotransmitter agent responsible for schizophrenia, implicating a complex interplay of systems. In view of classic antipsychotics' ability to block D2 receptors and reduce positive symptoms of schizophrenia, it is thought that the dopaminergic system plays a large role in producing these symptoms in schizophrenia. Similarly, atypical antipsychotics, which seem to improve both positive and negative symptoms, have led investigators to believe that serotonin also plays a role in schizophrenia due to their effects on the serotonin system (Biederman, Spencer, and Wilens, 1997).

Treatment

Treatment of PDD requires psychological and social approaches including special education and behavior therapy. Special education should be highly structured, individualized, and year round with emphasis on socialization, language, and self-care skills. Behavior therapy is used to improve cognitive, motor, and social skills. When these interventions are insufficient, targeting specific symptoms with medication can be extremely beneficial. The decision tree shown in Figure 1

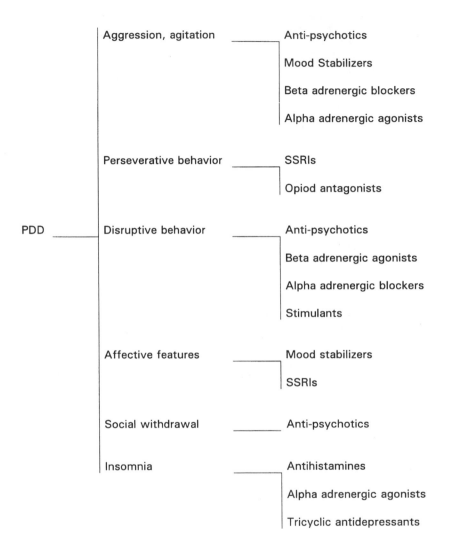

Figure 1 Treatment decision tree for pervasive developmental disorders.

summarizes common target symptoms and pharmacological interventions used in PDD.

Pharmacological interventions are the mainstay of treatment for psychotic disorders. Psychological and social therapeutic approaches are useful adjuncts to treatment. Illustrated in Figure 2 is the treatment decision tree for psychotic disorders.

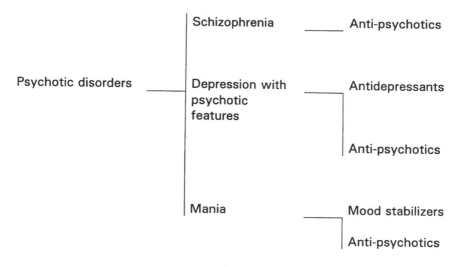

Figure 2   Treatment decision tree for psychotic disorders.

ANTIPSYCHOTICS

The typical antipsychotic medication classes consist of phenothiazines (e.g., thioridazine, chlorpromazine, fluphenazine), butyrophenones (e.g., haloperidol), indole derivatives (e.g., molindone), and thioxanthenes (e.g., thiothixene). All of these medications exhibit antagonistic action at the dopamine receptor site and produce similar therapeutic effects. There is no clear evidence that one typical antipsychotic agent is more effective than another. Medications are chosen based on their side effect profile. Haloperidol, for example, is a high-potency antipsychotic with less sedating effects than lower potency medications such as chlorpromazine, but use of haloperidol has a higher association with extrapyramidal symptoms. Typical antipsychotics are thought to be most effective in controlling the positive symptoms in psychotic disorder, which consist of hallucinations, delusions, formal thought disorders, inappropriate affect, and catatonic and aggressive behaviors.

The atypical antipsychotics category is comprised of risperidone, quetiapine, olanzapine, and clozapine. In addition to exhibiting dopaminergic antagonistic effects, these agents also exhibit serotonergic antagonistic properties. Preliminary studies are significant for similar benefits in treating positive symptoms, as with the typical antipsychotic

281

medications, but the atypical antipsychotics appear to exhibit greater beneficial effects on negative symptoms such as social withdrawal, apathy, blunted affect, anhedonia, and impoverished speech. The atypical agents also have a lower incidence of extrapyramidal side effects than typical antipsychotic medications (Biederman et al., 1997).

The typical antipsychotics are shown to be beneficial in treating symptoms of aggression, social withdrawal, hyperactivity, stereotypies, self-injurious behavior, and sleep disturbances. Some studies have even indicated improvement in language-acquisition skills. Among the different types of typical antipsychotics, the most studied in children is haloperidol. Many clinicians feel that the reduced sedating effects of haloperidol are beneficial in treating youth who are socially withdrawn and inattentive. There have been several double-blind, placebo-controlled studies measuring the effectiveness of haloperidol in children with autism. Campbell and associates (1978) published a study of 40 inpatient children age two to seven with autistic disorder. The children were randomly assigned to one of four groups based on treatment: haloperidol and behavioral language therapy; haloperidol alone; placebo and behavioral language therapy; and placebo alone. The children were followed over a 12-week period; the mean dose of haloperidol was 1.65 mg per day. Although the group on haloperidol showed more improvement than the placebo group, the group who received both haloperidol and behavioral language therapy made the most significant gains.

Another double-blind placebo-controlled study, by Cohen et al. (1980), consisted of 10 hospitalized children age two to seven with autism. The children were randomly assigned to either a placebo group or a haloperidol group (mean dose, 1.65 mg per day) for two-week intervals and then randomly reassigned over the course of eight weeks. The haloperidol-treated group exhibited fewer stereotypic movements and greater attention and compliance. Eight of the 10 children exhibited excessive sedation. The older children in the study had a robust response to medication. A multicenter study of 34 children age three to 16 with autism was conducted by Naruse and coworkers (1982). It was a double-blind crossover investigation of pimozide, haloperidol, and placebo. Pimozide and haloperidol were both more effective than placebo in controlling aggression.

The atypical antipsychotic medications are increasingly used in treating people with PDD due to the favorable side effect profiles and their therapeutic effects in targeting negative symptoms such as social

282

withdrawal. Risperidone is the most investigated atypical agent in the treatment of PDD. McDougle and associates (1998) did a double-blind placebo-controlled study of risperidone in adults with PDD. The study consisted of 31 adults randomly placed on either risperidone or placebo treatment for 12 weeks. The placebo-treated group showed no improvement, but the risperidone group exhibited improvement in repetitive behavior, aggression, anxiety, depression, and irritability. Open-trial studies of risperidone in children and adolescents with PDD have also yielded encouraging results (Findling, Maxwell, and Wiznitzer, 1997; McDougle et al., 1997; Nicolson, Avad, and Sloman, 1998). Mean dosing in these studies ranged from 1.1 to 1.8 mg per day. Case reports of olanzapine treatment of PDD are also promising and warrant systematic trials to further assess efficacy in this population (Krishnamoorthy and King, 1998).

It is important to define the etiology of the psychosis to effectively treat psychotic symptoms. Antipsychotics are the mainstays of treatment. Commonly used typical neuroleptics include thioridazine, chlorpromazine, and haloperidol. Antipsychotic use in childhood schizophrenia is the most studied. Pool and colleagues (1976) did a double-blind placebo-controlled loxapine-and-haloperidol study of 76 adolescents with schizophrenia. The mean dose of loxapine was 87.5 mg per day, and there were no significant differences in response to either loxapine or haloperidol. Extrapyramidal side effects occurred in about 70% of the youngsters on either medication, and about half experienced excessive sedation. Spencer and Campbell (1994) conducted a double-blind placebo-controlled study using 16 prepubertal children age five to 11 with schizophrenia and comparing haloperidol to placebo. The study lasted 10 weeks using a mean dose of 1.92 mg per day. All of the children improved on haloperidol, and 14 of the 16 children exhibited significant improvement.

As in PDD, there may be advantages to treating with atypical antipsychotic agents over typical agents. Kumra and associates (1996) did a double-blind clozapine–haloperidol comparison in 21 adolescents age 12 to 16 with schizophrenia. Only youths who had been nonresponsive to typical agents were included. After a six-week trial, clozapine was found to be strikingly superior to haloperidol in treating both positive and negative symptoms. The mean dose of clozapine was 176 mg per day, and the mean dose of haloperidol was 16 mg per day. Due to side effects of neutropenia and seizures, one third of the group had to discontinue use of clozapine. Siméon, Carrey, and Wiggings (1995) did an open-label investigation of seven youngsters age 11 to 17 with schizophrenia using risperidone at doses ranging from 1 to 4 mg per day. Six of the seven children demonstrated a robust response, but two experienced excessive sedation. In 1997, Armenteros and colleagues conducted an open pilot-study of risperidone (mean dose, 6.6 mg per day) in 10 adolescents with schizophrenia. After a two-week medication washout period, they were treated for six weeks with risperidone. Significant improvement was observed in positive and negative symptoms with no major adverse reaction.

Olanzapine is also undergoing initial studies in the treatment of childhood-onset schizophrenia. Kumra, Jacobsen, Lenane, Karp, et al. (1998) investigated olanzapine (mean dose, 17.5 mg per day) in eight adolescents for eight weeks in an open-label study. These youth had been treatment-refractory to typical antipsychotic medications. These adolescents exhibited mild improvement in negative symptoms with olanzapine treatment but marked improvement in positive symptoms.

Adverse effects from typical neuroleptic medication include dystonic reactions, tardive dyskinesia, and neuroleptic malignant syndrome. Monitoring children on typical antipsychotics includes obtaining baseline liver enzymes repeated every six months. Baseline abnormal involuntary movement scales (AIMs) should be performed and repeated every six months. Most dystonic reactions can be managed by lowering the dosage or using antiparkinsonian agents such as benzotropine. Discontinuance is necessary when symptoms of neuroleptic malignant syndrome or tardive dyskinesia occur. Clozapine in associated with agranulocytosis and seizures; therefore, a baseline electrocardiogram (ECG), EEG, complete blood count (CBC), and liver-function tests (LFTs) need to be obtained. CBCs require weekly monitoring and should be repeated every three months. An EEG should be repeated while at the optimal dose or if 300 mg per day has been exceeded. An association with hepatotoxicity in male pediatric patients treated with risperidone is reported (Kumra et al., 1997), and it is recommended that LFTs be repeated every three months. Baseline AIMs should be obtained, and the onset of amenorrhea and galactorrhea should be monitored in females.

ALPHA-ADRENERGIC AGONISTS

Alpha-adrenergic-stimulating agents inhibit noradrenergic activity. They are reportedly useful in treating symptoms of hyperactivity, impulsivity, and aggression in youngsters with PDD. Agents used are clonidine and guanfacine. Clonidine has a half-life of 2.5 hours, and guanfacine has a half-life of 16 hours. Guanfacine is less sedating and less hypotensive than clonidine and can be given in one daily dose because of guanfacine's longer half-life.

Studies of the effects of alpha-adrenergic agonists in youths with PDD are few but demonstrate promise. Frankhauser and colleagues (1992) performed a double-blind placebo-controlled study in eight boys age five to 13 years with autism using clonidine. Doses ranged from 0.15 mg per day to 0.20 mg per day in three divided doses. The clonidine-treated group exhibited improvement in hyperactivity and was less irritable. Another double-blind placebo-controlled study of transdermal clonidine (mean dose, 0.005 mg/kg per day) included nine males age five to 33 with autism (Jaselski et al., 1992). The patients using transdermal clonidine experienced some improvement in hyperactivity, aggression, social withdrawal, and stereotypies.

Pulse and blood pressure monitoring is essential during treatment with clonidine and should be checked at least twice at each dosage level. Contraindications to alpha-adrenergic agonist use are chronic renal failure and severe cardiovascular disease. Other side effects include dry mouth, dizziness, nausea, orthostatic hypotension, weakness, and agitation. When stopping alpha-adrenergic agonists, the medication should be tapered over a period of several days to weeks. Withdrawal symptoms include motor restlessness, tics, and increased blood pressure and pulse.

BETA-ADRENERGIC BLOCKING AGENTS

Beta-adrenergic blocking agents are used in controlling aggression by decreasing autonomic overreactivity. Propanolol and hadolol have been studied in individuals with PDD. Conner and associates (1997) did an open-label study using nadolol (mean daily dose, 2.5 mg/kg) in 11 developmentally disabled patients age nine to 24. Ten of the subjects exhibited a marked decrease in aggressive behavior. Open-label studies of propranolol have yielded similar results.

Contraindications to the use of beta-blocking agents include asthma, diabetes mellitus, hyperthyroidism, cardiac conduction defects, and tachycardia. Blood pressure and pulse should be checked before each dose until a therapeutic level is established. Propranolol should be carefully monitored when the pulse is below 60 beats per minute or the blood pressure drops below 80/50 mmHg. Dizziness, postural hypotension, and exercise intolerance are indications that the dosage should be monitored carefully. Other side effects include lethargy, onset of diabetes mellitus, depression, and bronchoconstriction. Beta-blocking agents can increase the blood levels of neuroleptics such as chlorpromazine and thioridazine.

SELECTIVE SEROTONIN REUPTAKE INHIBITORS

Abnormal serotonin levels in patients with autism, obsessive-compulsive disorder, and stereotypic movements lead to a theoretical interest in the use of SSRIs in treating PDD. SSRIs are found to ameliorate obsessive and compulsive symptoms by decreasing the synaptic reuptake of serotonin. SSRIs may also improve affective symptoms and self-injurious behavior.

A double-blind controlled study by Gordon, State, and Nelson (1993) compared clomipramine and desipramine to placebo in adult patients with PDD. Clomipramine was found to be superior to desipramine and placebo in controlling aggression, stereotypies, rituals, compulsive behaviors, and social relatedness. McDougle and associates (1996) did a double-blind placebo-controlled study of fluvoxamine in 30 adults with autism. After 12 weeks, half of the patients on fluvoxamine exhibited improvement in obsessions, maladaptive behavior, aggression, and language. In open-label studies, sertraline (Steingard et al., 1997) and fluoxetine (Bregman, Volkmar, and Cohen, 1991; Cook et al., 1992) also exhibit promising results.

The rule when using SSRIs is to start at the lowest possible dose and titrate slowly up in order to minimize the risk of adverse reactions such as agitation, restlessness, and irritability. Clomipramine is a tricyclic antidepressant and therefore requires ECG monitoring. Side effects may include anticholinergic effects, blood pressure changes, tachycardia, and increased risk for seizures. Side effects associated with SSRIs are an amotivational syndrome, behavioral agitation, and, rare but serious, "serotonin syndrome." Serotonin syndrome manifests by hyperthermia, rigidity, myoclonus, confusion, and delirium. Other potential side effects include apathy, agitation, and disinhibition.

NALTREXONE

Naltrexone is an opioid agonist that has been used in treating self-injurious behavior, hyperactivity, and poor social relatedness in people with PDD. Study findings are mixed as to the utility of naltrexone in treating PDD (Buitelar, Willemsen-Swinkels, and Van Engeland, 1998). Investigators found a modest improvement in hyperactivity and irritability for patients treated with naltrexone but no demonstrable effects in learning or social relatedness. Anecdotally, there are patients who appear to exhibit a good response to this medication. Naltrexone is not recommended for patients with Rett's disorder. Hepatotoxicity may be a rare side effect (Kumra et al., 1997).

STIMULANTS

There are a few open-label studies suggesting that stimulants may be of benefit in treating hyperactivity and inattention in high-functioning individuals with PDD (Quintana et al., 1995) and in more severely affected individuals not responding to educational and behavioral interventions. Administration of stimulants in this population must be done cautiously, because these patients may experience an exacerbation of stereotypies and disruptive behavior. Medications in this class include methylphenidate, dextroamphetamine, magnesium pemoline, and a newer drug, Adderall (a combination of dextroamphetamine salts). Most of the studies conducted have used methylphenidate. Anorexia, weight loss, irritability, insomnia, and dysphoria are side effects associated with stimulant usage.

MOOD STABILIZERS

Mood stabilizers can be useful in managing aggressive behavior and in treating affective features in PDD. Mood stabilizers are also used for augmentation of antipsychotics in treating schizophrenia. Children with PDD may have a family history of bipolar disorder, and, if aggression and irritability occur, these agents can be of benefit (Steingard and Biederman, 1987). Patients with PDD have a high incidence of seizure disorder, which may exacerbate behavioral problems. These children often improve on anticonvulsant types of mood stabilizers.

Mood stabilizers include lithium and the anticonvulsants carbamazepine, valproate, and Neurontin (gabapentin). Before initiating lithium, baseline thyroid profiles, creatinine, blood urea nitrogen (BUN), ECG, electrolytes, and CBC must be obtained. Possible side effects from lithium include gastrointestinal symptoms, renal damage, tremor, sedation, and decreased thyroid functioning. Monitoring for carbamazepine and valproate include LFTs, CBCs, BUN, and creatinine; carbamazepine also requires a urinalysis. All three of these medications require blood-level monitoring throughout their use. Rare side effects of carbamazepine may include bone-marrow suppression and liver dysfunction. Extremely rare side effects are Steven-Johnson syndrome and systemic lupus erythematosus. Uncommon side effects of valproate are liver toxicity, hyperammonemia, alopecia, neutropenia, thrombocytopenia, hyperglycemia, and pancreatitis.

Conclusion

Recent developments in the use of pharmacologic agents are leading to dramatic changes in the treatment of serious mental disorders in adolescents and to the practice of adolescent psychiatry. The caution in using typical antipsychotics at any age, but especially in youth, is lessened with the advent of atypical antipsychotics, but caution should not be discontinued. Treatments with these medications demonstrate clear benefits for adolescents with PDD and psychotic disorders, but they do not work for all youth with these disorders, and a few individuals develop serious side effects.

SSRI antidepressants are a clear improvement over tricyclic antidepressants in treating impulsive and compulsive thoughts and behaviors in adolescents. Their side effects are relatively minor, but treatment with these medications still requires skilled management and monitoring to ensure maximal benefit.

Other medications increasingly used in treating psychiatric disorders in adolescents—including stimulants, adrenergic blocking agents, and mood-stabilizing agents—also are improving symptom outcome and probably long-term prognosis. These too require skilled evaluation to determine the most appropriate medication, the most effective dose, and a careful consideration and monitoring of side effect potential.

Adolescent psychiatrists continue to play a significant role in the diagnosis and treatment of serious mental disorders in youth. There is an increasing need to have state-of-the-art knowledge of psychotropic medications to complement our diagnostic and psychotherapeutic skills.

REFERENCES

American Psychiatric Association (1994), *Diagnostic and Statistical Manual of Mental Disorders* (4th ed.). Washington, DC: APA.

Anderson, G. M., Freedman, D. X., Cohen, D. J., Volkmar, F. R., Hoder, E. L., McPhedran, P., Minderaa, R. B., Hansen, C. R. & Young, J. G. (1987), Whole blood serotonin in autistic and normal subjects. *J. Child Psychol. Psychiat.*, 28:885–900.

Armenteros, J., Whitaker, A., Welikson, M., Stedge, D. & Gorman, J. (1997), Risperdone in adolescents with schizophrenia: An open pilot study. *J. Amer. Acad. Child Adolesc. Psychiat.*, 36:694–700

Bartak, L., Rutter, M. & Cox, A. (1995), A comparative study of infantile autism and specific developmental receptive language disorder, I: The children. *Br. J. Psychiat.*, 126:127–145.

Biederman, J., Klein, R. G., Pine, D. S. & Klein D. F. (1998), Resolved: Mania is mistaken for ADHD in prepubertal children. *Amer. J. Child Adolesc. Psychiat.*, 37:1091–1099.

———— Spencer, T. & Wilens, T. (1997), Psychopharmacology. In: *Textbook of Child & Adolescent Psychiatry*, ed. J. M. Wiener. Washington, DC: American Psychiatric Press, 49:779–812.

Bloomquist, H. K., Bohman, M., Edvinsson, S. O., Gillberg, C., Gustavson, K. H., Holmgren, G. & Wahlstrom, J. (1985), Frequency of fragile X syndrome in infantile autism. *Clin. Genetics,* 27:113–117.

Bregman, J., Volkmar, F. & Cohen, D. (1991), Fluoxetine in the treatment of autistic disorder. *Scientific Proceedings of the Annual Meeting of the American Academy of Child and Adolescent Psychiatry,* 7:52.

Buitelar, J. K., Willemsen-Swinkels, S. & Van Engeland, H. (1998), Naltrexone in children with autism [Letter]. *J. Amer. Acad. Child Adolesc. Psychiat.*, 37:800–801.

Burd, L., & Kerbeshian, I. (1987), A North Dakota prevalence study of schizophrenia presenting in childhood. *J. Amer. Acad. Child Adolesc. Psychiat.,* 26:347–350.

Campbell, M., Anderson, L. T., Meier, M., Cohen, I. L., Small, A. M., Samit, C. & Sachar, E. J. (1978), A comparison of haloperidol and behavior therapy and their interaction in autistic children. *J. Amer. Acad. Adolesc. Child Psychiat.,* 17:640–655.

———— & Shay, J. (1995), Pervasive developmental disorders. In: *Comprehensive Textbook of Psychiatry*, ed. H. I. Kaplan & B. J. Sadock. Baltimore, MD: Williams & Wilkins, 37:2277–2294.

Cantwell, D. P., Baker, L., Rutter, M. & Mawhood, L. (1989), Infantile autism and developmental dysphasia: A comparative follow-up into middle childhood. *J. Autism Dev. Disord.,* 19:19–31.

289

Caplan, R., Guthrie, D., Gish, B., Tanguay, P. & David-Lando, G. (1989), The Kiddie Formal Thought Disorder Scale: Clinical assessment, reliability, and validity. *J. Amer. Acad. Child Adolesc. Psychiat.,* 28:408–416.

Chess, S. (1977), Follow-up report on autism in congenital rubella. *J. Autism Dev. Disord.,,* 7:69–81.

Cohen, I. L., Campbell, M., Posner, D., Triebel, D., Small, A. M. & Anderson, L. T. (1980), A study of haloperidol in young autistic children: A within-subjects design using objective rating scales. *Psychopharmacol. Bull.,* 16:63–65.

Commings, D. E. & Commings, B. G. (1991), Clinical and genetic relationship between autism-pervasive developmental disorder and Tourette's syndrome: A study of 19 cases.

Conner, D. F., Ozbaynak, K. R., Benjamin, S., Ma, Y. & Fletcher, K. E. (1997), A pilot study of nadolol for overt aggression in developmentally delayed individuals. *J. Amer. Acad. Child Adolesc. Psychiat.,* 36:826–834.

Cook, E. H. Jr., Rowlette, R., Jaselski, C. & Leventhal, B. L. (1992), Fluoxetine treatment of children and adults with autistic disorder and mental retardation. *J. Amer. Acad. Child Adolesc. Psychiat.,* 31:739–745.

————Leventhal, B. L. & Freedman, D. X. (1998), Free serotonin in plasma: Autistic children and their first degree relatives. *Biol. Psychiat.,* 24:488–491.

Evans, J. & Acton, W. P. (1972), A psychiatric service for the disturbed adolescent. *Br. J. Psychiat.,* 120:429–432.

Findling, R. L., Maxwell, K. & Wiznitzer, M. (1997), An open clinical trial of risperidone monotherapy in young children with autistic disorders. *Psychopharmacol. Bull.,* 33:155–159.

Frankhauser, M. P., Karumanchi, V. C., German, M. L., Yates, A. & Karumanchi, S. D. (1992), A double-blind placebo-controlled study of the efficacy of transdermal clonidine in autism. *J. Clin. Psychiat.,* 53:77–82.

Ghazinddin, M. & Tsai, L. Y. (1991), Depression in autistic disorder. *Br. J. Psychiat.,* 159:721–723.

Gillberg, C. (1995), *Clinical Child Neuropsychiatry.* Cambridge, England: Cambridge University Press.

——— & Srendsen, P. (1987), CSF monoamines in autistic syndromes and other pervasive developmental disorders of early childhood. *Br. J. Psychiat.,* 151:89–94.

———— Terenius, L., Hagberg, B., Witt-Engerstrom, I. & Eriksson, I. (1990), CSF beta-endorphins in childhood neuropsychiatric disorders. *Brain Dev.*, 12:88–92.

Gordon, C., State, R. & Nelson, J. (1993), A double-blind comparison of clomipramine, desipramine, and placebo in the treatment of autistic disorder. *Arch. Gen. Psychiat.*, 50:441–447.

Green, W. H., Campbell, M., Hardesty, A. S., Grega, D. M., Padron-Gayol, M., Shell, J. & Erlenmeyer-Kimling, L. (1984), A comparison of schizophrenic and autistic children. *J. Amer. Acad. Child Adolesc. Psychiat.*, 23:399–409.

Jaselski, C. A., Cook, E. H., Jr., Fletcher, K. E. & Leventhal, B. L. (1992), Clonidine treatment of hyperactive and impulsive children with autistic disorder. *J. Clin. Psychopharmacol.*, 12:322–327.

Kerbeshian, J. & Burd, L. (1996), Case study: Comorbidity among Tourette's syndrome autistic disorder, and bipolar disorder. *J. Amer. Acad. Child Adolesc. Psychiat.*, 35:681–685.

Kobayashi, R., Murata, T. & Yoshinaga, K. (1992), A follow-up study of 201 children with autism in Kyushu and Yamaguchi areas, Japan. *J. Autism Dev. Disord.*, 22:395–411.

Kolvin, I. (1971), Studies in childhood psychoses. I: Diagnostic criteria and classification. *Br. J. Psychiat.*, 118:381–384.

Krishnamoorthy, J. & King, B. H. (1998), Open-label olanzapine treatment in five preadolescent children. *J. Child Adoles. Psychopharmacol.*, 8:107–113.

Kumra, S., Frazier, J. A., Jacobsen, L. K., McKenna, K., Gordon, C. T., Hamburger, S., Smith, A. K., Albus, K. E., Alaghband-Rad, J., Lenane, M. & Rapoport J. L. (1996), Childhood-onset schizophrenia: A double-blind clozapine haloperidol comparison. *Arch. Gen. Psychiat.*, 53:1090–1097.

———— Herian, D., Jacobsen, L., Brigeglin, C. & Groethe, D. (1997), Case study: Risperidone-induced hepatotoxicity in pediatric patients. *J. Amer. Acad. Child Adolesc. Psychiat.*, 36:701–705.

———— Jacobsen, L. K., Lenane, M., Karp, B. I., Frazier, J. A., Smith, A. K., Bedwell, J., Lee, P., Malanga, C. J., Hamburger, S. & Rapoport, J. L. (1998), Childhood-onset schizophrenia: An open-label study of olanzapine in adolescents. *J. Amer. Child Adolesc. Psychiat.*, 37:377–385.

———— ———— ———— Zahn, T. P., Wiggs, E., Alaghband-Rad, J., Castellanos, F. X., Frazier, J. A., McKenna, K., Gordon, C. T., Smith, A., Hamburger, S. & Rapoport, J. L. (1998), "Multidimensionally impaired disorder": Is it a variant of very early-onset schizophrenia?. *J. Amer. Acad. Child Adolesc. Psychiat.,* 37:91–99.

McClellan, J. & Werry, J. S. (1997), Practice parameters for the assessment and treatment of children and adolescents with schizophrenia. *J. Amer. Acad. Child Adolesc. Psychiat.,* 36(10 suppl.):S177–S193.

McDougle, C., Holmes, J., Bronson, M., Anderson, G., Volkmar, F., Price, L. & Cohen, D. (1997), Risperdone treatment of children and adolescents with pervasive developmental disorders: A prospective, open-label study. *J. Amer. Acad. Child Adolesc. Psychiat.,* 36:685–693.

———— ———— Carlson, D. C., Pelton, G. H., Cohen, D. J. & Price, L. H. (1998), A double-blind, placebo-controlled study of risperidone in adults with autistic disorder and other pervasive developmental disorders. *Arch. Gen. Psychiat.,* 55:633–641.

———— Naylor, S. T., Cohen, D. J., Volkmar, F. R., Heninger, G. R. & Price, L. H. (1996), A double-blind, placebo-controlled study of fluvoxamine in adults with autistic disorders. *Arch. Gen. Psychiat.,* 53:1001–1008.

Naruse, H., Nagahata, M., Nakane, Y., Shirahash, K., Takesada, M. & Yamazaki, K. (1982), A multicenter double-blind trial of pimozide, haloperidol, and placebo in children with behavioral disorders using crossover design. *Acta Paedopsychiatrica,* 48:173–184.

Nicolson, R., Avad, G. & Sloman, L. (1998), An open trial of risperidone in young autistic children. *J. Amer. Acad. Child Adolesc. Psychiat.,* 37:372–376.

Pool, D., Bloom, W., Mielke, D. H., Roniger, J. J., Jr. & Gallant, D. M. (1976), A controlled evaluation of loxitane in seventy-five adolescent schizophrenic patients. *Curr. Ther. Res.,* 19:99–104.

Quintana, H., Birmaher, B., Stedge, D., Lennon, S., Freed, J. & Greenhill, L. (1995), Use of methylphenidate in the treatment of children with autistic disorder. *J. Autism Dev. Disord.,* 25:283–294.

Ritvo, E. R., Freeman, B. J., Pingree, C., Jorde, L. B., Mason-Brothers, A., Jones, M. B., McMahon, W. M., Petersen, P. B., Jenson, W. R. & Mo, A. (1989), The UCLA–University of Utah Epidemiologic Survey of Autism: Prevalence. *Amer. J. Psychiat.,* 146:1032–1036.

Ross, D. L., Klykylo, W. M. & Hitzemann, R. (1987), Reduction of elevated CSF beta-endorphins by fenfluramine in infantile autism. *Pediat. Neurol.,* 3:83–86.

Rutter, M. (1978), Diagnosis and definition. In: *Autism: A Reappraisal of Concepts and Treatment,* ed. M. Rutter & E. Schopler. New York: Plenum, 1:1–25.

Siméon, J. G., Carrey, N. J. & Wiggings, D. M. (1995), Risperidone effects in treatment-resistant adolescents: Preliminary case reports. *J. Child Adolesc. Psychopharmacol.,* 5:69–79.

Spencer, E. K. & Campbell, M. (1994), Children with schizophrenia: Diagnosis, phenomenology, and pharmachotherapy. *Schizophr. Bull.,* 20:713–725.

Stefanatos, G. A., Grover, W. & Geller, E. (1995), Autism and autistic-like conditions in Swedish rural and urban areas: A population study. *Br. J. Psychiat.,* 149:81–87.

Steinberg, D. (1985), *Psychotic and Other Severe Disturbances in Adolescent Psychiatry: Modern Approaches.* Oxford, England: Blackwell Scientific.

Steingard, R. & Biederman, J. (1987), Lithium responsive manic-like symptoms in two individuals with autism and mental retardation. *J. Amer. Acad. Child Adolesc. Psychiat.,* 26:932–935.

——— Zimnitzky, B., Demaso, D. R., Bauman, M. L. & Bucci, J. P. (1997), Sertraline treatment of transition-associated anxiety and agitation in children with autistic disorder. *J. Child Adolesc. Psychopharmacol.,* 7:9–15.

Tsai, L. Y. & Ghazinddin, M. (1997), Autistic disorder. In: *Textbook of Child & Adolescent Psychiatry,* ed. J. M. Wiener. Washington, DC: American Psychiatric Press, 18:255–280.

Volkmar, F. R. (1996), Childhood and adolescent psychosis: A review of the past 10 years. *J. Amer. Acad. Child Adolesc. Psychiat.,* 35:843–851.

——— Szatmari, P. & Sparrow, S. S. (1993), Sex differences in pervasive developmental disorders. *J. Autism Dev. Disord.,* 23:579–591.

Werry, J. S. (1991), Child and adolescent schizophrenia, bipolar, and schizoaffective disorders: A clinical and outcome study. *J. Amer. Acad. Child Adolesc. Psychiat.,* 30:457–465.

PART V

ISSUES IN ADOLESCENT CONSULTATION-LIAISON

16 PSYCHIATRIC CONSULTATION ON AN ADOLESCENT MEDICAL SERVICE

EVERETT DULIT

This chapter will offer an aerial view of the territory identified by the title, followed by fuller development of some selected themes included in that overview, then followed by some closing comments intended to leave the reader thinking about three issues that it might be helpful for the consultation/liaison (C/L) psychiatrist to think about while doing the work.

I shall begin with a list of medical conditions commonly seen on an adolescent medicine service and commonly brought to the attention of the C/L psychiatrist by pediatricians seeking an assessment and recommendations for treatment and/or management (Friedman et al., 1998, pp. 87–146). The intent of setting forth this list is to convey what seems to me to be the impressive breadth of such conditions (pp. 792–937). However, the list does not pretend to be all-inclusive; there are also the rare metabolic, hormonal, and/or developmental conditions seen, for example, once a decade that are not included on the list. When one of these is admitted, knowledge about that rare clinical condition suddenly becomes of central importance—commonly precipitating a race to the library by both pediatricians and consultant.

Clinical Conditions and Issues Seen on an Adolescent Medicine Inpatient Service

The suicide attempter. The depressed adolescent. The serious substance abuser. The conduct-disordered adolescent. (Note: The previous four conditions do tend to go together; with any one of those diagnoses, you commonly also have one or more of the others.) The sickle-cell patient, in painful crisis (i.e., with a sudden attack of pain). The diabetic or asthmatic patient, commonly admitted in the crisis that results when "control" of the illness is lost. The eating-disordered patient, with anorexia and/or bulimia. Obesity (especially extreme cases). Pelvic inflammatory disease (Friedman et al., 1998, pp. 1104–1107). That whole cluster of conditions in which individual psychology, affect states, and bodily symptoms strongly interact and intertwine—including conversion symptoms, psychophysiological phenomena, somatoform symptoms, Munchausen's syndrome, and frank malingering, all of those some form of significant "psychogenicity." Death and dying issues (e.g., end-stage cancers and renal disease). Therapies, notably for cancers, in which the treatment is so hard on the patient as to raise serious questions for all regarding how far to go. Trauma and the aftermath of trauma, including posttraumatic stress disorder (PTSD) and injuries that leave serious impairment (loss of limb or vision) affecting an entire life, sometimes precluding prior career choices (e.g., athletics). Lupus, commonly with frank psychiatric symptoms. Consent and refusal-of-treatment issues, which especially highlight judgments about the maturity/immaturity of the adolescent, taking note that key medical decisions for adolescent patients involve three significant "power centers" (parent, physician, adolescent patient) rather than the more usual two (doctor and parent with preadolescent child; doctor and patient with adult patient).

Another group of problems concerns staff-centered and staff-defined issues. Conflict among house staff, nursing staff, and patient over some requests for analgesics by patients claiming to be in pain (those conflicts deriving from staff concern about alleged overuse by patients, about alleged "recreational use" by patients, about control). Approach by staff to clear evidence of denial of illness by a patient. Approach to alleged compliance/noncompliance behavior, especially alleged lack of self-care that supposedly "keeps bouncing this patient back in here again—for us to have to start all over again getting their illness under control." One-to-one nursing monitoring for patients at high risk for suicide attempt and/or elopement. The handling of and the expression of anger by staff, of grief by staff, including especially strong staff reactions to death and dying, particularly for the especially liked, admired, beloved, endearing, respected patient. Dealing with staff (house staff, nursing staff, senior staff) who seem particularly "unpsychological-minded" and/or who seem particularly adversarial and/or angry and/or moralistic in their dealing with patients.

EVERETT DULIT

SUICIDE ATTEMPTERS

Good programs vary in the approach they take to the task of evaluating and treating adolescents seen in the immediate aftermath of a suicide attempt. I shall outline here the approach that has emerged in our program (Dulit, 1995) and that seems to us to have real merit in some of its leanings. There is surely room, however, for programs with honest differences of emphasis, all of them useful and effective even with the differences, especially if features that are less emphasized in other programs are balanced by other features that somehow manage to make up for what may seem to be missing.

We like to hospitalize virtually all suicide attempters seen in the ER. Some programs like to make the evaluation in the ER—often choosing the option (generally welcomed by patient and family) to send the patient home with a referral to outpatient treatment—as a way of "protecting" the inpatient service, which is felt to be chronically at risk of "overload." We lean in the direction of admitting all suicide attempters to our Adolescent Medicine Unit (not to the Psychiatry Inpatient Unit). That has the advantages of (a) giving top priority at first to assessing and treating the injury to the body (overdose, cutting, jumping, etc.), (b) transmitting the message "This is *serious!*" in a way and to a degree that sending the patient home does not, and (c) giving "the behavioral team" on the unit (one part-time psychiatrist and one full-time social worker) a chance to begin the process of identifying the "dynamic" of what happened from the adolescent's point of view and (very important!) identifying the dynamic of what is going on between the adolescent and the parent(s), at which interface we find much (most) of the psychological material that comes to seem critical in bringing about the crisis. We refer about 80% of our patients to outpatient treatment. About 5% to 10% we send home without further treatment, and about 5% to 10% we refer to a secure (locked) inpatient service for further evaluation and treatment. However, follow-up studies done on our patient population (compatible with data from other studies on similar patient populations; e.g., Trautman, Stewart, and Morishima, 1993) reveal that only a very small fraction (about 5%) actually follow through with an outpatient treatment that goes beyond two or three sessions. As a consequence, we work in the immediate aftermath of the attempt with the assumption that what we don't provide the patient probably won't get. That leads us to place a great deal of emphasis on trying to do an effective job of brief therapy in the time we do have (a few sessions at most).

As part of our evaluation, after an attempt by overdose of some medication from the family medicine cabinet, we like to ask: "At the time you took all those pills, were you trying or planning or expecting to end up dead?" If they say yes, our next question is: "Well, as it turned out [usually because they communicated to someone what they had done, in a kind of change of mind, though less frequently because they were discovered by chance to be sick or even comatose], clearly you didn't die. Are you glad of that or perhaps kinda sorry?" Obviously, answers at all in the "I'm sorry" direction are high-risk cases. They are rare. But, we are especially alert to the shrugged-shoulder response meaning "I don't know—maybe." These cases are not as rare, and clearly they are high risk also.

If the answer to "Were you trying or planning or expecting to end up dead?" is no or "not really," we like to ask: "Then what *were* you trying for?" Sometimes the patients' tendency is to think that we are really asking at that point for a confession that they did it to "get attention" and for a ritual of contrition ("I know I shouldn't have done it"). That tendency can be so great as to require real work to get them away from those cliches (Occasionally valid, to be sure) to a search for an answer that contains more of their own individual psychological truth. This often takes the form "I was just so upset—I had to do something!"—which makes the attempt then seem at core an outburst of relatively undifferentiated angry, distressed feeling, a kind of "cry to the heavens," to the fates, an explosion of anger, which is quite different from the more goal-directed manipulation (usually of parents) that the phrase "trying to get attention" usually connotes.

PSYCHOGENIC ILLNESSES

One important cluster of interconnected phenomena that will regularly engage the C/L consultant is the quite varied disorders that all come under the heading of "medical presentation but with psychogenic origins." The *Diagnostic and Statistical Manual of Mental Disorders, Fourth Edition* (*DSM–IV*; American Psychiatric Association, 1994) sorts these out into disorders named somatization, undifferentiated somatoform, conversion, pain, body dysmorphic, somatoform NOS, and hypochondriasis. However, there is also much of value, worth retaining, in the older categories: psychosomatic, psychophysiological, conversion, and malingering. The C/L psychiatrist should steep himself or herself in the literature on those conditions and on Munchausen's syndrome and Munchausen's-by-proxy.

Two important practical pieces of advice in relation to work with the foregoing kinds of cases are:

1.   Physicians (pediatricians) whose view of medical illness is primarily centered on well-defined medical illness arising out of clear biological causation can easily move toward thinking that psychological causation is relatively easy to change compared with biological causation, which feels to them more solid, real, objective, and not "just in the mind." Some things just in the mind can indeed be dramatically altered through psychological work with the patient, but some other psychological states may be exceedingly difficult to get people to change. Indeed, there may well be in the patient population a subgroup that expresses psychological conflict through bodily symptoms because of or as part of a worldview and an expressive style not at home with psychological material. As a consequence of that unpsychological-mindedness, they are likely to be particularly closed off to successful psychotherapy because of real incapacities beyond the usual mixed motivations and secondary gains. Nonetheless, some psychotherapy may be worth a try, partly because it's not easy to be sure of the prospects for success at the outset. One can sometimes be pleasantly surprised by a capacity for psychological-mindedness that emerges in the course of the work where one hadn't anticipated or perceived it at the outset. Also, in the course of trying for a psychotherapy, one can usually learn more about possible psychological roots of the illness than one can in a brief evaluation (Fritz, Mattison, and Spirito, 1993).

2.   Often it occurs that a patient is referred (e.g., with abdominal pain, with some gait disturbance) after a very extensive search for underlying objective organic pathology fails to reveal anything of significance (Webster, 1998). Increasingly, the physicians evaluating the patient come to think: "Maybe this is a case for psych?" In support of that possibility, house staff often mention some "stresses" in the patient's life that came at about the right time. Mostly the events and feelings nominated for consideration are fairly commonplace in the lives of adolescents. That doesn't completely rule them out for relevance, but it does definitely reduce the likelihood that the alleged "stress" was a

significant contributing factor. Always the C/L psychiatrist should try to make an independent positive diagnosis of possible psychogenicity (i.e., not primarily "by default" but because a persuasive line of thought positively suggestive of psychogenicity can be delineated). At the same time, however, it is important to urge continued work on the organic possibilities, considering that long-term follow-up studies (e.g., Slater, 1956) demonstrate that a surprisingly high percentage of patients (in the range of 30% to 50%) with a discharge diagnosis of psychogenic in an adult hospital practice, upon long-term follow-up, eventually turned out to have been suffering from a straightforward organic illness that hadn't emerged clearly enough at the time of the early hospitalization to be objectively discerned—and not because of bad work.

THE IMPOSSIBLE PATIENT: BORDERLINE CONDITION AND/OR SEVERE PERSONALITY DISORDER

Patients with some form of severe personality disorder and/or with borderline condition are not infrequently seen on an adolescent medicine service. For example, they may be admitted with one of the recurrent manipulative suicide attempts that are part of the *DSM–IV* definition of borderline personality disorder, or they may present with anorexia nervosa or with severe recurrent substance abuse. The terms personality disorder and borderline (and the ideas that go with them) tend not to be terms used by pediatricians, who are most at home with psychiatric disorders that are straightforwardly "medical" (like attention deficit hyperactivity disorder or childhood psychosis) or childhood difficulties that seem clearly to derive from negligent or faulty parenting. But borderline condition and the personality disorders tend to be neither clearly medical nor clearly the consequences of "bad parenting."

Pediatrics staff tend not to speak of these patients in diagnostic language. Instead, they may simply think and speak of the patient as "impossible!" When they do attempt to work with these patients, they tend to favor approaches centering on a tone of kindly reasonability— like the good parent, uncle, or aunt trying to "win over" a child who is being temporarily difficult. As is well recognized in psychiatry, such approaches tend not to work well with severe personality disorder, borderline condition certainly included. (Note that the borderline state is conceptualized in *DSM–III* and *DSM-IV* as a personality disorder. But there is also an earlier idea with much merit—an idea that treats the borderline state as a condition that can coexist with all other personality disorders, generally making them worse, thus also serving as a kind of severity marker.)

I favor education of pediatrics staff about borderline condition not with any expectation that they might thus become better equipped to treat the disorder, which is usually so very resistant to treatment even in experienced hands. The goal instead is primarily to help them to recognize when borderline condition might be the reason for the difficulty they are having with a particular "impossible patient" and thus to protect them against the likelihood that the almost inevitable failure of their psychological work with those patients might leave them unnecessarily discouraged about using their emerging psychological skills with patients who are not borderline and with whom they could be quite effective.

DEATH AND DYING ISSUES

Death and dying issues can hit house staff and nursing staff very hard, especially with a patient they like a lot and most especially when they're left with a sense that somehow they should have been able to do better. They commonly turn to the psychiatrist and the social workers for help with talking through feelings about the loss. The weekly staff conference can sometimes be used very effectively for a kind of group processing of the feelings—sharing, clarifying, helping people to find words for their thoughts and feelings, providing and getting mutual support, mourning the loss, and moving by the end of the conference some distance toward some closure on the experience. Ironically, psychiatrists, psychologists, and social workers who actually have much less experience with death and dying than the house staff are called upon to be "the strong ones." Somehow, the identification of us as workers on psychological ground creates an expectation to which we have to rise—and most often definitely do, partially by virtue of accepting the expectation as appropriate and as fitting our self-definition and partially by being more adept at and more experienced with doing the psychological work within ourselves that needs to be done to handle death and dying issues. In addition, I think age helps; seniors can be particularly useful here.

THE PSYCHOTIC ADOLESCENT

Sometimes an actively psychotic adolescent is admitted to an adolescent medicine service. Psychosis can be a background and accompaniment to suicidal behavior, or it can be a consequence of recreational use of psychotomimetic drugs ("tripping"). The presence of psychosis may be obvious and recognized at the time of admission, or it may emerge only after some time (hours, days) in the hospital. Whereas the actual hospital care appropriate for the psychotic adolescent would have been straightforward enough if the patient had been admitted to a psychiatry inpatient service, on an adolescent medicine service the mismatch between a major mental disorder and the usual focus of the working group (on organic medical disorders) can present major problems. House staff and nursing staff on an adolescent medicine unit do not define themselves as people who want to work with such patients, and they usually do not have adequate training for such work. Further, the ward is not "set up" for it—not only regarding staff expectations about behavior of patients but also regarding physical structure (locked vs. unlocked doors and windows, single rooms, seclusion rooms, restraints, etc.). House staff and nursing staff are often only minimally familiar with psychoactive medications—which commonly leads to using them gingerly (i.e., at dosages that are too low to be optimal or giving the medication only "when necessary" when a regular clock-based schedule would be better).

Two important tasks for the consultant when a psychotic adolescent is housed on an adolescent medicine service are (a) close monitoring of care, especially of medications, to get dosages up to and maintained at potentially useful levels and (b) getting the patient transferred to a psychiatry inpatient service as soon as possible, which can run into the difficulty that, once the patient is "safely" housed on a medical service, ER personnel with "hot cases" poorly housed in an ER may well be motivated to use any psychiatric beds that "open up" for one of those patients rather than for a patient "already being taken care of in house."

CONSENT AND REFUSAL ISSUES ON AN ADOLESCENT MEDICINE SERVICE

Consent and refusal decisions on an adolescent medicine service are clearly complicated by the status of the adolescent "in-between" childhood and adulthood. Can adolescents make their own health care decisions? Probably the basic mind-set of most medical personnel about that issue would be to identify the adolescent as "immature" in his or her thinking compared to the adult. And clearly some adolescents much prefer to have major medical decisions made by their parent(s). Further, the academically inclined student of cognitive development might well point to the fact that the average age for the emergence of fully developed abstract thinking is not until middle adolescence or even later than that. On this point, however, I hold a somewhat atypical point of view based on a judgment about my own extensive clinical experience working with adolescents in a medical setting. It seems to me that, if one sits down and takes seriously the challenge to really communicate well and honestly with an adolescent, and takes the time that is required, and works to bring out the best in the adolescent's capacity to think, one can, with a very wide range of adolescents (from very bright down to low-average intelligence) over a very wide range of ages (down to 15, 14, 13, 12), elicit a response within the same wide range of thoughtfulness and good sense one gets from a large unselected group of adults. A crucial point in this context is to remember that the judgments on complex medical matters that come from any large unselected group of adult patients will be no "gold standard." Foolish, ill-considered, wrongheaded ideas and decisions are commonplace in adult medical work. Ask any internist. As a consequence, my working stance is to take very seriously the input from adolescent patients, regarding both consent and refusal. When a decision is made by the adolescent patient or by the parent that seems to me to be quite wrongheaded and unwise, I take it as my responsibility to do my best to press for a reconsideration. There are no rules against trying openly to make a hard sell when the merits of what you are trying to press for seem unmistakably in the patient's best interests. Instead, it is my position that the doctor even has an obligation to give the patient and parents a chance to hear him or her thinking out loud at his or her best—and persuasively—about the key options that are involved. Of course, there are situations in which the key options are all shades of gray. In such cases, one tends to permit the patient to pick what seems to the patient "the right shade" of gray.

MEDIATING DIFFICULT INTERACTIONS BETWEEN PATIENTS AND NURSING STAFF: A PROBLEM IN SOCIAL PSYCHOLOGY

A recurrent problem on an adolescent medicine inpatient service is the clash between adolescent patient and nursing staff. Although each episode has its own unique features, one can also see an underlying social psychology here that persists and creates problems. There is a trend among adolescents (not universal, but typical) of being "breezy," irreverent, even rebellious, feeling put upon by adult rules especially when they conflict with the adolescent's agenda ("some action, man"). Some adolescents "push the envelope" as far as they think they can. On the other hand, there is a trend among nursing staff (not universal, but characteristic) of being highly respectful of "the rules" and "the right way," which are clearly very important in their work. They tend to be self-selected for the character and personality that make a good fit with that (very legitimate) emphasis in the culture of nursing. Those values are then greatly reinforced by training. Inevitably, that difference leads to ongoing tensions, with episodic flare-ups and hostilities. Patients particularly prone to become lightning rods for this kind of tension include (a) patients with sickle-cell disease asking for painkillers, (b) patients (e.g., diabetics, asthmatics) for whom nurses (and house staff) suspect noncompliance at home as a major causal factor behind repeated hospitalizations, which allegedly wouldn't be needed if the patient took proper care of the illness on his or her own at home, and (c) sexually active young women with pelvic inflammatory disease.

Studies of the hospital experiences of patients in pain repeatedly show a tendency of nursing and house staff to undermedicate. Sometimes, staff justify such holding back as a means of avoiding the development in the patient of tolerance or dependence or addiction. Commonly with sickle-cell adolescents, especially those close to "the street life," there is the suspicion that the patient is asking to be on the meds partially for "the buzz" instead of "really needing it." Sometimes a vicious cycle emerges in which nurses think the adolescent is asking for meds too soon, and they delay giving the requested dose. The adaptation of some adolescents to finding themselves repeatedly experiencing that kind of delay is to begin indeed asking for it early, before the pain gets really bad. That can lead to a kind of self-fulfilled prophecy, each "side" ending up with justification in reality for its suspicions of the other, each side feeling in the right and wronged by the other. It takes skillful work as mediator and would-be authority to help both sides get past that standoff.

As for the diabetics and asthmatics, sometimes noncompliance at home is indeed a significant "cause" of the need for hospitalization. But a certain amount of tolerance for the adolescent's understandable reluctance to accept the illness (even though he or she eventually must) and some skill at using the episode to build a better working alliance for "next time you go home" can help to get self-care onto a better track next time around. And the situation is further complicated by the fact that the illness in some diabetics and asthmatics is much more "brittle" than in others (i.e., the illness in those patients is somehow much more difficult to get and keep under control). As a consequence, the noncompliant label is sometimes attached to an adolescent patient quite mistakenly—an injustice that commonly stimulates resentment and interferes with the working relation between caretakers and patient.

In the case of the patients with pelvic inflammatory disease, clearly the situation makes the patient a lightning rod for those undercurrents of sexual moralizing that are an inevitable part of the worldview of some staff. That is always difficult to discuss, to alter, to soften, even in the best of intrastaff working relations. But one has to try.

ON COMMUNICATING ONE'S CONSULTATION OPINIONS AND JUDGMENTS TO PEDIATRICS STAFF

Essentially there are three ways, and all are very important. First is the longish note in the chart, written quite early, usually immediately after the first substantial block of time spent evaluating the case, usually the same day the referral is made, or the next day for referrals made late in the day. The second method is individual conversations with attendings, house staff, nursing staff, social workers, and sometimes with parents—whoever is of some substantial importance to the case. At first these conversations are largely data gathering, and then increasingly they include transmission of one's opinions to others. The third method is a case presentation conference at which a case is presented, interviewed, and discussed—either at a regularly scheduled (weekly) "behavior rounds" or at a conference specially called to deal with some particularly problematic case and/or crisis.

The long note written not too long after the referral is made (after the patient has been seen and some substantial judgment has been reached) has the great advantage of being available in the chart to be read by everyone connected with and interested in the case. Talk comes so naturally and easily to colleagues working together on a ward that the temptation is strong just to say what you want to say to staff and colleagues who happen to be there when you are. But on any modern hospital unit, the number of people significantly involved is quite substantial—with some of that group off-duty at any given time, returning later to hear what you had to say filtered through others. With such a process, the chance of message distortion and loss of crucial emphases is high. Having a coherent, balanced statement of your opinion, your thinking, and your differential diagnosis down on paper for all to read at any time serves everyone well. It becomes a common ground to which all can refer. It functions as both a communication and an organizer.

However, actually talking with key personnel makes possible yet another level of interchange—an attempt and an opportunity to deal with individual staff objections, reluctance, and adverse reactions to the patient or to the plan of action that is proposed. As with psychotherapy, the pathways to optimal outcome are far from clear at the outset, but often real progress can be made if only by showing to reluctant colleagues how much you value their genuine and willing participation.

A weekly behavior rounds at which a patient is presented for whom psychological or psychiatric or life difficulties are paramount provides a particularly favorable context for teaching and learning in an academic setting. The conference can be led jointly by the senior adolescent medicine physician and the consulting adolescent psychiatrist. A patient is chosen, preferably by house staff, whose questions about management provide a basic organizer for the conference. The tradition in pediatrics is not as comfortable with interview of the patient in a "public setting" as is the tradition in psychiatry. Clearly, however, such interviews can be done in a way respectful of the patient's privacy and sensitivities. Such interviews add immeasurably to the group's "feel" for the "real, live patient." They also provide a particularly favorable opportunity for demonstrating interview technique, notably for modeling an approach that feels to the patient more like an interesting conversation than like being "grilled"—an approach that gives the patient a chance to hear someone (the interviewer) thinking well and out loud about complex psychological matters (including some that seem central in the patient's life), the interviewer being comfortable with uncertainty but trying to open up various plausible lines of thought, always trying to think well, always trying to draw patient and staff into a group experience of thinking well. Such a conference can greatly facilitate communication and learning at multiple levels—through explicit teaching about particular conditions and through friendly adversarial jousting between psychiatrist and "ephebiatrician" that makes honest differences in stance and judgment come alive, which can teach how quite different views can all have some validity and which can teach about the art of synthesizing several partial truths into a yet larger truth.

MEDICAL EXPERTISE

The C/L psychiatrist is regularly exposed to communications about quite technical medical matters with which he or she is not really familiar. Sometimes those are communications made directly to him or her about a case. Sometimes they are conversations among others, or they are notes in the chart. Clearly, an ideal toward which the C/L psychiatrist has to strive is to progressively accumulate more and more technical knowledge about the wide range of illnesses encountered in the course of doing the work of psychiatric consultation. Inevitably, however, some material will arise that will be unfamiliar ground for the C/L worker—material about uncommon illnesses, about new and uncommon medical procedures, about special local conditions, and/or about treatment availability/unavailability. Sometimes lab results are presented with the clear intent to communicate something important about diagnosis or prognosis—the implications of which the psychiatry consultant doesn't confidently "get," not knowing the normal range for those chemistries. To do the work well, one must be able to ask for help on such occasions from knowledgeable others. Sometimes that is best done while a case is being presented at the major weekly conference, under which circumstances often many others in the room are secretly grateful that someone else asked. It's good if the consulting psychiatrist sometimes elects to be that courageous someone. Sometimes it's best done in private with a pediatrics colleague one regularly uses to "educate me, please, about—."

A small but illustrative matter: Often the C/L psychiatrist will be feeling very much the outsider when he or she hears conference comments in which unfamiliar initials play a key role: "This patient had a TPC, but the LN was low, so we had to do an NFP instead." I've taken to saying quietly in response: "NIP!" The reaction is usually a few moments of bewilderment and then a "What?"—to which I respond, also quietly, "No Initials, Please," that usually leads to cheerful laughter and a real improvement for a while.

309

Some Concluding Themes

1. *"It isn't fair!"*   Patients of any age can have the "It isn't fair!" reaction upon finding themselves ill, "singled out," stricken, impaired, different, abnormal. But adolescents do seem to have that reaction even more intensely. Adolescence is supposed to be a time of vibrant good health—a kind of a peak period for energy and stamina. But adolescence isn't that for most of the patients who need hospitalization on an adolescent medicine unit. Adolescence is normally a time of exquisite sensitivities about unfavorable comparisons between oneself and other adolescents regarding looks, skills, strength, and vigor. One is supposed to look "great" and feel "great" during adolescence. But the patients one sees on an adolescent medicine service generally do not. Part of the job of the behavioral specialist is to try to help these patients to confront those facts and feelings and to try to find a way to come to some livable resolution of those currents and cross-currents of anger and resentment, of shame and blame, of need for special care and hating the need for special care, of a normal wish for independence and of need for the continued dependence on parents that the illness forces on both parent and adolescent. The struggle for self-esteem is hard enough for unimpaired adolescents, given mass media presentations of unreachable ideals (of beauty, of daring, of skills). That struggle is yet more difficult for the seriously or chronically ill adolescent. At the same time, most studies of the chronically ill adolescent give grounds for optimism that putting together a livable package of self-esteem and as good a life as the illness permits is something that can indeed be and is being done by a substantial fraction of "real, regular adolescents" and not only by the exceptional youngster.

2. *On the creative use of banter.*   Among professionals who center their careers on work with adolescents, there tends to arise a certain style of relating and speaking with our patients that is worth pausing to listen to and to think about. It's a way of speaking and relating that includes a large component of banter, of joking, of saying serious things in a light way or at least an offbeat way. It's an art that comes to some people naturally, and it's an art that others can learn. It's a way of speaking that works very well to bridge the age gap, the power gap, and the education gap. It aspires to be interesting, even intriguing, to leave the adolescent thinking, to leave questions open, to model for the adolescent an adult thinking out loud and at his or her best about

the adolescent's situation. It emphasizes opening up possible lines of thought rather than being firm about conclusions. Often it leaves important questions quite unresolved ("It could be this way—or it could be that way—or it could be—"). It aspires to leave the adolescent thinking (and maybe even saying): "Hmm—I never thought about it that way before—." It may try to leave the cool and cocky adolescent a little bit unsettled (hence open to interaction), by throwing an occasional curve ball, and to leave the frightened adolescent feeling that in fact he or she is among friends. Part of the task of becoming a worker with adolescents is to find one's own way to some individualized version of that way of speaking and thinking.

3. *There are calmer waters just up ahead.* A colleague in adolescent medicine was asked at a conference: "What do you use as a criterion of success in your work with adolescents?" The colleague responded: "To get them safely through the teens and out the other side." It's a good answer. It includes the implication that the teenage years are turbulent waters—an important partial truth that is not true for all but true for many and especially for those who end up in professional hands—but it also includes the implication that there are calmer waters up ahead. And for those adolescents who live close to the street scene, the teens are a time that can be quite literally life-threatening—so much so that just getting them through and out of that decade alive can be a major achievement, with realistic grounds for hope of an easier time for all concerned, as the adolescent moves into and through the 20s.

REFERENCES

American Psychiatric Association. (1994), *Diagnostic and Statistical Manual of Mental Disorders* (4th ed.). Washington, DC: APA.

Dulit, E. (1995), Immediately after the suicide attempt. In: *Treatment Approaches in the Suicidal Adolescents*, ed. I. Zimmerman & G. Asnis. New York: Wiley, pp. 91–105.

Friedman, I., Fisher, M., Schonberg, S. K. & Alderman, E. (1998), *Comprehensive Adolescent Health Care*, 2nd ed. St. Louis, MO: Quality Medical Publishing–Mosby.

Fritz, G., Mattison, R. & Spirito, A. (1993), *Child and Adolescent Mental Health Consultation in Hospital, School and Court*. Washington, DC: American Psychiatric Association Press.

Slater, E. (1956), Diagnosis of hysteria. *Br. Med. J.*, 5447:1395–1399.

Trautman, P., Stewart, M. & Morishima, A. (1993), Are adolescent suicide attempters non-compliant with out-patient care? *Amer. Acad. Child Adolesc. Psychiat.*, 32:89–94.

Webster, M. (1998), Psychological problems manifested by somatic symptoms. *Adolesc. Med.*, 9:403–413.

THE AUTHORS

OLGA ACOSTA, PH.D. is Assistant Professor, University of Maryland School of Medicine, Department of Psychiatry, Baltimore; and Associate Director, Center for School Mental Health Assistance, Baltimore.

STEVEN ADELSHEIM, M.D. is Assistant Professor of Psychiatry, Pediatric Family and Community Medicine, University of New Mexico School Medicine; and Director, New Mexico School Mental Health Initiative for the New Mexico Department of Health.

STEWART ADELSON, M.D. is Clinical Assistant Professor of Psychiatry, Sanford and Joan Weill Medical College of Cornell University, New York; and Assistant Clinical Professor of Psychiatry, College of Physicians and Surgeons, Columbia University, New York.

KATHLEEN ALBUS is currently a graduate student in the Department of Psychology at the University of Delaware. She is working toward a degree in clinical psychology.

IRVING H. BERKOVITZ, M.D. is Clinical Professor in Psychiatry, UCLA School of Medicine, Los Angeles. He also maintains a private practice in the Los Angeles area.

ILEANA BERNAL-SCHNATTER, M.D. is Clinical Assistant Professor of Psychiatry, Division of Child and Adolescent Psychiatry, University of Medicine and Dentistry of New Jersey - Robert Wood Johnson Medical School, Piscataway.

313

ROBINDER KAUR BHANGOO, M.D. is Senior Staff Fellow, Pediatric and Developmental Neuropsychiatry Branch, National Institute of Mental Health, Bethesda, MD.

SHELLEY DOCTORS, PH.D. is Supervising Analyst and Faculty Member, Institute for the Psychoanalytic Study of Subjectivity; and Faculty and Supervisor, Institute for Child, Adolescent and Family Studies, New York, NY.

EVERETT DULIT, M.D. is Associate Clinical Professor of Psychiatry and Pediatrics, AECOM, New York; and Psychiatric Consultant, Adolescent Medicine, Montefiore Medical Center, New York.

AARON H. ESMAN, M.D. (Editor) is Professor of Clinical Psychiatry (Emeritus), Cornell University Medical College; and Faculty, New York Psychoanalytic Institute. He is editor of *Psychology of Adolescence: Essential Readings, and the Psychiatric Treatments of Adolescents,* and author of *Adolescence and Culture.*

ROBERT GAINES, PH.D. is Director of Child Therapy Service, Faculty, Supervisor of Psychotherapy, William Alanson White Institute, New York, NY; and Faculty, Director of Psychoanalytic Supervision, Manhattan Institute, New York, NY.

ROBERT HENDREN, D.O. is Professor and Director, Division of Child and Adolescent Psychiatry, University of Medicine and Dentistry of New Jersey-Robert Wood Johnson Medical School, Piscataway.

HARVEY HOROWITZ, M.D. is past president of the American Society for Adolescent Psychiatry and is in the private practice of Psychiatry and Psychotherapy in Ardmore, PA.

MARKUS J. P. KRUESI, M.D. is Professor of Psychiatry and Chief, Child and Adolescent Psychiatry, University of Illinois at Chicago Department of Psychiatry; and Director, Institute of Juvenile Research, Chicago.

MARSHA H. LEVY-WARREN, PH.D. is Associate Director, Institute for Child, Adolescent and Family Studies (ICAFS), New York; and author of *The Adolescent Journey.*

LAURA NABORS, PH.D. is Assistant Professor, Department of Psychiatry, and Research Consultant, Center for School Mental Health Assistance, University of Maryland School of Medicine, Baltimore.

GIL NOAM, PH.D. (HABIL), ED.D., is an Associate Professor of Psychiatry/ Psychology, and Education, Harvard University, Cambridge, MA. He is in private practice of Psychoanalysis and Child and Adolescent Psychology in Cambridge, MA.

BERNARD RAPPAPORT, M.D. is Assistant Clinical Professor of Psychiatry and Human Behavior, University of California at Irvine; and Medical Director of Behavioral Health, County of Orange Health Care Agency, Santa Ana, California.

NANCY RAPPAPORT, M.D. is Clinical Instructor at Harvard Medical School, Cambridge; and Child Psychiatrist Attending at Cambridge Hospital.

RICHARD RATNER, M.D. is Clinical Professor of Psychiatry & Behavioral Sciences, George Washington University School of Medicine, Washington; and Adjunct Professor, Georgetown University Law Center. He is in private practice in Washington, D.C.

MARK RIDDLE, M.D. is Associate Professor of Psychiatry and Pediatrics, and Director, Division of Child and Adolescent Psychiatry, Johns Hopkins University School of Medicine, Baltimore, MD.

RICHARD ROSNER, M.D. is Clinical Professor, Department of Psychiatry, New York University School of Medicine; and Medical Director, Forensic Psychiatry Clinic, Bellevue Hospital Center, New York City.

SRIRANGAM S. SHREERAM, M.D. is Instructor and Fellow, Child & Adolescent Psychiatry, University of Illinois at Chicago, Department of Psychiatry, Chicago.

NANCY TASHMAN, PH.D. is Assistant Professor, University of Maryland School of Medicine, Department of Psychiatry, Baltimore; and Consultant, Center for School Mental Health Assistance, Baltimore.

ROBERT WEINSTOCK, M.D., is a Clinical Professor of Psychiatry, and Psychiatrist, Student Health Service, UCLA.

The Authors

MARK D. WEIST, PH.D. is an Assistant Professor and Director of the School Mental Health Program (SMHP), Department of Psychiatry, University of Maryland.

DWIGHT V. WOLF, M.D., Assistant Professor, Division of Child & Adolescent Psychiatry, Department of Psychiatry & Behavioral Science, University of Texas Medical Branch, Galveston, TX.

CONTENTS OF VOLUMES 1-23

ABERASTURY, A.
   The Adolescent and Reality (1973)   2:415–423
ABRAMOWITZ, J., *see* FORT, MCAFEE, KING, HOPPE, FENTON, ABRAMOWITZ, WOODBURY, AND
      ANTHONY (1990)
AGLE, D.P., *see* MATTSSON AND AGLE (1979)
AMERICAN SOCIETY FOR ADOLESCENT PSYCHIATRY
   Position Statement on Training in Adolescent Psychiatry (1971)   1:418–421
ANDERSON, D. D.
   Family and Peer Relations of Gay Adolescents (1987)   14:162–178
ANDERSON, G., *see* FLEISHER AND ANDERSON (1995)
ANDERSON, R.
   Thoughts on Fathering: Its Relationship to the Borderline Condition in Adolescence
      and to Transitional Phenomena (1978)   6:377–395
ANTHONY, E. J.
   Self-Therapy in Adolescence (1974)   3:6–24
   Between Yes and No: The Potentially Neutral Area Where the Adolescent and His
      Therapist Can Meet (1976)   4:323–344
   Treatment of the Paranoid Adolescent (1981)   9:501–527
   The Creative Therapeutic Encounter at Adolescence (1988)   15:194–216
   The Long-Term Setting (1990)   17:99–108
   Treatment of a Narcissistically Disordered Adolescent: Some Theoretical and Thera-
      peutic Considerations (1998)   23:107–134
   see also BOOTS, GOODMAN, LOUGHMAN, AND ANTHONY (1990); FORT, MCAFEE, KING,
      HOPPE, FENTON, ABRAMOWITZ, WOODBURY, AND ANTHONY (1990)
APFEL, R. J., *see* FISHER AND APFEL (1988)
APTER, A., *see* MCKNEW, CYTRYN, LAMOUR, AND APTER (1982)
ARMENTANO, M., *see* HENDREN, ARMENTANO, GRATER, MIKKELSEN, SARLES, AND SOND-
      HEIMER (1997)
ARNSTEIN, R. L.
   The Adolescent Identity Crisis Revisited (1979)   7:71–84
   The Student, the Family, the University, and Transition to Adulthood (1980)
      8:160–170
   Overview of Normal Transition to Young Adulthood (1989)   16:127–141

317

ARONSON, M.
  Discussion (1998)   22:157–162
ASHWAY, J. A.
  The Changing Needs of Female Adolescents (1980)   8:482–498
ATKINSON, R.
  The Development of Purpose in Adolescence: Insights from the Narrative Approach
      (1987)   14:149–161
AUGER, N., *see* BOND AND AUGER (1982)
BACHRACH, L. L.
  Sociological Factors Associated with Substance Abuse among New Chronic Patients
      (1989)   16:189–201
BAITTLE, B., AND OFFER, D.
  On the Nature of Male Adolescent Rebellion (1971)   1:139–160
BAKER, H. S.
  Underachievement and Failure in College: The Interaction between Intrapsychic
      and Interpersonal Factors from the Perspective of Self Psychology (1987)
      14:441–460
  Dynamic Aspects of the Creative Process: Overview (1988)   15:217–219
  James Joyce and Stephen Daedalus: Object and Selfobject Relationships in the
      Successful and Blocked Creative Process (1988)   15:258–278
  If Rocky Goes to College: Dilemmas of Working-Class College Students (1988)
      16:70–91
BAKER, L., *see* ROSMAN, MINUCHIN, LIEBMAN, AND BAKER (1977)
BAKER-SINCLAIR, M. E., *see* WEIST AND BAKER-SINCLAIR (1997)
BALIKOV, H., *see* COHEN AND BALIKOV (1974)
BARAN, A., *see* SOROSKY, BARAN, AND PANNOR (1977)
BARGLOW, P., *see* WEISSMAN AND BARGLOW (1980); JAFFE AND BARGLOW (1989)
BARGLOW, P., ISTIPHAN, I.; BEDGER, J. E.; AND WELBOURNE, C.
  Response of Unmarried Adolescent Mothers to Infant or Fetal Death (1973)
      2:285–300
BARISH, J. I., *see* KREMER, PORTER, GIOVACCHINI, LOEB, SUGAR, AND BARISH (1971)
BARISH, J. I., AND SCHONFELD, W. A.
  Comprehensive Residential Treatment of Adolescents (1973)   2:340–350
BARNHART, F. D., *see* LOGAN, BARNHART, AND GOSSETT (1982)
BAYRAKAL, S.
  Sociocultural Matrix of Adolescent Psychopathology (1987)   14:112–118
BEDGER, J. E., *see* BARGLOW, ISTIPHAN, BEDGER, AND WELBOURNE (1973)
BEMPORAD, J., *see* HALLOWELL, BEMPORAD, AND RATEY (1989)
BENEDEK, E.
  Female Delinquency: Fantasies, Facts, and Future (1979)   7:524–539
  see also LOONEY, ELLIS, BENEDEK, AND SCHOWALTER (1985)
BENHAMOU, H.
  Discussion of Greenberg and Esman's Chapter (1993)   19:415–417
BENSON, R. M.
  Narcissistic Guardians: Developmental Aspects of Transitional Objects, Imaginary
      Companions, and Career Fantasies (1980)   8:253–264

BERGER, A. S., AND SIMON, W.

Sexual Behavior in Adolescent Males (1976)   4:199–210

BERKOVITZ, I. H.

Feelings of Powerlessness and the Role of Violent Actions in Adolescents (1981)
9:477–492

The Adolescent, Schools, and Schooling (1985)   12:162–176

Educational Issues in Adolescents: Therapeutic Potentials in School Programs:
Introduction to Special Section (1987)   14:479–482

Aggression, Adolescence, and Schools (1987)   14:483–499

Building a Suicide Prevention Climate in Schools (1987)   14:500–510

Value of Group Counseling in Secondary Schools (1987)   14:522–545

The Adolescent in the Schools: A Therapeutic Guide (1995)   20:343–363

See also FLEISHER, BERKOVITZ, BRIONES, LOVETRO, AND MORHAR (1987); PECK AND
BERKOVITZ (1987)

BERLIN, I. N.

Opportunities in Adolescence to Rectify Developmental Failures (1980)
8:231–243

Prevention of Adolescent Suicide among Some Native American Tribes (1985)
12:77–93

BERMAN, L. B., AND GOODRICH W.

Running Away from Treatment Observations and Admission Predictors for Hospitalized Adolescents (1990)   17:279–304

BERMAN, S.

The Response of Parents to Adolescent Depression (1980)   8:367–378

BERNDT, D. J., *see* FEINSTEIN AND BERNDT (1995)

BERNS, R. S., *see* KREMER, WILLIAMS, OFFER, BERNS, MASTERSON, LIEF, AND FEINSTEIN (1973)

BERNFELD, S. (trans. Julie Winter and Richard C. Marohn)

Concerning a Typical Form of Male Puberty (1995)   20:52–66

BERNSTEIN, N. R.

Psychotherapy of the Retarded Adolescent (1985)   12:406–413

Discussion of Fisher and Apfel's "Female Psychosexual Development: Mothers,
Daughters, and Inner Organs" (1988)   15:30–33

See also FISHER AND APFEL (1988)

BERTALANFFY, L. VON

The United Theory for Psychiatry and the Behavioral Sciences (1974)
3:32–48

See also GRINKER (1974)

BETTLEHEIM, B.

Obsolete Youth: Toward a Psychograph of Adolescent Rebellion (1971)
1:14–39

Discussion of Alfred Flarsheim's Essay (1971)   1:459–463

BLACK, S.

Minor Tranquilizer Use in Adolescents (1979)   7:402–409

BLINDER, B. J., AND CADENHEAD, K.

Bulimia: A Historical Overview (1986)   13:231–240

Contents of Volumes 1–23

BLOS, P.

The Generation Gap: Fact and Fiction (1971)   1:5–13

The Overappreciated Child: Discussion of E. James Anthony's Chapter (1976)
4:345–351

When and How Does Adolescence End: Structural Criteria for Adolescent Closure
(1971)   5:5–17

Modifications in the Classical Psychoanalytical Model of Adolescence (1979)
7:6–25

Modifications in the Traditional Psychoanalytic Theory of Female Adolescent Development (1980)   8:8–24

The Contribution of Psychoanalysis to the Psychotherapy of Adolescents (1983)
11:104–124

Masculinity: Developmental Aspects of Adolescence (1989)   16:5–16

See also BRAHM (1989); ESMAN (1989); RAKOFF (1989)

BLOTCKY, M. J., *see* LOONEY, BLOTCKY, CARSON, AND GOSSETT (1980)

BLOTCKY, M. J., AND LOONEY, J. G.

Normal Female and Male Adolescent Psychological Development: An Overview
of Theory and Research (1980)   8:184–199

BOND, T. C., AND AUGER, N.

Benefits of the Generic Milieu in Adolescent Hospital Treatment (1982)
10:360–372

BOOTS, S.; LOUGHMAN, S.; AND ANTHONY, E. J.

The Family Treatment during the Long-Term Inpatient Care of the Adolescent
(1990)   17:129–157

BONIER, R. J.

Staff Countertransference in an Adolescent Milieu Treatment Setting (1982)
10:382–390

BOROWITZ, G. H.

Character Disorders in Childhood and Adolescence: Some Consideration of the
Effects of Sexual Stimulation in Infancy and Childhood (1971)   1:343–362

The Capacity to Masturbate Alone in Adolescence (1973)   2:130–143

see also GIOVACCHINI AND BOROWITZ (1974)

BOWLBY, L. J.

Attachment Theory and Its Therapeutic Implications (1978)   6:5–33

BOXER, A. M., *see* WEISSMAN, COHEN, BOXER, AND COHLER (1989); WEIL AND BOXER (1990)

BOYER, B.

Interactions among Stimulus Barrier, Maternal Protective Barrier, Innate Drive
Tensions, and Maternal Overstimulation (1971)   1:363–378

Meanings of a Bizarre Suicidal Attempt by an Adolescent (1976)   4:371–381

BRADLEY, S. J.

Panic Disorder in Children and Adolescents: A Review with Examples (1990)
17:433–450

BRAHM, E.

Discussion of Peter Blos's Chapter (1989)   16:16–20

See also BLOS (1989)

BRANDT, L. M.

The Fairy Tale as Paradigm of the Separation-Individuation Crisis: Implications for Treatment of the Borderline Adolescent (1983)   11:75–91

BRETT, E., *see* WHISNANT, BRETT, AND ZEGANS (1979)

BRIONES, L., *see* FLEISHER, BERKOVITZ, BRIONES, LOVETRO, AND MORHAR (1987)

BROCKBANK, R.

Adolescent Psychodynamics and the Therapy Group (1980)   8:529–538

BROCKMAN, D. D.

Focal Analysis of a College Freshman (1986)   13:139–163

Psychoanalytic Assessment of Young Adults (1989)   16:246–258

The Fate of Don Juan: The Myth and the Man (1992)   18:44–62

BROWN, S.

Acting Out in Adolescence: Genesis and Some Treatment Implications (1978)   6:461–468

BRUCH, H.

Anorexia Nervosa (1977)   5:293–303

Island in the River: The Anorexic Adolescent in Treatment (1979)   7:26–40

BRULL, H. F.

The Psychodynamics of Drug Use: A Social Work Perspective (1976)   4:309–317

BRYT, A.

Developmental Tasks in Adolescence (1979)   7:136–146

BUCHANAN, R. W.

Discussion of Vivian M. Rakoff's Chapter (1989)   16:387–392

BUCKY, S. F., *see* SCHULLER AND BUCKY (1974)

BULLARD, D. M., JR.

Reflections on the Hospital Treatment of Adolescents at Chestnut Lodge (1990)   17:305–321

BURCH, C. A.

Identity Foreclosure in Early Adolescence: A Problem of Narcissistic Equilibrium (1985)   12:145–161

BURQUEST, B.

Severe Female Delinquency: When to Involve Family in Treatment (1979)   7:516–523

BURT, R. A., *see* MILLER AND BURT (1977)

BUTLER, K., *see* HENDREN AND BUTLER (1998)

BUYTENDORP, A. A.

In Memoriam: Sol Nichtern (1988)   15:ix–x

CADENHEAD, K., *see* BLINDER AND CADENHEAD (1986)

CAHILL, A. J.

Aggression Revisited: The Value of Anger in Therapy and Other Close Relationships (1981)   9:539–549

See also MEEKS AND CAHILL (1988)

CAHNERS, S. S., *see* STODDARD AND CAHNERS (1985); PAHLAVAN, AND CAHNERS (1985)

CANTWELL, D. P.

Use of Stimuli Medication with Psychiatrically Disordered Adolescents (1979)   7:375–388

CAPER, R. A.

The Interaction of Drug Abuse and Depression in an Adolescent Girl (1981) 9:467–476

CARLSON, G., *see* STROBER AND CARLSON (1982)

CARLSON, G. A.

Lithium Carbonate Use in Adolescents: Clinical Indications and Management (1979) 7:410–418

The Phenomenology of Adolescent Depression (1981)   9:411–421

CARLTON, B. S., *see* MILLER AND CARLTON (1985)

CARSON, D. I., *see* LEWIS, GOSSETT, KING, AND CARSON (1973); LOONEY, BLOTCKY, CARSON, AND GOSSETT (1980)

CASPER, R. C.

Treatment Principles in Anorexia Nervosa (1982)   10:431–454

Risk Factors for the Development of Eating Disorders (1992)   18:91–103

CAUGHEY, J. L.

Masking the Self: Fictional Identities and the Construction of Self in Adolescence (1988)   15:319–332

CAWELTI, J.

Contemporary Youth Consciousness: Emergent Themes in Recent American Fiction (1980)   8:288–300

CHABERT, C., *see* JEAMMET AND CHABERT

CHAVIS, D. A.

The Intensive Psychoanalytic Psychotherapy of a Severe Narcissistic Personality Disorder in Adolescence (1990)   17:109–128

CHIGIER, E.

Adolescence in Israel: Thoughts on the Middle-Class Urban Adolescent (1973) 2:435–444

CHORAS, P. T., *see* SHIELDS AND CHORAS (1982)

CLINE, D. W., *see* PETZEL AND CLINE (1978)

COHEN, J.

Learning Disabilities and the College Student: Identification and Diagnosis (1983) 11:177–198

Learning Disabilities and Adolescence: Developmental Considerations (1985) 12:177–196

Attentional Disorders in Adolescence: Integrating Psychoanalytic and Neuropsychological Diagnostic and Developmental Considerations (1993)   19:301–342

On the Uses and Misuses of Psychoeducational Evaluations (1997) 21:253–268

COHEN, R. S., *see* WEISSMAN AND COHEN (1985); WEISSMAN, COHEN, BOXER, AND COHLER (1989)

COHEN, R. S., AND BALIKOV, H.

On the Impact of Adolescence upon Parents (1974)   3:217–236

COHEN, T. B.

Analysis of Adolescents with Development Arrest (1981)   9:550–558

COHLER, B. J.

New Ways in the Treatment of Emotionally Disturbed Adolescents (1973) 2:305–323

The Significance of the Therapist's Feelings in the Treatment of Anorexia Nervosa (1977)   5:352–384
see also WEISSMAN, COHEN, BOXER, AND COHLER (1989)
COONS, F. W.
The Developmental Tasks of the College Student (1971)   1:256–274
COOPER, B. M., AND EKSTEIN, R.
Borderline Adolescent Girls in Rebellion against the Father (1978)   6:396–408
see also SOLOW AND COOPER (1974)
COPELAND, A. D.
Violent Black Gangs: Psycho- and Sociodynamics (1974)   3:340–353
An Interim Educational Program for Adolescents (1974)   3:422–431
The Impact of Pregnancy on Adolescent Psychosocial Development (1981) 9:244–253
The Effect of Childhood Sexual Trauma on Female Psychological Development: An Overview (1988)   15:34–45
Childhood Symptoms of Maladjustment: A Prognostic Indicator of Adolescent Psychopathology (1993)   19:394–400
Adolescent Psychiatry: Present Status and Future Trends (1995)   20:77–86
COSTELLO, J. L., *see* MASTERSON, LULOW, AND COSTELLO (1982)
CRABTREE, L. H., JR.
Minimal Brain Dysfunction in Adolescents and Young Adults: Diagnostic and Therapeutic Perspectives (1981)   9:307–320
CRABTREE, L. H., JR., AND LEVINSON, D. F.
Recurrent Large-Group Phenomena: Studies of an Adolescent Therapeutic Community (1980)   8:512–528
CURTISS, G., *see* MAROHN, LOCKE, ROSENTHAL, AND CURTISS (1982)
CYTRYN, L., *see* MCKNEW, CYTRYN, LAMOUR, AND APTER (1982)
DAILY, S. AND REDDICK, C.
Adolescent Day Treatment: An Alternative for the Future (1993)   19:523–540
DAMOND, M., *see* SIGAFOOS, FEINSTEIN, DAMOND, AND REISS (1988)
DAVIDSON, H.
The Role of Identification in the Analysis of Late Adolescents (1974) 3:263–270
DAVIS, M., AND RAFFE, I. H.
The Holding Environment in the Inpatient Treatment of Adolescents (1985) 12:434–443
DECINA, P., *see* KRON, DECINA, KESTENBAUM, FARBER, GARGAN, AND FIEVE (1982); SACKEIM, DECINA, AND MALITZ (1982)
DE LEON, G.
The Therapeutic Community Perspective and Approach for Adolescent Substance Abusers (1988)   15:535–556
DERDEYN, A. P., AND WATERS, D. B.
Parents and Adolescents: Empathy and the Vicissitudes of Development (1977) 5:175–185
DEUTSCH, A., AND MILLER, M. J.
Conflict, Character, and Conversion: Study of a "New Religion" Member (1979) 7:257–268

DIMPERO, R., *see* JONES, PEARSON, AND DIMPERO (1989)

DIXON, K. N.

Group Therapy for Bulimia (1986)   13:391–404

DOCTORS, S.

The Symptom of Delicate Self-Cutting in Adolescent Females: A Developmental
View (1981)   9:443–460

DOHERTY, M. B. *see* ROSENTHAL AND DOHERTY (1985)

DOUGHERTY, D., *see* PORT, HARROW, JOBE, AND DOUGHERTY (1997)

DYRUD, J. E.

To Tell the Truth in Retrospect (1977)   5:422–428

EASSON, W. M.

Depression in Adolescence (1977)   5:257–275

EHRLICH, A., *see* ESPINOZA AND EHRLICH (1989)

EISENBERG, L.

The Relativity of Adolescence: Effects of time, Place, and Persons (1980)
8:25–40

EKSTEIN, R.

The Schizophrenic Adolescent's Struggle toward and against Separation and Individuation (1973)   2:5–24

From the Language of Play to Play with Language (1976)   4:142–162

A Note on the Language of Psychotic Acting Out: Discussion of L. Bryce Boyer's
Chapter (1976)   4:382–386

The Process of Termination and Its Relation to Outcome in the Treatment of
Psychotic Disorders in Adolescence (1978)   6:448–460

As I Remember Her: Anna Freud, 1895–1982 (1983)   11:5–8

The Adolescent Self during the Process of Termination of Treatment: Termination,
Interruption, or Intermission? (1983)   11:125–146

see also COOPER AND EKSTEIN (1978)

ELLIS, W., *see* LOONEY, ELLIS, BENEDEK, AND SCHOWALTER (1985)

ELSON, M., AND KRAMER, J. F.

Introduction—Vulnerable Youth: Hope, Despair, and Renewal (1980)
8:267–269

ERIKSON, E.

Reflections (1983)   11:9–13

ERLICH, H. S.

Adolescents' Reactions to Rabin's Assassination: A Case of Patricide? (1998)
22:189–205

see also KLEIN AND ERLICH (1978)

ESCOLL, P. S., *see* SMARR AND ESCOLL (1973, 1976)

ESMAN, A. H.

Changing Values: Their Implications for Adolescent Development and Psychoanalytic Ideas (1977)   5:18–34

Adolescent Psychopathology and the Rapprochement Phenomenon (1980)
8:320–331

The Study of Lives: Discussion of Tashjian and Shaw (1982)   10:99–105

A Developmental Approach to the Psychotherapy of Adolescents (1985)
12:119–133

Giftedness and Creativity in Children and Adolescents (1986)　　13:62–84
Art and Psychopathology: The Message of "Outsider" Art (1988)　　15:160–181
Discussion of Peter Blos's Chapter (1989)　　16:21–25
Borderline Personality Disorders in Adolescents: Current Concepts (1989)　　16:319–336
G. Stanley Hall and the Invention of Adolescence (1993)　　19:6–20
Adolescence and Society (1995)　　20:89–108
Editor's Introduction (1998)　　22:vii–viii
In Memoriam: Peter Blos, Ph.D. (1998)　　22:xiii–xv
Shakespeare's Adolescents (1998)　　22:25–37
Discussion (1998)　　22:162–164
In Memoriam: Derek Miller, M.D. (1998)　　23:vii–viii
see also GREENBERG, HAIMAN, AND ESMAN (1987); BLOS (1989); BRAHM (1989); GREENBERG (1993)

ESPINOZA, R. L., AND EHRLICH, A.
Personality, Family Relationships, and Moral Development in Chicano and Black Adolescent Gang Members (1989)　　16:216–227

ESSER, G., see SCHMIDT, LAY, ESSER, AND IHLE (1998)

FAJARDO, B.
Psychoanalytic Developmental Perspectives on the Treatment of a Young Adult (1993)　　19:343–356

FARBER, S., see KRON, DECINA, KESTENBAUM, FARBER, GARGAN, AND FIEVE (1982)

FARNSWORTH, D. L.
Adolescence: Terminable and Interminable (1973)　　2:31–43

FEINBERG, H. B., see REICH AND FEINBERG (1974)

FEINER, A. H., see LEVENSON, FEINER, AND STOCKHAMER (1976)

FEINSILVER, D. B.
The Family Meeting as a Darkroom: Countertransference Issues with Severely Disturbed Adolescents (1985)　　12:509–523

FEINSTEIN, C. B.
Early Adolescent Deaf Boys: A Biophysical Approach (1983)　　11:147–162
see also SIGAFOOS, FEINSTEIN, DAMOND, AND REISS (1988)

FEINSTEIN, C. B., AND LYTLE, R.
Observations from Clinical Work with High School Aged, Deaf Adolescents Attending a Residential School (1987)　　14:461–477

FEINSTEIN, S. C.
In Memoriam: William A. Schonfeld (1971)　　1:v–vi
The Cult Phenomenon: Transition, Repression, and Regression (1980)　　8:113–122
Why They Were Afraid of Virginia Woolf: Perspectives on Juvenile Manic-Depressive Illness (1980)　　8:332–343
Manic-Depressive Disorder in Children and Adolescents (1982)　　10:256–272
Reflections of the Editor Emeritus (1995)　　20:xiii–xxiii
Adolescent Affective Disorders (1995)　　20:7–21
In Memoriam (1998)　　22:ix–21
see also KNOBEL, SLAFF, KALINA, AND FEINSTEIN (1973); KREMER, WILLIAMS, OFFER, BERNS, MASTERSON, LIEF, AND FEINSTEIN (1973)

Contents of Volumes 1–23

FEINSTEIN, S. C., AND GIOVACCHINI, P. L.

In Memoriam: Arthur A. Miller (1973)   2:v

In Memoriam: Donald W. Winnicott (1973)   2:363

In Memoriam: Judith Baskin Offer (1977)   5:v

FEINSTEIN, S. C. AND BERNDT, D. J.

Assimilating Piaget: Cognitive Structures and Depressive Reaction to Loss (1995) 20:23–28

FEINSTEIN, S. C.; GIOVACCHINI, P. L.; AND JOSSELYN, I. M.

Introduction (1974)   3:99–102

FEINSTEIN, S. C., AND MAROHN, R.

In Memoriam: Roy W. Grinker, Jr. (1993)   19:xi–xii

Editors' Introduction (1993)   19:3–5, 257–258, 359–360, 445

FENTON, W., *see* FORT, MCAFEE, KING, HOPPE, FENTON, ABRAMOWITZ, WOODBURY, AND ANTHONY (1990)

FIELDING, J. E., *see* HANSEN, MALOTTE, AND FIELDING (1987)

FIEVE, R., *see* KRON, DECINA, KESTENBAUM, FARBER, GARGAN, AND FIEVE (1982)

FISHER, C. P.

Beyond Identity: Invention, Absorption, and Transcendence (1992) 18:448–460

FISHER, S.

Some Observations on Psychotherapy and Creativity (1981)   9:528–538

FISHER, S. M., AND APFEL, R. J.

Female Psychosexual Development: Mothers, Daughters, and Inner Organs (1988) 15:5–29

see also BERNSTEIN (1988)

FISHER, S. M., AND SCHARF, K. R.

Teenage Pregnancy: An Anthropological, Sociological, and Psychological Overview (1980)   8:393–403

FLAHERTY, L. T.

To Love and/or to Work: The Ideological Dilemma of Young Women (1982) 10:41–51

A Model Curriculum for Teaching Adolescent Psychiatry (1989)   16:491–520

In Memoriam: Richard C. Marohn, M.D. (1997)   21:xi–xii

FLARSHEIM, A.

Resolution of the Mother-Child Symbiosis in a Psychotic Adolescent (1971) 1:428–458

see also BETTELHEIM (1971)

FLEISHER, S. J.; BERKOVITZ, I. H.; BRIONES, L.; LOVETRO, K.; AND MORHAR, N.

Antisocial Behavior, School Performance, and Reactions to Loss: The Value of Group Counseling and Communication Skills Training (1987) 14:546–555

FLEISHER, W. P., AND ANDERSON, G.

Dissociative Disorders in Adolescence (1995)   20:203–215

FORT, D.; MCAFEE, L.; KING, R.; HOPPE, W.; FENTON, W.; ABRAMOWITZ, J.; WOODBURY, C.; AND ANTHONY, E. J.

Long-Term Group Psychotherapy with Adolescent Inpatients (1990)   17:158–201

FRAIBERG, S.

The Adolescent Mother and Her Infant (1982)   10:7–23

FRATTAROLI, E. J.

The Lunatic, the Lover, and the Poet: A Study of Shakespeare's Conception of
    Creativity (1988)   15:221–246

FREEDMAN, D. X.

On the Use and Abuse of LSD (1971)   1:75–107

FREEDMAN, J., *see* SHAPIRO AND FREEDMAN (1987)

FREEDMAN, J. A., *see* ROSSMAN AND FREEDMAN (1982)

FRENKEL, R. S.

Late Adolescence: Spock and the Ego-Ideal (1988)   15:46–64

FRIEDMAN, E. J.

Neuroendocrine Aspects of Bulimia (1986)   13:422–427

FRITSCH, R. C., AND GOODRICH, W.

Adolescent Inpatient Attachment as Treatment Process (1990)   17:246–263

FRITSCH, R. C.; HOLMSTROM, R. W.; GOODRICH, W.; AND RIEGER, R. E.

Personality and Demographic Differences among Different Types of Adjustment
    to an Adolescent Milieu (1990)   17:202–225

FULLERTON, C. S.; YATES, B. T.; AND GOODRICH, W.

The Sex and Experience of the Therapist and Their Effects on Intensive Psychother-
    apy of the Adolescent Inpatient (1990)   17:272–278

GADPAILLE, W. J.

Adolescence: Developmental Phase or Cultural Artifact (1977)   5:143–150
Psychosexual Developmental Tasks Imposed by Pathologically Delayed Childhood:
    A Cultural Dilemma (1978)   6:136–155

GALATZER-LEVY, R. M.

The Analysis of an Adolescent Boy (1985)   12:336–360
Clinical Institute: Perspectives in the Treatment of Adolescents and Youth (1985)
    12:293–295
Adolescent Violence and the Adolescent Self (1993)   19:418–441

GALUSZKA, F.

Art and Inspiration (1988)   15:134–147

GARBER, B.

Mourning in Adolescence: Normal and Pathological (1985)   12:371–387
The Learning Disabled Adolescent: A Clinical Perspective (1992)
    18:322–347
Parent Loss in Childhood and Adult Psychopathology (1997)   21:101–118
The Child and Adolescent Literature about the Death of a Parent (1995)
    20:217–236

GARDNER, H., AND WOLF, C.

The Fruits of Asynchrony: A Psychological Examination of Creativity
    (1988)   15:96–120

GARDNER, R. A.

The American Educational System and the Psychological Development of the
    Adolescent (1990)   17:19–35

GARGAN, M., *see* KRON, DECINA, KESTENBAUM, FARBER, GARGAN, AND FIEVE (1982)

GARNER, D. M.

Cognitive Therapy for Bulimia Nervosa (1986)   13:358–390

GEDO, J. E.

Portrait of the Artist as Adolescent Prodigy: Mozart and the Magic Flute (1988)
15:288–299

GIOVACCHINI, P. L.

Fantasy Formation, Ego Defect, and Identity Problems (1971)   1:329–342

The Adolescent Process and Character Formation: Clinical Aspects—with Reference to Dr. Masterson's "The Borderline Adolescent" (1973)   2:269–284

Character Development and the Adolescent Process (1973)   2:402–414

The Difficult Adolescent Patient: Countertransference Problems (1974)
3:271–288

Madness, Sanity, and Autonomy (1976)   4:46–59

Productive Procrastination: Technical Factors in the Treatment of the Adolescent
(1976)   4:352–370

Psychoanalytic Perspectives on Adolescence, Psychic Development, and Narcissism
(1977)   5:113–142

Discussion of Dr. Richard Marohn's Chapter: A Critique of Kohut's Theory of
Narcissism (1977)   5:213–235

The Borderline Aspects of Adolescence and the Borderline State (1978)
6:320–338

The Sins of the Parents: The Borderline Adolescent and Primal Confusion (1979)
7:213–233

Sociocultural Factors, Life-Style, and Adolescent Psychopathology (1980)
8:65–78

Creativity, Adolescence, and Inevitable Failure (1981)   9:35–59

The Borderline Adolescent as a Transitional Object: A Common Variation (1985)
12:233–250

Introduction: Countertransference Responses to Adolescents (1985)
12:447–448

Countertransference and the Severely Disturbed Adolescent (1985)
12:449–467

Psychic Discontinuity during Adolescence: Discussion of Panel Presentations,
American Society for Adolescent Psychiatry, May 1986 (1987)
14:417–422

see also KREMER, PORTER, GIOVACCHINI, LOEB, SUGAR, AND BARISH (1971); FEINSTEIN,
GIOVACCHINI (1973,1977); FEINSTEIN, GIOVACCHINI, AND JOSELYN (1974)

GIOVACCHINI, P. L., AND BOROWITZ, G. H.

An Object Relationship Scale (1974)   3:186–212

GLENN, J.

Dora as an Adolescent: Sadistic and Sadomasochistic Fantasies (1998)
22:141–157

Reply to Discussions (1998)   22:164–168

GLUCKMAN, R. M.

Physical Symptoms as a Mask for Emotional Disorders in Adolescents (1993)
19:384–393

GODENNE, G. D.

From Childhood to Adulthood: A Challenging Sailing (1974)   3:118–127

Education and Social Reality: Present and Future (1993)   19:21–30

Forming a Therapeutic Alliance with Teenagers (1995)   20:289–298

Hearing the S.O.S.: Assessing the Lethality of a Youth in Distress (1997)
    21:211–233

GOLD, L., *see* WESTEN, LUDOLPH, SILK, KELLAM, GOLD, AND LOHR (1990)

GOLDBERG, A.

On Telling the Truth (1973)   2:98–112

GOLDMAN, H. H., *see* RIDGELY, GOLDMAN, AND TALBOTT (1989)

GOLOMBEK, H., AND KORENBLUM, M.

Brief Psychoanalytic Psychotherapy with Adolescents (1995)   20:307–324

GOLOMBEK, H., AND MARTON, P.

Adolescents over Time: A Longitudinal Study of Personality Development (1992)
    18:213–284

GOLOMBEK, H.: MARTON, P.; STEIN, B.; AND KORENBLUM, M.

Personality Functioning Status during Early and Middle Adolescence (1987)
    14:365–377

see also KORENBLUM, MARTON, GOLOMBEK, AND STEIN (1987); MARTON, GOLOMBEK,
    STEIN, AND KORENBLUM (1987); STEIN, GOLOMBEK, MARTON, AND KORENBLUM
    (1987); STEIN, GOLOMBEK, MARTON, AND KORENBLUM (1990)

GOODMAN, D., *see* BOOTS, GOODMAN, LOUGHMAN, AND ANTHONY (1990)

GOODRICH, W.

The Severely Disturbed Adolescent: Hospital Treatment Processes and Patterns of
    Response (1990)   17:226–245

see also BERMAN AND GOODRICH (1990); FRITSCH AND GOODRICH (1990); FRITSCH,
    HOLMSTROM, GOODRICH, AND RIEGER (1990); FULLERTON, YATES, AND GOODRICH
    (1990)

GOODSITT, A.

Narcissistic Disturbances in Anorexia Nervosa (1977)   5:304–312

GORDON, J. S.

Running Away: Reaction or Revolution (1979)   7:54–70

GOSSETT, J. T., *see* LEWIS, GOSSETT, KING, AND CARSON (1973); LOONEY, BLOTCKY, CARSON,
    AND GOSSETT (1980); LOGAN, BARNHART, AND GOSSETT (1982)

GOTTLIEB, R. M.

Boarding School Consultation: Psychoanalytic Perspectives (1992)
    18:180–197

The Current Crisis in Psychotherapy at Boarding Schools: Protecting the Interests
    of the Child and of the School (1998)   23:233–246

GRAFF, H.

Clinical Perspectives on Managed Care (1993)   19:508–516.

GRALNICK, A.

Adolescence, the Adolescent, and Hospital Treatment (1989)   16:397–411

GRATER, S., *see* HENDREN, ARMENTANO, GRATER, MIKKELSEN, SARLES, AND SONDHEIMER
    (1997)

GRAY. S. H.

Developmental Issues in Young Adulthood: Psychoanalytic Perspectives (1990) 17:328–337

GREENACRE, P.

Differences between Male and Female Adolescent Sexual Development as Seen from Longitudinal Studies (1976)   4:105–120

GREENBERG, L., AND ESMAN, A.

The Role of Interdisciplinary Consultation: Countertransference during the Acute Psychiatric Hospitalization of the Adolescent (1993)   19:401–414

GREENBERG, L.; HAIMAN, S.; AND ESMAN, A. H.

Countertansference during the Acute Psychiatric Hospitalization of the Adolescent (1987)   14:316–331

GREENBERG, R.

Psychiatric Aspects of Physical Disability in Children and Adolescents (1974) 1:298–307

Psychiatric Aspects of Physical Disability: Impact on the Family (1979)   7:281–288

GREENWOOD, E. D.

The School as Part of the Total Hospital Community: A Summary (1974) 3:435–438

GRINBERG, L.

Identity and Ideology (1973)   2:424–434

GRINKER, R. R., JR., *see* GRINKER, GRINKER, AND TIMBERLAKE (1971)

GRINKER, R. R., SR.

In Memoriam: Ludwig von Bertalanffy (1974)   3:41

The Borderline Syndrome (1978)   6:339–343

see also HOLZMAN AND GRINKER (1977)

GRINKER, R. R., SR.; GRINKER, R. R., JR.; AND TIMBERLAKE, J.

"Mentally Healthy" Young Males: Homoclites (1971)   1:176–255

GRYGOTIS, D. C. AND SCHWARZ, E. D.

Adolescent Partial Hospitalization: A Developmental Perspective (1995) 20:381–396

GUNDLACH, R. A., *see* LITOWITZ AND GUNDLACH (1987)

GUNTHER, M. S.

Acute-Onset Serious Chronic Organic Illness in Adolescence: Some Critical Issues (1985)   12:59–76

HAGIN, R. A., *see* SILVER AND HAGIN (1985)

HAIMAN, S, *see* GREENBERG, HAIMAN, AND ESMAN (1987)

HALLER, L. H.

Before the Judge: The Child-Custody Evaluation (1981)   9:142–164

HALLOWELL, E. M.; BEMPORAD, J.; AND RATEY, J. J.

Depression in the Transition to Adult Life (1989)   16:175–188

HALMI, K. A., AND LARSON, L.

Behavior Therapy in Anorexia Nervosa (1977)   5:323–351

HALPERIN, D. A.

Arthur Rimbaud: The Poet as an Adolescent (1987)   14:63–81

Master and Apprentice: The Mentoring Relationship in the Development of Adolescent Creativity (1988)   15:279–287

HALPERIN, D.; LAURO, G.; MISCIONE, F.; REBHAN, J.; SCHNABOLK, J.; AND SHACHTER, B.

Countertransference Issues in a Transitional Residential Treatment Program for Troubled Adolescents (1981)   9:559–577

HANSEN, D. B.

Discussion of Dr. Carol Nadelson's Presentation: Women in Leadership Roles (1987)   14:42–47

HANSEN, W. B.; MALOTTE, C. K.; AND FIELDING, J. E.

Tobacco and Alcohol Prevention: Preliminary Results of a Four-Year Study (1987) 14:556–575

HARDING, R. K., *see* LOONEY, HOWARD, AND HARDING (1987)

HARROW, M. *see* PORT, HARROW, JOBE, AND DOUGHERTY (1997)

HAUSER, P. M.

Our Anguished Youth: Baby Boom under Stress (1980)   8:270–280

HAUSER, S. T. AND LEVINE, H. A.

Relatedness and Autonomy in Adolescence: Links with Ego Development and Family Interactions (1993)   19:185–227

HECHTMAN, L.; WEISS, G.; PERLMAN, T.; AND TUCK, D.

Hyperactives as Young Adults: Various Clinical Outcomes (1981)   9:295–306

HENDREN, R. L. AND BUTLER, K.

Impulse Control Disorders in Adolescents (1998)   22:85–112

HENDREN, R. L.; ARMENTANO, M.; GRATER, S.; MIKKELSEN, E. J.; SARLES, R.; AND SONDHEIMER, A.

Adolescent Psychiatry Training: Guidelines for Child and Adolescent Psychiatry Residents, General Psychiatry Residents, and Medical Students (1997) 21:409–435

HERZOG, D. B.

Is Bulimia an Affective Disorder? (1986)   13:428–436

HOFMANN, A. D., AND LEWIS, N. R.

The Needle of Caring, the Thread of Love: Creative Writing on an Adolescent Medical Ward (1981)   9:88–116

HOLMSTROM, R. W., *see* FRITSCH, HOLMSTROM, GOODRICH, AND RIEGER (1990)

HOLZMAN, P. S.

Discussion—Vulnerable Youth: Hope, Despair, and Renewal (1980) 8:309–314

HOLZMAN, P. S., AND GRINKER, R. R., SR.

Schizophrenia in Adolescence (1977)   5:276–290

HOPPE, W., *see* FORT, MCAFEE, KING, HOPPE, FENTON, ABRAMOWITZ, WOODBURY, AND ANTHONY (1990)

HORAN, R.

Masked I Go Forward—Play Research and Creativity: Overview (1988) 15:301–305

The Semiotics of Play Fighting at a Residential Treatment Center (1988) 15:367–381

HOROWITZ, H. A.

Psychiatric Casualties of Minimal Brain Dysfunction in Adolescents (1981) 9:275–294

Creativity and Adolescence: Introduction to Special Section (1988)   15:67–76

Editor's Introduction (1993)   19:79–85

In Memoriam: John Bowlby (1992)   18:xi–xii

In Memoriam: Herman D. Staples, M.D. (1997)   21:xiii–xv

HOROWITZ, H. A.; OVERTON, W. F.; ROSENSTEIN, D.; AND STEIDL, J. H.

Comorbid Adolescent Substance Abuse: A Maladaptive Pattern of Self-Regulation (1992)   18:465–483

HOROWITZ, M. A.

Adolescent Daydreams and Creative Impulse (1998)   22:3–23

HOWARD, B. L., *see* LOONEY, HOWARD, AND HARDING (1987)

HOWARD, K. I., *see* OFFER, OSTROV, AND HOWARD (1986); SCHONERT-REICHL, OFFER, AND HOWARD (1995)

HUMPHREY, L. L.

Family Dynamics in Bulimia (1986)   13:315–332

IHLE, W., *see* SCHMIDT, LAY, ESSER, AND IHLE (1998)

ISENBERG, P., *see* SCHNITZER, ISENBERG, AND ROTHMAN (1978)

ISTIPHAN, I., *see* BARGLOW, ISTIPHAN, BEDGER, AND WELBOURNE (1973)

JACKSON, H. C.

Moral Nihilism: Developmental Arrest as a Sequela to Combat Stress (1982) 10:228–242

JAFFE, C. M.

A Hierarchical Model of Adolescent Development: Implications for Psychotherapy (1997)   21:3–33

JAFFE, C., AND BARGLOW, P.

Adolescent Psychopathology and Attachment Research: Mutual Contributions to Understanding (1989)   16:350–371

JAFFE, S.L.

Adolescent Substance Abuse: Assessment and Treatment (1998)   23:61–71

JEAMMET, P.

Some Reflections by Way of Conclusion (1986)   13:524–534

JEAMMET, P., AND CHABERT, C.

A Psychoanalytic Approach to Eating Disorders: The Role of Dependency (1998) 22:59–84

JENNINGS, J. *see* PEARSON, JENNINGS, AND NORCROSS (1998)

JOBE, T. *see* PORT, HARROW, JOBE, AND DOUGHERTY (1997)

JOHNSON, C., AND MADDI, K. L.

The Etiology of Bulimia: Biopsychosocial Perspectives (1986)   13:253–273

JONES, J. M.; PEARSON, G. T.; AND DIMPERO, R.

Long-Term Treatment of the Hospitalized Adolescent and His Family: An Integrated Systems-Theory Approach (1989)   16:449–472

JORDAN, J. V.

The Relational Self: Implications for Adolescent Development (1993) 19:228–239

JOSEPHSON, A. M. AND ERICKSON, W. D.

The Effect of Paternal Huntington's Disease on Male Adolescence (1992) 18:306–321

JOSSELSON, R.

Identity Diffusion: A Long-Term Follow-Up (1987)   14:230–258

Identity Formation in Adolescence: Implications for Young Adulthood (1989)
16:142–154

JOSSELYN, I. M.

Etiology of Three Current Adolescent Syndromes: A Hypothesis (1971)
1:125–138

Implications of Current Sexual Patterns: An Hypothesis (1974)   3:103–117

see also FEINSTEIN, GIOVACCHINI, AND JOSSELYN (1974)

KALINA, E.

The Adolescent Aspect of the Adult Patient (1976)   4:387–392

see also KNOBEL, SLAFF, KALINA, AND FEINSTEIN (1973)

KALOGERAKIS, M. G.

The Sources of Individual Violence (1974)   3:323–339

Developmental Issues and Their Relation to Due Process in the Family Court (1979)
7:497–502

Adolescent Analyzability Reconsidered (1997)   21:271–288

Adolescent Violence - Twentieth Century Madness: A Critical Review of Theories
of Causation (1998)   22:251–275

KANDLER, H. O.

Comprehensive Mental Health Consultation in the High Schools (1979)
7:85–111

KAPLAN, E. H.

The Dilemma of Disposition: Psychiatric Decision Making and the College-bound
High School Senior (1982)   10:469–483

Career Change in Early Adulthood: Developmental Considerations (1989)
16:259–277

KATZ, P.

Cultural Differences and Work Ethic (1980)   8:100–112

The First Few Minutes: The Engagement of the Difficult Adolescent (1990
17:69–81

The Psychotherapeutic Treatment of Suicidal Adolescents (1995)
20:325–341

Adolescence, Authority, and Change (1997)   21:49–65

Establishing the Therapeutic Alliance (1998)   23:89–105

KATZ, S.H.

The Role of Family Interactions in Adolescent Depression: A Review of Research
Findings (1998)   23:41–58

KAUFMAN, L.

The Rationale for the Family Approach with Adolescents (1986)   13:493–509

KELLAM, A., see WESTEN, LUDOLPH, SILK, KELLAM, GOLD, AND LOHR (1990)

KELLY, J. B.

Observations on Adolescent Relationships Five Years after Divorce (1981)
9:133–141

KELLY-BYRNE, D.

Word Child: Transformations in Play Story (1988)   15:333–345

KENDALL, P. C., see RONAN AND KENDALL (1990)

KENISTON, K.

Youth as a Stage of Life (1971)   1:161–175

KERNBERG, O. F.

Cultural Impact and Intrapsychic Change (1976)   4:37–45

Psychoanalytic Psychotherapy with Borderline Adolescents (1979)
7:294–321

The Diagnosis of Narcissistic and Antisocial Pathology in Adolescence (1998)
169–186

KERNBERG, P. E.

Psychoanalytic Profile of the Borderline Adolescent (1979)   7:234–256

KESTEMBERG, E.

Adolescent Pathology: Commencement, Passage, or Catastrophe (1986)
13:455–466

KESTENBAUM, C. J.

Current Sexual Attitudes, Societal Pressure, and the Middle-Class Adolescent Girl
(1979)   7:147–156

Adolescents at Risk for Manic-Depressive Illness (1980)   8:344–366

Children and Adolescents at Risk for Manic–Depressive Illness: Introduction and
Overview (1982)   10:245–255

Putting It All Together: A Multidimensional Assessment of Psychotic Potential in
Adolescence (1985)   12:5–16

Childhood Trauma Revisited: Interruption of Development (1995)
20:125–138

see also KRON, DECINA, KESTENBAUM, FARBER, GARGAN, AND FIEVE (1982)

KHAN, M. M. R.

To Hear with Eyes: Clinical Notes on Body as Subject and Object (1974)
3:25–40

KING, J. W.

Teaching Goals and Techniques in Hospital Schools (1974)   3:419–421

see also LEWIS, GOSSETT, KING, AND CARSON (1973); WEINER AND KING (1977)

KING, J. W., AND MEEKS, J. E.

Hospital Programs for Psychiatrically Disturbed Drug-Abusing Adolescents (1988)
15:522–534

KING, R., *see* FORT, MCAFEE, KING, HOPPE, FENTON, ABRAMOWITZ, WOODBURY, AND AN-
THONY (1990)

KIRSHNER, L. A.

The Developmental Function of Acting Out in Three Adolescents (1989)
16:337–349

KLEIN, H., AND ERLICH, H. S.

Some Psychoanalytic Structural Aspects of Family Function and Growth (1978)
6:171–194

KLEIN, H., AND LAST, U.

Attitudes toward Persecutor Representation in Children of Traumatized and Non-
traumatized Parents: Cross-cultural Comparison (1978)   6:224–238

KLERMAN, G. L.

Adaptation, Depression, and Transitional Life Events (1980)   8:301–308

KLUFT, R. P. AND SCHULZ, R.

Multiple Personality Disorder in Adolescence (1993)   19:259–279

KLUMPNER, G. H.

On the Psychoanalysis of Adolescents (1976)   4:393–400

A Review of Freud's Writings on Adolescence (1978)   6:59–74

KNOBEL, M.; SLAFF, B.; KALINA, E.; AND FEINSTEIN, S. C.

Introductions from the First Panamerican Congress on Adolescent Psychiatry (1973)
2:391–401

KOBAK, R. R.

Attachment and the Problem of Coherence Implications for Treating Disturbed
Adolescents (1993)   19:137–149

KOHEN-RAZ, R.

Developmental Patterns of Higher Mental Functions in Culturally Disadvantaged
Adolescents (1974)   3:152–167

Special Education Needs at Adolescence (1977)   5:460–487

KOHUT, H.

Remarks on Receiving the William A. Schonfeld Distinguished Service Award
(1980)   8:51–53

KOLB, J. E., AND SHAPIRO, E. R.

Management of Separation Issues with the Family of the Hospitalized Adolescent
(1982)   10:343–359

see also SHAPIRO AND KOLB (1979)

KORENBLUM, M.

Diagnostic Difficulties in Adolescent Psychiatry: Where Have We Been, and Where
Are We Going? (1993)   19:58–76

KORENBLUM, M.; MARTON, P.; GOLOMBEK, H.; AND STEIN, B.

Disturbed Personality Functioning: Patterns of Change from Early to Middle Adolescence (1987)   14:407–416

see also GOLOMBEK AND KORENBLUM (1995) GOLOMBEK, MARTON, STEIN, AND KOREN-
BLUM (1987); MARTON, GOLOMBEK, STEIN, AND KORENBLUM (1987); STEIN, GOLOM-
BEK, MARTON, AND KORENBLUM (1987); STEIN, GOLOMBEK, MARTON, AND
KORENBLUM (1990)

KRAMER, J. F., see ELSON AND KRAMER (1980)

KRASNOW, C. G.

Joseph Conrad's The Shadow Line: From Late Adolescence to Early Adulthood
(1989)   16:202–215

KREMER, M. W.; PORTER, R.; GIOVACCHINI, P. L.; LOEB, L.; SUGAR, M.; AND BARISH, J. I.

Techniques of Psychotherapy in Adolescents: A Panel (1971)   1:510–539

KREMER, M. W.; WILLIAMS, F. S.; OFFER, D.; BERNS, R. S.; MASTERSON, J.F.; LIEF, H. I.; AND
FEINSTEIN, S. C.

The Adolescent Sexual Revolution (1973)   2:160–194

KRON, L.; DECINA, P.; KESTENBAUM, C. J.; FARBER, S.; GARGAN, M.; AND FIEVE, R.

The Offspring of Bipolar Manic–Depressives: Clinical Features (1982)
10:273–291

LADAME, F.

Introduction—Today's Adolescent Psychiatry: Which Adolescents to Treat and
How? (1986)13:449–454

Depressive Adolescents, Pathological Narcissism, and Therapeutic Failures (1987)
14:301–315

LAGE, G.

Self Psychology Perspectives on Adolescents (1997)   21:305–316

LAMIA, M. C.

The Revision of Object Representation in Adolescent Males (1982)
    10:199–207

LAMOUR, M., *see* MCKNEW, CYTRYN, LAMOUR, AND APTER (1982)

LARSON, L., *see* HALMI AND LARSON (1977)

LASSERS, E., AND NORDAN, R.

Separation-Individuation of an Identical Twin (1978)   6:469–479

LAST, U., *see* KLEIN AND LAST (1978)

LAUFER, M.

Studies of Psychopathology in Adolescence (1973)   2:56–69
A View of Adolescent Pathology (1977)   5:243–256
On Reconstruction in Adolescent Analysis (1980)   8:460–468
Adolescent Psychopathology and Aims of Treatment (1986)   13:480–492

LAURO, G., *see* HALPERIN, LAURO, MISCIONE, REBHAN, SCHNABOLK, AND SHACHTER (1981)

LAY, B., *see* SCHMIDT, LAY, ESSER, AND IHLE (1998)

LEITENBERG, H., AND ROSEN, J. C.

A Behavioral Approach to Treatment of Bulimia Nervosa (1986)   13:333–357

LERNER, H.

Discussion (1998)   23:134–142

LEVENSON, E. A.; FEINER, A. H.; AND STOCKHAMER, N. N.

The Politics of Adolescent Psychiatry (1976)   4:84–100

LEVI, L. D., *see* STIERLIN, LEVI, AND SAVARD (1973)

LEVINE, E. M.

Rural Communes and Religious Cults: Refuges for Middle-Class Youth (1980)
    8:138–153

LEVINE, E. M., AND SHAIOVA, C. H.

Anomie: Influence on Impulse Ridden Youth and Their Self-destructive Behavior
    (1977)   5:73–81

LEVINE, S. V.

Youth and Religious Cults: A Societal and Clinical Dilemma (1978)   6:75–89
Adolescents, Believing and Belonging (1979)   7:41–53
The Psychological and Social Effects of Youth Unemployment (1982)
    10:24–40
The Role of Psychiatry in the Phenomenon of Cults (1980)   8:123–137
The Myths and Needs of Contemporary Youth (1987)   14:48–62
Cults Revisited: Corporate and Quasi-Therapeutic Co-optation (1992)
    18:63–73

LEVINSON, D. F., *see* CRABTREE AND LEVINSON (1980)

LEWIS, J. M.

The Adolescent and the Healthy Family (1978)   6:156–170
The Impact of Adolescent Children on Family Systems (1986)   13:29–43

LEWIS, J. M.; GOSSETT, J. T.; KING, J. W.; AND CARSON, D. I.

Development of a Protreatment Group Process among Hospitalized Adolescents
    (1973)   2:351–362
see also LOONEY AND LEWIS (1983)

LEWIS, M.

Adolescent Psychic Structure and Societal Influences: A Biopsychosocial Model (1982)   10:125–139

LEWIS, N. R., *see* HOFMANN AND LEWIS (1981)

LICHTENBERG, J. D.

Continuities and Transformations between Infancy and Adolescence (1982)   10:182–198

The Relational Matrix: The Contributions of Infant Research to a Psychodynamic Developmental Psychology (1993)   19:106–120

LIEBMAN, R., *see* ROSMAN, MINUCHIN, LIEBMAN, AND BAKER (1977)

LIEF, H. I., *see* KREMER, WILLIAMS, OFFER, BERNS, MASTERSON, LIEF, AND FEINSTEIN (1973)

LIFTON, R. J.

Proteus Revisited (1976)   4:21–36

LITOWITZ, B. E.

The Speaking Subject in Adolescence: Response to Theodore Shapiro's Essay (1985)   12:312–326

LITOWITZ, B. E., AND GUNDLACH, R. A.

When Adolescents Write: Semiotic and Social Dimensions of Adolescents' Personal Writing (1987)   14:82–111

LOBEL, L.

A Study in Transitional Objects in the Early Histories of Borderline Adolescents (1981)   9:199–213

LOCKE, E. M., *see* MAROHN, LOCKE, ROSENTHAL, AND CURTISS (1982)

LOEB, L.

Intensity and Stimulus Barrier in Adolescence (1976)   4:255–263

see also KREMER, PORTER, GIOVACCHINI, LOEB, SUGAR, AND BARISH (1971)

LOEB, L. R.

Traumatic Contributions in the Development of an Obsessional Neurosis in an Adolescent (1986)   13:201–217

LOEB, L. R., AND LOEB, F. F. JR.

A Psychodynamic Approach to the Early Diagnosis of Manic-Depressive Disorder in Adolescent (1992)   18:348–364

LOGAN, W. S.; BARNHART, F. D.; AND GOSSETT, W. T.

The Prognostic Significance of Adolescent Interpersonal Relationships during Psychiatric Hospitalization (1982)   10:484–493

LOHR, N., *see* WESTEN, LUDOLPH, SILK, KELLAM, GOLD, AND LOHR (1990)

LOONEY, J. G.

Adolescents as Refugees (1979)   7:199–208

Research Priorities in Adolescent Psychiatry: Report of the Committee on Research of the American Society for Adolescent Psychiatry (1985)   12:104–114

President's Preface (1988)   15:xi–xii

see also MILLER AND LOONEY (1976); BLOTCKY AND LOONEY (1980)

LOONEY, J. G.; BLOTCKY, M. M.; CARSON, D. I.; AND GOSSETT, J. T.

A Family Systems Model for Inpatient Treatment of Adolescents (1980)   8:499–511

LOONEY, J. G.; ELLIS, W.; BENEDEK, E.; AND SCHOWALTER, J.

Training in Adolescent Psychiatry for General Psychiatry Residents: Elements of a Model Curriculum (1985)   12:94–103

LOONEY, J. G.; HOWARD, B. L.; AND HARDING, R. K.

Homoclites Revisited: The Search for Identification in Hospitalized Young Adult Patients (1987)   14:137–148

LOONEY, J. G., AND LEWIS, J. M.

Competent Adolescents from Different Socioeconomic and Ethnic Contexts (1983) 11:64–74

LORANDOS, D. A.

Adolescents in Residential Treatment: A Six-Year Comparison (1990) 17:473–478

LOUGHMAN, S., *see* BOOTS, GOODMAN, LOUGHMAN, AND ANTHONY (1990)

LOVE, R. L., AND WIDEN, H. A.

Short-Term Dynamic Psychotherapy: Another Kind of Learning on Campus (1985) 12:327–335

LOVETRO, K., *see* FLEISHER, BERKOVITZ, BRIONES, LOVETRO, AND MORHAR (1987)

LUDOLPH, P., *see* WESTEN, LUDOLPH, SILK, KELLAM, GOLD, AND LOHR (1990)

LULOW, W. V., *see* MASTERSON, LULOW, AND COSTELLO (1982)

LYTLE, R., *see* FEINSTEIN AND LYTLE (1987)

MCAFEE, L., *see* FORT, MCAFEE, KING, HOPPE, FENTON, ABRAMOWITZ, WOODBURY, AND ANTHONY (1990)

MCCARTNEY, J. R.

Adolescent Depression: A Growth and Development Perspective (1987) 14:208–217

MCCAFFERTY, C. M.

President's Preface (1993)   19:ix–x

MCCAUGHAN, D. L.

Teaching and Learning Adolescent Psychotherapy: Adolescent, Therapist, and Milieu (1985)   12:414–433

MCKNEW, D. H., JR.; CYTRYN, L.; LAMOUR, M.; AND APTER, A.

Fantasy in Childhood Depression and Other Forms of Childhood Psychopathology (1982)   10:292–298

MADDI, K. L., *see* JOHNSON AND MADDI (1986)

MALITZ, S., *see* SACKHEIM, DECINA, AND MALITZ (1982)

MALMQUIST, C. P.

Juveniles in Adult Courts: Unresolved Ambivalence (1979)   7:444–456

MALOTTE, K., *see* HANSEN, MALOTTE, AND FIELDING (1987)

MARKIN, R., *see* VILLELA AND MARKIN (1987)

MAROHN, R. C.

Trauma and the Delinquent (1974)   3:354–361

Discussion of Aaron H. Esman's Chapter (1977)   5:35–38

The "Juvenile Impostor": Some Thoughts on Narcissism and the Delinquent (1977) 5:186–212

A Psychiatric Overview of Juvenile Delinquency (1979)   7:425–432

Adolescent Rebellion and the Task of Separation (1980)   8:173–183

John Wesley Hardin, Adolescent Killer: The Emergence of Narcissistic Behavior Disorder (1987)   14:271–296

Violence and Unrestrained Behavior in Adolescents (1990)   17:419–432

On Becoming an Adolescent Psychotherapist: How Am I Going to Work with These Kids? (1992)   18:369–380

Editor's Preface (1995)   20:ix–xi

Comments on Dr. Siegfried Bernfeld's Paper "Concerning a Typical Form of Male Puberty" (1995)   20:66–75

Failures in Everyday Psychotherapy (1997)   21:289–303

A Reexamination of Peter Blos's Concept of Prolonged Adolescence (1998) 23:3–19

see also WINTER AND MAROHN (trans.) (1995)

MAROHN, R. C.; LOCKE, E. M.; ROSENTHAL, R.; AND CURTIS, G.

Juvenile Delinquents and Violent Death (1982)   10:147–170

MAROHN, R. C.; OFFER, D.; OSTROV, E.; AND TRUJILLO, J.

Four Psychodynamic Types of Hospitalized Juvenile Delinquents (1979) 7:466–483

MARTIN, A. D.

Learning to Hide: The Socialization of the Gay Adolescent (1982)   10:52–65

MARTIN, R., *see* PROSEN, TOEWS, AND MARTIN (1981); TOEWS, MARTIN, AND PROSEN (1981); TOEWS, PROSEN, AND MARTIN (1981)

MARTON, P.; GOLOMBEK, H.; STEIN, B.; AND KORENBLUM, M.

Behavior Disturbance and Changes in Personality Dysfunction from Early to Middle Adolescence (1987)   14:394–406

see also GOLOMBEK, MARTON, STEIN, AND KORENBLUM (1987); KORENBLUM, MARTON, GOLOMBEK, AND STEIN (1987); STEIN, GOLOMBEK, MARTON, AN KORENBLUM (1987); STEIN, GOLOMBEK, MARTON, AND KORENBLUM (1990)

MASSIE, H. N.

Intensive Psychodynamically Oriented Treatment of Two Cases of Adolescent Psychosis (1988)   15:487–504

MASTERSON, J. F.

The Borderline Adolescent (1973)   2:240–268

The Borderline Adolescent: An Object Relations View (1978)   6:344–359

Tracking the Borderline Triad (1986)   13:467–479

Paradise Lost - Bulimia, A Closet Narcissistic Personality Disorder: A Developmental, Self, and Object Relations Approach (1995)   20:253–266

see also KREMER, WILLIAMS, OFFER, BERNS,MASTERSON, LIEF, AND FEINSTEIN (1973)

MASTERSON, J. F.; BAIARDI, R.; FISHER, R.; AND ORCUTT, C.

Psycotherapy of Borderline and Narcissistic Disorders in the Adolescent: Establishing a Therapeutic Alliance (1992)   18:3–25

MASTERSON, J. F.; LULOW, W. V.; AND COSTELLO, J. L.

The Test of Time: Borderline Adolescent to Functioning Adult (1982) 10:494–522

MATTSSON, A., AND AGLE, D. P.

Psychophysiologic Aspects of Adolescence: Hemic Disorders (1979) 7:269–280

MAUK, G. W.

A Light Unto the Darkness: The Psychoeducational Imperative of School-Based Suicide Postvention (1998)   23:179–205

MECHLING, J.

On the Relation between Creativity and Cutting Corners (1988)   15:346–366

MEEKS, J. E.

Adolescent Development and Group Cohesion (1974)   3:289–297

Inpatient Treatment of the Violent Adolescent (1985)   12:393–405

see also KING AND MEEKS (1988)

MEEKS, J. E., AND CAHILL, A. J.

Therapy of Adolescents with Severe Behavior Problems (1988)   15:475–486

MEISSNER, W. W.

Adolescent Paranoia: Transference and Countertransference Issues (1985) 12:478–508

MEYER, N.

Lost Boys Wandering around the Peter Pantheon (1985)   12:46–58

MIKKELSEN, E. J., *see* HENDREN, ARMENTANO, GRATER, MIKKELSEN, SARLES, AND SOND- HEIMER (1997)

MILLER, A. A.

Identification and Adolescent Development (1973)   2:199–210

see also FEINSTEIN, GIOVACCHINI, AND MILLER (1971); FEINSTEIN AND GIOVACCHINI (1973)

MILLER, D.

The Drug-Dependent Adolescent (1973)   2:70–97

Early Adolescence: Its Psychology, Psychopathology, and Implications for Therapy (1978)   6:434–447

Treatment of the Seriously Disturbed Adolescent (1980)   8:469–481

Adolescent Suicide: Etiology and Treatment (1981)   9:327–342

The Termination of Treatment of Adolescents (1990)   17:82–90

Adolescent Suicide: Etiology and Treatment (1993)   19:361–383

Diagnostic Assessment and Therapeutic Approaches to Borderline Disorders in Adolescents (1995)   20:237–252

Psychiatric Contributions to Improve the Effectiveness of Juvenile Justice (1998) 22:113–140

MILLER, D., AND BURT, R. A.

On Children's Rights and Therapeutic Institutions (1977)   5:39–53

MILLER, D., AND CARLTON, B. S.

The Etiology and Treatment of Anorexia Nervosa (1985)   12:219–232

MILLER, D., AND LOONEY, J. G.

Determinants of Homicide in Adolescents (1976)   4:231–254

MILLER, D.; VISOTSKY, H. M.; AND CARLTON, B. S. (1994)   26–43

MILLER, M. D.

Therapeutic Effects of a Near-Death Experience in Anorexia Nervosa (1993) 19:489–501

MILLER, M. J., *see* DEUTSCH AND MILLER (1979)

MINTZ, T.

Clinical Experience with Suicidal Adolescents (1981)   9:493–496

MINUCHIN, S., *see* ROSMAN, MINUCHIN, LIEBMAN, AND BARKER (1977)

MISCIONE, F., *see* HALPERIN, LAURO, MISCIONE, REBHAN, SCHNABOLK, AND SHACHTER (1981)

MITCHELL, J. E., *see* PYLE AND MITCHELL (1986)

MITCHELL, J. R.
Normality in Adolescence (1980)   8:200–213

MOREAU, D. L.
A Model Adolescent Consultation Service in a Psychiatric Teaching Hospital (1992)
18:381–389

MORHAR, N., *see* FLEISHER, BERKOVITZ, BRIONES, LOVETRO, AND MORHAR (1987)

MUIR, B. J.
The Development of Personal Individuality: Limited Treatment Goals in an Psychoanalytic Hospital (1986)   13:510–523

MUNICH, R. L.
Some Forms of Narcissism in Adolescents and Young Adults (1986)
13:85–99

MUSLIN, H. L.
Romeo and Juliet: The Tragic Self in Adolescence (1982)   10:106–117

NADELSON, C. C.
Women in Leadership Roles: Development and Challenges (1987)   14:28–41
Teenagers in Distress (1989)   16:53–69

NAGERA, H.
Adolescence: Some Diagnostic, Prognostic, and Developmental Considerations
(1973)   2:44–55

NEFF, L.
Chemicals and Their Effects on the Adolescent Ego (1971)   1:108–120

NEWMAN, K.
Bonnie and Clyde: A Modern Parable (1971)   1:61–74

NEWMAN, L. E.
Transsexualism in Adolescence: Problems in Evaluation and Treatment (1973)
2:144–159

NEWMAN, M. B., AND SAN MARTINO, M. R.
Adolescence and the Relationship between Generations (1976)   4:60–71

NICHTERN, S.
Introduction: The Educational Needs of Adolescents in Psychiatric Hospitals (1974)
3:389–390
The Therapeutic Educational Environment (1974)   3:432–434
The Missing Adolescent (1980)   8:54–64
The Sociocultural and Psychodynamic Aspects of the Acting-Out and Violent
Adolescent (1982)   10:140–146
The Pursuit of the Fantasy Family: Generational Aspects (1983)   11:27–34
Gandhi: His Adolescent Conflict of Mind and Body (1985)   12:17–23
see also BUYTENDORP (1988)

NORCROSS, J. *see* PEARSON, JENNINGS, AND NORCROSS (1998)

NORDAN, R., *see* LASSERS AND NORDAN (1978)

NOVICK, J.
Termination of Treatment in Adolescence (1977)   5:390–412

OFFER, D.

The Mystery of Adolescence (1987)   14:7–27

see also BAITTLE AND OFFER (1971); KREMER, WILLIAMS, OFFER, BERNS, MASTERSON, LIEF, AND FEINSTEIN (1973); OFFER AND OFFER (1977); OSTROV AND OFFER (1978); MAROHN, OFFER, OSTROV, AND TRUJILLO (1979); SCHONERT-REICHL, OFFER, AND HOWARD (1995)

OFFER, D., AND OFFER J. B.

Three Developmental Routes through Normal Male Adolescence (1976) 4:121–141

OFFER, D.; OSTROV, E.; AND HOWARD, K. I.

Self-Image, Delinquency, and Help Seeking Behavior among Normal Adolescents (1986)   13:121–138

OFFER, D., AND VANDERSTOEP, E.

Indications and Contraindications for Family Therapy (1974)   3:249–262

OFFER, J. B., AND OFFER, D.

Sexuality in Adolescent Males (1977)   5:96–107

see also OFFER AND OFFER (1976)

OLDHAM, D. G.

Adolescent Turmoil: A Myth Revisited (1978)   6:267–279

OLDS, J.

The Inpatient Treatment of Adolescents in Milieu including Younger Children (1982)   10:373–381

OSORIO, L. C.

The Psychoanalysis of Communication in Adolescents (1977)   5:422–448

OSTROV, E., AND OFFER, D.

Loneliness and the Adolescent (1978)   6:34–50

see also MAROHN, OFFER, OSTROV, AND TRUJILLO (1979); OFFER, OSTROV, AND HOWARD (1986)

OVERTON, W. F.; STEIDL, J. H.; ROSENSTEIN, D.; AND HOROWITZ, H. A.

Formal Operations as a Regulatory Context in Adolescence (1992) 18:502–513

PAHLAVAN, L., *see* STODDARD, PAHLAVAN, AND CAHNERS (1985)

PALGI, P.

Death of a Soldier; Sociocultural Expressions (1976)   4:174–198

PALOMBO, J.

The Cohesive Self, the Nuclear Self, and Development in Late Adolescence (1990) 17:338–359

PANNOR, R., *see* SOROSKY, BARAN, AND PANNOR (1987)

PEARSON, G. T.

Long-Term Needs of Hospitalized Adolescents (1987)   14:342–357

PEARSON, G.T., JENNINGS, J., AND NORCROSS, J.

A Program of Comprehensive School-Based Mental Health Services in a Large Urban Public School District: The Dallas Model (1998)   23:207–231

see also JONES, PEARSON, AND DIMPERO (1989)

PECK, M. L.

The Loner: An Exploration of a Suicidal Subtype in Adolescence (1981) 9:461–466

PECK, M. L., AND BEROKOVITZ, I. H.

Youth Suicide: The Role of School Consultation (1987)   14:511–521

PEPPER, B., *see* RYGLEWICZ AND PEPPER (1989)

PERL, E.

Breaking Up or Breaking Away: The Struggle Around Autonomy and Individuation Among Adolescent Daughters of Divorce (1997)   21:83–99

Snatching Defeat from the Jaws of Success: Self-Destructive Behavior as an Expression of Autonomy in Young Women (1998)   23:143–167

PERLMAN, T., *see* HECHTMAN, WEISS, PERLMAN, AND TUCK (1981)

PEROSA, L. M.; SIMONS, R.; AND PEROSA, S. L.

The Family Perceptions of Young Adults with Putative Risk for Schizophrenia (1997)   21:165–181

PEROSA, S. L., *see* PEROSA, SIMONS, AND PEROSA (1997)

PETZEL, S. V., AND CLINE, D. W.

Adolescent Suicide: Epidemiological and Biological Aspects (1978) 6:239–266

PETZEL, S. V., AND RIDDLE, M.

Adolescent Suicide: Psychosocial and Cognitive Aspects (1981)   9:343–398

PFEFFER, C. R.

Clinical Dilemmas in the Prevention of Adolescent Suicidal Behavior (1988) 15:407–421

PHILIPS, I., AND SZUREK, S. A.

Youth and Society: Conformity, Rebellion, and Learning (1974)   3:140–151

PHILLIPS, E., *see* SALGUERO, YEARWOOD, PHILLIPS, AND SCHLESINGER (1980)

PHILLIPS, R. E.

The Creative Moment: Improvising in Jazz and Psychotherapy (1988) 15:182–193

POLIER, J. W.

The Search for Mental Health Services for Adolescents (1974)   3:313–322

POLLAK, O.

Youth Culture, Subcultures, and Survival (1974)   3:49–53

Perspectives on Family Life and Social Change (1980)   8:79–84

PONTON, L. E.

A Review of Eating Disorders in Adolescents (1995)   20:267–285

Adolescent Mood Disorders (1997)   21:183–207

PORT, J.; HARROW, M.; JOBE, T.; AND DOUGHERTY, D.

Thought Disorders in Adolescent Schizophrenia: Toward an Integrative Model (1997)   21:119–164

PORTER, R., *see* KREMER, PORTER, GIOVACCHINI, LOEB, SUGAR, AND BARISH (1971)

POTOK, C.

Rebellion and Authority: The Adolescent Discovering the Individual in Modern Literature (1976)   4:15–20

PROSEN, H., *see* TOEWS, MARTIN, AND PROSEN (1981); TOEWS, PROSEN, AND MARTIN (1981); TOEWS, MARTIN, AND PROSEN (1985)

PROSEN, H.; TOEWS, J.; AND MARTIN, R.

The Life Cycle of Family: Parental Midlife Crisis and Adolescent Rebellion (1981) 9:170–179

PUTNAM, N.

Revenge or Tragedy: Do Nerds Suffer from a Mild Pervasive Development Disorder? (1990)   17:51–68

PYLE, R. L., AND MITCHELL, J. E.

The Prevalence of Bulimia in Selected Samples (1986)   13:241–252

RAFFE, I. H., *see* DAVIS AND RAFFE (1985)

RAFFERTY, F. T.

The Evolution of Two-tiered Health Care (1990)   17:7–18

RAFFERTY, F. T., AND STEFFEK, J. C.

A Group Approach with the Hapless Adolescent (1977)   5:429–441

RAKOFF, V. M.

The Illusion of Detachment (1978)   6:119–129

History of Adolescent Disorders (1980)   8:85–99

A Reconstruction of Identity (1981)   9:22–32

Discussion of Peter Blos's Chapter (1989)   16:26–30

The Emergence of the Adolescent Patient (1989)   16:372–386

Friendship and Adolescents (1992)   18:104–117

Creativity and Productivity in Adolescents (1993)   19:46–57

Trauma and Adolescent Rites of Initiation (1995)   20:109–123

Nietzsche and the Romantic Construction of Adolescence (1998)   22:39–56

see also BLOS (1989); BUCHANAN (1989)

RANGELL, L.

Seventeen: A Developmental View (1989)   16:92–117

RANSOHOFF, R.

The Borderline Adolescent Grows Up (1978)   6:409–419

RASCOVSKY, A.

Filicide and the Unconscious Motivation for War (1974)   3:54–67

RASHKIS, H. A., AND RASHKIS, S. R.

I. An Investigation of the Influence of Parental Communications of Adolescent Ego Development (1981)   9:227–235

II. Parental Communication, Readiness of Adolescents to Leave Home, and the Course of Treatment (1981)   9:236–243

RASHKIS, S. R., *see* RASHKIS AND RASHKIS (1981)

RATEY, J. J., *see* HALLOWELL, BEMPORAD, AND RATEY (1989)

REBHAN, J., *see* HALPERIN, LAURO, MISCIONE, REBHAN, SCHNABOLK, AND SHACHTER (1981)

REDL, F.

Emigration, Immigration, and the Imaginary Group (1976)   4:6–12

REICH, R., AND FEINBERG, H. B.

The Fatally Ill Adolescent (1974)   3:75–84

REISS, D., *see* SIGAFOOS, FEINSTEIN, DAMOND, AND REISS (1988)

RENSHAW, D.

Adolescent Sex and AIDS (1998)   23:171–178

RIDDLE, M., *see* PETZEL AND RIDDLE (1981)

RIDGELY, M. S.; GOLDMAN, H. H.; AND TALBOTT, J. A.

Treatment of Chronic Mentally Ill Young Adults with Substance Abuse Problems: Emerging National Trends (1989)   16:288–313

RIEGER, R. E.

The Significance of the Attachment Process in Brain-damaged Adolescent Psychiatric Patients (1990)   17:264–271

see also FRITSCH, HOLMSTROM, GOODRICH, AND RIEGER (1990)

RINSLEY, D. B.

Theory and Practice of Intensive Residential Treatment of Adolescents (1971)   1:479–509

Special Education for Adolescents in Residential Psychiatric Treatment (1974)   3:392–418

Borderline Psychopathology: The Concepts of Masterson and Rinsley and Beyond (1981)   9:259–274

The Adolescent, the Family, and the Culture of Narcissism: A Psychosocial Commentary (1986)   13:7–28

A Review of the Pathogenesis of Borderline and Narcissistic Personality Disorders (1988)   15:387–406

RIZZUTO, A.-M.

I, Me, Myself: The Subjective Aspect of Identity (1992)   18:419–447

ROBINSON, L. H.

Adolescent Homosexual Patterns: Psychodynamics and Therapy (1980)   8:422–436

In Defense of Parents (1990)   17:36–50

ROBITSCHER, J.

The Commitment of Minors: Problems of Civil Liberties (1979)   7:457–465

RODEN, M.M., *see* RODEN AND RODEN (1982)

RODEN, R. G., AND RODEN, M. M.

Children of Holocaust Survivors (1982)   10:66–72

RONAN, K. R., AND KENDALL, P. C.

Non-Self-controlled Adolescents: Applications of Cognitive-Behavioral Therapy (1990)   17:479–505

ROSE, G. J.

Maternal Control, Superego Formation, and Identity (1971)   1:379–387

ROSEN, J. C., *see* LEITENBERG AND ROSEN (1986)

ROSENSTEIN, D. AND HOROWITZ, H. A.

Attachment, Personality, and Psychopathololgy (1993)   19:150–176

ROSENSTEIN, D.; HOROWITZ, H. A.; STEIDL, J. H.; AND OVERTON, W. F.

Attachment and Internalization: Relationship as a Regulatory Context (1992)   18:491–501

ROSENTHAL, M. J.

Filial Obligation in Adolescence: An Orientation (1977)   5:151–174

Sexual Differences in the Suicidal Behavior of Young People (1981)   9:422–442

ROSENTHAL, P. A.

Delinquency in Adolescent Girls: Developmental Aspects (1979)   7:503–515

Changes in Transitional Objects: Girls in Midadolescence (1981)   9:214–226

see also ROSENTHAL AND ROSENTHAL (1982)

ROSENTHAL, P. A., AND DOHERTY, M. B.

Psychodynamics of Delinquent Girls' Rage and Violence Directed toward Mother (1985)   12:281–289

ROSENTHAL, R., *see* MAROHN, LOCKE, ROSENTHAL, AND CURTISS (1982)

ROSENTHAL, S., AND ROSENTHAL, P. A.

Koro in an Adolescent: Hypochondriasis as a Stress Response (1982) 10:523–531

ROSMAN, B. L.; MINUCHIN, S.; LEIBMAN, R.; AND BAKER, L.

Input and Outcome of Family Therapy in Anorexia Nervosa (1977) 5:313–322

ROSNER, R.

Report of the Accreditation Council on Fellowships in Adolescent Psychiatry (1997) 21:389–407

ROSSMAN, P. G.

Psychotherapeutic Approaches in Depressed, Acting-Out Adolescents: Interpretive Tactics and Their Rationale (1982)   10:455–468

ROSSMAN, P. G., AND FREEDMAN, J. A.

Hospital Treatment for Disturbed Adolescents: The Role of Parent Counseling Groups (1982)   10:391–406

ROTENBERG, C. T.

Creativity and the Transformational Process (1988)   15:247–257

ROTHMAN, S. *see* SCHNITZER, ISENBERG, AND ROTHMAN (1978)

ROTHSTEIN, D. A.

On Presidential Assassination: The Academia and the Pseudo-Community (1976) 4:264–298

The Academe, the Pseudo-Community, and the Army in the Development of Identity (1983)   11:35–63

ROUX, N., *see* VILLENEUVE AND ROUX (1995)

RYGLEWICZ, H., AND PEPPER, B.

Compromised Development: The Complex Plight of Young Adults with Mental/ Emotional Disorders (1989)   16:278–287

SACKHEIM, H. A.; DECINA,; AND MALITZ, S.

Functional Brain Asymmetry and Affective Disorders (1982)   10:320-335

SALGUERO, C.; YEARWOOD, E.; PHILLIPS, E.; AND SCHLESINGER, N.

Studies of Infants at Risk and Their Adolescent Mothers (1980)   8:404–421

SALZ, A.

Kibbutz Sasa: Nurturing Children at Risk (1993)   19:469–448

SALZMAN, L.

Adolescence: Epoch or Disease (1974)   3:128–139

SANCHEZ, E. G.

Factors Complicating the Psychiatric Diagnosis of Adolescents (1986) 13:100–115

SANDERS, J.

Principles of Residential Treatment: Staff Growth and Therapeutic Interaction (1985)   12:361–370

Severely Emotionally Disturbed Children: Fore*seeing*, Avoiding, and Ameliorating Their Pain (1993)   19:446–468

346

Residential Treatment of Severely Disturbed Children (1995)   20:397–408
SANDLER, J.
Comments on the Self and Its Objects (1992)   18:395–406
SAN MARTINO, M.R., *see* NEWMAN AND SAN MARTINO (1976)
SARGENT, D. A.
A Contribution to the Study of the Presidential Assassination Syndrome (1976)
    4:299–308
SARLES, R., *see* HENDREN, ARMENTANO, GRATER, MIKKELSEN, SARLES, AND SONDHEIMER
    (1997)
SARLES, R. M.
President's Preface (1992)   18:ix
SAVARD, R. J., *see* STIERLIN, LEVI, AND SAVARD (1973)
SCHARF, K. R., *see* FISHER AND SCHARF (1980)
SCHILDKROUT, M. S.
The Pediatrician and the Adolescent Psychiatrist (1974)   3:68–74
SCHIMEL, J. L.
Adolescents and Families: An Overview (1979)   7:362–370
Psychotherapy with Adolescents: The Art of Interpretation (1986)
    13:178–187
The Role of Humor as an Integrating Factor in Adolescent Development (1992)
    18:118-126
SCHLESINGER, N., *see* SALGUERO, YEARWOOD, PHILLIPS, AND SCHLESINGER (1980)
SCHMIDT, M.H., LAY, B., ESSER G., AND IHLE, W.
Psychosomatic and Depressive Symptoms from Age Eight to Age Eighteen (1998)
    23:73–86
SCHNABOLK, J., *see* HALPERIN, LAURO, MISCIONE, REBHAN, SCHNABOLK, AND SHACHTER
    (1981)
SCHNALL, D. , AND YOUNGERMAN, J.
Disadvantaged Adolescents Separating from Home and Hospital: Spanning the
    Antipodes through Paradox (1989)   16:435–448
SCHNEIDER, S.
Impingement of Cultural Factors on Identity Formation in Adolescence (1992)
    18:407–418
SCHNITZER, R.; ISENBERG, P.; AND ROTHMAN, S.
Faces in the Crowd: Portraits and Racial Youth (1978)   6:195–223
SCHNURR, R. G.
Psychological Assessment and Discussion of Female Adolescents with Trichotillo-
    mania (1988)   15:463–470
SCHONERT, K. A.
Sex Differences in Moral Reasoning among Emotionally Disturbed Adolescents
    (1992)   18:198–212
SCHONERT-REICHL, K. A.; OFFER, D.; AND HOWARD, K. I.
Seeking Help from Informal and Formal Resources During Adolescence: Sociode-
    mographic and Psychological Correlates (1995)   20:165–178
SCHONFELD, W. A.
Foreword (1971)   1:vii–viii

Adolescent Development: Biological, Psychological, and Sociological Determinants (1971)   1:296–323

Depression in Adolescents (1995)   20:31–38

see also FEINSTEIN (1971); BARISH AND SCHONFELD (1973)

SCHOWALTER, J., *see* LOONEY, ELLIS, BENEDEK, AND SCHOWALTER (1985)

SCHULLER, A. B., AND BUCKY, S. F.

Toward Prediction of Unsuccessful Adaptation in the Military Environment (1974)   3:85–95

SCHWARTZ, E. D.; KOWALSKY, J. M.; AND HANUS, S.

Malignant Memories: Signatures of Violence (1993)   19:280–300

SCHWARTZ, K. M.

The Meaning of Cults in Treatment of Adolescent Issues (1986)   13:188–200

SCHWARTZBERG, A. Z.

Overview of the Borderline Syndrome in Adolescence (1978)   6:286–297

Adolescent Reactions to Divorce (1980)   8:379–392

Divorce and Children and Adolescents: An Overview (1981)   9:119–132

The Adolescent in the Remarriage Family (1987)   14:259–270

Adolescent Substance Abuse: Introduction (1988)   15:505–507

Editor's Introduction (1993)   19:505–507

Sherman C. Feinstein, M.D.: Editor, Adolescent Psychiatry, 1973 to 1994 (1995)   20:3–5

SCHWARZ, E. D., *see* GRYGOTIS AND SCHWARZ (1995)

SEIDEN, A. M.

Sex Roles, Sexuality, and the Adolescent Peer Group (1976)   4:211–225

SHACHTER, B., *see* HALPERIN, LAURO, MISCIONE, REBHAN, SCHNABOLK, AND SHACHTER (1981)

SHAIOVA, C. H., *see* LEVINE AND SHAIOVA (1977)

SHAPIRO, E. R.

Research on Family Dynamics: Clinical Implications for the Family of the Borderline Adolescent (1978)   6:360–376

Introduction: The Adolescent, the Family, and the Hospital (1982)   10:339–342

see also KOLB AND SHAPIRO (1982)

SHAPIRO, E. R., AND FREEDMAN, J.

Family Dynamics of Adolescent Suicide (1987)   14:191–207

SHAPIRO, E. R., AND KOLB, J. E.

Engaging the Family of the Hospitalized Adolescent: The Multiple Family Meeting (1979)   7:322–342

SHAPIRO, R. L.

Family Dynamics and Object-Relations Theory: An Analytic, Group-interpretive Approach to Family Therapy (1979)   7:118–135

SHAPIRO, T.

Adolescent Language: Its Use for Diagnosis, Group Identity, Values, and Treatment (1985)   12:297–311

SHARFSTEIN, B.

Adolescents and Philosophers: A Word in Favor of Both (1978)   6:51–58

SHARFSTEIN, S. S.

Financing Child and Adolescent Mental Health Care (1993)   19:517–522

SHARPNACK, J.D., *see* MAUK AND SHARPNACK (1998)

SHAW, J. A.

Adolescents in the Mobile Military Community (1979)   7:191–198

Adolescence, Mourning, and Creativity 1981)   9:60–77

The Postadolescent Crisis of John Stuart Mill (1982)   10:85–98

Narcissism, Identity Formation and Genocide (1998)   22:211–226

SHEININ, J. C.

Medical Aspects of Eating Disorders (1986)   13:405–421

SHIELDS, J. D., AND CHORAS, P. T.

Treatment of the Hospitalized Adolescent: Management of Regression during Discharge (1982)   10:407–424

SHIELDS, R. W.

Mutative Confusion at Adolescence (1973)   2:372–386

SIGAFOOS, A. D.; FEINSTEIN, C. B.; DAMOND, M.; AND REISS, D.

The Measurement of Behavioral Autonomy in Adolescence: The Autonomous Functioning Checklist (1988)   15:432–462

SILK, K., *see* WESTEN, LUDOLPH, SILK, KELLAM, GOLD, AND LOHR (1990)

SILVER, A. A., AND HAGIN, R. A.

Outcomes of Learning Disabilities in Adolescents (1985)   12:197–213

SIMON, W., *see* BERGER AND SIMON (1976)

SIMONS, R., *see* PEROSA, SIMONS, AND PEROSA (1997)

SINAIKO, H.

Plato's Laches: Courage, Expertise, Psychotherapy, and Adolescence (1986)   13:44–61

SINGER, M.

Family Structure, Disciplinary Configuration, and Adolescent Psychopathology (1974)   3:372–386

SLAFF, B.

History of Adolescent Psychiatry (1981)   9:7–21

Creativity: Blessing or Burden? (1981)   9:78–87

History of Child and Adolescent Psychiatry Ideas and Organizations in the United States: A Twentieth-Century Review (1989)   16:31–52

Thoughts on Short-Term and Single-Session Therapy (1995)   20:299–306

In Memoriam: Sherman C. Feinstein, M. D. (1998)   22:ix–xii

see also KNOBEL, SLAFF, KALINA, AND FEINSTEIN (1973)

SMARR, E. R., AND ESCOLL, P. J.

The Youth Culture, Future Adulthood, and Societal Change (1973)   2:113–126

The Work Ethic, the Work Personality, and Humanistic Values (1976)   4:163–173

SNYDER, S.

Movies and the Adolescent: An Overview (1992)   18:74–90

SOLNIT, A. J.

Obstacles and Pathways in the Journey from Adolescence to Parenthood (1983)   11:14–26

SOLOW, R. A.

Planning for Education Needs (1974)   3:391–393

Psychopharmacology with Adolescents: A Current Review (1978)   6:480–494

SOLOW, R. A., AND COOPER, B. M.

Therapeutic Mobilization of Families around Drug-induced Adolescent Crises (1974)   3:237–248

SONDHEIMER, A.

Anticipation and Experimentation: The Sexual Concerns of Mid Adolescence (1982) 10:208–227

SONDHEIMER, A., *see* HENDREN, ARMENTANO, GRATER, MIKKELSEN, SARLES, AND SONDHEIMER (1997)

SONIS, M.

Aichhorn Revisited: A Report on Acting-Out Adolescent Behavior (1979) 7:484–496

SOROSKY, A. D.

Psychopharmacology and the Adolescent: An Introduction (1979)   7:373–374

Introduction: An Overview of Eating Disorders (1986)   13:221–229

SOROSKY, A. D.; BARAN, A.; AND PANNOR, R.

Adoption and the Adolescent: An Overview (1977)   5:54–72

SOROSKY, A. D., AND STICHER, M. B.

Trichotillomania in Adolescence (1980)   8:437–454

Introduction/Adolescent Suicidology (1981)   9:323–326

SOSIN, D. A.

The Diary as a Transitional Object in Female Adolescent Development (1983) 11:92–103

STAPLES, H. D.

In Memoriam: Dedication to Margaret S. Mahler (1987)   14:xi–xiii

Reflections on the History of Adolescent Psychiatry (1995)   20:39–49

STEFFEK, J. C., *see* RAFFERTY AND STEFFEK (1977)

STEIDL, J. H.; HOROWITZ, H. A.; OVERTON, W. F.; AND ROSENSTEIN, D.

Family Interaction as Regulatory Context in Adolescence (1992)   18:484–490

STEIN, B.

Personality Functioning and Change in Clinical Presentation from Early to Middle Adolescence (1987)   14:378–393

Consistency and Change in Personality Characteristics and Affect from Middle to Late Adolescence (1990)   17:404–414

Working with Adolescent Victims of Ethnic Cleansing in Bosnia (1998) 22:227–240

see also GOLOMBEK, MARTON, STEIN, AND KORENBLUM (1987); KORENBLUM, MARTON, GOLOMBEK, AND STEIN (1987); MARTON, GOLOMBEK, STEIN, AND KORENBLUM (1987)

STEIN, M. H.

Day Treatment for Serious Mental Illness (1993)   18:541–550

STICHER, M. B., *see* SOROSKY AND STICHER

STIERLIN, H.

The Adolescent as Delegate of His Parents (1976)   4:72–83

Treatment Perspectives on Adolescent Runaways (1977)   5:413–421

STIERLIN, H.; LEVI, L. D.; AND SAVARD, R. J.
Centrifugal versus Centripetal Separation in Adolescence: Two Patterns and Some
of Their Implications (1973)   2:211–239
STOCKHAMER, N. N., see LEVENSON, FEINER, AND STOCKHAMER (1976)
STOCKING, M.
Catastrophe and the Capacity to Withstand It: An Adolescent Responds to Personal
Tragedy (1989)   16:412–434
STODDARD, F. J., AND CAHNERS, S. S.
Suicide Attempted by Self-Immolation during Adolescence. II. Psychiatric
Treatment and Outcome (1985)   12:266–281
STODDARD, F. J.; PAHLAVAN, K.; AND CAHNERS, S. S.
Suicide Attempted by Self-Immolation during Adolescence. I. Literature Review,
Case Reports, and Personality Precursors (1985)   12:251–265
STONE, M. S.
Special Problems in Borderline Adolescents from Wealthy Families (1983)
11:163–176
Suicide in Borderline and Other Adolescents (1992)   18:289–305
STROBER, M., AND CARLSON, G.
Predictors of Bipolar Illness in Adolescents with Major Depression: A Follow-Up
Investigation (1982)   10:299–319
SUGAR, M.
Network Psychotherapy of an Adolescent (1971)   1:464–478
Adolescent Confusion of Nocturnal Emissions as Enuresis (1974)   3:168–185
Group Process in the Management of a High School Crisis (1974)   3:362–371
Introduction to Chaim Potok's Address (1976)   4:13–14
Therapeutic Approaches to the Borderline Adolescent (1979)   7:343–361
Sexual Abuse of Children and Adolescents (1983)   11:199–211
Diagnostic Aspects of Underachievement in Adolescents (1987)   14:427–440
Subtle Classroom Abuse in an Adolescent Inpatient Program (1988)
15:422–431
Developmental Anxieties in Adolescence (1990)   17:385–403
Late Adolescent Development and Treatment (1992)   18:131–155
Education and Poverty: Problems and Possibilities (1993)   19:31–45
Facets of Adolescent Sexuality (1995)   20:139–161
Adolescents and Disaster (1997)   21:67–81
Section Editor Introduction (1998)   22:207–209
Adolescent Genocide (1998)   22:241–250
see also KREMER, PORTER, GIOVACCHINI, LOEB, SUGAR, AND BARISH (1971)
SUTTON-SMITH, B.
Creativity and the Vicissitudes of Play (1988)   15:307–318
SZUREK, S. A., see PHILIPS AND SZUREK (1974)
TABACHNICK, N.
The Interlocking Psychologies of Suicide and Adolescence (1981)   9:399–410
TALBOTT, J. A., see RIDGELY, GOLDMAN, AND TALBOTT (1989)
TASHJIAN, L. D.
Aspects of Internalization and Individuation: James Joyce's Portrait of the Artist
as a Young Man (1982)   10:75–84

TIMBERLAKE, J., *see* GRINKER, GRINKER, AND TIMBERLAKE (1971)

TOEWS, J.

Adolescent Developmental Issues in Marital Therapy (1980)   8:244–252
see also PROSEN, TOEWS, AND MARTIN (1981)

TOEWS, J.; MARTIN, R.; AND PROSEN, H.

III. The Life Cycle of the Family: Perspectives on Psychotherapy with Adolescents (1981)   9:189–198

Death Anxiety: The Prelude to Adolescence (1985)   12:134–144

TOEWS, J.; PROSEN, H.; AND MARTIN, R.

II. The Life Cycle of the Family: The Adolescent's Sense of Time (1981) 9:180–188

TOLCHIN, J.

Telephone Psychotherapy with Adolescents (1987)   14:332–341

TOLPIN, P. H.

Some Psychic Determinants of Orgastic Dysfunction (1971)   1:388–413

TRAD, P. V.

The Psychotherapeutic Pathway to Adaptive Individuation for Adolescents Confronting Conflict (1997)   21:317–346

Anxiety, Depression, and Psychosomatic Disorders: Developmental Arrhythmias in Adolescent Mothers (1995)   20:179–202

TRUJILLO, J., *see* MAROHN, OFFER, OSTROV, AND TRUJILLO (1979)

TUCK, D., *see* HECHTMAN, WEISS, PERLMAN, AND TUCK (1981)

TYSON, P.

Developmental Roots of Adolescent Disturbance (1998)   23:21–39

VANDERSTOEP, E., *see* OFFER AND VANDERSTOEP (1974)

VAN PUTTEN, T.

Antipsychotic Drugs in Adolescence (1979)   7:389–401

VILLELA, L., AND MARKIN, R.

Adolescent Film Preferences: The World of Purple Rain: A Psychodynamic Interpretation (1987)   14:119–132

VILLENEUVE, C.

The Awareness of the Past in Adolescence (1997)   21:35–47

VILLENEUVE, C. AND ROUX, N.

Family Therapy and Some Personality Disorders in Adolescence (1995) 20:365–380

VON FOERSTER, H.

On Constructing a Reality (1988)   15:77–95

On Seeing: The Problem of the Double Blind (1993)   19:86–105

WALLACE, M. E., *see* WALLACE AND WALLACE (1985)

WALLACE, N. L., AND WALLACE, M. E.

Transference/Countertransference Issues in the Treatment of an Acting-Out Adolescent (1985)   12:468–477

WALSH, B. T.

Medication in the Treatment of Bulimia (1986)   13:437–445

WARNER, B. S., *see* WEIST AND WARNER (1997)

WATERS, D. B., *see* DERDEYN AND WATERS (1977)

WEIL, N. H., AND BOXER, A. M.
Who Mothers Young Mothers? Treatment of Adolescent Mothers and Their Children with Impaired Attachments (1990)   17:451–472
WEINE, S. M.
The Game's the Thing: Play Psychotherapy with a Traumatized Young Adolescent Boy (1997)   21:361–386
WEINER, M. F., AND KING, J. W.
Self-Disclosure by the Therapist to the Adolescent Patient (1977)   5:449–459
WEINSTEIN, N.
Liberty and Mental Health: A Philosophical Conflict (1979)   7:433–443
WEINTROB, A.
Foreword: Replenishing ASAP's Vines: Vintage and Nonvintage Wines (1998) 23:ix–xii
WEISBERG, P. S.
Demographic, Attitudinal, and Practice Patterns of Adolescent Psychiatrists in the United States (1978)   6:90–118
WEISS, G., see HECHTMAN, WEISS, PERLMAN, AND TUCK (1981)
WEISSMAN, S., AND BARGLOW, P.
Recent Contributions to the Theory of Female Adolescent Psychological Development (1980)   8:214–230
WEISSMAN, S., AND COHEN, R. S.
The Parenting Alliance and Adolescence (1985)   12:24–45
WEISSMAN, S. H.; COHEN, R. S.; BOXER, A. M.; AND COHLER, B. J.
Parenthood Experience and the Adolescent's Transition to Young Adulthood: Self Psychological Perspectives (1989)   16:155–174
WEIST, M. D., AND BAKER-SINCLAIR, M. E.
Use of Structured Assessment Tools in Clinical Practice (1997)   21:235–251
WEIST, M. D., AND WARNER, B. S.
Intervening Against Violence in the Schools (1997)   21:349–360
WELBOURNE, C., see BARGLOW, ISTIPHAN, BEDGER, AND WELBOURNE (1973)
WELLS, L. A.
Common Issues of Late Adolescence and Young Adulthood in Medical Students (1989)   16:228–245
WERKMAN, S. L.
Introduction: The Effect of Geographic Mobility on Adolescents (1979)   n 7:175–177
Coming Home: Adjustment Problems of Adolescents Who Have Lived Overseas (1979)   7:178–190
WESTEN, D.; LUDOLPH, P.; SILK, K.; KELLAM, A.; GOLD, L.; AND LOHR, N.
Object Relations in Borderline Adolescents and Adults: Developmental Differences (1990)   17:360–384
WHISNANT, L.; BRETT, E.; AND ZEGANS, L.
Adolescent Girls and Menstruation (1979)   7:157–171
WIDEN, H. A.
Phase-specific Symptomatic Response to Sibling Loss in Late Adolescence (1987) 14:218–229
The Risk of AIDS and the College Psychotherapist (1989)   16:473–487
see also LOVE AND WIDEN (1985)

WILLIAMS, C. K.
  Poetry and Consciousness (1988)   15:121–133
WILLIAMS, F. S.
  Discussion of Rudolf Ekstein's Chapter (1973)   2:25–30
  Family Therapy: Its Role in Adolescent Psychiatry (1973)   2:324–339
  The Psychoanalyst as Both Parent and Interpreter for Adolescent Patients (1986)
    13:164–177
  see also KREMER, WILLIAMS, OFFER, BERNS, MASTERSON, LIEF, AND FEISNTEIN (1973)
WILSON, C. P.
  The Psychoanalytic Psychotherapy of Bulimic Anorexia Nervosa (1986)
    13:274–314
WILSON, M. R., JR.
  A Proposed Diagnostic Classification for Adolescent Psychiatric Cases (1971)
    1:275–295
  In Memoriam: Dana L. Farnsworth (1905–1986) (1987)   14:xv–xvi
WINNER, E.
  The Puzzle of Art (1988)   15:148–159
WINNICOTT, D. W.
  Adolescence: Struggling through the Doldrums (1971)   1:40–50
  Delinquency as a Sign of Hope (1973)   2:364–371
  see also FEINSTEIN AND GIOVACCHINI (1973)
WINTER, J. AND MAROHN, R. C. (trans.)
  Vienna Psychoanalytic Society Minutes - February 15, 1922   20:51–52
WISEMAN, H. AND LIEBELICH, A.
  Individuation in a Collective Community (1992)   18:156–179
WOLENSKY, R. P.
  College Students in the Fifties: The Silent Generation Revisited (1977)
    5:82–95
WOLF, C., *see* GARDNER AND WOLF (1988)
WOLF, E. S.
  Sigmund Freud: Some Adolescent Transformation of a Future Genius (1971)
    1:51–60
  Tomorrow's Self: Heinz Kohut's Contribution to Adolescent Psychiatry (1980)
    8:41–50
  Adolescence: Psychology of the Self and Selfobjects (1982)   10:171–181
WOODALL, C.
  The Body as a Transitional Object in Bulimia: A Critique of the Concept (1987)
    14:179–189
WOODBURY, C., *see* FORT, MCAFEE, KING, HOPPE, FENTON, ABRAMOWITZ, WOODBURY, AND
    ANTHONY (1990)
WYNNE, L. C.
  The Epigenesis of Relational Systems: A Revised Developmental Perspective (1993)
    19:240–254
YATES, B. T., *see* FULLERTON, YATES, AND GOODRICH (1990)
YEARWOOD, E., *see* SALGUERO, YEARWOOD, PHILLIPS, AND SCHLESINGER (1980)
YOUNG-EISENDRATH, P.
  The Interpretive Community of Self (1993)   19:177–184
YOUNGERMAN, J., *see* SCHNALL AND YOUNGERMAN (1989)

354

ZARETSKY, I. I.

Youth and Religious Movements (1980)   8:281–287

ZASLOW, S. L.

Countertransference Issues in Psychotherapy with Adolescents (1985) 12:524–534

ZEANAH, C. H.

Subjectivity in Parent-Infant Relationships: Contributions from Attachment Research (1993)   19:121–136

ZEGANS, L., *see* WHISNANT, BRETT, AND ZEGANS (1979)

ZINNER, J.

Combined Individual and Family Therapy of Borderline Adolescents: Rationale and Management of the Early Phase (1978)   6:420–427

355

Author Index

A

Abikoff, H., 184, 192, *202, 207*
Ablon, J. S., 224, 225, *242*
Acton, W. P., 273, *290*
Adams, P. B., 193, *203*
Addy, C. L., 222, *234*
Adleman, H. S., 82, *89*
Aichhorn, A., 41, *45*
Ainsworth, M., 54, *66*
Al-Shabbout, M., 219, 220, *236*
Alaghband-Rad, J., 277, 283, *291, 292*
Albus, K. E., 283, *291*
Alderman, E., 297, 298, *311*
Alderman, J., 221, *239*
Aldershof, A. L., 226, *234*
Alegria, M., 75, 77, 81, *88*
Alessi, N., 222, *240*
Allen, A. J., 187, 188, *202*
Alpert, J. L., 81, *86*
Alsobrook, J. P., 244, *268*
Altshuler, L., 231, *239*
Aman, M. G., 191, *202*
Ambrosini, P., 214, 219, *232, 240*
Anastopoulos, A. D., 181, *202*
Anderson, G., 278, 283, *289, 292*
Anderson, J. C., 244, 246, *265*
Anderson, L. T., 282, *289, 290*
Andreasen, N. C., 224, *240*
Andrews, J. A., 213, *238*
Angold, A., 216, *232, 245, 266*
Anker, J. A., 217, *234*
Ansseau, M., 259, 260, *265*
Anthony, E. J., 41, *45*

Appelbaum, P. S., 168, *171*
Appiah, A., 52, 54, *66*
Apter, A., 263, *265*
Apter, J. T., 221, *232*
Armenteros, J., 194, 204, 284, *289*
Armstrong, D., 83, *89*
Arndt, S. V., 187, 188, *202*
Arnsten, A., 189, 190, *204, 206*
Aron, C., 149, *157*
Arsanow, J. R., 216, *232*
Asbell, M. D., 189, *206*
Asche, B., 262, *266*
Astrachan, B. M., 200, *207*
Avad, G., 283, *292*

B

Bagley, C., 182, *202*
Baker, L., 276, *290*
Balach, L., 250, 262, *266*
Baldessarini, R., 186, 187, *211, 202*
Ballach, L., 216, *232*
Barbey, J. T., 220, *232*
Bard, B., 150, *158*
Barker, M., 185, *205*
Barkley, R. A., 77, *89,* 181, 182, *202*
Barlow, S. H., 121, *130*
Barnhill, L. J., 190, *206*
Baron, H. A., 255, *268*
Barrickman, L., 187, 188, *202*
Bartak, L., 276, *289*
Bass, J., 75, 76, *86, 87*
Bassham, G., 151, *157*

Baudhiun, M., 226, *236*
Bauman, M. L., 286, *293*
Beaundry, M. B., 216, *232*
Beck, J. C., 76–77, *88*
Beck, N. C., 213, *236*
Becquemont, L., 220, *232*
Bedwell, J., 284, *291*
Beedy, J., 56, *68*
Begg, D. J., 182, *208*
Behar, D., 197, *211*
Behr, R., 194, *205*
Bell, R. M., 80, *87*
Bell-Dolan, D. J., 244, 246, *265*
Belluci, P. A., 76, *87*
Benjamin, S., 285, *290*
Bennett, D. S., 192, 197, *208*
Bennie, E. H., 228, *238*
Benson, D., 124, 126, *131*
Berenson, A. B., 215, *241*
Bergmann, A., 4–6, *23,* 49, *67*
Bergner, P. E., 227, *233*
Berney, T., 257, 258, *265*
Bernstein, D. A., 121, *131*
Bernstein, G., 244, 248, 249, 251, 252,
    254, 255, 261, *265, 269*
Bertrand, L., 182, *202*
Biederman, J., 179, 181–183, 186–190,
    199, 201, *202, 205, 210–211,* 215,
    219, 224, 225, *232, 242,* 253, 255,
    258, 259, 263, *265, 267,* 277, 279,
    282, 287, *289, 293*
Biggs, J. T., 225, *242*
Bilo, L., 195, *203*
Binder, M., 263, *265*
Bird, H. R., 76, *86,* 181, *203,* 244, 248,
    251, *265*
Birkett, M., 222, *232*
Birmaher, B., 216–220, *232, 236, 238,*
    239, 250, 262, *266,* 287, *292*
Birmaher, M. D., 218, *241*
Bishop, K., 149, 153, *157*
Black, B., 262, *266*
Bloom, W., 283, *292*
Bloomquist, H. K., 274, *289*
Blos, P., 4, 5, *22,* 39, *45,* 49, *66*
Blum, H. M., 75–77, *88*
Bohman, M., 274, *289*

Bolitho, F., 182, *202*
Bond, L. A., 81, *86*
Borchardt, C. M., 244, 248, 254, 255,
    265
Borgstedt, A. D., 183, 184, 200, *207*
Borst, S., 56, *67*
Botteron, K. N., 216, 226–228, 230,
    233, 235
Boulos, C., 187, *203, 207,* 216, 218,
    233, 237
Bower, S., 225, *241*
Bowers, M. B., Jr., 221, *239*
Bowlby, J., 63, *66*
Bowring, M. A., 224, *233*
Boyd, J. H., 244, *268*
Boyle, M. H., 75–77, *88,* 180, *203*
Bradley, S., 262, 263, *267*
Braiman, S., 244, *270*
Bregman, J., 286, *289*
Brent, D., 250, *266*
Brigeglin, C., 287, *291*
Brodsky, L., 230, *240*
Brodsky, M., 262, *266*
Bromet, E. J., 224, *233*
Bronson, M., 283, *292*
Brooks-Gunn, J., 7, *23*
Brosen, K., 220, 221, *233, 236*
Brown, J., 189, 198, *209*
Brown, R. T., 185, *203*
Brown, W. A., 222, *233*
Brownstein, H. H., 76, *87*
Brumaghim, J. T., 183, 200, *207*
Bryt, A., 39, *45*
Bucci, J. P., 286, *293*
Buchanan, C. M., 110, *117*
Buchsbaum, Y., 214, *239*
Buitelar, J. K., 287, *289*
Burd, L., 273, 278, *289, 291*
Burgess, A. G., 183, *208*
Burgess, A. W., 183, *208*
Burke, J., 76, *86,* 213, *233,* 244, *268*
Burke, K., 76, *86,* 213, *233*
Burke, P. M., 248, *268*
Burlingame, G. M., 121, *130*
Burroughs, J., 226, 231, *241*
Busner, J., 183, 184, 199, *206, 207*
Butler, P. M., 256, *268*

Byles, J. A., 75–77, *88*
Byrne, C., 75–77, *88*

C
Cadman, D. T., 75–77, *88*
Caffman, L. M., 188, *209*
Calabrese, J. R., 231, *233*
Calderon, R., 216, *238*
Callaghan, M., 182, *208*
Campbell, M., 190, 193, 194, *203–204,* 227, *233,* 273, 276, 282, 283, *289–291, 293*
Canino, G., 76, *86,* 181, *203,* 244, 248, 251, *265*
Cantwell, D. P., 76, *86,* 190, 199, *204,* 213, *233,* 276, *290*
Caplan, G., 81, *86*
Caplan, R., 275, *290*
Capozzoli, J. A., 190, 191, *206,* 218, *236*
Carlson, D. C., 283, *292*
Carlson, G., 199, *204,* 213, 216, 218, 222, 224, 225, *232,* 233, 234, *241*
Carmody, T., 216, 218, 220, *234*
Carr, L. G., 217, *234*
Carrey, N. J., 283, *293*
Castellanos, F. X., 277, *292*
Chandler, M., 63, *67*
Chappell, P. B., 189, 190, *204*
Chess, S., 274, *290*
Chestnut, E. C., 217, *234*
Christian, K., 219, 220, *238*
Chung, M., 221, *239*
Clarke, G., 214, 218, 225, 238, *241*
Cloninger, C. R., 195, *210*
Coffey, B. J., 253, 256, 257, *266*
Coffin, W. S., 116, *117*
Cohen, D., 189, 190, *204, 206,* 278, 283, 286, *289, 292*
Cohen, I. L., 282, *289, 290*
Cohen, J., 180, *204*
Cohen, P., 75–77, 81, *88, 89,* 180, *204*
Cohler, B. J., 52, *66*
Cole, J. O., 220, *240*
Collins, ., 227, *233*
Colliver, J. D., 182, *211*

Comer, J. P., 81, *86*
Commander, M., 256, *266*
Commings, B. G., 278, *290*
Commings, D. E., 278, *290*
Compas, B. E., 81, *86*
Conner, D. F., 285, *290*
Conners, C. K., 193, *204,* 250, *267*
Connor, D., 189, 190, 195, 199, 201, 202, *204*
Cook, E., 252, 261, *269*
Cook, E. H., Jr., 279, 285, 286, *290, 291*
Coons, H. W., 184, *207*
Cooper, C. R., 37, *46*
Cooper, M. A., 226, *235*
Cooper, T. B., 217, 226–228, *233–235*
Copeland, D. R., 256, *268*
Copping, W., 218, *241*
Corcoran, C. M., 213, *236*
Costello, E. J., 216, *232,* 245, *266*
Cowdry, R. W., 198, *205*
Cowen, E. L., 121, *130*
Cox, A., 276, *289*
Coyle, J. T., 218, *236*
Crawford, J. W., 75–77, *88*
Crossette, B., 170, *171*
Crouse-Novak, M., 213, *237*
Crowley, T. J., 184, 188, *209*
Cueva, J. E., 194, *204*
Cuffe, S. P., 222, *234*
Cully, M., 250, 262, *266*
Cummings, N. A., 122–123, 128, *130*
Curtis, S., 182, *203*

D
Dachille, S., 220, 221, *240*
Damore, J., 193, 194, *204*
Danforth, H., 226, *241*
Dantzer, R., 253, *266*
David-Lando, G., 275, *290*
Davidson, J., 222, *237, 241*
Davies, M., 244, *270*
DeAntonio, M., 225, *241*
DeBattista, C., 220, *240*
Delaney, M. A., 192, 193, 196, *208*
Delito, J. A., 193, 194, *204*

Dell, L., 183, *206*
DeLong, G. R., 226, *234*
Delpit, L., 110, *117*
Delucchi, G. A., 231, *233*
Demaso, D. R., 286, *293*
Denckla, M. B., 189, 198, *209*
Detrinis, R. B., 218, *236*
DeVane, C. L., 189, *207*
Diamond, B. L., 169, *171*
Dicker, R., 192, 193, *209*
Dinicola, V. F., 218, *241*
Dolinsky, A., 244, *270*
Domeshek, L. J., 259–261, *268*
Donovan, S. J., 193, 194, *205*
Douglass, R., 76, *87*
Dryfoos, J., 75, 77, 78, *87,* 121, *130*
Dubois, C., 216, *237,* 255, 256, 260, 261, *269*
Dulcan, M., 182, 198, *205*
Dulit, E., 299, *311*
Dummit, E. S., 262, *266*
Durlak, J. A., 128, *130*

E
Earls, F., 79, *87*
Eccles, J. S., 110, *117*
Edelbrock, C. S., 181, *202*
Edvinsson, S. O., 274, *289*
Efron, D., 185, *205*
Eison, A. S., 259, *266*
Elia, J., 197, *207*
Ellickson, P. L., 75, 80, *87*
Elliot, G., 110, *117,* 187, *205,* 217, *234*
Elterich, G., 216, *232*
Emde, R., 11, *23*
Emslie, G., 216, 218, 220, *234, 241*
English, A., 84, *87*
Enzer, N., 80, *89*
Epstein, J., 151, *158*
Erikson, E. H., 4, *23,* 49, 50, 55–58, 60–61, *66*
Eriksson, I., 279, *291*
Erlenmeyer-Kimling, L., 273, *291*
Ernst, M., 190, *204*
Escoll, P., 4–6, *23*
Esman, A., 31, *46*

Eth, S., 170, *172*
Evans, J., 273, *290*
Evans, S. E., 183, 184, *205, 209*
Ewing, C., 143, *157*

F
Fagan, J., 153, *157*
Fairbanks, J. M., 262, *266*
Fallahi, C., 213, *236*
Famularo, R., 253, *266*
Faraone, S., 181, 182, *203,* 215, 224, 225, *232, 242*
Faust, D., 120, *131*
Fava, M., 222, *241*
Fay, A., 121, *131*
Feehan, M., 244, 248, 250, 251, *267*
Feinberg, T. L., 213, *237*
Feldman, M., 150, *158*
Feldman, S., 110, *117*
Fennig, S., 224, *233*
Fenton, T., 253, *266*
Ferguson, H. B., 216, 218, *237, 241,* 254–256, *269*
Ferro, T., 222, *234*
Fetner, H. H., 227, *234*
Findling, R., 221, *238,* 283, *290*
Fine, C., 181, *203*
Fine, E. M., 181, *209*
Finkelstein, R., 213, *237*
Finney, J. W., 120, *132*
Fischer, K. W., 55, *68*
Fischer, M., 181, *202*
Fish, B., 227, *233*
Fisher, M., 297, 298, *311*
Fisher, P., 76, *89,* 216, *240*
Fisher, W. W., *289*
Fitzpatrick, P. A., 183, 200, *207*
Flaherty, L. T., 120, 125, *131*
Flavell, J. H., 160, *171*
Fleming, J. E., 180, *203*
Fletcher, K. E., 181, *202,* 285, *290, 291*
Flood, J. G., 187, *211*
Flory, M., 76, *89*
Foot, P., 170, *171*
Francis, G., 244, 246, *266*
Franck, G., 259, 260, *265*

Frankel, L. S., 255, *268*
Frankhauser, M. P., 285, *290*
Fras, I., 191, *205*
Frazier, C., 149, 153, *157*
Frazier, J., 225, 226, *235,* 277, 283, 284, *291, 292*
Freed, J., 287, *292*
Freedman, D. X., 278, 279, *289, 290*
Freedman, M., 116, *117*
Freeling, K., 151, *158*
Freeman, B. J., 273, *292*
Freeman, R., 225, 226, *241*
Freud, A., 4, *23,* 51, *66*
Freud, S., 4, 7, *23,* 51, *66*
Fried, J., 220, 221, *240*
Friedman, I., 76, *87,* 297, 298, *311*
Friedman, L. M., 219, 220, *238*
Friesen, S., 221, *238*
Fristad, M. A., 225, 226, *242*
Fritz, G., 301, *311*
Fruehling, J., 199, *206*
Furman, E., 5, *23*

G
Gadow, K. D., 202, *205*
Gaines, R., 27, 30, *45*
Galatzer-Levy, R., 4–6, *23*
Gallagher, S., 75, 76, 86, *87*
Gallant, D. M., 283, *292*
Garcia, M., 219, 220, *236*
Gardner, D., 198, *205,* 218, *233*
Gardner, D. M., 255–261, *267*
Garfinkel, B. D., 254, 255, *265*
Garfinkel, L., 229, *234*
Garfinkel, M., 229, 231, *234, 235*
Garland, A., 82, *87, 89*
Garland, E. J., 194, *205*
Garrison, C. Z., 222, *234*
Garrison, E. G., 120, *131*
Gastfriend, D. R., 186, *205*
Gatsonis, C., 76, *87,* 216, 222, *237*
Gauthier, B., 255, 256, *269*
Geist, D. E., 186, 199, *211*
Gelenberg, A., 227, *234*
Geller, B., 195, *205,* 216–218, 224–228, 230, *233–235, 240, 241*

Geller, E., 276, *293*
Gendreau, P. L., 180, *210*
George, L. K., 244, *268*
Gephart, J., 77, *88*
Geraets, I., 260, 261, *269*
Gerard, M. A., 259, 260, *265*
German, M. L., 285, *290*
Gershon, S., 226, 229, *240*
Ghazinddin, M., 273, 278, 279, *290, 293*
Ghuman, H., 120, 127, *132*
Gillberg, C., 200, *205,* 272, 274, 279, *289–291*
Gilligan, C., 33, *46,* 52, *67,* 110, *117,* 163, *172*
Gish, B., 275, *290*
Gittleman-Klein, R., 257, *266–267*
Glantz, M. D., 182, *211*
Glaser, G., 76, *88*
Gleicher, H. B., 78, 79, *88*
Gnagy, E., 183, 184, *209*
Goethals, G., 53, *68*
Goldstein, P. J., 76, *87*
Goldston, D., 216, *237*
Gonzalez, A., 189, 191, *210*
Gonzalez, N., 190, *204*
Goodman, G., 122, *131*
Goodman, S. H., 75, 77, 81, *88*
Goodman, W., 244, *268*
Goodyer, I. M., 216, *235*
Gordon, C., 277, 283, 286, *291, 292*
Gorman, J., 284, *289*
Gould, M. S., 76, *86, 89,* 181, *203,* 216, *240,* 244, 248, 251, *265*
Graae, F., 254, 255, *267*
Graham, D., 216, *235*
Gram, L. F., 220, *236*
Grayson, P., 222, *234*
Green, S. H., 256, *266*
Green, W. H., 186, 190, *205,* 226, 228, *235,* 273, *291*
Greenacre, P., 7, *23*
Greenberg, J. R., 26, *46*
Greenblatt, D. J., 220, *235*
Greenhill, L., 184, 185, *210,* 287, *292*
Greenstein, J., 183, 184, *208*
Grega, D. M., 273, *291*

Greist, J. H., 226, *236*
Griffin, S., 190, *210*
Grisso, T., 154, *157*
Groethe, D., 287, *291*
Groh, C., 193, *206*
Grossman, J. A., 214, *239*
Grotevant, H. D., 37, *46*
Grover, W., 276, *293*
Guevremont, D. C., 181, *202*
Gustavson, K. H., 274, *289*
Guthrie, D., 216, *232,* 275, *290*
Gutierrez-Casares, J. R., 218, *240*

H
Hadley, S. W., 121, *131*
Haffey, W. G., 121, *130*
Hagberg, B., 279, *291*
Hager, R., 143, *157*
Hajal, F., 193, 194, *204*
Halbreich, U., 222, 237, *241*
Halperin, S. F., 76, *87*
Hamburger, S., 197, *207,* 277, 283, 284, *291, 292*
Hamel, L., 190, 191, *206*
Hammond, R. W., 216, *240*
Han, Y., 120, 127, *132*
Hansen, C. R., 278, *289*
Hansen, J. G., 221, *233*
Hardesty, A. S., 273, *291*
Hardin, M. T., 263, *269*
Harding, M., 190, *210*
Harmatz, J., 186, *202,* 220, *235*
Harrington, M., 155, *157*
Harrison, R. J., 189, 199, 201, 202, *204*
Harrison, W., 222, *233, 241*
Härtter, S., 220, *235*
Hastings, E., 120, 127, *132*
Heath, J., 226, *235*
Hellerstein, D. J., 222, *237*
Hendren, R. L., 183, *206*
Henggeler, S., 153, *157*
Heninger, G. R., 286, *292*
Henry, D., 182, *208*
Herbert, M. B., 216, *235*
Herian, D., 287, *291*
Herrmann, K. J., 187, 188, *202*

Hersen, M., 244, 246, 248, *267, 269*
Herzog, D. B., 191, *210*
Hibbs, E. D., 197, *207*
Hickey, P., 122, *131*
Hicks, R., 82, *89*
Hiemke, C., 220, *235*
Higgins, R., 53, *68*
Hightower, A. D., 121, *130*
Hill, J. C., 180, *206*
Himmelhoch, J., 229, 231, 234, *235,*
Hitzemann, R., 279, *292*
Hoagwood, K., 201, 202, *211*
Hodde-Vargas, J. E., 183, *206*
Hoder, E. L., 278, *289*
Hoeper, E. W., 213, *236*
Holmes, J., 283, *292*
Holmgren, G., 274, *289*
Holttum, J., 226, 229, *240*
Hops, H., 213, *238*
Hornig, C. D., 244, 246, *269*
Horowitz, H., 170, *172*
Horrigan, J. P., 190, *206*
Horst, E., 53n, 57, *67*
Horwitz, S. M., 75, 77, 81, *88*
Hoven, C. W., 75, 77, 81, *88*
Huertas-Goldman, S., 181, *203,* 244, 248, 251, *265*
Hughes, C. W., 216, 218, 220, *234*
Hulsizer, D., 58, *67*
Hunt, J., 197, *211*
Hunt, R. D., 189, *206*
Hurley, M., 149, *157*
Hynd, G. W., 182, *209*

I
Iancu, I., 263, *265*
Ingram, J., 262, *266*
Inhelder, B., 12, *23*
Isaac, G., 224, *236*
Isaac, M. T., 195, *210*
Isojarvi, J. I. T., 194, 195, *206,* 229, *236*
Iyengar, S., 214, *240*

J
Jackson, C., 123, *132*
Jackson, K. L., 222, *234*

Jacobs, D., 76–77, *88*
Jacobsen, L., 277, 284, 287, *291, 292*
Jacobson, E., 7, *23*
Jacobson, S. J., 226, *236*
Jain, U., 219, 220, *236*
Jarman, F., 185, *205*
Jaselski, C., 285, 286, *290, 291*
Jefferson, J. W., 226, *236*
Jellinek, M. S., 186, *205*
Jensen, P. S., 202, *206*
Jenson, W. R., 273, *292*
Jeppsen, U., 220, *236*
Jetton, J. G., 182, *203*
Jiang, H., 259–261, *268*
John, R., 228, *238*
Johnson, J., 76, *89,* 244, 246, *269, 270*
Johnson, K., 226, *236,* 255, *268*
Johnston, H. F., 199, *206*
Jones, E., 39, *46*
Jones, K., 226, *236*
Jones, M. B., 273, *292*
Joorabchi, B., 253, *267*
Jordan, J., 52, *67*
Jorde, L. B., 273, *292*
Joshi, A. R. T., 190, 191, *206*
Joshi, P. T., 190, 191, *206,* 218, *236*

K
Kalikow, K., 244, *270*
Kalogerakis, M., 153, *157*
Kanner, A., 258, *267*
Kantor, S., 42, *46*
Kaplan, L. J., 4, *23,* 39, *46*
Kaplan, S. L., 183, 184, 199, 202, *206–207*
Karajgi, B., 192, 193, *209*
Karambelkar, J., 216, *232*
Karno, M., 244, *268*
Karp, B. I., 284, *291*
Karumanchi, S. D., 285, *290*
Karumanchi, V. C., 285, *290*
Kasen, S., 180, *204*
Kashani, J. H., 213, *236,* 244, 246–248, 250, 251, *267*
Katic, M., 216, 228, *237, 239*

Kaufman, J., 250, *266*
Kay, S. R., 197, *207*
Kazchin, A. E., 248, *269*
Kazdin, A. E., 244, 246, *267*
Keary, A., 155, *157*
Keck, P. E., 231, *242*
Keck, P. E., Jr., 229, 231, *238–239*
Keller, M. B., 218, *236*
Keller, M. D., 218, *241*
Kelly, J., 244, 248, 250, 251, *267*
Kelly, K. L., 199, *204*
Kemph, J. P., 189, *207*
Kentgen, L. M., 262, *266*
Kerbeshian, I., 273, *289*
Kerbeshian, J., 278, *289, 291*
Kessler, R. C., 213, *236*
Keys, S. G., 120, *131*
Keysor, C. S., 197, *207*
Khan, A., 191, *210*
Khandelwal, S. K., 227, *236*
Khetarpal, S., 250, *266*
Kiely, K., 224, 225, *242*
Kilkenny, R., 56, *68*
King, B. H., 283, *291*
King, C. A., 222, *240*
King, R., 263, *265, 269*
Kinscherff, R., 253, *266*
Klass, E., 184, *207*
Klein, D., 257, *266–267*
Klein, D. F., 193, 194, *205,* 277, *289*
Klein, D. N., 222, 224, *234, 237, 238*
Klein, R. G., 184, 192, *202, 207,* 216, 218, *236,* 241, 254–262, *266–267,* 277, *289*
Kleinman, M., 76, *89*
Klorman, R., 183, 184, 200, *207*
Klykylo, W. M., 279, *292*
Knee, D., 186, *202*
Knott, V., 255, 256, 260, 261, *269*
Kobayashi, R., 275, *291*
Kocsis, J. H., 222, *237, 241*
Koehler-Troy, C., 225, *237*
Kohlberg, L., 57, *68,* 162, *172*
Kolvin, I., 273, *291*
Koplewicz, H. S., 216, *241,* 258, *267*
Koppelman, J., 69, *73,* 124, *131*
Koran, L., 222, *241*

Kovacs, M., 76, *87,* 213, 215, 216, 222, 224, 225, *233, 237*
Kowatch, R. A., 216, 218, 220, *234*
Kraepelin, E., 222, *237*
Kramer, M., 244, *268*
Kramer, R., 193, *204*
Kranzler, H. R., 259, 260, *267*
Krishnamoorthy, J., 283, *291*
Kruesi, M. J. P., 179, 181, 183, 189, 192, 193, 197, 198, 200, 201, *207, 209, 210*
Kumra, S., 277, 283, 284, 287, *291–292*
Kupeitz, S., 184, *206*
Kuperman, S., 187, 188, *202*
Kusiak, K. A., 199, *204*
Kutcher, S., 187, *203, 207,* 216, 218, 228, *233, 237,* 239, *241,* 253, 255–261, *267, 268*
Kwasnik, D., 182, *202*
Kye, C., 217, *238*

L
Laatikainen, T. J., 194, 195, *206,* 229, *236*
LaLonde, C., 63, *67*
Lampert, C., 225, 226, 231, *241*
Langley, J. D., 182, *208*
Lanza-Kaduce, L., 153, *157*
Lara, M. E., 75, *87*
Last, C. G., 244, 246, 248, *265–267, 269*
Latz, J. R., 191, *207*
Laughren, T. P., 202, *206*
Lavik, N. J., 256, *268*
Lazarus, A. A., 121, *131*
Lazarus, J. H., 228, *238*
Leaf, P. J., 75, 77, 81, *88*
Lear, J. G., 69, *73,* 78, 79, *88,* 124, 125, *131*
LeBot, M. A., 220, *232*
Leckman, J. F., 189, 190, *204,* 244, *268*
Lee, P., 284, *291*
Lelio, D. F., 181, 189, 192, 193, 198, *207, 210*
Lelon, E., 215, *232*
Lenane, M., 277, 283–284, *291, 292*

Lennon, S., 287, *292*
Leonard, H., 202, *206,* 252, 261, *269*
Leong, G. B., 169, 170, *172–173*
Levanthal, B. L., 279, 285, 286, *290, 291*
Leverich, G. S., 231, *239*
Levin, G. M., 189, *207*
Levine, M., 143, *157*
Levitan, J., 193, 194, *204*
Levy-Warren, M. H., 4, *23*
Lewinsohn, P. M., 76, *89,* 213, 214, 222, 224, 225, *237, 238, 240*
Lewis, D., 76, *88,* 150, *158*
Liebowitz, M. R., 244, 246, *269*
Lifton, R. J., 61, *67*
Lightfoot, S. L., 110, *117*
Links, P. S., 75–77, *88*
Locke, B. Z., 244, *268*
Luby, J., 216, 224, 225, *235*
Luebbert, J. F., 192, 193, 196, 197, *208*
Lupatkin, W., 216, 217, *239*
Lynch, K. A., 189, 190, *204*

M
Ma, Y., 285, *290*
Macbeth, J. A., 165, *172*
Mackenzie, S., 253, *267*
Magnus, R. D., 221, *238*
Mahler, M. S., 4–6, *23,* 49, *67*
Major, L. F., 191, *205*
Malanga, C. J., 284, *291*
Malone, R. P., 192, 193, 196, 197, *208*
Manassis, K., 262, 263, *267*
Mandoki, M. W., 220, 221, *238*
March, J. S., 250, 252, 261, 263, *267, 269*
Marcus, R., 221, *238*
Marcus, S. C., 200, *208*
Marks, R. E., 191, *202*
Marohn, R. C., 1–2, *2,* 4–6, *23,* 25–26, *46*
Martin, J., 216, *240,* 262, *266*
Marton, P., 187, *203,* 216, *237*
Mason-Brothers, A., 273, *292*
Masters, K., 190, *208*
Mattes, J., 193, *208*

Mattison, R., 301, *311*
Mawhood, L., 276, *290*
Maxwell, K., 283, *290*
Mazuire, C. M., 221, *239*
Mazzie, R., 220, 221, *240*
McAdams, D. P., 61, *67*
McAllister, J. A., 213, *236*
McCarthy, J. F., 83, *89*
McCauley, E., 216, *238, 248, 268*
McClellan, J., 277, *292*
McConville, B. J., 219, 220, 231, *238, 242*
McCracken, J. T., 191, *207*
McDonald, J., 110, *117*
McDougle, C., 283, 286, *292*
McElroy, S. L., 229, 231, *238–239, 242*
McGee, R., 182, *208*, 244, 246, 248, 250, 251, *265, 267*
McGlashan, T. H., 224, *239*
McGronagle, K. A., 213, *236*
McHugh, T., 229, *234*
McKenna, K., 277, 283, *291, 292*
McKenzie, N. S., 250, *266*
McKeown, R. E., 222, *234*
McLaughlin, J., 151, *158*
McLeer, S. V., 182, *208*
McMahon, W. M., 273, *292*
McManus, M. A., 77, *88*
McNabb, J., 216, *232*
McPhedran, P., 278, *289*
Meehl, P. E., 120, *131*
Mehta, K., 75, 76, 86, *87*
Meier, D., 110, *117*
Meier, M., 282, *289*
Melanbaum, R., 225, *237*
Melander, H., 200, *205*
Mellits, E. D., 189, 198, *209*
Melloni, R. H., 189, 199, 201, 202, *204*
Melo, R., 195, *203*
Melton, G., 153, *157*
Mennin, D., 224, 225, *242*
Meyer, D. A., 225, *242*
Meyer, V., 220, 221, *240*
Michalos, C., 170, *172*
Mick, E., 182, *203*, 215, *232*
Midgley, C., 110, *117*
Mielke, D. H., 283, *292*

Mikalauskas, K., 231, *239*
Mikulich, S. K., 184, 188, *209*
Milich, R., 121, *131*
Miller, M. O., 154, *157*
Miller, R. D., 170, *172*
Miller, W., 260, 261, *269*
Milner, J., 254, 255, *267*
Minderaa, R. B., 189, *206, 278, 289*
Minnery, K. L., 219, 220, 231, *238, 242*
Mitchell, J., 216, *238, 248, 268*
Mitchell, S. A., 26, *46*
Mo, A., 273, *292*
Moffitt, T. E., 77, *88*
Moreau, D., 76, *89*
Morishima, A., 299, *311*
Morrell, W., 226, 231, *241*
Moscoso, M., 181, *203, 244, 248, 251, 265*
Moss, S. J., 248, *268*
Mullins, D., 256, *268*
Munasifi, F., 230, *240*
Mundy, E., 224, 225, *242*
Murata, T., 275, *291*
Murphy, D. A., 183, 184, *208*
Murphy, K. R., 182, *202*
Murphy, M., 58, *67*
Murphy, S. M., 261, *268*
Murrill, L. M., 197, *207*
Murthy, R. S., 227, *236*
Musick, J. S., 52, *66*
Myers, C. P., 120, 127, *132*
Myers, J. K., 244, *268*
Myers, K., 216, *238*
Myers, W., 183, *208*

N
Nada-Raja, S., 182, *208*
Nagahata, M., 282, *292*
Nakane, Y., 282, *292*
Nappi, C., 195, *203*
Narrow, W. E., 75, 77, 81, *88*
Naruse, H., 282, *292*
Nasr, F. N., 216, *232*
Naylor, M., 222, *240*
Naylor, S. T., 286, *292*
Neer, S., 216, 266

Nelson, J., 221, *239,* 286, *291*
Nestadt, G., 244
Newacheck, P. W., 77, *88*
Newcorn, J., 181, *203*
Nicolson, R., 283, *292*
Nielson, K. K., 221, *233*
Nietzel, M. T., 121, *131*
Noam, G., 53, 55, 57, 58, 63, 64, *67–68*
Noyes, R., 188, *202*
Nunes, E. V., 193, 194, *205*
Nye, S., 156, *158*

O

Obrosky, S., 222, *237*
O'Donnell, D., 190, *210*
Offer, D., 4, *23,* 53, *68*
Offord, D. R., 75–77, 80, *88,* 180, *203*
Ogbu, J. U., 52, *68*
Olfson, M., 200, *208*
Oligny, P., 180, *210*
Ollendick, T. H., 120, *132*
Olsen, L., 123, *132*
Orrison, W. W., 183, *206*
Orvaschel, H., 244, 246–248, 250, 251,
    267
Overall, J. E., 194, *204,* 255, *268*
Overton, W. R., 170, *172*
Owen, R., 261, *268*
Ozbayrak, K. R., 189, 199, 201, 202,
    204, 285, *290*

P

Padron-Gayol, M., 273, *291*
Pagan, A., 181, *203,* 244, 248, 251, *265*
Pakarinen, A. J., 194, 195, *206,* 229,
    236
Papart, P., 259, 260, *265*
Papatheodorou, G., 218, 228, *239, 241*
Parker, J. D. A., 250, *267*
Parker, J. L., 220, 221, *238*
Parson, T., 84, *88*
Partridge, F., 244, 248, 250, 251, *267*
Pataki, C. S., 199, *204*
Paulauskas, S., 76, *87,* 213, *237*
Pauls, D. L., 244, *268*
Peabody, R., 151, *158*

Pearson, J., 216, *235*
Pederson, W., 256, *268*
Pedro-Carroll, J. L., 121, *130*
Pelham, W. E., 183–184, *205, 208, 209*
Pelton, G. H., 283, *292*
Penuel, W. R., 54, 62, *68*
Perel, J., 216, 217, *232, 239*
Perrin, S., 244, 246, *267*
Perry, P. J., 187, 188, *202*
Perry, R., 194, *204*
Petersen, P. B., 273, *292*
Peterson, A. C., 33, *46*
Peterson, B. S., 183, *208*
Pfeffer, C. R., 259–261, *268*
Pfefferbaum, B., 255, 256, *268*
Pfister, K., 182, *203*
Philips, I., 80, *89*
Piaget, J., 12, *23, 24*
Pincus, H. A., 200, *208*
Pincus, J., 76, *88,* 150, *158*
Pine, D. S., 262, *266,* 277, *289*
Pine, F., 4–6, *23,* 49, *67*
Pingree, C., 273, *292*
Poh, C., 227, *233*
Poillion, M. J., 122, *131*
Pollack, S., 168, *172*
Pollock, M., 225, *237*
Pool, D., 283, *292*
Pope, H. G., 231, *239*
Popper, C. W., 187, 199, *205, 208,* 217,
    234
Porter, P. J., 78, 79, *88*
Posner, D., 282, *290*
Post, R. M., 231, *239*
Powell, J., 79, *87*
Powers, S., 56, *68*
Poznanski, E. O., 214, *239*
Prendergast, M., 256, *266*
Preskorn, S. H., 217, 221, *238, 239*
Price, D. T., 217, *234*
Price, L., 283, 286, *292*
Prichep, L., 150, *158*
Pries, R., 76–77, *88*
Puente, R., 193, *208*
Puig-Antich, J., 214, 216, 217, 220,
    221, *239, 240*
Puopolo, P. R., 187, *211*

Q

Quaskey, S., 189, 198, *209*
Quintana, H., 216, *232,* 287, *292*
Quitkin, F. M., 193, 194, *205*

R

Rabinovich, H., 220, 221, *240*
Racine, Y., 180, *203*
Rae, D., 76, *86,* 213, *233,* 244, *268*
Rae-Grant, N. I., 75–77, *88*
Ragueneau, I., 220, *232*
Rahdert, E., 182, *211*
Rakel, R. E., 261, *268*
Rall, T. W., 256, *268*
Rao, U., 216, *232, 239–240,* 259, 260, *270*
Rapaport, M. D., 199, *204*
Rapaport, J., 179, 197, *207, 209,* 244, *270,* 277, 283, 284, *291, 292*
Rasmussen, B. B., 220, *236*
Rasmussen, S., 244, *268*
Ratner, R., 151, 156, *158*
Ratzoni, G., 263, *265*
Reed, K., 216, *237*
Reeder, A. I., 182, *208*
Reftoff, S., 182, *211*
Regier, D., 75, 76, 77, 81, 86, *88,* 213, *233,* 244, *268*
Reich, T., 224, *240*
Reid, J. C., 213, *236*
Reiter, S., 255–261, *267, 268*
Resnicow, K., 83, *89*
Reuman, D., 110, *117*
Rey, J. M., 180, *209*
Rey-Sanchez, F., 218, *240*
Reynolds, C. R., 250, *268*
Ribera, J., 181, *203,* 244, 248, 251, *265*
Ricciuti, A., 197, *211*
Rice, J., 224, *240*
Richards, C., 76, *87,* 222, *237*
Richardson, E., 150, *158*
Richmond, B. O., 250, *268*
Riddle, M. A., 189, 190, *204,* 217, *240,* 252, 261, 263, *265, 269*
Rifkin, A., 192, 193, *209*
Riggs, P. D., 184, 188, *209*

Rintelmann, J., 216, 218, 220, *234*
Ritvo, E. R., 273, *292*
Rizzotto, L., 254, 255, *267*
Robbins, D. M., 76–77, *88*
Roberts, N., 216, *237,* 255, 256, *269*
Roberts, R. E., 213, *238, 240*
Robins, L. N., 79, 80, *87, 89,* 244, *268*
Rohde, P., 76, *89,* 214, 225, *238*
Roniger, J. J., Jr., 283, *292*
Roose, S. P., 220, *232*
Rosenbaum, J., 222, *237, 241*
Rosenberg, D. R., 226, 229, *240*
Rosenberg, L. A., 189, 198, *209*
Rosenberg, T. K., 213, *236*
Rosenstein, D., 170, *172*
Rosner, R., 142, *142,* 168, *172*
Ross, D. L., 279, *292*
Rothschild, G. H., 193, *204*
Rowlette, R., 286, *290*
Rubio-Stipec, M., 181, *203,* 244, 248, 251, *265*
Rundell, J. R., 215, *242*
Rush, J., 216, 218, 220, *234*
Rutter, M., 273, 276, *289, 290, 293*
Ryan, N., 214, 216, 217–221, 232, *236, 238,* 239, *240–242,* 262, *266*
Ryan, P. J., 76, *87*
Ryback, R. S., 240, *240*

S

Sachar, E. J., 282, *289*
Safer, D. J., 181, 200, 202, *209*
Sales, B., 154, *157*
Salzman, C., 256, *269*
Samit, C., 282, *289*
Sanchez-Lacay, A., 181, *203,* 244, 248, 251, *265*
Sanford, M., 180, *203*
Scahill, L., 189, 190, *204,* 263, *269*
Schafer, R., 4, 5, *24,* 34, *46*
Schatzberg, A. F., 220, *240*
Schecter, D., 28, 29, *46*
Schimel, J., 42, *46*
Schlitt, J., 69, *73,* 125, *131*
Schloredt, K., 216, *238*
Schmidt-Lackner, S., 225, *241*

Schneier, F. R., 244, 246, *269*
Schoener, E. P., 180, *206*
Schonberg, S. K., 297, 298, *311*
Schonert-Reichl, K., 53, *68*
Schoonover, S. C., 227, *234*
Schreier, H. A., 191, *209*
Schuchter, M. D., 217, *234*
Schultze, E., 189, 190, *204*
Schumacher, E., 188, *202*
Schwartz, H., 142, *142*
Scott, K., 183, *208*
Secher, S. M., 216, *235*
Seeley, J. R., 76, *89,* 213, 214, 222, 224, 225, *237–238, 240*
Seizman, A., 263, *265*
Seligman, S., 57, *68*
Semrad, E., 109, *117*
Semrud-Clikeman, M., 182, *209*
Sesman, M., 181, *203,* 244, 248, 251, *265*
Sexon, S. B., 185, *203*
Shader, R. I., 220, *235*
Shafer, M. E., 123, *132*
Shaffer, D., 76, 80, 82, *87, 89,* 216, *240,* 244, *270*
Shain, B. N., 222, *240*
Shanock, S., 76, *88*
Shanok, R., 57, *68*
Shapiro, R., 28, *46*
Shapiro, T., 31, *46,* 227, *233*
Shaw, K., 249, 251, *265*
Shay, J., 276, *289*
Shell, J., 273, *291*
Shelton, R., 222, *237*
Sherbourne, C. D., 75, *87*
Shirahash, K., 282, *292*
Siegel, M. G., 120, *131*
Sienna, M., 181, *203*
Silva, J. A., 169, 170, *172–173*
Silva, P. A., 244, 246, 248, 250, 251, *265, 267*
Silva, R., 190, *204*
Simeon, J., 216, *237*
Siméon, J. G., 218, *241,* 254–257, 260, 261, *269,* 283, *293*
Simms, R. M., 199, *207*
Simpson, G. M., 227, *233*

Singer, H. S., 189, 198, *209*
Slater, E., 302, *311*
Sloman, L., 283, *292*
Small, A. M., 193, 194, *203, 204,* 282, *289, 290*
Smallish, L., 181, *202*
Smith, A., 277, 283, 284, *291, 292*
Smith, B. H., 183, 184, *209*
Smith, C., 76–77, *88*
Smith, L., 153, *157*
Snarey, J., 57, *68*
Soriano, J., 182, *203*
Sorter, M. T., 219, 220, 231, *238, 242*
Sparrow, S. S., 273, *293*
Spencer, E. K., 283, *293*
Spencer, T., 182, 186, 188–190, 199, 201, *210–211,* 279, 282, *289*
Spindler, G., 110, *117*
Spindler, L., 110, *117*
Spirito, A., 301, *311*
Sprich, S., 181, *203*
Springer, C., 156, *158*
Srendsen, P., 279, *291*
St. Germaine, A., 78, 79, *88*
Staghezza, B., 76, *86*
Stallings, P., 250, *267*
State, R., 286, *291*
Stedge, D., 284, 287, *289, 292*
Stefanatos, G. A., 276, *293*
Steidel, J. H., 170, *172*
Stein, M. A., 182, *211*
Steinberg, D., 273, *293*
Steinberg, L., 110, *117*
Steiner, H., 194, 201, *210*
Steingard, R., 182, 186, 188–191, 199, *210, 211,* 286, 287, *293*
Stern, D. N., 6, 7, *24*
Stewart, J. W., 193, 194, *205*
Stewart, M., 299, *311*
Stiffman, A. R., 79, *87*
Stoewe, J. K., 181, 183, 189, 193, 201, *210*
Stoff, D., 197, *211*
Stott, F. M., 52, *66*
Strakowski, S. M., 231, *242*
Strauss, C. C., 244, 246, 248, *265, 266, 269*

Strober, M., 218, 224–226, 231, *233, 236, 237, 241, 242*
Strupp, H. H., 121, *131*
Suarez-Orozco, C., 51, *68*
Suarez-Orozco, M., 51, *68*
Sugai, K., 257, *269*
Sullivan, A., 110, *117*
Sullivan, H. S., 26, 28, 31, 36, 39, *46–47*
Sullivan, K., 250, *267*
Sullivan, M. R., 255, *268*
Summer, G. S., 220, 221, *238*
Sun, K., 225, 226, *235*
Susser, E. S., 193, 194, *205*
Svadjian, H., 224, 228, 229, *242*
Swanson, J., 184, 185, 190, 199, *204, 210*, 252, 261, *269*
Szalai, J., 216, 228, *239, 237*
Szasz, T. S., 122, *131*
Szatmari, P., 75–77, *88*, 180, *203*, 273, *293*

T
Takesada, M., 282, *292*
Tallmadge, J., 77, *89*
Tamplin, A., 216, *235*
Tancer, N. K., 216, *241*, 262, *266*
Tanguay, P., 275, *290*
Tanner, J. M., 10, *24*
Tapia, M. A., 220, 221, *238*
Tapia, M. R., 220, 221, *238*
Taylor, A., 181, *203*
Taylor, C., 58, *67*
Taylor, J., 110, *117*
Taylor, L., 82, *89*
Temple, D. L., 259, *266*
Terenius, L., 279, *291*
Tereszkiewicz, L., 84, *87*
Thase, M. E., 222, *232, 241*
Thatte, S., 260, 261, *269*
Thomas, B., 226, *235*
Thomas, H., 75–77, *88*
Thompson, J. W., 200, *208*
Thompson, L. L., 184, *209*
Thornell, A., 182, *203*
Todd, R. D., 216, *235*

Tome, M. B., 195, *210*
Torres, D., 220, 221, *240*
Trad, P., 36, *47*
Trautman, P., 76, *89, 299, 311*
Treder, R., 216, *238*
Tremblay, R., 180, *210*
Triebel, D., 282, *290*
Trommer, B., 182, *211*
Tsai, L. Y., 273, 278, 279, *290, 293*
Tucker, S. G., 226, *242*
Turbott, S. H., 191, *202*
Tyrer, P., 261, *268*

U
Uhde, T. W., 262, *266*
Uris, P. F., 120, *131*

V
Vaden-Kiernan, M., 75, 77, 81, *88*
Vaillant, G. E., 63, *68*
Vallano, G., 183, *208*
Van Engeland, H., 287, *289*
Vargas, L.A. 183, *206*
Varley, C. K., 184, 185, *210*
Varma, V. K., 227, *236*
Vaughan, R. D., 83, *89*
Velez, C. N., 76, *89*
Verda, M., 188, *202*
Vestergaard, P., 227, *241*
Vieland, V., 82, *89*
Viesselman, J. O., 226, *241*
Vigil, J. D., 54, *68*
Vistisen, K., 220, *236*
Vitaro, F., 180, *210*
Vitiello, B., 197, 201–202, *206, 211*
Vodde-Hamilton, M., 183, 184, *208*
Volkmar, F., 273, 275, 278, 283, 286, *289, 292, 293*
von Frenckell, R., 259, 260, *265*
von Knorring, A., 200, *205*
von Moltke, L. L., 220, *235*

W
Wagner, K. D., 215, 218, 219, *232, 236, 241*
Wahlstrom, J., 274, *289*

Walkup, J. T., 218, *236*
Waller, J. L., 222, *234*
Walsh, T., 244, *270*
Walter, H. J., 83, *89*
Ward, B., 187, *207,* 216, *237*
Warner, B. S., 125, *131*
Warner, V., 250, *269*
Warren, M. P., 7, *23*
Waterman, G. S., 216, *232,* 262, *266*
Waterman, P., 83, *89*
Waterman, S., 217, *238*
Watson, J. P., 195, *210*
Waxman, R., 120, 124, 126, 127, *131*
Weber, W., 182, *203*
Webster, M., 301, *311*
Weigmann, H., 220, *235*
Weinberg, N. Z., 182, *211*
Weinberg, W. A., 216, 218, 220, *234*
Weinstock, R., 169, 170, *172–173*
Weisburg, H., 151, *158*
Weiss, R. E., 182, *211*
Weissman, M. M., 214, 216, *240, 242,* 244, 246, 250, *269*
Weist, M., 75, 79, *89,* 120, 123–128, *131–132*
Welikson, M., 284, *289*
Weller, E., 214, 217, 218, 224–226, 228, 229, *236, 239, 241, 242*
Weller, R. A., 214, 217, 224–226, 228, 229, *239, 241, 242*
Wender, E. W., 181, *211*
Werry, J., 190, *204,* 273, 277, *292, 293*
Wertsch, J. V., 54, 62, *68*
West, S. A., 219, 220, 231, *238, 242*
Whitaker, A., 244, *270,* 284, *289*
Whitmore, E. A., 184, *209*
Whittle, B., 82, *87, 89*
Wickramaratne, P., 214, *242,* 250, *269*
Wigal, S., 184, 185, *210*
Wigfield, A., 110, *117*
Wiggins, D., 255, 256, 260, 261, *269,* 283, *293*
Wiggs, E., 277, *292*
Wilens, T., 279, 282, *289*
Wilens, T. E., 179, 182, 183, 186–190, 199, 201, *203, 210–211*
Willemsen-Swinkels, S., 287, *289*

Williamdon, S., 181, *203*
Williams, M., 225, 226, *235*
Williams, S., 182, *208,* 244, 246, 248, 250, 251, *265, 267*
Williamson, B. S., 217, *238*
Williamson, D. E., 214, 216, *232, 240*
Winner, L., 153, *157*
Winnicott, D. W., 63, *68*
Wise, M. G., 215, *242*
Witkovsky, M. T., 199, *206*
Witt-Engerstrom, I., 279, *291*
Wiznitzer, M., 283, *290*
Wolf, E. S., 4, *24,* 63, *68*
Wolkenfield, F., 197, *207*
Wolkow, R., 263, *267*
Woodbury, M., 181, *203,* 244, 248, 251, *265*
Woodward, C. A., 75–77, *88*
Woolston, J. L., 263, *269*
Work, W. C., 121, *130*
Wozniak, J., 224, 225, *242*
Wright, V., 186, *202*
Wyman, P. A., 121, *130*

Y
Yager, T., 76, *86*
Yamazaki, K., 282, *292*
Yates, A., 285, *290*
Yates, E., 217, *234*
Yaylayan, S., 226, *241*
Yeager, C., 150, *158*
Yonkers, K., 222, *237*
Yoshinaga, K., 275, *291*
Young, E., 218, *233*
Young, J. G., 278, *289*
Young, R. C., 225, *242*
Yudell, R. S., 183, 184, *209*

Z
Zahn, T. P., 277, *292*
Zambenedetti, M., 193, 194, *204*
Zarin, D. A., 200, *208*
Zhao, S., 213, *236*
Ziegler, V. E., 225, *242*
Zima, B., 75, *87*
Zimerman, B., 225, 226, 228, *235*

AUTHOR INDEX

Zimnitzky, B., 286, *293*
Zisook, S., 222, *237*
Zito, J. M., 181, 200, *208, 209*
Zucker, H., 27, *47*
Zwier, K. J., 259, 260, *270*

Subject Index

A

adolescence
  development leading up to, 28–30
  early, 6–13, 21
  late, 17–22
  middle, 13–17, 21
  psychoanalytic theory of, 1–2
adolescent medicine inpatient service,
    310–311
  clinical conditions seen in, 297–304
  issues seen in, 297–298, 303–309
advising program in Cambridge, 109,
    111–117
age of majority, 165–166. *See also*
    competence
aggression, assessment of, 197–198
aggressive children and adolescents, 99,
    192
alpha-adrenergic agonists, 188–190,
    284–285
alprazolam, 254–255
American Academy of Pediatrics
    (AAP), 164–166
American Society for Adolescent Psychi-
    atry (ASAP), 150–151
anticonvulsant drugs, 193–195
antidepressants
  nontricyclic, 187–188, 217–222
  tricyclic, 185–187, 198, 216–218,
    257–259
antipsychotic drugs, 190–191, 271,
    281–284
anxiety disorders
  classification/nosology, 243–244
  comorbidity, 247–248
  developmental issues, 245–247
  diagnostic assessment, 248–251
  drug therapy, 243, 252–264
  epidemiology, 244–245
Asperger's disorder, 272, 273, 278
at-risk populations, programs targeting,
    81, 110, 129
attachment disorder, reactive, 276
attention deficit/hyperactivity disorder
    (ADHD), 179
  anxiety disorders and, 245, 248
  clinical presentation, 181–182
  diagnosis, 180, 182, 277
  drug therapy, 188–191, 195, 198, 199
    alpha-2 adrenergic agonists,
      188–190
    antidepressants, 184–186, 188, 198
    antipsychotics, 190–191
    stimulants, 183–185
autism, 278–279
autonomy, 34, 35

B

behavior disorders
  classification/nosology, 179–180
  clinical presentation, 180–181
  comorbidity, 181, 182, 201, 215–216,
    248
  diagnostic assessment, 182–183
  drug therapy, 183–202

behavior disorders *(continued)*
  combination, 199
  duration, 200
  placebo, 196
  research issues, 200–202
  epidemiology, 180–181
behavioral consultation model, 81
belonging, 54–58
  case material, 58–60, 63, 64
benzodiazepines, 253–257
beta-blockers, 195–196, 252–253,
    285–286
biochemical correlates, 278–279
bipolar disorder, 223–224
  clinical presentation and assessment,
    224–225, 277
  drug therapy, 225–231
bodily changes during puberty, 7, 8, 10,
    11
borderline conditions, 302–303
bupropion, 187, 188
buspirone, 259–261

C
Cambridge Rindge and Latin High
    School (CRLS), 111–117
capital punishment, juvenile, 149–152,
    159, 169–171
carbamazepine, 193, 194, 229–230
Center for School Mental Health Assis-
    tance (CSMHA), 124
child mental health, questionable as-
    sumptions in, 119–125
"chumship," 31, 60
clomipramine, 257–259
clonazepam, 254
clonidine, 188–190, 199
clozapine, 283–284
cognitive development, Piaget's stages
    of, 160–162
cognitive maturation, 30–31
commitment, civil, 167
community consultation model, 81
community mental health centers
    (CMHCs), 120
competence, 159–160, 171

civil, 163
to stand trial, 139–142, 153–154
concrete operational stage, 161–162
conduct disorder (CD), 179
  diagnostic assessment, 182–183
  drug therapy, 184, 185, 189–196,
    198, 201
  epidemiology, 180–181
  placebo treatment, 196
  relation to oppositional defiant disor-
    der, 179
confidentiality and privacy, 98–99
consultation/liaison (C/L) psychiatrists,
    297, 300–302. *See also* adoles-
    cent medicine inpatient service
  medical expertise, 309
consultation models, 81
consultation opinions and judgments,
    communicating, 307–309
consultation with school districts, 96–97

D
death and dying issues, 303
death penalty, juvenile, 149–152, 159,
    169–171
dependence *vs.* independence, 34, 35,
    43. *See also* separation-
    individuation
depression. *See also* dysthymic disorder
  clinical presentation and assessment,
    214–216, 222–223
  comorbidity, 215–216, 248
  drug therapy, 216–223
  major, 213–222
desipramine, 185–187
developmental disorders. *See* pervasive
    developmental disorders
developmental theory. *See also* interper-
    sonal (developmental) theory
  clinical applications, 40–45, 62–66
diagnosis, negative aspects of, 122
differentiation, 29, 30, 35. *See also* sepa-
    ration-individuation
disabilities, services for students with,
    94, 99
droperidol, 191

drug abuse, 103–104
drug therapy. *See also specific drugs and disorders*
  augmentation strategies, 221–222, 231
dysthymic disorder, 222–223

E
Erikson, E.
  on adolescence, 55–56
  epigenetic model of life cycle, 54–56
  on identity development, 49–52, 54
expanded school mental health (ESMH), 124–126
  role for child and adolescent psychiatrists, 129–130
  stakeholder involvement and collaboration, 126–127
  youth needs and services offered, 127–129

F
families, and community mental health centers, 120
family therapy, multisystemic, and juvenile delinquency, 153
feminist theory, intimacy, identity and, 52
  intimacy, identity and, 52
fifty-minute session, the, 121–122, 127
fluoxetine, 188, 218–220, 262, 263
forensic psychiatry
  defined, 135–136
  ethics in, 168–169
  four-step approach to, 137–139
  vs. therapeutic psychiatry, 135–137
formal operational stage, 161–162

G
gabapentin, 230
gangs, 32–33
Gault, case of, 146–148
genital phase and genital sexuality, 4, 6, 14, 16, 20–22
group identification, 54. *See also* belonging, sense of

groups, adolescents traveling in, 13. *See also* gangs
guanfacine, 189–190

H
haloperidol, 281–283

I
identification(s), 60–63
  parental, 17–18, 38–39
identity, 60–63
  as self-chosen, 54, 58, 60, 64
identity concept, challenged, 52–54
identity crisis, as normative *vs.* pathological, 53
identity development, 54
  historical psychoanalytic perspective on, 49–52
imipramine, 254
independence. *See* dependence *vs.* independence
infancy, and interpersonal theory on, 28–29
informed consent and refusal, 163–166, 304–305
insanity and the insanity defense, 154–156, 170
insight, 64, 65
institutionalization, involuntary, 167
interpersonal (developmental) theory, 25–27, 29, 30, 45
  clinical applications, 40–45
  and cognitive maturation, 30–31
  and development leading up to adolescence, 28–30
  developmental progression, 27–28
  and peer relationships, 31–33
  and puberty, 33–34
  and relational developmental theory, 26–27
interpersonal view of adolescence, 39–40
intimacy
  development of a sense of, 3–5, 12, 16–17, 21, 22
  identity formation and, 52
  need for, 32

J
juvenile court system, 156
and adult courts, 144–146, 149–153,
156, 159–160
origins and principles, 143–144
recent history, 148–153
role of psychiatrists, 153–156

L
Landau-Kleffner's syndrome, 276
language disorders, 276
latency period, defined, 55
life cycle, 53–56, 58
lithium, 192–193, 225–228, 230

M
managed care, 121–123
Medicaid, 102, 106
medical inpatient service. *See* adolescent medicine inpatient service
medical model, 81–82
mental health, child and adolescent
questionable assumptions in, 119–124
mental health care
long-term, continuous *vs.* intermittent/
episodic, 122–123, 128
overcoming barriers to, 76–78, 83–84
mental health consultation model, 81
mental health professionals
biases, 120, 129
as service providers, 121, 129
as specialists, 123–124
methylphenidate (MPH), 183–184, 187,
191, 198
mirtazapine, 221
monamine oxidase inhibitors (MAOIs),
220
mood stabilizers, 287–288. *See also specific drugs*
moral development, conceptions of,
162–163
mutual-inclusive self, 57, 58, 64

N
naltrexone, 286–287
nefazodone, 221

New Mexico School Mental Health Initiative (SMHI), 104–106
nursing staff, mediating difficult interactions between patients and,
305–307

O
obsessive-compulsive disorder (OCD),
243–244
Office of Juvenile Justice and Delinquency Prevention, 144, 148
olanzapine, 284
oppositional defiant disorder (ODD),
179
drug therapy, 189, 193–195
epidemiology, 180–181

P
parental authority, 37–38
parental identifications, 17–18, 38–39
parental relationship, renegotiation of
the, 34–39
parents, working with, 42–43
peer groups, culture, and relationships,
31–33, 38, 60. *See also* groups
permission, parents allowing adolescents, 36, 37
personality disorders, severe, 302–303
pervasive developmental disorders
(PDD), 271
assessment, 273–274
biochemical correlates, 278–279
classification, 272
developmental issues, 275
differential diagnosis, 275–277
epidemiology, 273
treatment, 279–280
drug therapy, 271, 279–288
pharmacologic treatment. *See* drug
therapy
pindolol, 195–196
posttraumatic stress disorder (PTSD),
103
comorbidity with behavior disorders,
181, 182
preoperational stage, 160–161

prevention programs in schools,
128–129
previewing, 36–37
Primary Mental Health Project (PMHP),
121
privacy. *See* confidentiality and privacy
promotion, of adolescents by parents,
36, 37
propranolol, 195–196
psychoanalytic identity theory, 49–52.
See also separation-
individuation
psychoanalytic technique, 25
psychodynamic therapy, 25, 64
psychogenic illnesses, 300–302
psychosis, 275
in adolescent medical service,
303–304
assessment, 273–275
classification, 272–273
differential diagnosis, 276–278
drug therapy, 271, 280–284, 288
epidemiology, 273
puberty, 7–8, 10
bodily changes during, 7, 8, 10, 11
interpersonal context of, 33–34
interpersonal theory and, 33–34
sexuality during, 33–34
public health approaches, combined
with child psychiatry, 79–80

R
"recapitulation theory," 39
refusal of treatment, 163–164, 167
relational developmental theory, 26–27
research on adolescents, legal and ethical issues in, 166–167
Rett's disorder, 272
rights and privileges, adolescent, 159
risperidone, 191, 282–284

S
sameness-difference theme, 16
schizophrenia
biochemical correlates, 279
comorbidity, 278
drug therapy, 283–284
epidemiology, 273
school-based health centers (SBHCs),
69–72, 75, 125
history, 77–78
in New Mexico, 102–103
as unique opportunities to reach
youth, 77, 79–80, 85–86
school-based mental health care
need for models of, 80–83
in New Mexico, 101–107
recommended components of new
models, 83–85
visits to, for mental health problems,
81
school-based mental health clinics, on-
site, 91–93, 98–100
family focus, 95
identifying students in need, 98–99
patients and families served by,
93–94
services, 95–98
school districts, consultation with,
96–97
School Mental Health Initiative (SMHI),
104–106
School Mental Health Program
(SMHP), 124–126
school staff, collaboration with clinicians, 127
selective serotonin reuptake inhibitors
(SSRIs), 217–222, 261–264,
286, 288. *See also* fluoxetine
self, sense of
development and redefinition of, 3–5,
7, 10–11. *See also* separation-
individuation
self-mutilating behavior, 9–11
self psychological perspective, 1–2, 25
separation anxiety, 246, 253
separation-individuation, 34
case material, 9–11, 14–16, 18–22
in early adolescence, 6–13, 21
in late adolescence, 17–22
in middle adolescence, 13–17, 21
theories of, 4–6
sertraline, 219

sex, adolescent
  laws regarding, 167–168
sexuality, during puberty, 33–34
somatoform disorders, 300–302
special education model, 81
State Children's Health Insurance Plan
  (SCHIP), 106–107
stimulants, 183–185, 287
suicide attempters, 299–300
supportive therapy, 64

T
tardive dyskinesia, 284
teachers, and mental health care,
  123–124
therapeutic binds, 65
therapeutic models and methods, 64
therapeutic relationship, 41–45
therapy. *See also* developmental theory,
  clinical applications
  interpersonal theory and, 40–43, 45
    case material, 43–45
  psychodynamic, 25, 64
  supportive, 64
  terminating, 128
  working with parents, 42–43
therapy sessions, length of, 121–122,
  127–128

thioridazine, 191
Tourette's disorder, 278
training, clinical
  school as optimal area for, 127
treatment, mechanisms for engaging students in, 84
treatment refusal, 163–164, 167
tricyclic antidepressants (TCAs)
  for anxiety disorders, 257–259
  for behavior disorders, 185–187, 198
  for depression, 216–218

U
underachievement. *See* academic
  performance
University of Maryland's School Mental
  Health Program (SMHP),
  124–125

V
valproate/valproic acid, 193–195,
  228–229
venlafaxine, 221

Y
Youth and Family Centers, 72–73